THE PIRATE
SANTOS

CURSE OF THE TREASURE COAST

BY
PATRICK S. MESMER

ACKNOWLEDGEMENTS AND THANKS

This work is dedicated to Tricia; My loving wife and the light of my life. Special thanks to Steve Carr for his unwavering support and knowledge, Michael and Sandy Storm, my loving cousin Michelle Moore, Steve Sparks, Jeff Whitman, Ken and Michelle Cook, Jim Shettleroe, Willie Willette, Hal and Terry, Corky, Michael Phillips, Jim McCormick and the rest of the wonderfully supportive staff at Gilbert's Bar- House of Refuge, all of my workmates, and everyone else who enjoys a good story.

FOREWORD

I'm with my love the sea again- the place of water and sky;

I need a sloop tight under me and the stars to steer it by

The steering's pull; the cry of wind; my hand in hers so tight;

The gray of morning turns to dawn; her waves capped with white

I'm with my love the sea again, where seagulls hunt and dive;

Her waves break high on cool sand and speed a sandpiper's stride

White clouds glide; palm fronds bend; thoughts grow old and wise;

The smell of brine in the thick salt air, the shine of my love's eyes

I'm with my love the sea again; her sweet voice calls to me;

The hours I spend along her shores; the love of life so free

My trip will end as all things do; my true love at my side;

Although my time here is short, her vastness never dies

SANTOS ALVAREZ
1715

NASSAU, BAHAMAS
1765

The beautiful sunsets still move me after all of these years; the way that, at the end of a gorgeous day, the oranges and reds blend into explosions of color rising far into the sky like slow moving ships sailing toward heaven. I am an old man now and simple things of such magnificent beauty bring me greater joy than ever before. I have seen my life through the years as a continual chain of events that were originally random occurrences, but now comprise the story of my existence. Things have indeed changed; it is now the year of our lord seventeen sixty- five, and I have recently entered my seventy-seventh year. One might say that I am, in fact, too old and have long outlived my usefulness, but that is an opinion I will dispute. I can still sail a ship single-handedly and thrash a man one quarter my age in a fair fight.

It has been nearly twenty years since I lost my wife to a plague of pox that swept through the filthy streets of Jamaica, an event that troubled and damaged me so badly that I procured passage on the first ship available to this place, and have called it my home ever since.

Life has been good to me here in the small island town of Nassau, especially since I was able to bring plenty of silver with me to help make my life one of ease.

The bustle of constant commerce in the streets is rather soothing to my old soul. The English do not care for my fugitive brethren here, but wealth does indeed have its advantages, and I am, for the most part, left alone. If I let myself sit idle for too long my mind always regresses back to the sandy, desolate beaches of La Florida and the many years of strife and subsistence I spent there.

Time passes quickly, especially in the closing chapter of our fragile existence. In retrospect, my time here seems to have transpired in the wink of an eye; a flash of light in a rainstorm; a renegade star falling in a cerulean night sky. In the course of recorded history, my contribution to the annals of history may, in the long run, prove to be insignificant, but I believe that an accurate account of my exploits will prove to be entertaining to a certain percentage of the populace. I have noticed of late that my powers of recollection are beginning to fail, so I have chosen to record the exploits of my life before they fade into oblivion and are lost forever. As I look back through the years, I realize that I was fortunate to have been a part of a very special and turbulent time in history. Not only have I managed to accumulate great wealth, but I have also had the chance to cavort with many of the most interesting people the world has known.

I have haunted many beautiful and remote milieus in my time; from my native home of La Habana to the most diminutive of the remote Caribbean islands. These were all wondrous places in their individual ways, but there will always be one that remains close to my heart for all eternity. This, my friends, is the wild and forbidding coast of La Florida. In my opinion, my famous predecessor, Juan Ponce de León, did not name this magnificent land merely for the Easter holiday and the stunning array of plant life on the ground, but also for the dazzling cloud formations that resemble hyacinths floating in a pool of water. They are fluid; constantly changing and fast moving and, for some reason, seem closer to us than anywhere else. My experiences of this land and her forbidding and ancient beauty have enhanced my life and enriched my existence beyond all of my wildest childhood hopes.

Many perceive the "Land of Flowers" as a vast, uninhabitable quagmire. In my view, she possesses an unspoiled natural splendor that is irresistible to men who prefer the solace of a mangrove swamp to the endless prattle and squawk of other humans. Her savannahs, lakes, and streams teem with countless inhabitants ranging from the great black bear to the curious raccoon, snakes of all colors and sizes, magnificent golden cats with long tails, ferocious reptiles who swallow men whole, and more varieties of birds than can be counted. Her terrain holds a wonderful but threatening beauty all its own, from the tight clumps of palmetto and sea grapes flourishing along her windswept coasts, to the seemingly endless miles of long leaf slash pine forests.

The greatest impression on my life was formed not solely by the beauty of this wondrous land, but also by the relationships I made with the native people who once inhabited her shores. These resilient people of ancient origins maintain their existence from the seemingly endless bounty of fish, animals, and plants that La Florida provides. It is to these misunderstood and ultimately doomed souls and the exquisite land on which they dwell that I dedicate this tale. I hope that someone someday may read it and remember them. This may indeed occur due to the fact that I am somewhat famous as an "entrepreneur" of sorts. My name is Santos Alvarez, and this is my story.

PART ONE

CUBA 1710

CHAPTER 1
LA HABANA

I saw her face again, as I had nearly every night for the last two weeks. She always appeared in the same way; her face twisted with hatred, her eyes mocking and accusatory. Her features appeared to be native in origin and very beautiful in an ethereal and exotic way, but her dark, wild stare terrified me. Her bronze skin was painted with three parallel, white stripes on both sides of her face extending from just below her eyes to a point on each side of her chin. Her nose was pierced in the center with a thin "u" shaped piece of gold pointing downward, a small ball mounted to each end. Her hair was very long; black as night and cascading over her shoulders, barely concealing her breasts. In every dream her lips moved constantly as if speaking, but I heard no sound. Just as it seemed that I would begin to understand her strange words, I would awaken abruptly, drenched in sweat.

My eyes opened as the morning sun warmed my face, its rays filtering through the thin, billowing curtains over the large window in my bedroom. Our servant, Badu, had opened the wooden *rejas* the night before to allow the cool night air in. The first thought that came to me was that I had closed my eyes for only a few moments and it was still the night before. I looked around the small room and stretched my arms above my head, at the same time opening my mouth in a wide yawn.

Who was she? I wondered.

Below me were the sounds of movement in the rooms on the first floor of our large house. I laid my head back down on my soft pillow and contemplated going back to sleep for a while. Thoughts of my plans for the day came, and I decided that it was time to rise. In one motion, I pulled the covers aside and sat up, feeling the coolness of the smooth wood floor against the bottoms of my bare feet. I stood and walked across the room, taking a quick glance out the sun- filled window at the veranda and street below. I turned to glance at my reflection in the tall mirror next to my bed. My eyes were puffed with the residue of sleep and my dark hair was shooting out in all directions. I smiled at the thought of my beloved Dorathea seeing me this way, so I wetted my palm with a broad sweep of the tongue and tried to smooth it down into the respectable appearance of a gentleman. I pulled on a clean set of stockings and breeches and grabbed a shirt from the closet, looking at myself intensely in the mirror as I hastily buttoned it up. Satisfied with my appearance, I ran to the large wooden door of my bedroom and turned the latch handle with both hands, pulling it open. I immediately smelled food cooking in the kitchen area of the house, and felt my stomach growl with hunger. I bounded down the steps two at a time.

The sun shone through the lace curtains on the windows and hit the floor, creating a decorative silhouette of distorted floral designs on everything in the room. Maria stood at the water basin, her back to me as she peeled a large orange she had picked earlier from the tree in the garden. Its fresh fragrance hit my nose and I again felt the rumble of hunger pangs. Maria was a short, plump woman with a bright disposition who lived just outside of town and came to help with the domestic chores for a few hours each day. She had dark skin with very long hair that was tied into a tight bun on her head, and wore a white work dress with leather sandals on her feet. She had worked for my father for many years since my mother died.

"*Buenos días*, Santos," Maria said with cheerful sternness as she continued her task, not looking up at me. "Go clean your face and hands before you eat. *Su padre* will be here shortly, and he would not care to see your dirty fingers."

"*Sí Maria!*" I said brightly and ran through the open back door to the yard.

I was greeted by the sweet aroma of the white gardenias that lined the winding brick walkway, and the long vines of yellow, bell-shaped morning glories that grew through the bars of the tall wrought iron fence. I paused for a moment and drew in a deep breath, surveying the dazzling array of brightly colored flowers in the large, well-kept garden. Along the rear border of the yard were the tall, looming coquina pillars of the back gate, where the sweet-smelling white mariposa jasmine bushes grew. They were my favorite because their wonderful scent was strongest in the evening hours when the air was cooler. I heard the low buzz of the bees as they busily toiled, hopping from fragrant flower to flower, their golden bodies shimmering in the morning sun. I took in the beautiful sight of the huge gumbo limbo trees with their meandering, leafy branches and gnarled and twisting trunks that stood every twenty feet around the garden's perimeter. Over my head, the broad leaves of the majestic coconut palms swayed in the morning breeze. My gaze then fell on the tall marble statue that constituted the centerpiece of the garden: a Roman beauty dressed in a wrap that barely concealed her buxom figure; her face permanently etched in an expression of thoughtful neutrality; her mouth turned slightly upward in an almost imperceptible, knowing smile.

It was already warm and humid, but this was normal for a July morning in La Habana. A familiar voice called from the kitchen doorway, so I looked back toward the house.

"Santos!"

My father was a handsome man of forty-five years with intense brown eyes that could project both fearlessness and sensitivity. He had a bald head with short graying hair on the sides, and kept a short, neatly manicured "*barbas de chivo*" beard on his face. He was not a tall man, but carried himself in a regal manner that suggested intelligence and importance, and wore the clothes of a gentleman, with white ruffles on his elegant waistcoat and breeches with high white socks and fine leather shoes. He wore a "*corbata*" wrapped around his neck and looped through a buttonhole of his coat.

"Good morning, Papa!" I said brightly, walking to him as he waited with outstretched arms. He embraced me warmly, laughing out loud in his warm, friendly way. I felt the physical strength of the man that had always awed me as he tightened his grip around my shoulders. "How is my son this morning?" he said in his resonant voice.

"I'm well, Papa. Are you staying home today? The weather is so beautiful and perfect for fishing." I said cheerfully.

As he gazed into my eyes the smile left his face, and he slowly shook his head.

"I told you last night that I cannot go with you today, Santos. I have a meeting with Señor Pena this morning. Besides that, you have to go to school."

I lowered my head in mock frustration, for I already knew what he would say, and kicked the dirt with my shoe, showing my disappointment.

"I don't want to go to lessons, Papa. I want to stay with you today."

"Santos," he said with a tone of sternness in his voice, "you know better."

"Yes, father," I answered.

I took his outstretched hand in mine and together we walked back into the house through the open door.

Our home was in the section of the city in which lived the more wealthy members of *"la sociedad,"* the Spanish born *"peninsulares."* Many prominent people resided there, including *Gobernador* Laureano José de Torres Ayala a Duadros Castellanos himself, as well as most of the other important members of the colonies governing class. Father was a very well respected man with many friends and associates in La Habana, and had used his influence to get me admitted to the fine Jesuit school to learn the arts, reading, and math skills. He had also privately arranged for me to learn foreign languages, including English and French. A few months earlier, I had expressed my feelings to him about this.

"Father, why must I learn the tongues of our enemies when most of the other boys at the school rarely do their assignments at all?" I had asked him, barely concealing the indignation in my voice.

"Santos, I hold you to a higher standard than those boys. You must remember that you are an Alvarez, and life will be challenging for you. You must prepare yourself for the increasingly unpredictable future. We are still at war with the *Gran Alianza,* and I believe that the conflict will only worsen with time. Someday you may find that the skills you are learning will prove to be valuable."

I had never known my mother because she had died during a scourge of cholera that ravaged our island when I was very young. My father had been left with the dual responsibilities of raising me and maintaining his position to provide for us. It is my belief that this was the reason he was not only very active in my academic career, but insisted on controlling my day to day personal life as well. I was a child of privilege in a society in which birth and lineage meant all, and my father did his best to remind me of that as often as he could. He sheltered me from the realities of the harsh outside world, while at the same time preparing me for what he said were "the rigors of life ahead." He carefully scrutinized anyone who tried to get close to me, including my childhood friends, and would often make the decision whether they were "worthy." This would always make me angry for a time, until he did something generous and caring to melt away my resentment. I often wondered why he was so fervent, but I loved him very much and considered him the most important person in my life.

After breakfast we walked out to the stable at the side of the great house. The carriage stood waiting for us, and Badu was already perched on the high seat behind the two stout mares. I had known the man my whole life, and knew that he had been with my father for many years and was a trusted and valued part of our household. He had the blackest skin that I had ever seen and an easy, broad smile, and dressed in the formal style of a house servant. Father often made it clear to me that Badu was not "owned," but was a hard-working man who was like a member of our family. He could have procured a "slave" to do the day to day menial tasks like many of the other prominent men did on a regular basis, but he did not agree with the institution and spoke out vehemently against it. This did not endear him to many of the men of La Habana, and the whispers behind closed door were rampant.

With a quick snap of the leather reins, we started the short journey to the ornately decorated, high arched doorways of the Jesuit school. As the carriage bounced along the rough road, my father spoke.

"You know that you have to do what is right, Santos. You have no choice. I only want the best for you, and I want you to have the good things in life. Please do as I ask and learn how to be a virtuous man."

I gave him my best bored expression and rolled my eyes. This speech had been delivered to me nearly every day of my sixteen years, and I knew that an argument with him would never end well. He finished his tirade, and we continued our bumpy ride in uncomfortable silence, turning onto Acosta Street and passing the "*Iglesia del Espiritu Santo*" Church. As we bounced and joggled along through the winding shell rock covered streets, I gazed absently out the window at the buildings and people of La Habana. My mind wandered, and I contemplated the dreams that I had been having and the frightening expression on the Indian woman's face.

I thought of my own desires; the strongest of which being that I could sail away on one of the great ships in the harbor. I had always loved the ocean and admired the men who lived on it, frequently making my way to the shoreline to spend hours just watching the water. I felt drawn to the endless expanse of open sea that was just outside the protective walls of the city. I had read all of the books on seamanship and sailing that the brothers possessed at the Jesuit school, and had talked to many experienced sailors whenever I could, often annoying them with my incessant questions.

Every aspect of our life in La Habana revolved around the sea, and I had decided early in life that I would someday be sailing to some far-off place. The only problem with my decision was that my father would have none of it. He claimed that the true keys to power and success were to be found on dry land through political and financial means. I knew that we would never agree on this.

Father had long ago told me that La Habana was a very important place for *Madre España*. This was due to our island's strategic position in the Caribbean and its proximity to *el canal de las Bahamas*, a northbound "river in the sea" that the great explorer Juan Ponce De Leon had discovered in the year fifteen-thirteen. This natural current coursed through the ocean just to the north of us, and was the reason so many sailing vessels visited the port of La Habana on their shipping routes.

I loved to go to *el puerto* and watch the ships as they proudly glided in through the narrow channel between the two mighty forts to trade, restock, or careen their great hulls. My favorites were the treasure galleons that sailed in frequently for provisions and maintenance. These great behemoths were magnificent and majestically ornate in appearance, and I watched in absolute awe as they came in. They had huge crews of men and traveled in groups called *flotillas*. It was said that the treasures of the world were transported on them to *Madre España* every year, and I believed it. I watched as they were loaded with silver, gold, and other treasures that came from such faraway places as Peru and the Orient.

The waterfront was active as a beehive while men of all sorts ran everywhere performing a multitude of tasks, all of them preparing for the great voyages on which they would soon be embarking. At low tide, huge vessels were painstakingly "hoved down" on their sides to enable the sailors to clean the barnacles and seaweed from their undersides. The men would then begin the arduous process of scorching and scraping the wood's surface to rid it of the persistent *toredo* worms which, if left unattended, would eventually consume the ship from under the crew's feet. The hull would then be coated with black sulfur pitch and cow's hair before being covered with "sacrificial" wood sheathing. I was amazed at how vigorously these tough men worked in the hot sun.

There were so many different kinds of people there; noblemen, scalawags, rascals, slaves, Indians, and even pirates. I had been watching them from my hiding places for years: rough looking men with dark, darting eyes and colorful dress who drank together in the common houses. There was no proof that these men were of ill repute, but I knew it to be so in most cases, as did most of the other citizens of the colony. It seemed that everyone needed something from La Habana, and for this reason it had become the most important port in all of the Caribbean.

We soon arrived at our destination. As the carriage stopped in front of the Jesuit school, I kissed father goodbye and entered the large building, making my way through the dark hallways and trying to avoid the stern looks of the passing monks on my way to the classroom. My Latin teacher, Brother De Luis, glared at me with disdain as I took my seat at one of the high wooden desks in the front row. He was a short, plump man with small, mean eyes, and wore the simple, brown robe of the church. His hair was cut in a ring around his head, exposing his glistening, bald pate.

"Ah Santos; how nice of you to join us today. I suppose that being the son of the Finance Minister excuses you from being at your lesson on time. I think that you will need to see me later to explain yourself."

As the monk's chastising words came in the grating, nasal voice that I had grown to hate, I found that I could do nothing but sheepishly look down at my desk. My ears caught a barely audible snicker of contempt behind me, and my anger flared. I whirled my head around and met the grinning countenance of Allejandro Ruiz sitting in the back row. He was slightly larger than me, with shoulder length red hair and a pale, rough complexion due to an adolescent skin condition on his otherwise plain featured face. His mouth was curved in an arrogant half-smile, an expression that had become very familiar to me over the last two years. His father was a *Criollo*; a working class, native born citizen of the colony, and an officer in the army in charge of the defenses around La Habana.

Allejandro had always had a critical attitude toward me. At first, it bothered me so much that I sought advice from my father on how to best deal with it. Upon hearing Allejandro's last name, he gave me a knowing, slightly weary expression and tried his best to explain the nature of the animosity between classes in La Habana. He assured me that it was not personal and that, due to our family's position and standing in the social order, I would have to learn to cope with undeserved criticism from members of the "lower" class. I did not understand this concept, but was temporarily reassured by my father's insight and calming words.

Two weeks earlier, I was kicking a ball around in the large parade ground next to the school with some of the other boys. Being somewhat of a natural athlete, I had successfully stolen possession of the ball from Allejandro, who immediately retaliated by pushing me roughly from behind, nearly causing me to stumble. This made me angry, and I whirled on him, thrusting both hands into his chest and sending him tumbling to the ground. He went into such a violent rage that spit flew from his mouth as he screamed.

"You motherless son of a dog!" he howled, "You think you are so special in your big house! Everyone hates you here!"

I then did the worse thing I could do. I burst out with laughter at his words. Leaping to his feet, he started to run toward me, but two of his friends restrained him.

"*Mi padre* says that your father is a criminal who milks the profit from those who really work for a living! He should be hung in the square!"

I stared at him in stunned silence, not believing what I had heard. Allejandro's friends held him back, giving me a few moments to try and sort out exactly what he had said. My father was my whole world, and this insolent fool had just insulted him in front of the other boys. The air was suddenly filled with the sound of a bell ringing, the signal for us to return to afternoon lessons. I looked into Allejandro's sneering face and felt my resentment grow.

Fearing reprisal from the cruel monks, I successfully held my temper at bay, but the seed had been planted. As we all ran back to the doorway by the garden, I had to repeatedly tell myself that I did not want to upset my father by fighting in school. Later, I was so proud of myself that I told him of the whole affair. He just looked at me and shook his head slowly, then gave me a big hug as he congratulated me for my self-control.

"Santos," he said in his gentle voice, "you have the Alvarez anger in you. You must learn to control it. If you do not, you will pay dearly for impulsively acting on it."

Now here I was, two weeks later, feeling the rising temper that my father had warned me about. Allejandro met my gaze defiantly and continued his insolent grinning. I made a silent promise to push the boy from my thoughts and turned my attention back to the front of the classroom. I fought against the wrathful feelings that were now clouding my thoughts. As soon as lessons ended, I quickly made my way back out to the street and started toward home.

"Hey!"

It was a familiar voice. I knew who it belonged to before I turned.

He was there with two other boys, and I knew what he wanted. I turned slowly and met his arrogant gaze and that smug smile.

"Are you on your way home?" he asked in a mocking, sarcastic voice.

"Why do you hate me, Allejandro?" I asked. "You have always been against me."

He smiled at this, then gave his friends a quick glance.

"I know a little about you, Santos. I know that you think that you're better than all the rest of us. I figure that you need to be taught a lesson about how things really are."

"Ah, Allejandro," I answered. I think that you have already answered that question by coming here with three against only me. You are showing your true bravery."

"I also know something else about you, Santos. I know about the curse on your family," he said with a triumphant look on his face.

I felt a spark of shame and embarrassment. I knew exactly what he was talking about. I had been hearing whispers of it for years and thought it a ridiculous and unfair excuse by the uneducated, superstitious rabble for resentment against my family. The curse was well known in La Habana, especially in the darker, more forbidding neighborhoods where the slaves and Indians practiced the old religions.

"You are as ignorant and foolish as a child, Allejandro, believing in such superstition!" I sneered at him, feeling the hold over my temper weakening.

He then made a snorting sound like an irate bull and charged at me recklessly. Having caught me off guard, he hooked his arm around my torso and we both tumbled to the hard shell rock surface of the road. The pain of the impact momentarily took my breath away, and I felt a dark plume of anger grow in my mind. I quickly regrouped, slipping out of his grasp and spinning away. I sprang to a half-standing crouch, my fists raised to fighting position. He got to his feet and paused, glaring at me defiantly as his chest heaved with exertion. He then lowered his shoulder and made another reckless charge at me. This time I was ready, easily sidestepping him, and then driving my knee into his side. He let out a loud grunt of pain and fell to his knees. My blood was now high and fury possessed me, so I lashed out with my clenched fist, catching him solidly in the center of his face. His head jerked back with the impact, and blood sprayed from both nostrils. He brayed in shock and pain and fell to the ground, his face buried in his hands.

The beast inside of me was now loose, and I whirled on the other two shocked boys, screaming like an animal. They both saw that I was shaking with rage. Glancing quickly at each other for affirmation, they both turned tail and fled down the road, leaving Allejandro on the ground, his hand over his broken nose as blood poured down his shirt.

I turned and quickly strode away from the place, anger and frustration blocking any rational thoughts in my head. I knew that my father would soon learn of the incident and that he would be bitterly disappointed at my part in it. I could see the frown of disapproval on his face, and dreaded the endless lecture that was sure to follow. Taking deep breaths, I desperately tried to calm myself as I reluctantly walked toward home.

I soon arrived at the house and saw an elegant horse and carriage tethered at the front of the house. It seemed that my father and I had company, and my distraught feelings instantly melted as I realized who it was. I smiled in wonder at the way the fates had worked in my favor. I needed a diversion more than ever, and one had been delivered to my doorstep.

CHAPTER 2
DORATHEA

I walked in through the open front door of the house and saw my father seated at his huge, ornately carved mahogany desk in the great room. Across from him sat a very well dressed man I knew very well. The visitor had a full head of white hair and darkly tanned skin that crinkled like leather at the corners of his eyes and mouth when he smiled. The two men were sharing a laugh at some humorous exchange and both looked up as I entered.

"Santos! We have been honored with a visit from our friends, the Peñas!" my father said, a wide smile on his face.

"*Buenas tardes* Señor Peña," I said, "It is an honor to see you."

Even as I addressed the two men in front of me, I could see her out of the corner of my eye, sitting by the window in my comfortable rocking chair enjoying the sunlight radiating through the clear glass. I tried to ignore the mischievous smile that made me want to grin.

"*Hola Santos!*" she said brightly. Her sing-song voice was so pleasurable to me that it caused me to blush uncontrollably.

"*Cómo estás,* Señorita Dorathea, it has been a long time. ." I stammered clumsily, tripping over my words. My eyes fell to the floor in shame and embarrassment. It had indeed been a long time, and I was unprepared for the wave of mixed emotions that suddenly overcame me.

She let out a low barely suppressed laugh that mercifully broke the awkward silence that I had created with my schoolboy nervousness.

I stood there stupidly, staring at my shoes in embarrassment. I was truly an idiot.

"Father, do you mind if I go out for a walk?" she said brightly, "Santos will accompany me."

"Umm, I suppose it will be all right. Señor Alvarez and I have many important matters to discuss. Be careful and don't go too far away from the house," he said, eyeing me suspiciously.

As we walked out onto the hard packed shell rock road she moved closer to me, carefully looking over her shoulder to make sure her father wasn't watching.

"Father doesn't trust me at all," she said. "He hates all of the boys who come around to court me."

Dorathea Peña was the most beautiful girl in all of La Habana. She had long flowingly rich brown hair and beautifully expressive eyes, and was sought after by every young man in the colony. Our families had always been close, so she and I had been brought together at a very early age and had spent many of our childhood hours together. This girl had been the other half of me, my closest friend and soul mate for several years of my life as a child.

She had not always been a ravishing beauty. It seemed that only a few short years had passed since she had been a gangly, awkward young creature with limbs that seemed too long and a silly, shrill laugh. As children, we had explored all of the dark, hidden parts of our city as great adventurers, fighting monumental battles as soldiers and renegades. Dorry and I were so close that we swore allegiance to one another, and often shared our deepest thoughts and opinions on adult society as we perceived it. The thing that most endeared me to her was her sense of humor and the way our minds seemed to work together. We fought like devils, as children often do, and had shown each other our darkest emotions in the heat of anger. Our spats never lasted long, for she could easily melt my resolve with a simple smile and a sound punch in the shoulder before bolting away. I would give chase, and together we would whirl off into another adventure. It was such a simple, wonderful time, and the world seemed huge and endless with possibilities. I loved my friend more than life itself, and I wanted to be her consort forever. I recall how truly innocent and happy we were and how precious that gift was.

As we grew older our families demanded more and more of our time and we gradually grew apart. I was sent to learn from the brothers at *Iglesia Parroquial del Espíritu Santo*, and Dorry to the nuns from the *Convento de Santa Clara de Asís* in preparation for our "adulthood." The melancholy I suffered at the loss of her company caused a definite change in me, and I believe it was at this point in my life that I began to develop a cynicism and coldness toward others that proved hard to escape in my later years. I became my father's student, and spent most of my time pursuing male duties and activities. It seemed that both Dorry and I had settled into the strict social roles of colonial society. Time passed, and I watched from afar as she transformed from a graceless tomboy into a striking and reserved young woman like a summer butterfly. The new distance between us made me sad, and I wished that I could go to her. I saw her often, but it seemed that there was a wide river between us. I hadn't spoken to her intimately in nearly four years.

It was one of those beautiful days that were as close to perfect as could be. We walked toward the open fields at the far end of the street. She turned to me, a mischievous expression on her cherubic face.

"Follow me, Santos!" she cried and ran off into the tall grass and flowers. I ran after her like a happy, obedient dog.

We were soon lying side by side on our backs in a field watching the white clouds roll along with gentle slowness against the light blue expanse of the sky. With the sun warming our faces and the cool breeze blowing through our clothes and hair, we chattered away blindly, our conversation randomly bouncing from subject to subject, leading us to wherever it meandered. We were behaving as if the years apart had been erased, and we were still children.

"Santos, did you miss me? Do you still love me after all of these years?" she teased in her musical voice.

The question startled me and I did not answer right away, so she persisted.

"You do love me; I know it. I can see it as clearly as I can see that cloud right over there," she said teasingly.

"Which cloud? The sky is full of them," I said.

She paused and pointed her finger toward a big one to the west of us.

"That one there, the one that looks just like *Padre* Ramirez!" she said.

I looked at it and realized how accurate her observation had been and started to laugh. It did in fact resemble the old coot! I could not contain myself and began to giggle helplessly, quivering uncontrollably at the hilarity of the image. My laughter proved to be infectious and she joined in, and soon we were both howling like little fools there in the middle of that field.

"Dorry, I have missed you," I said. "My father is so dominating, and he makes me very angry. I am so sorry that things have changed between us. I used to love our time together."

I felt the sadness well up all at once as the realization struck me that our childhood had nearly passed. She placed her hand on my cheek and spoke softly.

"Santos, I have missed you as well. I wish that things could be as they were, but you know that they can never be. You must do as he says right now because he loves you as only a father can, and wants the best for you."

With that, she gave me a sad smile.

"The reason that I wanted to see you today is that I want you to explain the talk that I have heard."

I looked at her, confused.

"What talk?" I asked.

"The people speak of a curse on your family," she said, her expression changing to one of dark concern.

I shook my head in frustration.

"Oh, not that nonsense again. It is nothing, no more than an old tale spun by the city spinsters."

"Santos, they say that you will carry it, that you will fall victim to the scourge that has plagued your ancestors for generations."

I started to get angry.

"They will say anything to get at my father! His political foes will stop at nothing to discredit him in any way possible!" I retorted.

Dorathea started to cry.

"Please Santos, I only tell you this out of concern. The people are very superstitious and even though the stories may not be true, they can hurt you."

I was very frustrated now. I had heard stories of the curse from others since I was a child, but had been too young to understand it and how it affected me. My father had never discussed it, and the one time I had asked him about it he had responded with such explosive anger that I never asked again. He curtly informed me that it was a plot by his enemies to sabotage his career, and that such fables were very detrimental.

I could see him in my mind, his finger pointing up in the air as it always did when he was trying to make a point that he wanted me to never forget.

"Reason should always prevail when dealing with such mythology and innuendo," he would retort.

I didn't like the look in his eyes and grew to hate the very mention of the curse and tried to completely shut it out of my life. I actually knew very little about it; only that many men from my family had supposedly suffered premature engagements with fate as a result of it.

But there were those dreams.

I had been having them since I was very young, and they were always the same; the beautiful native woman and her scowling countenance speaking in her unintelligible language. Was this woman with her sharp, black eyes part of the curse? Was it real?

Dorathea could sense the distress in my thoughts, and her eyes softened.

"I'm sorry, Santos. I just get very defensive when others talk about you. You are still very dear to my heart, even though we have grown apart. I have missed you in my life."

I gazed into her eyes for a long moment, and then slowly bent my head to hers. I could feel her breath on my skin; the soft caress of it sending a thrill through me. Our lips met in warm union and we hung there, pausing in a perfect moment of connection. The flood of feelings was too much for us and we pulled apart, momentarily taken aback, both of our faces flushing crimson.

"Santos, we have to get back," she said, standing up and smoothing her dress with her hands.

"Dorathea, please," I said in a pleading voice "I am sorry."

She looked at me for along moment, and then her face broke into a grin.

"My father would kill you if he saw that."

We both laughed. She took my hand, and together we walked back toward the house.

CHAPTER 3
<u>DREAMS</u>

A few days later I was walking in the forest west of the city on one of my solitary excursions. I had been "escaping" in this manner for years, seeking solace from what I felt to be the confining spaces of my life. It seemed to me that I did my best thinking in the wilderness where there were no other people. Animals and birds had always held a sacred place in my heart, so I tried to remain as quiet as possible with the hope of encountering them on the trails that I knew. I thrilled to hear the songs of finches or parakeets high in the trees, or catch a glimpse of the small rodents called *hutias*, or the wily mongoose as he hunted snakes. I never told my father of the true nature of my wanderings because he feared for my safety in the uninhabited areas of the island and would have forbidden me to go. As far as he knew, I was staying to the areas within the colony's protective walls. There had always been the threat of thieves preying on unsuspecting travelers who strayed too far from the safety of the city, but I was not worried because I carried the long skinning knife that my father had given me for protection a year earlier.

This particular morning, I was on a high ridge in a large grove of thick Caribbean slash pines, and had paused to enjoy the fragrance of their branches. There was a thin layer of fog that hung over the tops of the trees down the hillside below me; a few lonely, high palms the only things penetrating it. The colors were awe inspiring from my high vantage point. I could see brilliant red displays of huge royal poinciana trees and clusters of acacia, white oak and yellow tulip; their trunks and branches covered with thick blankets of sprawling vines and resurrection fern. I heard a familiar song in the branches of a tree in front of me, and looked up to see a small bird with a white throat, gray breast and a red lower body. It was a *tocororo*, and I whistled in an attempt to call it. It looked down and answered, nervously stepping from leg to leg before flitting off into the trees in a flurry of motion. As I looked over this magnificent expanse of blue sky and fauna, I knew then that God was there with me, and that this place was one of his most wonderful creations.

Moving forward through a section of very thick ferns, I stepped into a small open space between two huge kapok trees. My heart leapt with alarm as I heard a strange hissing sound a few inches from my face. I quickly scanned the green leaves in front of me, and stopped. I found myself looking into the green, slotted eyes of a good sized boa snake that was wrapped around a crooked, low-hanging branch. My jerky reaction caused me to trip on some tree roots and I stumbled, tumbling head over heels down a steep embankment through sharp brambles. I couldn't believe my stupidity and cursed loudly. Moving quickly to get upright again, I furiously pulled the thorny branches from my clothes.

After making sure that I wasn't hurt, I looked up and was surprised to see a skeletal wooden framework sticking up through the thick underbrush. It appeared to be what was left of a shelter. Now covered in spider webs, its top row was decorated by three worn, wooden masks that had been carved into grotesque facial expressions. The faded dye still showed the stark colors that originally adorned them, and the blank holes of their eyes stared off at nothing. I looked down and recoiled in fear as I found myself staring into the grinning countenance of a dirty, worn human skull. I was in some sort of ancient encampment that had obviously been abandoned for a long time. As I was growing up, my father had told me stories of the *Taino* people. They were the original inhabitants of the island, but I had never actually seen any of them. According to him, most of these natives had been very docile and could not withstand the power of the conquistadors. Their population was decimated within a few short years. When he told me this story he would grow sad, and stare off as if in deep thought.

I sat for a long time, my hands wrapped around my knees, and thought of the people who once lived their lives right where I sat. Where had they all gone? What did they think of? Did they have the same hopes and dreams as I did? My father had told me that when the Spanish first arrived on the island many of them had taken *Taino* wives, and that many of the *criollo* families of La Habana were of "mixed" heritage. The *criollo* boys at the school differed in appearance from the rest of us, and I often wondered if the Indian blood of the lost *Taino* people ran in their veins.

It was very breezy and the sun had begun to set, the afternoon shadows growing longer on the ground before me. I sat in that deserted place of long ago, listening to the sound of the wind rustling through the fronds of the slash pine and high coconut palms. I closed my eyes and took in a deep breath of fragrant air, and my thoughts drifted to the magical afternoon I had spent with Dorathea. She had come back into my life so suddenly after years of distance, and I was both thrilled and a little confused. It was like something infinitely precious had been forever lost, only to be miraculously rediscovered. It was incredible to me that we had both shared the same desire and longing for each other after so many years. My heart now ached that she was not with me, and I knew that I never wanted to lose her again.

I frowned as I recalled the concern she had shown about the ridiculous curse that had supposedly been cast on my family. I loved her, but how could she believe in such superstition? My thoughts then clouded as I remembered the frightening dreams I had been having. Could there be some truth to it? I quickly pushed the fooling notion away.

Suddenly, I heard something. Cocking my head to the wind, I recognized the distant pealing of the *Castillo* bell and the loud, thickly muffled boom of cannon fire. Sensing that something was very wrong, I got to my feet and ran down the path as fast as I could back toward the city. As I drew closer, gasping with exertion, the sounds grew louder.

By the time I reached the west gate of the city it was very late afternoon, with darkness fast approaching. I saw people hurrying out of their homes, heading toward the water, many of them carrying lanterns. I grabbed the shoulder of a man running past me, pulling him to a stop.

"What is this? What is happening?" I demanded.

"The treasure ships are coming! There is talk that they have captured pirates!" he said, his eyes filled with excitement.

I felt a surge of excitement.

I had been exposed to pirate lore throughout my life. The city was constantly on guard from these scofflaws, and the soldiers in the fort were continually vigilant for strange vessels in the harbor. La Habana had been attacked and completely sacked many times in the past, and each time it had taken the city years to recover. The residents were terrified of the "fiends of the sea" and constantly buzzed fearfully about the havoc that these brigands could wreak at any time.

The attitude was different in the school yard, however, where my schoolmates and I idolized these criminals and tried to emulate their bravery in pretend battles, running at each other with wooden sabers, demanding money and treasure. We had all heard of the exploits of fearsome Englishmen like Henry Avery and Henry Morgan of Jamaica, who had successfully preyed upon the King's treasure galleons for years. Even though they were the most hated men we knew, my friends and I secretly admired their free spirits and freedom from the constraints of the law. How innocent and foolish we were!

I knew where I wanted to go. I followed *Calle Malecon* to the northern edge of the city and the great *Castillo De San Salvador* fortress. A full moon shone brightly, lighting the landscape in a thousand shades of blue, so I had no need for a lantern. I approached the high coquina wall and searched for a way to climb to the top. The men of the city, along with their slaves, had recently completed construction of these protective barriers as a deterrent to attacks on La Habana. I found a place where a small wooden storage building had been erected very close to the wall, so I pulled myself to the top of it. I sat on its flat wide surface, my legs dangling against the walls outside face. I will never forget the sight I beheld.

Millions of stars glimmered against the night sky. The strong ocean breeze rifled my hair and whistled through my clothes. As I looked at the breathtaking beauty before me, the still air was rocked by a terrific explosion from across the harbor. I could see a bright red glow, as a large signal fire blazed from the top tier of *Castillo Del Morro*, the other great fortress on the opposite side. A short distance out into the sea, beyond the opening to the harbor, two huge galleons rose and fell with the swells. I realized that the sound I had heard was from the firing of cannon in the fort that were saluting their arrival, and that the fire had been built to help guide them into the dark passage. Normally the ships would have waited until the daylight hours to navigate into the harbor of La Habana, but there were signs of possible foul weather approaching. I watched for at least an hour as the two lumbering vessels navigated the small entrance in the darkness, each one slowly making its way into the channel.

It was such a wonderful night, with the cool wind softly carrying the salty scent of the sea. I loved this spot. Whenever I was here, my mind grew distant and filled with thoughts and dreams. I lay down on my side and looked out over the roiling, crashing waves and closed my eyes. Slowly, I drifted off into sleep.

He gazed down at the courtyard from his window high in the temple and focused on nothing, his thoughts wandering aimlessly. The sun blazed with the relentless intensity of a ceremonial fire. He experienced a wave of envy as he watched two men conversing with an attractive young woman near the far wall of the huge parade ground, marveling that they could take for granted the freedom so recently stolen from him. The comforting sounds of music wafted up from the street; the rhythmic beat of a rattle and flute playing a familiar melody that momentarily transported him to an earlier, happier time.

How could he have been such a fool?

Looking down at his multi-colored robe lying on the dusty floor of the room, he shook his head in frustration at the grim reality of his situation. His gaze shifted to the low table by the window at the ceremonial knife that was used in the daily rituals. It was about two hands in length and carved from black obsidian; its jade-encrusted handle shaped in the form of a small, grinning demon. The demon's hands held the blade out from its torso and served as the weapon's handle. He smiled as he remembered the night of its origin.

He had been the High and Holy leader, the "Tlatoani," for only a short time before the great change happened - the event that had changed his life forever.

This knife had, over each consecutive year of its use, taken at least twenty thousand hearts from daily sacrifices in the tonally, or "animating spirit" ritual. This energy sustained the orbit of the sun, and was transmitted through human blood, so the heart was required to provide endless food for the Sun God "Huitzilpochtli." A steady supply of this life supporting organ would always insure the proper movement of the sun.

He picked it up and gripped it in his hand, marveling at the way it fit in his palm and at its perfectly balanced weight. He felt the familiar pulse of the object's raw energy surge through him as he held it. Was he not a great King? How could this have happened in such a short time? He pursed his lips together as the events of the past few months ran through his head, seemingly for the hundredth time. He was the most powerful ruler that his people had ever known, and had ruled decisively, with authority that was never questioned.

I woke with a start as I felt myself falling, and quickly righted myself. The dream had seemed so real, but looking back on it now, it made no sense at all. I knew that it was very late, so I reluctantly jumped down from the wall and made my way back into the city. As I hurried through the streets and darted in between houses my mind kept returning to the dream and the questions that it presented. Who was the man? The more I thought of it, the more I disregarded it as one of those nonsensical scraps that occur in the somnolent world.

As I approached our house, I saw that all of the windows were bright with amber lantern light. There was a carriage with two fine horses in front of it. I recognized it and immediately felt dread. I ran to the house, bounding up the short shell path, and burst through the door.

"Father?" I called out. "Are you here?"

Hearing nothing, I started up the beautifully polished wooden staircase, where I was surprised to be greeted by Carlos Rodriguez, the cities only *médico*. He was a short, plump middle aged man with greasy, graying hair and a kind face. He smiled and placed his hands on my shoulders, holding me back.

"Santos, my boy," he said in a low voice. I looked into his eyes and did not like the look of concern and pity I saw.

"What is it? " I demanded. "Why are you here in our house?" I tried to push past him.

"I want to see my father."

"Santos, wait," he said, "Your father has taken ill."

I looked at him in bewilderment. "Taken ill? He was fine this morning."

"Santos, I do not know what it is. It came upon him suddenly. The servant, Badu, came to me in great urgency. He said that your father had suffered some sort of attack. I came as quickly as I could."

The door was open slightly and the light from inside shone through the space. I slid past the portly man, pushed the door open and could not believe what I saw. My first thought was that this could not be the man that I saw just this morning. His skin was ashen, and his eyes were large and bloodshot. He looked as if he was having trouble breathing, and I saw a blood stained kerchief in his hand.

"Father!" I cried out, "What has happened to you?"

He looked at me, his red eyes strained and pleading.

"My son, you have come!"

He raised his outstretched arms to me and I ran to him, embracing him. The tears came, stinging my eyes and running down my cheeks.

He whispered into my ear, his voice feeble.

"Santos, I have to tell you something. You must be quiet and listen to me."

"Father, I don't understand," I said in a quavering voice, "what are you saying?"

He looked over my shoulder at señor Rodriguez.

"Could you please leave us for a few moments? I need to talk to my son privately."

"Yes, Señor Alvarez," Carlos said, "I will be right outside if you need me."

The man turned and walked out of the room, pulling the door closed as he left.

My father looked at me for a long moment as if trying to decide what to say.

"Santos, you must listen to me. The Lord has executed his will today for reasons only He knows. For some reason He has stricken me today and I think that I may know why."

I looked at him and made my best effort to say nothing, although my frustration was growing.

"I believe it is the curse."

I tried to cover the disappointment that I perceived at his words. For some reason, I felt something close to betrayal.

"Father, please. You have just taken ill. You will feel better tomorrow."

He coughed violently, bringing his hand to his mouth. I winced at the sound of it, and he continued speaking as if I had said nothing.

"I know that you have heard the rumors among the people. I need to tell you that when I first heard of the curse on our family, I did not believe it at all. Then, as I grew older, I learned of the terrible things that happened to our ancestors. Now I fear that I have fallen victim to it. As far as I know, the curse began with an ancestor of ours who bravely fought with the great conquistador, Hernán Cortés."

"Are you speaking of Donato Alvarez, the soldier?"

He looked at me with sad eyes, the tiny veins of blood in them betraying his pain.

"Yes my son. His story has been passed down through our family for nearly two centuries. I learned it from my father."

"But how can it be true?" I asked, shaking my head in disbelief. "How could you believe anything so terrible? We have always been soldiers for God and have lived our lives in a fine and righteous way."

"My son, please hear me out!" he said and grabbed my arm so hard that it hurt. He bent his head and coughed again on the blanket next to him. I was shocked to see a thin spray of blood on it.

"Father! I will get Señor Rodriguez." I started toward the door.

"No! You must listen!"

I felt helpless and hot, the blood rushing to my face.

He hacked loudly in an attempt to clear his throat and started speaking again.

"As you know, Donato continued the conquest of the Aztec people with the small army of Cortés. During the arduous march back toward the sea, he fell violently ill for no apparent reason. Despite the fact that he confessed all of his sins to the Brothers and to God himself, he soon died a horrible death, twisting in agony from an unknown pain that seemed to take hold of his very being. One of his fellow soldiers overheard his desperate confession, and the rumors began to spread of a terrible curse.

Donato had a son back in *Madre España* who, upon reaching the proper age, followed in his father's footsteps and travelled to *Nueva España* to help extend the realm and share in the wealth. He lived many years in Portobello, married, and had two fine sons and a daughter. At the pinnacle of what was a happy, successful life he inexplicably took ill and died of the same violent illness. The same has been true of all of the male members of our family since."

I could only stare at him.

"All this talk of curses, Father. I think that you are ill and that you will feel better when you recover from this affliction."

"No, Santos! You must take heed!"

I started to get angry. How could he, my own father, be throwing this nonsense into my face like the boys at school had for years? It was more than I could bear or even comprehend so I moved to the door, pulled it open and ran from the room. I found Señor Rodriguez sitting patiently on a chair on the landing, waiting for our visit to be over.

I looked at him intensely.

"What is wrong with him? He makes no sense."

The *médico* hung his head in frustration.

"I do not know, Santos. I have never seen anything like it. He was in good health this morning, as you know, and now this," he said sadly, gesturing toward the bedroom door.

"I will sleep downstairs tonight, Señor Rodriguez, please let me know if there is any change. Maria will get you whatever you need, just ring the bell."

"Goodnight, Santos," he said.

CHAPTER 4
CHANGE

I made myself as comfortable as possible on the large, cushioned chair in the room where my father worked, but sleep was elusive. Every time I did manage to nod off I would very soon awaken; my mind a torrent of confused thoughts. My world seemed to be coming apart all at once, and it terrified me.

What was happening to us? Why had he become so sick? Had someone poisoned him? Could my father's story be true?

My head ached with exhaustion. I shifted my body on the soft curves of the chair and closed my eyes, finally drifting off.

He was above average height among his people, with dark skin and a powerful, smoothly toned body that he loved to adorn with the colorful royal robes and accoutrements of his position. He had a long face with brown eyes, kind features, and an easy smile which made him very attractive to women. On his chin was a rough, shortly trimmed beard, rare among his kind, and his hair was jet black, cut just above his ears.

He turned his head slowly toward a sound behind him. It was a feminine voice, in the native tongue that the young Spanish soldier standing guard outside his rooms could not understand. A young, beautiful, dark-haired girl entered the room and stood before him, her eyes downcast. He rose to his feet in unabashed nakedness.

"Cualli, you have come to me." he said.

The girl did not raise her eyes, for it would have been very disrespectful to do so. She was scantily clothed in a colorful robe that barely concealed the golden brown skin of her tautly muscled body and ample bosom. He could have any woman in the kingdom he desired, but of his two true wives, she was his favorite. She spoke in a low, careful tone.

"Yes, Tlatoani. A slave informed me that you requested my presence. The invaders nearly prevented my coming to you."

His eyes clouded and he felt rage and frustration at the impudence of the newcomers. How could these men be so audacious after he had welcomed them with all the grace and respect of his kingdom? He hated the feeling of helplessness as his authority and influence were diminished by these strange men.

He had been warned of their coming by messengers from the massacre at Cholula, and had become immediately anxious. At first, he had believed that they were emissaries of the gods and that their leader was the feather- headed Quetzlcoatl, the boundary maker between earth and sky, returning to his rightful place in the great city of Tenochtitlan. This event had been predicted by the priests of the Templo Mayer and seemed to be inevitable. As they had accurately predicted, the pale, hairy ones had recently recruited thousands of the hated Tlaxcalans, sworn enemies of his people. Those same Tlaxcalans were at that very moment heading toward them. He had pondered the best course of action, and had decided that welcoming them with open arms was the only solution to avoid disruption of the city. He had arranged a wondrous reception of hundreds of warriors in full regalia for when the advancing throng arrived at the causeway leading to the great metropolis.

The king suppressed these dark emotions and gazed down at the girl's lovely form, realizing that he needed to forget his troubles, if only for a few minutes. He took her hand and gently guided her to his private chamber, where the mats of his bed lay on the stone floor. Sitting down on the soft surface, he pulled her to him, her youthful body molding with his, and they made passionate love.

After his lust was spent, the King lay back on the mat and stared at the ceiling. His dark thoughts returned now. What would become of his empire now that these white devils had taken advantage of his kindness? Had he angered the Gods? Had he not been a great and fair ruler?

My eyes opened, and the images sank back into the recesses of my mind. The dream had been so real that I felt that I had been there. I raised my head from the chair, feeling my back twinge slightly because of the uncomfortable position I had slept in. The sun shone through the gauzy curtains over the windows, and I smelled food cooking. Stretching my arms up into the air to relax my muscles, I rose from the couch. Walking into the kitchen, I stopped behind Maria, busy at some task, and gazed at the back of her white dress, noticing that she was not singing softly like she usually did in the morning.

"Maria, is everything all right? Why are you so quiet this morning?"

There was a pause, and then she spoke.

The words that came out were not recognizable and seemed to come not from her, but from all directions. I felt a familiar stab of fear as I realized that I had heard the strange, nonsensical cadence before.

She slowly turned her head and I saw that it was not Maria at all.

This face was mottled and gray like a dead thing, and to my horror I recognized it. This was the same Indian woman from my dreams, but she had undergone a terrible transfiguration. This was no longer the countenance of an angry, beautiful native woman. Glaring at me was a figure from my deepest nightmares with black, empty sockets where the eyes should have been. Her mouth was open in a hideous red grin and her teeth were black stubs. She appeared very long dead.

"*Good morning, boy,*" it whispered in a rough hiss that sounded like dry leaves.

I screamed louder than I ever had in my life.

Someone shook me by the shoulders. My eyes flew open and I found myself looking up into the flushed face of Señor Rodriguez.

"Santos! Are you all right?" he said.

I could only stare at him in confusion. Another voice came from behind him, this one belonging to a woman.

"Santos! You had a nightmare!"

I turned my head and saw Maria; not the horrible creature I had just seen, but Maria.

I breathed a sigh of relief, and sat up. I then put my hands over my face.

"I am so sorry," I stammered, "I don't know what happened."

"It is fine, Santos," Maria said in her own soothing voice, "We understand completely. You are under a great strain with your father's sudden illness."

She walked over and kneeled down beside me, her hand reaching out to stroke my sweat-covered hair.

"Poor boy," she cooed softly. They both gazed at me intently, worried expressions on their faces.

"I'm all right," I said, my voice shaking slightly.

"Why don't you go for a walk before breakfast to get some air?" Señor Rodriguez said.

I walked slowly down the street toward the waterfront, trying to make sense of the terrible dream. My head was still hurting and I longed for something to distract my thoughts. I could hear drums beating, and I wondered if they had something to do with the treasure galleons that I had seen enter the harbor the night before. As I drew closer to *el puerto*, I could see that a large number of locals had gathered near one of the mighty ships that sat moored in the shallows of the harbor. As I approached, I admired the carving of the ship's hull and the intricate rigging that ran in every direction.

There was a ceremony going on with much commotion. I could see that the soldiers were leading a group of men down the cargo ramp to the dock. I made my way to the rear of the crowd and tried to get a glimpse of them, remembering what the hysterical man had told me last night about "prisoners." I strained my neck and saw that the soldiers had arranged themselves in a protective circle around these unfortunates, their pikes held at the ready, and were leading them toward the Government house. The locals from the town were hurling oaths at the men and gesturing wildly as they passed.

The prisoners walked in the center, the chains that bound their hands and feet rattling and their defiant eyes glaring at the crowd as they passed. My first impression was that they were the strangest, filthiest lot that I had ever laid eyes on. They carried themselves with an air of smugness, and clung close together as if in solidarity, marching steadily behind a man whom I took to be their captain. He was older than the rest and looked as though he had been severely beaten. His face was distorted with battered features, and blood ran down his cheeks and neck from a swollen, blackened left eye and a badly injured ear. His long brown hair was streaked with gray and tied behind his head, and he walked with a rolling gait. He was dressed as an English gentleman, albeit a filthy one, complete with a full waistcoat, large brass buttons and breeches with high leather boots. Despite his injuries, he glared defiantly at anyone who met his gaze and snarled like an animal. In my angry mood, I was secretly impressed with his bravery and defiant attitude in the face of the jeering crowd. These were real pirates!

Following him were two rough looking fellows who had taken up their colors and were brazenly displaying it as they walked along, despite the glares of the Spanish guards. The flag was made of black silk and emblazoned with what looked like a skeleton soldier with a long sword extended before it. Most of the men had dark, sun-parched skin and wore rags for clothes, with long bandanas tied around their heads like turbans. I was surprised and shocked to see that the majority of them wore no shoes on their feet. I remember this most vividly because, in my young impressionable state, I could not imagine walking the rough streets without my fine leather shoes. They were a desperate lot numbering about twenty, and as diverse a group as I had ever seen. Among them were several Africans who appeared to be part of the crew. It seemed like they were representative of all nationalities, each dressed in the crudest way imaginable.

As they passed in front of me, I was assaulted by their foul odor, a mixture of sweat, unwashed bodies, alcohol, and untreated wounds that could make any man's eyes water. I started to gag in revulsion. I looked up with bleary eyes and noticed one pirate who looked different in that he was markedly younger than the rest, appearing not much older than myself. He was a little taller than I and considerably thinner, with a rather gaunt and vacant expression, and appeared to be walking with a limp. It occurred to me that, in another life, he could have been one of my schoolmates. He had long blond hair that was, like the captain's, tied behind his head and he was clothed in the same fashion as the others save for a bright yellow shirt with its sleeves removed. He turned his head and caught my gaze for a moment, and I felt a twinge inside as my eyes met his. His cold countenance was marked by a bright raised scar that ran down the side of his left cheek, giving his once innocent face a chilling demeanor. I could have sworn that he gave me the hint of smile as if we were sharing some sort of private joke.

The strange procession quickly passed by and I turned away, trying to make sense of all that I had seen. In my imagination, I had always seen sea pirates as heroic criminals, not this ragtag collection of pitiful misfits. I moved away from the jeering mob, looking for an escape. Just as I broke free I found myself standing face to face with none other than my nemesis, Allejandro Ruiz. My heart sank at this unwanted and awkward confrontation, and I tried to look away.

"Ah Santos, my friend," he said, his voice dripping with sarcasm, "I see that you've come to witness Spain's justice on her mortal enemies."

His nose was bandaged and bruised from our earlier encounter. I looked at him briefly, and then quickly averted my eyes. "They don't look vicious to me. More like half-starved animals."

"I wouldn't let your friend, the *Gobernador*, hear that talk, little Santos."

I glared at him contemptuously. "Allejandro, I wish that you would just leave me alone. I do not want to talk to you, now or ever."

"I saw your precious Dorothea today," he said, continued smiling in his insolent way. "You are a lucky man, Santos. She is as sweet as the heavens can produce."

I felt the familiar anger growing again, as it had in our earlier encounter, and tried desperately to suppress it. I did not reply, so he continued to speak.

"You had best be careful though, Santos. There are others who have their eye on that little creat. ..."

He did not get the last word out. I moved like a cat, driving my fist into his face, splitting his lip like a tomato and spraying blood across his face. He had no time to react, and for the second time that week hit the ground as the result of my anger. This time, however, he did not move. A woman who had witnessed the blow screamed and ran to him.

"You've killed him!" she bellowed.

More people came and gathered around Allejandro's still body, as I stood stupidly rubbing my fist.

Then, he shifted and groaned and I knew that he was not dead. I heard clapping and laughter and spun around quickly. I could not believe what I saw. The sound was coming from the pirate captain and his men, who had just witnessed my moment of weakness. They were applauding as if they had just seen a play. The old sea dog actually winked at me! The soldiers grumbled and barked orders for the condemned men to be silent.

Suddenly I heard a man's deep voice call out, "Santos, come quickly! It's your father!" I recognized the voice of Badu, our servant. He was running toward me from the direction of our house.

"What has happened?" I demanded.

"Just come with me," he said and I saw tears streaming down his dark face.

CHAPTER 5
THE MEDALLION

Badu and I ran to the house as fast as we could, each of us panting heavily as we reached the walkway that led to the house. I left him doubled up and gasping for breath and quickly ran through the open doorway. As I approached the stairway that led to the upper rooms, I paused, suddenly dreading what I might find. I waited for Badu to join me, and together we slowly made our way up the stairs. I was covered in cool sweat and sick with fear as we approached the partially open door of my father's bedroom. There was little light, but I caught a quick glimpse of the bed where he laid, his body blocked from view by Señor Rodriguez. The physician had just pulled the blanket up over his face. I could see the covered lumps of his legs and noticed that one bare foot had slipped out from beneath the bedspread. Tears formed in my eyes and I felt an overwhelming sense of hopelessness. I began to sob quietly. Señor Rodriguez turned and gave me a sad smile, his head slowly nodding his understanding.

"What happened?" I blurted out.

"He has joined our Father in Heaven, Santos. I am sorry; I could do nothing."

His voice broke with emotion. "It's as if something evil overcame his very soul and snatched him from our midst."

"So, he is dead?" I asked in a timid voice, not quite comprehending what he had said.

"I am sorry, Santos." the doctor stammered as he shook his head back and forth in bewilderment.

We all remained silent for a few moments and stared at the motionless form on the bed. Tears streamed down my cheeks as full realization of his death set in.

"I want to spend a few minutes alone with him," I said, my voice breaking.

"Certainly, Santos. Badu and I will wait outside."

The two men left the room. I slowly approached the bed not wanting to accept the fact that he was truly gone. I bent and took the corners of the blanket between my fingers and pulled it down, exposing his countenance, gasping in shock at what I saw. The skin of his face was mottled with blotches and drawn tight to his skull as if he had been disease-ravaged for months. His sightless eyes were partially open and staring straight ahead and his mouth was agape; his purple tongue poking out like some sort of snake.

How could this be? Had I not seen him only a few hours before? Was this wasted condition even possible in such a short time? My mind reeled, and I thought I was going to pass out.

"Father, why have you left me?" I asked aloud. I sat and wept for close to an hour next to the body of this man who had been my whole life.

The door creaked as someone entered the room. I did not look up and soon became aware of a presence standing near me by the bed. I looked out of the corner of my eye and saw that it was Badu.

"The doctor, he leave." Badu said in his low, gravelly voice. "He say he'll be bock soon."

I said nothing and stared at my father's ravaged face.

Badu continued to speak.

"Master Santos, I got to tell you sumtin."

I looked up at his dusky face, its contours shiny in the clear light of the whale oil-soaked wick that burned in the lantern by his bed.

"What is it, Badu?" I said shakily.

"The master tell me sumtin' to tell you if he pass an' I steel round."

He looked at me gravely. "I promise him."

"Go on," I said, "tell me."

"He say for me to tell you he always love his son, and dat you need to listen to what I got to say."

With that, he walked across the room toward the door to my father's closet. This was the same one that I, as a child, had been forbidden to go near. I remembered my father's sharp tone when I had asked, with youthful curiosity, about its contents.

"*Santos, you stay away from this door,*" he had said with a grave expression on his face. "*If I ever see you near it I will punish you severely.*"

Badu paused, fishing in the front pocket of his breeches with one hand. He pulled out a small, black key. He held it up, showing it to me.

"He knew I wouldn't lose it," he said, smiling and glancing over at my father's body. He pushed the key into the old lock. When he tried to turn it there was some resistance from years of neglect, but he tried again and it unlocked. He pulled the door open, its hinges creaking in protest. He then disappeared from view into the dark interior of the closet. I could hear bumping and knocking as he tried to locate something, then I heard him drag something from the top shelf. As he emerged into the dim light of the room, I could see that he held an object in the crook of one arm. He crossed the room to the desk next to me and set it down on its polished wooden top. He then looked at me, a resigned expression on his dark face.

"Dere," he said, "you get dis. Now I done his biddin'. Can I go?"

"Why do you want to go, Badu? What do you think happened to him?"

He looked at me for a long time as if weighing an important decision in his mind, and then spoke.

"I believe dat dere is evil here."

"What did you say?" I asked incredulously.

"Your papa had a curse on him, boy. De demons took him."

"Badu, listen to yourself," I said, anger growing. "You don't actually believe that do you?"

He smiled at me, flashing his white teeth and said "Your papa believe it. He told me to warn you dat you next, Santos. I go now."

With that, he turned and hurriedly left the room. I stared at the door for a short time, scarcely believing what had just happened. I slowly walked to the box that Badu had left on the table and softly caressed its smooth mahogany surface. I felt uneasy about its contents and looked up at my father's body on the bed. Taking a deep breath, I undid the crude latch on the front of the box and slowly lifted the heavy lid, looking down at what lay inside.

The entire inside of the box was lined with soft, black velvet. In the center was a simple gold medallion on a long chain. The thing was very old looking and appeared to be hand- made. It was triangular and thicker on one side than the other, its face etched with two large intersecting lines that may have represented a cross. In the spaces to the upper left and lower right of the cross were two oval shapes that almost looked like eyes. It could have been the effect of grief at the loss of my father, but I was sure that some odd energy emanated from the medallion that I could not identify; one as tangible as anything I had ever felt. I picked it up and held it front of my face to admire its rough beauty.

"So this is what you wanted to give me," I said out loud.

As if by instinct, I slipped the chain over my head and let the medallion hang on my chest. For some strange reason I felt a surge of reassurance as it softly bounced against my body, as if I had established some connection with it. I turned and looked at my father's corpse and thought of the man who had been my best friend, my mentor, everything to me. I walked to the bed and lay down next to him as I was overcome with sadness. Burying my head in my arms, I broke into great wracking sobs until I drifted off to sleep.

The sun poured in through the open window as the sounds of the riot outside came to their ears.

The young priestess sensed the distressed thoughts of her lover and tried to soothe his turbulent thoughts by caressing his smooth chest.

"Do not worry, Tlatoani. The gods will prevail and rid us of this scourge."

He smiled and stroked her hair, realizing that he loved her more than any of the women he had known.

She continued to speak, her soothing voice calming him.

"We, the holy ones, have prayed for deliverance, and for vengeance against these invaders."

With this she reached for her shift on the floor and pulled from it on object that was wrapped in cloth.

"My love, I give this to you for protection against the evil that has darkened your soul. It has very old power from my ancestors, the ancient ones."

The King took it from her hand and carefully pulled back the cloth. Inside was an amulet attached to a long handmade gold chain. The amulet had three sides and was nearly as large as half of his palm. It was the most beautiful thing he had ever seen.

"What is this?" he asked her.

"It has been in my possession since I was child. When my mother's mother was very young she was exploring outside the gates of the city and became lost in the forest to the south. She was gone for days- so long that the people had given up on her as lost. After fourteen moons had passed, she miraculously appeared at the gates, unharmed. Around her neck was the amulet.

When questioned by the priests on how she had survived in the wild place, she told them that she had become very lost and was crying and hungry. A great storm was moving in and she could hear the sounds of the wild animals as they lurked in the jungle all around her. When it seemed that all was lost, there was a great clap of thunder, and a staggering bolt of lightning lit the entire sky, striking the ground very close to where she was hiding. She crept over to where this had happened and discovered that the lightning had unearthed a large statue of a holy man. It was beautiful and she stared at it for a long time, feeling awestruck.

Next to the statue was a large hole in the ground, and from it emerged a beautiful spirit; high priestess of the ancient ones. This spirit slipped the amulet around the girl's neck and embraced her, lifting her off the ground and high into the heavens. As they flew, the spirit priestess told her that the amulet would keep her from all evil as long as she possessed it. She warned the little girl to protect it with her life.

The priestess then flew to the gates of the city and deposited the girl safely for the guards to find her. She became the most powerful shaman in the city and passed the amulet down to her daughter, who was my mother and this is how I came to have it. I give this to you,

Tlatoani, with fear and dread in my heart because I do not know how it will affect your soul, but it is all I have. Take it and it will protect you."

The King, still wrapped in an embrace with his naked Cualli, awoke to the sound of heavy boots on the stone floor of the hallway outside. El Capitan Pedro de Alvarado blew into his room like a windstorm, accompanied by three soldiers and his female native interpreter. Dressed in the full royal armor of his rank, he was a red haired, boisterous man who spat out words in a clipped, staccato voice. The people knew him as "Tonatiuh." This name meant "Red Sun," and was given because of his flaming hair color and explosive manner.

"Get up!" he barked as the interpreter struggled to translate.

"Things have changed. The people do not yet understand that we now rule this kingdom. There are fights erupting everywhere in the city. You must give them a message of solidarity."

The King looked up at the Spaniard with a baleful, resigned expression. "I can do nothing, Tonatiuh, because your men continually enrage the people by your oppression and cruelty. When your leader, Cortes, repaid my good will with all of his treachery the people saw it as sign of my weakness." He let out a sad, resigned laugh. "My power is as good as gone."

Alvarado snorted disdainfully and walked to the window, looking out at the throng below.

"You are the great Moctezuma!" he said, waving his hand in a sweeping motion, his high, piercing voice dripping with sarcasm as the interpreter struggled to convert his words. "They love you and throw flowers when you pass. All you need do is wave one of your holy hands and the beast will be quelled! You must do it now, because there is a mob forming as we speak. You will don the sacred regalia and present yourself to the heathens outside or we will all suffer!"

With that, Alvarado curtly turned and left the room, his party following behind.

"He is an evil, stinking creature," Cualli said, in anger, "I hate him."

The King gazed at her, a sad expression on his face. "Cualli, you are a great priestess, but I fear that it is too late for us."

He called his slaves in to prepare him for the impending presentation by thoroughly washing his body. As he waited for them, he rinsed his face in the small basin near the large window that overlooked the plaza. He paused and stared at his reflection in the pool of water. He was the Sovereign, and he had been a virtuous one. Perhaps the people would listen to him and stop the fighting, and the scourge of the Spanish would pass like a bad season of harvest. He alone had the power to restore his beautiful empire and the vision of the eagle with the snake to its former glory.

As the slaves prepared him by cleaning, and then anointing his body with the sacred colors, he and Cualli sang all of the holy songs together. The robes and jewelry came next. As they were carefully arranged on him, his young bride suddenly burst into tears.

"Do not go out there my King," she pleaded, her voice choked with emotion. "It is too late!"

She fell to her knees, clinging to his robes as he moved away from her.

"I must go. The people will listen to me."

He waved a command to the slaves, who each took one of Cualli's arms, holding her back.

"Tlatoani, please wear the amulet! It will protect you!" she pleaded, and held it out toward him, the fine chain hanging down between her fingers.

He looked into her tear-filled eyes.

"I will wear it, Cualli." He reached out and took it from her outstretched palm. He then handed it to one of the slaves, who quickly moved behind him to fasten the small chain around his neck.

The King then smiled and turned away, making his way to the opening that led to the great precipice of the temple. As he moved, the sun glinted off the surface of the medallion.

"Cualli, do not worry. My powers are greater than any ancient conjuring. The Gods will protect and guide me."

The roar of the thousands of people outside was nearly deafening as he walked out into the sunlight, his hands raised in supplication. He immediately sensed that something had changed and felt a moment of fear. The people that he could see were not looking back with the same joy and adoration that he was accustomed to receiving. He knew then that his time had come, and he raised his face to the great Calchiuhtlicue, to whom he had devoted his life.

He closed his eyes and let her sacred warmth bathe his skin.

He had been a good King.

This was the last thought he had before the stones began to strike him.

My eyes snapped open with a start to the sound of someone knocking on the door. Momentarily confused, I looked around to see where I was. I soon realized that I was still lying next to my father's body.

"Yes?" I called out.

"Santos! Are you all right?"

It was the muffled voice of the *médico*.

"Y-yes," I stammered, "I'll just be a moment."

I rubbed my face in my hands. The dream had been vivid and terrifying, and I struggled to find some sort of meaning. I stood and looked down at the crumpled, wasted remains of what had been, only a few hours before, the most important person in my life. I felt great despair in my soul and knew that I had to leave; to get outside and alone for a while to sort things out.

"Thank you for this gift, Father. I do not understand the significance of it, but I anticipate that I will someday. I will treasure and respect it always." I turned and ran from the room, the golden medallion bouncing against my chest.

CHAPTER 6
TAKEN IN THE NIGHT

The night air was cool and windswept, with patches of gray clouds that moved quickly across the sky, intermittently obscuring the stars in their path. I ran aimlessly down the street, wet, salty tears burning my eyes and blurring my vision. My mind raced in many different directions, and I felt as though I had never been so confused. My father was gone and I had no one. How could this strange disease have taken his life so quickly? Why had Badu run from me like a scared child after giving me the medallion? Who were these people I kept dreaming about? It seemed as if everyone I knew believed that I had been touched by some ancient curse over which I had no control. My entire world had been turned upside down, and I had no friends to turn to for help and understanding. I thought of Dorathea, and quickly realized that it was much too late to go to her. I vowed to find her when daylight came. She would know what to do.

I saw amber lantern light glowing from the windows of a building, and quickly recognized the tavern that I had passed many times. I heard raucous laughter coming from inside, so I walked to the side of the doorway and peered into its murky interior. Many men sat at long tables, engaged in loud conversation as they drank and puffed on long cigars. It was obvious to me from their loud merriment that most of them were intoxicated by the spirits that were sold there. I had never tasted alcohol, but had seen others, including my father, use it on occasion. The place was filled with smoke and there was a group of unkempt musicians in the far corner playing a rowdy tune with their stringed instruments.

Two soldiers sat at the table nearest me, and were speaking loudly to each other to be heard over the din of the music. I didn't intend to eavesdrop on their conversation, but I heard them mention something about the pirates that I had seen at the square a few hours earlier. My interest was piqued and I couldn't resist listening in. I sat down on the porch by the door and pretended that I was resting and waiting for someone inside. One of the soldiers had a very gruff voice and spoke with a harsh tone as though he were very angry.

"The *bastardos* did it. They surprised and overpowered those careless guards, killing two of them in the process. I cannot believe that the *Soldados del Rey* have allowed this to happen."

I listened in disbelief. Had the pitiful men that I had seen really escaped? I listened intently as the man continued.

"When I catch them I will kill every one myself, and then hang them by a gibbet on the channel," he grumbled. "Do they really think that they will be successful in escaping our island?"

"Let's go," the other soldier said. "It's going to be a long night."

With that the men got up and strode through the door, walking past me and into the moonlight. I watched as they made their way down the street, weapons clanking at their sides.

The news amazed me, and I nearly forgot about my situation until I felt the amulet bouncing against my chest. The desperate, sad feelings quickly returned as I was reminded of the terrible tragedy that had befallen me. I knew where I wanted to go. I ran the entire length of the street and across many back alleys toward my secret place by the sea to try to sort out my turbulent, grief-filled feelings. The light from the moon and countless stars was brilliant, so I soon found the low building by the wall. I climbed to my familiar place on top of the edifice. The wind blew stiffly from the north and the ocean roared with ceaseless persistence. I sat down on the walls' hard surface, wrapping my arms around my knees as I gazed out over the rough surface of the water. I soon experienced a feeling of calmness that was both familiar and comforting, and my eyes scanned the night horizon for the lights of an approaching ship that would take me away from all of this pain. The turmoil of the waves seemed to mirror the furor in my head, and I began to appreciate the magnitude of what had happened. My hands instinctively rose to grasp and caress the amulet that now hung around my neck, and I felt a wave of confusion and sorrow. I lowered my head and began to sob.

'Why have you left me here alone, father?" I asked aloud, my voice choked with pain.

Suddenly, I heard a sound; a man's laugh, and I strained my eyes to see where it had come from. I saw a small light a short distance away. It quickly disappeared, and then reappeared a few seconds later. Apprehension washed over me as I realized that I was not alone in my private place. I stood up and walked along the top of the wall toward the glow, being careful not to lose my balance in the semi-darkness. As I drew closer, the light grew stronger and the voices became clearer. I could see that its source was on the ocean side of the wall. I found myself looking down on a small campfire with several men sitting around it on logs of driftwood. The curved tendrils of the fire whipped nearly horizontal in the stiff breeze, its light illuminating the men's features. I recognized several of them from earlier that day, so I lowered myself to a crouch to avoid detection. My heart leapt with fear as I realized that I had stumbled on the hiding place of the fugitive pirates. They were speaking to each other in a kind of talking whisper as if they were trying to be quiet. I grew very frightened and excited at the same time. It was like a scene from one of my dreams.

Suddenly, I heard a calm voice directly behind me.

"'Ello there, mate. I'm Calico Jack."

I was completely stunned and spun my head around. The last thing I remember was the face of my attacker. It was the boy that I had seen earlier with the gang of pirates. His face looked different now; hard edged and calculating, with the same hint of a smile. The blow to the side of my head was swift and hard, and I saw a dazzling flash of light before darkness enveloped me.

PART TWO

A BOY NO MORE

CHAPTER 7
PRISONER

I came to gradually, darkness slowly giving way to muddled half-light, instantly becoming aware of a stench that filled my nostrils; that of salty air mixed with semi-rotted food. I could not see in the inky darkness save for a very thin, sharp line of light that made its way down the wall in front of me. I tried to move but realized that my hands were bound behind my back. As I struggled to break free, I saw fine dust particles floating through the beam of light, so I looked up and saw a long crack above my head between the wall and the ceiling. I got the sense that I was confined in some small area, possibly a storage room. My center of gravity shifted, and I realized that I was on board some sort of sailing vessel. My stomach churned with unease, and I felt dizzy and nauseous.

Where was I? What had happened? Had I been kidnapped? I sat there for what seemed like hours, unable to move. Just as I was preparing to shout out, I heard someone, or something approaching. There was a heavy step followed by a dragging sound, then a wooden clunk. The pattern repeated- heavy step; dragging sound; clunk.

Then there was the sound of fingers fumbling with some sort of metallic latch, followed by the groan of rusted hinges as the small door was pulled open, allowing a flood of light to pour in, temporarily blinding me. I raised my head and, through squinted eyes, tried to see who my captor was. A spit of words flew from the person's mouth, and I struggled to recognize the language. At first, I had no idea what the unintelligible jumble was. I heard a few words of English, but it still made no sense.

As my eyes grew accustomed to the pale light, I saw that its source was a lantern with a large candle inside its glass. I found myself gazing into the countenance of my captor, and I gasped with shock at his appearance. He was a man of middle age with a craggy, pock-marked face that was more than half covered by a long, scraggly beard. He had a mop of bedraggled hair that was almost completely gray and fell around his face to his shoulders, giving him the appearance of an ancient wizard from one of the books in my father's library. His mouth was thin and turned downward at each end in a cruel, permanent frown, and his eyes were blazing slits that flashed with malevolence in the dull lamplight. He wore a loose, ragged tunic and a wide cloth belt that held up his breeches. He scrutinized me for a moment and then took one step forward, entering the tiny room. As he looked me up and down, I saw his face transformed by a menacing smile, his brown rotted teeth showing in an erratic pattern.

"Why, yer just a whelp," he chortled, "Cap'n been better to bust yaar skull and leave yaar stiff for the gulls." With that, he threw his head back and let out a terrible laugh that to me sounded like evil incarnate, and my flesh crawled with fear and revulsion. He backed out of the room and disappeared from my sight, and I heard him rummaging about in some unseen part of the room outside. I looked wildly around the room in the dim light to find any means of escape, and was dismayed to see that there were no openings other than the door itself. I was being held in a small storage room with three thick wooden rafters that ran across the ceiling. The foul man returned to the doorway and dropped a heavy wooden bowl to the floor in front of me. Part of its contents spilled out onto the floor.

I became aware of the faint aroma of steamy broth, my stomach leapt as the sickness overtook me. Involuntarily, I twisted my body and bent over to the side to vomit on the dusty floor. My stomach was empty, so the violent heaves yielded little but strings of saliva.

"Ha! Yer a lubber, that's certain!" he said in a condescending manner. I felt myself growing angry at my helplessness.

"Who are you?" I shouted. "I demand that you release me now."

With a burst of energy that took me by surprise, the man lashed out with his foot, kicking me savagely in my midsection. I saw bright lights as intense pain shot through my body, the breath leaving my lungs in a rush as I crumpled to the floor.

"Drag yer arse 'ere me Spanish mate. Nuff said, yae?"

I tried to respond, but my throat was so dry that all I could muster was a croak.

"Ah ye dog," my captor growled, and reached out a hand, grabbing my arm roughly and dragging me across the small room on my knees. I was amazed at the strength in his arms. There was a scraping sound and a sharp grunt, and in one deft motion, he was behind me. In a matter of seconds, the knot holding my wrists was undone and I was pushed to the hard wooden floor, landing roughly on my open palms.

"Ye best eat yer grub, mate. It's all you'll be ge'en, innit," he said in a mockingly calm voice.

"Who are you?" I cried out. "Where have you taken me?"

He turned from me and made his way out the small door
of the room and I saw, to my surprise, that one of his legs was
missing. In its place was a wooden post and cup that was
carved smooth and attached to his body just above his right
knee. He walked with a dragging sort of hop that I
recognized as the source of the strange sound that I had heard
earlier. He pulled the door closed with a loud slam, once again
plunging me into darkness. From the other side of the door, I
could hear that terrible cackle of laughter.

I knew that I had to get something into my empty
stomach so I fumbled in the darkness until my fingers found
the wooden container in the center of the floor; I reached
inside and grabbed at the contents, finding a soft chunk of
some unidentifiable meat and a piece of soggy biscuit soaked in
brine. I raised it to my mouth and bit into its bland,
tastelessness, attempting to savor it as much as possible.
Afterward, I rolled over on my back and stroked my sore
abdomen where the cruel man had kicked me.

"You will pay for that, my friend." I said softly.

Now that I had time to think, I began appraise my
situation from a practical standpoint. I was a prisoner here;
that was for sure. I had seen some of these men before, in La
Habana just the day before. I thought of the boy whose
prowess I had sorely misjudged, and the old man who had
held his head regally high as the townspeople and
soldiers jeered at them as they were paraded to the
Government house.

How had they escaped?

I leaned back against the wall and tried to quiet my mind.
The amulet emitted palpable warmth against my chest, and I
instinctively raised my hand to caress it.

She was there, floating in the darkness, glaring at me with burning hatred in her eyes. Her raw beauty was evident, and I could see why the man in my dream desired her so. Her face bore the familiar white markings and her black, lustrous hair fell over her shoulders. I looked away, hoping that the unwelcome vision would disappear.

When I turned my gaze back, my heart leapt with fear. She had transformed back into the rotting, corpse-like demon. Her eyes were now black and shiny, and her skin gray and mottled. She opened her mouth as if she was going to scream, exposing those brown, rotted teeth. I then heard her terrible, whispering voice in my mind.

"You are where you belong, boy. I will have you soon!"

My eyes snapped open, and I cursed myself for having fallen asleep. I had no idea how much time had elapsed, but I frantically tried to formulate a plan for another visit from the one-legged man. I looked around the room and saw that the only object at my disposal was the wooden bowl he had brought, so I grabbed it and rose to my feet. After a short time I heard the strange, shuffling gait of his approach. The metallic latch groaned and the door slowly pulled open.

"The Cap'n wants ter see you, mate," he growled in that same rough, measured tone.

I said nothing in response, so he pulled the door open wider. Light poured into the room from his lantern and he peered into the room. His eyes swept the interior and I could see him shudder with surprise.

Wot in bloody 'ell?" he said, and stepped fully into the room. I looked down on him from above where I had wedged my small body in between the ceiling rafters. Just as he started to look up, I let myself fall, simultaneously bringing the full weight of the wooden bowl down on his skull with all the force I could muster. He let out a loud groan and crumpled to the floor, his hands flying to his head. I scrambled over to him and grabbed his collar with both of my hands, pulling him up and slamming his head into the wall hard, my enraged face now inches from his. Gone was the arrogant look, and in its place an expression of pain and fear.

"You stupid old fool!" I hissed, "Where have you brought me?"

Blood now poured down over his face from the gash on his cranium and was matting the gray hair of his hair and beard.

"You've cracked me skull, ya!" he howled.

I pulled him back and slammed him to the wall again.

"I asked you a question! Tell me!" I demanded.

"Yer aboard the *Night'n'gale*," he moaned, "under Cap'n Brattock."

"Brattock? Is he the man I saw taken in La Habana?"

The old man just looked at me blankly and said, "Capn's ne'er been took."

That was when I was struck with something heavy, and all of the lights went out.

CHAPTER 8
CAPTAIN BRATTOCK

I awoke with a start to find my hands again bound behind my back. I was seated on the floor in an upright position with my back leaning against a smoothly finished wooden wall. The breeze from an open set of small, hinged glass windows hit my face, and I reflexively sucked in the sweet pureness of it. It was wondrous compared to the dank foul odor that had filled my previous tiny prison. I glanced around and saw that I was now on the upper deck of the ship in one of the cabins. The sky was visible through the windows and I could see white clouds slowly moving across it. I quickly realized that this was an illusion caused by the ships forward progress.

I looked around the room and saw that it was cluttered, but fairly elegantly furnished, especially for a ship full of criminals on the sea. Every surface was littered with various objects that all seemed to be of the highest quality: silk bolts of cloth, a wide assortment of firearms, fine china, swords, and a large globe on a spindle, just like the one my father kept on his great desk in La Habana. A tall bureau stood by the wall; each compartment stuffed with rolled up charts and other documents. There were several wooden chairs and, in the center of the room, a finely crafted table on which lay a large map. On top of it lay a black hat with a long red feather fixed to the brim.

The door pushed open with the creak of iron hinges and a large man walked in, his heavy heels rapping on the wooden floor. He turned and stared directly at me. He was an imposing figure. Tall and slender with a darkly tanned and weathered face, he appeared to be in his third or fourth decade of life. He had long dark hair streaked with thin lines of gray and tied behind his head. Under his nose was a trimmed mustache, and the on his chin was a small, neatly braided beard about six inches long. On his chest was large diamond-encrusted crucifix that hung from a long, gold chain around his neck.

"How's the fine lad this morning? he asked in a deep, resonant voice.

I glared at him defiantly, not saying a word.

"I am commander of this vessel of miscreants," he said. He looked at me for a long moment without saying anything, as if waiting for me to respond. His appearance was more like one of the crew. He was dressed more casually than I would have expected for a ship's captain, wearing a loose, crimson shirt tucked into black breeches.

"You do speak English, don't you?"

I was scared and angry, and maintained my silence, answering him with a defiant stare.

"I apologize for Rupert's behavior down in the hold. He's not quite right, you know? Tends to be a tad abusive with the guests."

He was English, but his accent was unlike Rupert's, and I knew that he came from a different class of people than my one-legged friend below decks.

He turned and walked across the room and began to shuffle some papers on the table, his back turned toward me.

"You nearly killed him, you know," he said pointedly, a hint of humor in his voice.

I felt the soreness of my ribcage where "Rupert" had kicked me.

"I'll finish the job when next we meet," I said.

He spun around and gazed at me, then burst into hysterical laughter.

"You could certainly outrun him." the captain said, now nearly choking with mirth.

My temper flared at his impertinence.

"Where are you taking me?" I demanded in a sharp tone.

He suddenly grabbed a wooden chair with no arms and spun it around, planting it backwards squarely in front of me. He straddled the seat and sat with his arms resting on the back of it and looked directly into my eyes, an expression of mock astonishment on his face. He began to speak as if he had not heard me at all.

"You are from a wealthy family, are you not?"

I did not answer him, but glared back with contempt, trying my best to conceal my fear. This man truly scared me.

He continued. "You may fetch a good ransom from your parents."

"If its ransom you are considering for my kidnapping, you will be disappointed. My father is dead," I said flatly.

He continued as if I had said nothing. "You speak the King's English fairly well. You must have been properly schooled."

I said nothing. He continued to examine me as if I was a rare animal that he had captured in a snare.

"I thought of letting the men kill you, but my heart could not justify taking the life of one so innocent and frail."

My face reddened with anger at these words.

"I will soon show you how frail I am," I said.

"Aah, you have a temper, my Spanish friend. You will make a fine addition to the crew of the *Nightingale*. She's a fine sloop, as you can see, with seventy-five able hands and fourteen guns."

My eyes widened at this.

"I would never join a gang of murdering criminals. You will all hang for your foul deeds."

He laughed again, throwing his head back.

"You certainly can defend yourself. My men told me of how you soundly thrashed that boy in La Habana," he said.

As he said this, I recalled the fight with Allejandro in the square.

"What is that amulet around your neck? It looks like an ancient piece of treasure. It is from the Indians of New Spain, I think."

There was a moment of panic as I tried to look down at my chest. Was this criminal going to steal it from me?

"Do not worry, boy. I do not need your trinkets. I have plenty to go around. I am merely inquiring of its origins."

"It belonged to my father," I said, tears welling in my eyes. "He is dead now."

"I see. I too lost my father at a young age," he said.

My anger flared yet again and I began to shout, at the same time straining against the tethers on my wrists.

"Who are you and where are you taking me?"

He smiled and laughed and said, in an almost cheerful voice, "I am Captain Bartholomew Brattock, originally of Whyte, slayer of the enemies of Queen Anne."

"Pirates are the enemies of all governments," I said.

"Ah, this is where you are mistaken, my brash young friend," he said, his tone sharpening a bit. "I am not a common "pirate" as you so boldly put it, but a mere privateer and business man with Letters of Marque from the admiralty."

"You are a cruel, godless criminal. My father says that you should all be hanged."

I paused as I realized what I had said; the memory of my father's death filled my exhausted brain.

"What is your name, boy?" he asked.

I looked down at the floor as the defiance seemed to drain from my body.

"Santos. Santos Alvarez."

"Ah, a fine Spanish name. Normally, one who bears such a brand would quickly find my blade. But I like you, young Santos Alvarez. I think I will spare you for now."

With that he rose from the chair, opened the door and walked out, pulling it closed behind him.

I felt such a sense of foreboding that I could not find ease for one second. The man had spared me to play with like a cat plays with a fat mouse, most likely to return later for the kill.

What was going to happen to me? Was I a slave? My heart ached as I thought of my father and what he would do to these foul men. My eyes again clouded with grief and frustration over his loss and the complete devastation of life as I knew it. I hung my head, and salty tears ran down my face.

It was then, as the sweat poured down my chest, that I again became conscious of the weight hanging around my neck. The amulet bounced lightly against me as I moved and seemed to radiate odd warmth that penetrated my chest and soon spread to my very soul, the sensation giving me a sense of comfort and strength.

Why hadn't they taken it from me? They certainly had plenty of opportunities to do so when I was unconscious. I hung my head and let exhaustion carry me away.

She was there in the darkness. Her mouth moved in that same terrifying way and the vengeful look in her black eyes brought back the sense of foreboding that I had grown so accustomed to. I tried to reach out to her with my mind and communicate; to let her know that I meant her no harm, and that she should move on to her resting place. She seemed to know that I was doing this and pushed me away, and I felt a wave of black hatred that made my blood run cold. I knew then that she possessed a power greater than anything that I could ever overcome, and that she wanted to kill me.

I was abruptly awakened from my nocturnal struggles by the rusted creaking of door hinges. Two men burst into the room, both very rough in appearance, and took positions on each side of me. The smaller of the two bent down and untied my wrists and each grabbed one of my arms, roughly pulling me to my feet. I was dragged out through the door, the brilliance of the day's light blinding me and the heavy smell of the sea coming to my nose.

"Bring him hither, mates. We've much work to do this day."

I was thrown down to the deck, sprawled on my stomach on the hard wooden surface of the deck.

I then heard the hysterical laughter of many men and felt a stab of panic. I looked up to see six or seven pirates standing around me. They all looked at me; their faces marked with derisive sneers, and it quickly became evident to me that I was the current subject of entertainment.

They were dressed in the same way as the pirates I had seen at La Habana. Most of them were barefoot, and more than a few donned loose stocking caps that hung halfway down their backs. Many wore either the short blue jackets common to British naval seaman or finely tailored silk shirts with breeches or trousers made of canvas. Others were clothed in nothing but filthy rags. Their faces were weather beaten and almond-colored from years in the blazing sun, and they all seemed to possess the same swarthy toughness of experienced seamen.

"Aye, this is the one 'oo nearly ended poor Rupert's trip," I heard someone say.

I turned and saw that it was the older boy, "Calico Jack" he had called himself, who had hit me on the wall in La Habana. He was leaning against the rail with his arms crossed; a smug, arrogant look on his face.

"Let's see this little Spanish girl dance for Rupert," he continued, "Maybe his pretty face will get bruised."

Many men laughed at this. I felt a surge of anger and glared at him. He returned my gaze with one of silent scorn. I knew then that he was going to be trouble for me. I looked past the men toward the front of the ship and saw Captain Brattock leaning against the rail, looking amused as he watched the developments.

I felt like a small rabbit about to be pounced upon by a wolf. The instincts that I had developed during the years of training from my father came to me, and I began to look for the weakest link in my situation.

"Let Rupert 'ave another go at him," one of them barked.

The pirates standing around me separated, and I saw the man who had been my captor glaring at me from a position on the deck about fifteen feet away. His head was wrapped in crude bandages from the blow I had given him with the wooden bowl. The blood from his wound had seeped through, giving him an even more bizarre appearance. In his hand was a large boarding hook with three prongs and a rope tied to it that was used to pull a ship closer during an attack on a prize. He waved it threateningly as he slowly advanced toward me with his hobbling gate. The men began to cheer him on as I crouched into a fighting stance. I turned to look at Captain Brattock and was met with a self-satisfied, expectant grin. I knew that I would have to fight for my life.

CHAPTER 9
PROVING GROUND

Rupert leered at me, his narrow, bloodshot eyes filled with hatred and a crooked, menacing grin on his face that showed his rotting teeth through parched lips. I boldly met his gaze, remembering something that my father had taught me. Men like Rupert had been the subject of derision for most of their lives and had great reserves of untapped resentment and anger. If such a man were an adversary in a fight, one way in which to unsettle his thinking was to tap into these reserves. I changed my hard expression to a smile, putting on my best expression of sarcastic defiance. I could see that my insolence was achieving the desired effect as he began to visibly tremble with rage, and I knew that he was indeed near the breaking point.

"Rupert," I shouted out loud, surprising the men so that they all turned their attention to me. "Did I not show you at our first meeting what becomes of men who provoke me?"

A couple of the sailors laughed at this and the whole tenor of the event seemed to change. As I expected, this put the man over the edge. He bellowed like some great animal and made a mad rush at me, at the same time raising the hook menacingly over his head. I shifted my position so that I was closer to the ornately carved wooden rail that surrounded the entire upper deck and crouched down lower. He quickly closed the distance between us and brought the hook down with savage force. I waited until the very last minute, and then spun away from him and around to his right side. He was much larger than me, but slow and unstable due to his wooden leg. The hook smashed into the top of the wooden rail, two of the barbed ends sinking in and holding fast from the force of the blow. With all of my might, I pushed Rupert toward the rail. Before he even realized what was happening, his weight shifted and he lost his balance. He hit the rail and pitched forward over it, falling headfirst toward the salty waves below. Fortunately for him, the rope from the hook tangled around his body and he jerked to a sudden stop, his body thudding against the side of the hull just above the water line. He bawled with pain and surprise as his bulk swung back and forth above the frothy sea.

The whole thing happened so fast that the sailors sat in stunned silence. Captain Brattock broke it with a clap of his hands.

"Bravo! An impressive showing for young Santos!"

I stared in disbelief as I saw him laughing. The men looked at him, and as the ridiculousness of the situation sank in, began to howl and hoot with amusement. Suddenly, I found myself surrounded by them as they congratulated me, slapping my back with approval and shaking my hand. This was entirely unexpected and I was at a loss as to how I was supposed to react. The pirates then led me to the area of the deck in front of the forecastle where a large number of the crew had assembled in a large circle.

"A dram for all!" Captain Brattock shouted, answered quickly by a wild cheer from the men. I looked through the crowd of men and met the gaze of young Calico Jack, noticing that he was the only one not laughing. He stared at me as if he were analyzing an insect. I quickly looked away and actually began to enjoy the attention and praise that I was receiving. As the rum was passed around, a ragtag band of three musicians took their place in the center of the circle and struck up a boisterous song- a tune that I did not recognize. An old man with a grizzled, unshaven face and rags for clothes played an ancient looking fiddle and danced around like some sort of dervish. He was accompanied by another wearing a long stocking cap and a brightly striped tunic, who banged on a stringed instrument with a long neck that I had never seen before. A small African man kept time on a small drum that looked like an animal skin pulled over a wooden bowl and tied tightly with cords. After the first refrain of the piece, the fiddler began to sing in a high, reedy voice. Many of the sailors began to clap and stomp their feet on the wooden deck in time with the ditty and were singing along. I was relaxing a bit and actually found myself tapping my toe in time at the infectious enthusiasm of the song.

Fiddler: *Me bonnie bunch o' roses, O!*

Crew: *Go down! Te blood red roses. Go down!*

Fiddler: *It's time for us to roll an' go!*

Crew: *Go down! Te blood red roses, O!*

I could never in my wildest reveries imagine a more sundry gathering of men in one place. I watched as several of them pulled Rupert up over the railing and helped him untie the knot around his chest. He was moaning in pain as he slowly got to his feet.

"Captain!" he groused, "the little Spaniard, e' don't fight fair! Give me another chance, please?"

Captain Brattock gave out another belly laugh.

"Rupert, I see you dropped your scabbard into the drink. What will you do, run him through with your pine leg?" he said.

The sailors around him burst into laughter at this, and Rupert hung his head in shame.

"Or better yet," the Captain continued, "maybe I will give you another chance so little Santos can put you back over the side to find your lost property!"

The men laughed even harder at this.

The wild dancing and festivities continued for hours. The whole upper deck was a mad flurry of activity as scores of men ran about in drunken revelry, chattering to each other in various languages. No less than ten of them slapped me on the shoulders and said encouraging things to me in whatever dialect they spoke.

"Way at 'eem mate. Ole Rupert 'ad it comin,'" said a grizzled old sailor dressed in brightly colored rags.

One of the African sailors approached me and flashed a broad smile.

"Hey mon, Rupert- he sorry he met you, is he!" he said as he punched my shoulder. He wore a large cutlass in his belt and had a brace of pistols strapped across his chest. I felt the deck under me pitch slightly as a sea breeze blew through my hair. I looked out over the roiling sea at the horizon and smiled as a thought occurred to me.

What in God's name had I gotten myself into?

I saw Rupert on the far side of the deck looking at me with resentment and shame, and noticed for the first time how small and vulnerable he appeared. I realized that the crippled man had most likely been the brunt of many jokes and pranks by the men for quite some time, so I felt a sudden wave of pity for him. I left the men by the "foc'sle," as the English sailors called it, and walked over to him.

"Rupert," I said, surprising the men standing around us. "I am regretful of the way our disagreement went. I did not mean to embarrass you. Please forgive me."

There was silence as I extended my hand. Rupert looked at me, suspicion and confusion filling his red eyes. He slowly raised his hand and I gripped it, noticing how much he trembled. The sailors looked at me and there was an awkward pause. Then, all at once, they let out a loud, animated cheer. I looked at the Captain, who smiled and gave me an almost imperceptible nod of approval.

As I walked away, a hand grasped my arm. It was the one who had knocked me out on that wall, the boy who called himself Calico Jack. I could feel that he had a very strong grip. He leaned close to my ear and spoke in a venomous whisper.

"That was very clever, boy. I see that you are brilliant at dispatching half-wits, but the real test will come soon. You'd best steer clear of the Captain. Let this be fair warning."

He gave my arm a quick shake and was gone.

CHAPTER 10
THE PIRATES LIFE

After the fight with Rupert, I seemed to have achieved a certain amount of respect among the crew. I learned very soon that I was expected to work with them, so I spent time familiarizing myself with the ship's workings. Even though I considered myself a captive and found the work to be difficult and tedious, it was a good opportunity to explore and learn about a real wind-born vessel, something that I had wanted to do since I was very young. My father had always forbidden me to venture aboard the great ships as they rested in port because of what he called the "bad influence of sailing men." I suspected that his real intention was to keep my head in the books and safe on dry land.

I was fascinated by the huge canvas sails that seemed to be under so much tension that they would burst and be torn asunder by the relentless wind of the open sea. I marveled at the agility of the sailors as they climbed through the intricate, spider-web tangle of rigging. I could not understand how each rope had an origin, an end, and an important purpose. I quickly took to the routine of the day-to-day work maintaining the ship and keeping it on course. The labor was non-stop and grueling, and in the evenings I would stumble to a comfortable place I had found near some large piles of neatly corded rope and quickly fall asleep, exhausted from the day's toil. When the weather permitted I preferred to rest in the open air of the upper deck because I found the odor of the men and the animals below to be intolerable.

I ate what all of the men ate. Our daily rations amounted to a small amount of watery broth and hardtack, a biscuit made from flour and salt. Occasionally the meals included meat, but only when the ship was near a port or after a prize ship with turtles or livestock aboard was taken. Hardtack was very tough and lasted a long time without spoiling, which made it the ideal food for long sea voyages. This rock-hard food was most often crawling with small, brown insects called weevils that bored holes through it as they fed on the yeast. A sailor would often have to completely submerge his biscuit, and then skim the insects of the surface of the water before he ate it. One could also put his biscuit near an open fire, the heat driving the intruders out. This was the common shipboard fare that Rupert had introduced me to when I was held prisoner.

The ages of the pirates ranged widely; from that of the cook who, like Rupert, appeared to be in his late sixties and sported a rough wooden crutch for a right leg, to the boy no older than thirteen years who sat on a barrel near me tying knots in a large piece of rope. Surprisingly, there were not as many open disputes between the men as would be expected with such a mixture of races, ages and nationalities. I learned that these men had signed actual articles of behavior that consisted of "rules of conduct" regarding firearms, shares from prizes, voting on new Captains, restrictions on gambling, fighting, leaving the ship before the conscription time, and benefits for injured men. One rule that I found particularly interesting was the total ban of women on board at any time. When I asked Captain Brattock about this he explained that there was no worse situation for bad feelings and jealousy among the men than when one of them had a female to keep him company. Men would often fight to the death over this.

I noticed that there were many Africans among the crew who spoke to each other in what sounded like French. They appeared to be treated as equals by the pirates. I was surprised at their audacious behavior as they brazenly walked among the crew. This was in sharp contrast to the way they were treated in La Habana. I had visited the slave market many times with Badu and could remember feeling sad for the people that were bought and sold there. Even though I was raised to believe that Africans were property and therefore destined to be servile, I felt sadness and pity as I saw the tears of mothers and fathers whose children were sold away to the highest bidder from some distant sugar plantation on another island. I considered Badu a family member, and I was very confused about the whole enterprise. I remember asking my father about the strange institution of slavery, and his response had been delivered in the usual slightly agitated, pragmatic way.

"Santos, there are some things that you will not understand until you are older. Men like Badu are irreplaceable members of our society. They were often taken from the most terrible and uncivilized places in the world and given a chance to be productive members of an enlightened society."

"What if they do not want this? What if they want to stay where they were born?" I asked.

"Most of the Africans are very well taken care of by their owners, Santos. They have much better lives with proper guidance and exposure to a developed culture."

I could see that my father was uncomfortable with the subject, so I let it go. From then on I accepted the institution as something that would always be around and one that I did not quite understand.

It was very early in the morning and a thick fog had rolled in over the sea's flat horizon. This was my first night on "watch" and I was trying to remain as vigilant as possible as I peered out through the dense haze. The long hours of this post gave me plenty of time to think about my new situation. I was still full of fear, anxiety, and confusion at the strange turn of events that had befallen me. I stood on the deck and gazed out at the ocean, hoping to catch a glimpse of the sail of a Spanish ship that would take me back to my dear Dorathea. What would happen to me? Would I ever see my home again? These dark thoughts filled my mind as the salty sea breeze blew through my hair and clothes. After what seemed like an eternity, the grayness of morning broke. I was suddenly startled by a noise.

"The Captain requests your presence in his cabin."

The voice sounded like rusted hinges on a door. I turned to see nothing. Confused, I looked down and saw the shortest man I had ever seen in my life. He was no larger than a six or seven year old child, but sported a full beard and long hair that jutted out from under his stocking cap. Over his left eye was a grimy patch held by a thin strap wrapped around his head. I followed him into the Captain's quarters, the same room where I had previously found myself a captive. The dwarf did not enter, but stood beside the entry, so I walked in.

"The door, please," the Captain said in his deep, gruff voice.

I pulled it closed behind me. As my eyes adjusted to the dim light of the cabin, I heard a scraping sound. He pulled the wooden-framed chair across the floor, gesturing to me with a sweep of his broad hand.

"Please take a pew, Santos."

I looked at him warily for a moment, and then sat down as he walked to the far side of the table and took his own seat. Picking up an open bottle of rum, he poured a small amount of it into a large, crystal goblet. Downing it in one gulp, he slammed the goblet to the table, the sound startling me. He gave me a mischievous, satisfied smile before he spoke.

"Santos Alvarez, you are an interesting one indeed. You are very good at defending yourself, boy. The first thing I want you to know is that I have no intention of harming you. I have actually taken a liking to you."

He paused for a moment and let out a low chuckle.

"That was very entertaining, what you put old Rupert through," he said.

"I'm glad you enjoyed it so, but your entertainment could have killed me," I said with a sarcastic tone that seemed to both surprise and amuse him.

He smiled again and looked at me intently, then began to nod his head slowly.

"Yes, yes, that could well have happened. But it did not."

I gazed back at him defiantly for few moments, and then spoke.

"Who is that young looking fellow with the blonde hair who seems to hate me? I think that he would like to slit my throat as I sleep."

"Ah, you must mean Jack. Oh, excuse me; he calls himself "*Calico*" Jack. He is an ambitious one, and clever as a rat. I would avoid the likes of him if I were you, Santos."

"Why does he detest me?" I asked.

"I believe that he is threatened by you, Santos. He is an excellent hand and a very able seaman, but I do not trust him."

"What are you going to do with me?" I asked.

"Santos, I have to explain something to you. I am a man of trade. I am responsible for every man you see out there. I was not born into this by an aristocratic ancestry; I took it by proving myself. If I do not deliver what we need and the prizes come far and few between, they will replace me with another. They are a superstitious lot, and the tide can turn on a Captain overnight. That is the way of the Brethren."

He leaned toward me, looking directly into my eyes.

"I would like you to reconsider my first offer and take the oath. I am much more serious this time than I was the first."

He sat down in a chair by the small bay window that opened to the sea. Turning his face toward it, he closed his eyes, letting the sea breeze blow through his hair. At that moment, he looked older and more vulnerable to me and I felt my original disdain weaken a bit. He continued to speak as he gazed out the window.

"You are both a good fighter and have intelligence. This is rare among men, especially in one so young. I think that you will look at it differently when you hear what I have to offer. I treat my men as well as any Captain of the Brethren. Even Rupert was paid handsomely for the loss of his leg during an unfortunate incident a few years ago. I paid him four hundred pieces of eight. The loss of an arm pays even higher: six hundred pieces."

I was taken aback by this. I pictured Rupert hobbling around the deck.

"That is very reassuring, Captain."

"I am prepared to pay you, Santos," he continued. "I will start you out at one hundred pieces. This is the same pay as a talented sail-mender."

As I listened to Captain Brattock, I felt the warmth of the amulet hanging around my neck and thought of my father. I cut him off and spoke.

"I have to be honest with you, sir. Even though I was brought aboard your ship against my will, I have been treated well since my initial imprisonment by your men. In my opinion, these poor souls you have here will eventually end their misguided existence when they meet the hangman's noose in a Spanish court. I will never consider joining you and your men, Captain. It is my opinion that, even though I am impressed with their tenacity and resourcefulness, most of the men here are murderers and thieves."

Even I was surprised at the audacity of my speech. The Captain looked at me with wide eyes and a mock exasperated expression. He then let out a loud, raucous laugh.

"Oh my gods, you amuse me Santos, with your high and mighty nobleness. I would like to tell you about myself. When I was a child, my family lived in an area near the London docks. My father was a tailor with a very small income, so we were very poor. To make matters worse, he was a slave to the demon rum and often spent on it what was left of his meager pay. There were five of us cramped in a one-room hovel, with a table, two chairs, and some straw for a bed.

Despite the squalor, we were content with just having each other; that is, until the plague came to our door. The first to go was my sister Lenore, and then, a few weeks later, my little brother Samuel. My mother was hysterical with grief over this and very hard to deal with. Many nights, my father chose not to come home, preferring instead to stay and commiserate over his bad fortune with his mates at the pub. A short time later, he disappeared as completely as if he had been cast off the face of the earth. I learned from some local boys that he had been pressed into military service aboard a sea-going vessel. Upon hearing this news, my mother suffered a breakdown that reduced her to a crying mess. While I was out stealing food from the local street merchants so we could eat, she hung herself from a rafter.

I found myself truly alone with nowhere to go. Lying about my age, I joined the English Navy at the ripe old age of fifteen. I spent three long years suffering at the abusive hands of the officers before I decided that I had taken enough, and smashed a Lieutenant in the head with a large gaff, cracking his skull and sending him over the side. Oh, I was angry all right, Santos; I was a killer in training."

He paused and poured himself another portion of the rum, downing it in one large swig.

"I was beaten within an inch of my life by those fine officers and thrown overboard for dead. The cold water revived me, and I managed to find a piece of floating wreckage on which I drifted aimlessly for days in the open sea. I would have perished if I hadn't been rescued by some Spanish sailors of questionable occupation.

For the next few years I served as a galley slave on their pirate vessel. I endured all of their abuse, and secretly took every opportunity to learn their methods. One particularly cruel bastard used to enjoy beating me regularly for no apparent reason. With each savage blow he delivered, I promised myself to unleash the hounds of hell on him and one day claim retribution.

Later, as the drunken Spaniards were getting supplies at a small island in the Bahamas, I managed to escape. Pretending that I was a shipwreck survivor, I was able to gain passage to the island of Jamaica. There I met old Captain Henry Morgan himself, just before he perished from drink and consumption. He took a liking to me and helped me sign onto a British privateer.

I spent the next ten years preying on Spanish ships, eventually working my way up to Captain. One of my fondest memories was when we took a Spanish sloop as a prize and I found myself standing face to face with that same bastard who used to beat me every day.

Let me tell you, it was not his lucky day, Santos.

After chasing him around the deck for a while for amusement, I tied him to the mainmast and watched him shriek with pain as my men tortured him. I then had him hung from the yardarm of his own ship.

Santos, I found in these rough men the family that I never had, and have been a faithful member of the Brethren for most of my life. I have also become very wealthy in the process, and own a great deal of property in Jamaica. I know one thing for certain; I hate the English and the Spanish with equal sentiment. I can honestly tell you, Santos, that if I had encountered you on a Spanish prize that I intended to take, I would not have hesitated to run you through and leave what is left to the sharks. You may say that this is cold and wrong-headed, but it is all I know."

I stared at him for a long moment, not knowing what to make of his story. I had to admit that I was in awe of him, and even respected his honest, brutal outlook. He seemed to be part animal, devoid of the insecurities that plagued normal men. I realized then that he was stronger than all of the merchant cheats that my father had dealt with over the years. It occurred to me then that he was not a pretender, but a living, breathing *"boucanier"* like the ones from our childhood games. He was a murderer, a cunning thief, a shrewd businessman, an experienced seaman, and a gentleman. I admired him, but knew that I could never be like him.

"I am sorry for the unfortunate circumstances of your upbringing, Captain, but I regret to say that I cannot stay. I would be grateful if you were to let me off at the next port of call."

At this the Captain again burst into riotous laughter.

"Port of call", you say? Santos, no man on this boat has the ability to amuse me as you do. It has been many months since I have had good conversation. Most of my men are so illiterate that they cannot spell their own names. Here, let me show you something."

With this he walked to the far edge of the cabin, pausing in front of a large, rectangular object that was covered by a sheet of red satin. He grabbed a corner of it and pulled it away, uncovering what lay underneath. I was astonished by what I saw. It was a fancy, wooden bookcase full of volumes. At least forty books were lined up in neat rows on five shelves, with the works of literary masters like Robert Herrick, Shakespeare, and Cervantes right before my eyes. It was as if I were in our library back in my home in La Habana. Captain Braddock sensed my appreciation of them and smiled.

"Gold and silver doubloons are not the only treasures to be plundered from English and Spanish transports. They are at your disposal, Santos. I want you to enjoy them."

He laughed heartily, then turned and walked out of the cabin leaving me to peruse my new treasure.

CHAPTER 11
GHOST WOMAN

Many days passed without incident as the relentless
Caribbean sun and salty sea breeze chafed my pale skin. I made
the most of the daily routine aboard the ship and did my best
to learn everything I could about its inner workings. I was
forced to work from dusk till dawn, performing many menial
tasks under the supervision of a burly English fellow named
Chamford, whose nearly unintelligible instructions were
difficult to decipher.

"Lift the skin up, mate, and put into the bunt the slack of
the clews, not too taut but just right, the leech and foot rope
and body of the sail; being careful not to let it get forward
under or hang down abaft!"

If I didn't understand him the first time, he would get
very angry and snarl at me menacingly.

I soon realized that most of the pirate crew consisted of
men with extensive seafaring experience who worked as hard
as any men when required, but took whatever chance they
could to be lazy. Most were prone to drink and violence,
many of them having wounds and missing limbs. Shipboard life
consisted of periods of very hard work followed by long
durations of inactivity under the hot sun during which the
men traded stories, slept on the open deck, or played dice,
cards, or a game called "backgammon." The art of swearing
and creative blaspheming was at first shocking to me due to
my religious upbringing, but I soon grew used to it and, at
times, found it quite amusing. Creative cursing is indeed an art
form that I have grown to respect over the years.

The navigation of the ship interested me greatly. Brattock
explained to me that even though the charts and maps strewn

about his cabin were beautifully detailed, they were often inaccurate. He took sightings from the deck every mid-day with a quadrant, an instrument for measuring the altitude of celestial bodies. This was a small object made of brass consisting of a ninety degree graduated arc with a movable radius for measuring angles. There was a plumb bob tied to it to ensure that it was held at a true ninety degree angle. He explained to me the concept of latitude, and how he could determine where we were by using his quadrant to take the altitude of the sun as it came to its greatest height. He then made a simple "correction" for the position of the sun north or south of the equator according to the date and the season. I found this fascinating and assisted him whenever I could, often peppering him with so many questions that he became weary of them.

I knew that my "friendship" with the Captain had become the subject of discussion and gossip among the men, and saw more than a few looks of contempt every day from the worst of them, especially from Calico Jack. I was always careful to wear the amulet hidden under my shirt, but some of the more unsavory men were so bold that they stared at the lump on my chest and smiled like wolves. I knew that if any of these low men tried to steal it, I would kill him. Whenever I engaged any of them in conversation, my hand would instinctively rise to cover and protect it.

After the sun went down, the deck was much cooler and lit with the amber glow of large lanterns that swayed in the ocean breeze. When I was not on watch I would go to a secluded corner below decks, light a candle and read a book from the large bookshelf in Captain Brattock's cabin. One night, I had completed a book and needed a replacement, so I ventured to his quarters. I found that he was present, so I knocked lightly on the door.

"Come in, damn your eyes," he said in a gruff voice. As soon as I entered the room, I could smell a strong scent of wine and knew that he was very drunk.

"You there, Santos. What do you want?" he said with a slur.

"I've finished this book and would like to get another, if it's all right." I said in a quiet voice.

"Which one did you read?" he said.

"King Lear, by Shakespeare."

"Ah, yes. A fine one," he said, "Did you like it?"

"Yes, I did," I answered.

He leaned back in his chair, his bleary eyes betraying his intoxication, and stared at the ceiling.

"I often feel like Lear, Santos, unable to trust even my closest mates. Oh, for a daughter with the devotion of Cordelia!" he said, raising his hand with a dramatic flair.

I quickly pulled one of the books from its place and moved toward the door.

"Santos, please stay and talk. I have no one with a brain on this godforsaken sloop of war," he said.

I reluctantly took my place in the wooden chair facing him. I didn't enjoy talking to him when he was drunk because he didn't listen well, only wanting me to hear his opinions.

The conversation lasted for at least two hours, with the Captain expounding about everything from the evils of the royalty, to religion, and then to privateering and piracy. As he spoke, he gulped wine from a large decanter by his side, his voice rising and falling with his passion about whatever subject we were discussing. I did my best to parry his stubborn opinions, but the drunker he became the harder it was to get a word in. He finally grew pensive, and spoke softly as he absently cleaned his fingernails with his large knife.

"My men and I cruise these waters for a reason, you know. The great ocean stream in the Bahama Channel runs just to the west of here; along the coast of "La Florida" as the Spanish bastards call it. There are a great many vessels wrecked on that coast, boy. You don't want to be one of them, let me tell you. There are hundreds of miles of coast with nothing there but low scrub pine. If the Spaniards don't get you the tribes of cannibals just waiting for some poor soul to wash up on the godforsaken beach will. I've been there and have seen it myself."

There was a long pause as I thought of the barren coast of La Florida and how forbidding it must have been.

"Santos," he said, "can I tell you something in confidence?"

Unable to believe what I was hearing, I stared at the man who had kidnapped and twice nearly killed me.

"All right sir," was all I could muster.

"There's a rat among my crew who is, at this very moment, plotting my demise. What do you think of that?"

I didn't know what to say. My thoughts immediately went to the strange "Calico Jack" as the most likely suspect, but I said nothing.

"I don't know, Captain," I said. "I am not as familiar with the men as you are, but if I hear anything I will tell you."

The Captain did not reply because he had passed out where he sat. His head was down, resting on his arms on the table, and he was snoring peacefully. I quietly got up from the chair and, picking up the large book that I had originally come for, made my way through his door and into the night.

I went back to my quiet place below decks and made myself comfortable, leaning back on the pile of rope and propping the large book on my chest in front of my face in order to read by the poor light of the small candle. I soon became drowsy and found it hard to keep my eyes open.

She was there, laughing at me with that terrible smile, the stark white lines on her dark, beautiful face.

"You will be with me soon, boy," her terrible, rasping voice taunted.

I tried to turn and run, but my legs would not work. It was as if I were being held in one place by some unseen force.

"I will show you the force of my power this very night, boy!"

I woke to the sound of a rodent skittering across the wooden floor in front of me. I shook my head to rid myself of the visions conjured in the dream. What was wrong with me? I set the book down and got up, wending my way up the small stairway to the deck. I walked to the rail and looked out over the dark sea. My thoughts inevitably turned to the only person that I really missed. Her beautiful face filled my daytime dreams and my heart ached with the loss of her. What would my sweet Doratea think of this bizarre new life into which I had been thrust? Did she pine for me in my sudden unexplained absence? Was there any type of search going on to find me? I stood by the deck and gazed at the horizon, my mind a torrent of emotion. Would I ever get back home?

I took in a deep breath of the briny air and walked slowly across the deck as the cool night breeze gently rippled my hair and shirt. The sea was strangely calm with no sound save for the endless rhythm of the waves as they gently slapped the hull. The swaying lanterns gave their soft light, casting long shadows and leaping across the wooden surface of the deck like strange demons in a macabre dance. I felt ill at ease as I progressed along the port side of the ship. I thought it odd that there was no one about and I supposed that the Captain would be furious that no one was at watch. Slowly, I walked toward the bow and saw that there were no lights in any of the windows. There was an unusual sensation on my chest, and I became conscious that my father's amulet was emitting that odd, familiar warmth. I slipped my hand under my shirt and caressed its rough surface.

Was the whole ship asleep?

I stared into the darkness ahead of me, and heard a sound that did not quite fit in. It was a woman's voice, singing softly. The words were unrecognizable but the melody was hauntingly beautiful. I peered ahead and noticed a strange, barely detectable greenish light shining from behind the forecastle wall. A niggling of fear crept into my heart as I slowed my pace toward the peculiar illumination. The singing got louder and the glow grew brighter, and I realized that whatever was there was moving toward me. As it slowly came into view, I gasped in horror, falling backwards onto the deck.

The spirit's features were placid, but seemed to tremble as if concealing something terrible just beneath its surface. The corners of her black mouth were turned up in an almost imperceptible smile of satisfaction, and I could see that, in life, she had indeed possessed a dark, exotic beauty. My eyes met hers, and my heart leapt with fear as I found myself caught in their black emptiness. They seemed to see straight into my very soul, and I felt myself being drawn in. With some effort, I pulled away and lowered my head. The sad, beautiful melody grew louder and seemed to fill my head, as tears sprang out of my eyes and ran down my cheeks.

It was not a person, but a figure from hell in the form of the native woman from my dreams. I grabbed the skin of my arm and pinched it hard; trying to wake up. Her form was bathed in the sickly greenish radiance that shone out from her in all directions. She moved in a terrifyingly slow and unnatural way as if completely underwater, her loose shift waving and pulsating as if there were no force binding her to the earth.

"This cannot be! Why do you come before me like this? Why do you haunt me so?" I screamed, not daring to look up. "What do you want?"

At first, she offered no answer, and as her form dissipated into the now blinding green light, I heard her thin, unearthly reply in my head:

"*I want your soul, boy, your soul.*"

CHAPTER 12
PRIZE

I heard a man shout and my eyes snapped open abruptly. The dream had been one of the most terrifyingly vivid yet, and I shuddered as I recalled it. The morning sky was a heavy gray color, and my hand instinctively rose to my breast to examine the familiar shape of the amulet. Its surface was against my skin, as if it had lain near the hearth of a fire.

The shout came again, this time clearly.

"Prize!" one of the crew shouted. I leapt to my feet at the same time trying to shake the grogginess of sleep. The deck was a mass of confusion with pirates running about in a mad rush like a hive of angry bees. I ran to the nearest man that I recognized, a grizzled looking fellow of about forty years with a long silver streaked beard. I grabbed his shoulder and pulled his face to mine, the smell of alcohol nearly overcoming me.

"What is it?" I said, "What has happened?"

"Why, there's a prize about, mate! Tis' a fine mornin' lad!"

He gawked at me, his bleary, red veined eyes wide with excitement.

"A prize?" I demanded. "What do you mean?

He pointed off the due south.

"There."

At first I saw nothing on the gray horizon of the morning, and then I noticed a small spot of white. As I hooded my eyes with my open hand to block the sun's glare I could make out billowing sails. I looked toward the bow and saw Captain Brattock standing on the highest point of the forecastle gazing out over the expanse of sea through his spy glass. He turned and brayed at the crew with the loud voice of authority.

The Captain had transformed from the jovial, relaxed and somewhat inebriated man I knew into something different. Dressed for battle, he wore a long black frock coat which was unbuttoned and billowing in the wind at his sides, exposing a brace of fine pistols strapped across his chest. On his head was his broad, black hat with an eagle feather protruding from its brim at an angle. He waved his long scabbard in front of him as he ran back and forth across the deck, shouting orders at the men. His face was animated, and there was a gleam of excitement in his eye about the impending encounter with the prize ship. His appearance was very intimidating, and I could now see why he was such an effective leader in battle. He had become a cunning predator about to pounce on his prey.

"Ho lads! Look handsomely now, there's booty to be had!"

A loud cheer went up from the men. I saw that they had instantly become united as one, and were now focused on the single purpose of conquest. A few of them sprang up onto the rigging to get a better view.

"Bear downward before the wind!" Brattock bawled as the sloop turned slowly toward the direction of the prize. We were quickly underway at a fast clip, and the sails of our quarry soon became more clear and distinct.

"Why is she alone? Where's the rest of the flotilla?" he howled. He turned his head toward me, his eyes glinting with predatory excitement.

"You'll be havin' a reunion, boy! She's Spanish!"

I was both shocked and excited at this news, and I immediately ran to the rail, my hands gripping its surface as I tried to catch a glimpse of the vessel. Brattock paced up and down along the rail, a hungry look of anticipation in his cold eyes, letting loose a continuous mixture of order's and oaths, none of which I completely understood.

"Keep those guns ready, lads. I'll not send a broadside unless forced. She's a fine lady and we'll use her right if we can board! Strike the colors, boys! We'll make the bastards kiss the gunner's daughter! Ready the guns, lads!" he barked.

I could hear the low rumble and feel the vibration of the deck as the cannons were rolled into place below decks.

There was a rustling, flapping sound to my left, and I saw that one of the pirates was running a flag up the main mast. I looked closely and saw that it bore the distinctive red cross on a white field; the symbol of New Spain. My heart sank as I realized what the pirates were doing. They intended to sidle up to the ship as a friend in disguise; a foul but effective tactic of which I had heard of back home. Nearly half an hour passed before we were close enough to see that it was indeed one of King Philip's merchant vessels. It was considerably larger than the *Nightingale*, and I recognized its design as that of a Dutch flute about eighty feet long and sporting two main masts. I had seen ships of this kind being loaded and unloaded many times in *el puerto* in La Habana.

Captain Brattock had most of the men, including the Africans, down below decks, leaving only the ones with makeshift uniforms in plain sight. The unsuspecting ship drew closer and "hove to" in a gesture of good will as they viewed the friendly colors. I could see men in finely tailored clothes standing on the deck looking toward us, and I watched the expressions of apprehension appear on their faces as we drew nearer. This ship was at least three times as large as the *Nightingale*, but not as well gunned. I looked at the name painted on the bow: she was the *Cristobal*.

"Lower the boats!" Captain Brattock suddenly yelled.

I watched them drop quickly down to the water level, each boat filled with eight to ten men apiece, each rowing off swiftly toward the unsuspecting vessel. As they drew close to the hull, shots rang out and I gasped with shock as one of the well-dressed sailors clutched his stomach and pitched forward off the deck, hitting the water head first. Shouts of surprise and anger erupted as the pirates leaped into action by throwing grapple hooks from their pirogues up onto the deck of the flute, tugging them until they held fast. Frantically, they leapt from the boats and began to climb her side. A few Spanish sailors had seen this and were leaning over the side, shooting pistols straight down into the pirate's faces. I saw two men fall dead into the roiling water.

The whole event unfolding before me was overwhelming to my young, impressionable mind. I had never witnessed such graphic violence in my young life and felt sick at the sight of it. I ran to the edge of the deck and vomited over the side as tears ran down my face. The noise of the vicious fighting was so vile to me that I could not comprehend it. I turned and looked back at the center of activity through bleary, unbelieving eyes. I heard a buzzing sound by my right ear and something very small, fast and heavy hit me in the cheek like a vicious bee sting, twisting my head to one side. My hand rose to my face and I felt a warm, sticky sensation. I pulled it away and saw that my fingers were covered in blood. I had been shot! I felt lightheaded and nearly fell to the deck in a near faint. I probed the wound with my fingers and realized that I had been grazed by an errant musket ball.

I turned and ran to the hatch and hurriedly descended the stairway. I saw the gunners by the forward cannons crowded around the portholes waiting to line up their next shot. I heard the command to fire and they let loose a deafening blast from the huge gun, the recoil kicking it back on its chocks. The men then cheered loudly as they heard the tell-tale screams of pain and panic and splintering wood from the prize. I found a hiding spot by some barrels and slid in behind them, wrapping my arms around my legs and holding my eyes shut as the blood from the wound on my face ran down my shirt. I reached up and clutched the amulet hanging on my chest and prayed for the spirit of my father to help me. For some reason this calmed me somewhat, as I felt the warmth of its magic once again permeate my body.

I was surprised at how quickly the attack ended. I became aware that terrifying sounds of the battle had waned, so I unsheathed the small sword that Captain Brattock had given me and crept out of my hiding place. Slowly, I made my way back toward the main stairway and past the gun deck, noting that it was now vacant save for a few injured men who leaned against the wall and groaned. I could hear the footsteps of men running and shouting on the main deck above, so I made my way up the stairs one at a time and poked my head up through the hatch. I looked around at the absolute mayhem taking place and quickly realized that there was an excellent chance that no one had noticed my earlier act of cowardice. I pulled myself up to the deck and walked toward a large group of men gathered near the bow. The prize ship was pulled up very close to the rail of the *Nightingale* and tied off with grappling hooks and rope. I could see that many men were aboard the heavily damaged *Cristobal* and had commenced the process of looting her. Men were carrying crates and chests up to her deck and smashing them open, discarding whatever contents they considered useless over the side in to the water.

"Santos!"

It was Captain Brattock. He had spotted me, so he strode over. He had blood on his fine coat and was drenched in sweat from the exertion of the battle.

"You are hurt! Did you take a ball?" he inquired as he took note of the wound on my face and my blood stained tunic.

"I- I think so," I stammered, "It's not serious."

He reached out and poked at the gash. As he did this I grimaced and yelped in pain.

"Ah, it's not bad. The ball grazed your face and kept going. It'll leave a scar, that's for sure. That pretty face of yours will have character now!"

The men around him burst into laughter at this as they beheld my pitiful state.

Captain Brattock turned his attention away from me and focused it on a group of men on their knees in a row, hands tied behind their backs. I realized that they were several prisoners that had been taken from the *Cristobal*.

"Gentlemen!" the Captain roared at them, "Here is one of your countrymen! He is one of your attackers!"

I glared at him angrily as the pirates howled with laughter, and some of the prisoners looked up at me. There were seven of them, and I could see that four were badly wounded. They were all filthy with grime and blood and wore exhausted, scared looks on their faces. I looked back at Captain Brattock.

"These men fought bravely for only being twelve in number," he continued, "and it is unfortunate that five of them met their fate when all they had to do was capitulate."

My eyes quickly moved from one face to the next, and I suddenly froze as I realized that I recognized two of them. One of them was Miguel Mejia, a small ferret-faced man with a broad mustache who I had heard my father describe as a "trader in commodities." He had been an infrequent visitor to our home for years.

I remembered that the man had always had a shifty way about him and always spoke with a sarcastic sneer. My father had never really trusted Miguel, but had explained to me that "business was business." The other man was Carlos Anguiano, a very fat and small featured man whom I had seen at the *embarcadero* many times over the years, but did not really know personally.

Miguel stared at me in disbelief, his wide eyes standing out against the filth of the battle on his face. I watched his eyes take in the sight of me; first at the wound on my face and my blood soaked tunic, then at the sword that I gripped tightly in my hand.

"I cannot believe it," he said out loud, "what in the name of God are you doing with these men?"

"Silence!" Captain Brattock barked before I could answer and pushed Miguel in the back with his foot so that he pitched forward on the deck. His face struck the wooden surface of the deck, and he let out a loud grunt.

"Captain!" I shouted brazenly. "I know that man! Please show him mercy!"

Captain Brattock laughed out loud at this.

"Santos, please. These men are our prisoners. You will have your chance to torture them later!"

There was yet another roar of laughter from the surrounding pirates.

I stared back at Miguel and Carlos helplessly. I wanted to cry out that I, too was a prisoner, but I quickly quelled the urge. I did not dare to appear weak in front of my captors.

"Take these dogs below," Captain Brattock bellowed, "They will be interrogated later."

The seven men were jerked up to their feet and roughly pushed to the hatchway as the pirates jeered insults at them. I felt as if I would die right where I stood. How could I have been such a coward?

CHAPTER 13
A PLEA FOR MERCY

I crept as quietly as I could down the stairway to the gun deck, then down the hatch to the storage deck, being careful not to spill the pitcher of water that I had drawn from one of the large wooden casks. As I made my way through an open doorway to the main hold, I could make out the shadowy figures of the prisoners lined up against a low wall. There were only two small ports for light and air to enter the room, so it was hard to see anything clearly. The men were sitting against the wall facing the ports and I could hear the sound of their chains dragging across the wooden floor as they moved. I detected the smell of human waste and grew apprehensive.

"Miguel?" I whispered.

"Santos Alvarez? Is it you?" he answered in a voice filled with fear and frustration.

"Yes, it is me."

"You have some explaining to do, my young friend."

I was surprised at the level of anger and disrespect that I heard in his voice.

"Keep your voices down!" I whispered hoarsely. "I have some water."

I tipped the pitcher of fresh water to the mouth of the first man in line. He reached his hands up to steady it to his lips, the chains hanging from his wrists rattling noisily.

"Senor Mejia, you must understand that I, like yourself, am a prisoner here. I was taken by force from the shoreline in La Habana," I said.

"Is that so, boy? If that is the case why are you not here next to us in chains?" Miguel hissed; his voice sharp with anger.

I heard the other men shuffle and groan with agreement. There was something in his voice, something understated that I could not at first pinpoint.

"Miguel, I have come down here to see if I can help you. What can I do?" I said.

"You can slit the throat of that English dog Brattock in his sleep and set us free," he answered.

"Miguel, if I even tried such a thing we would all be killed immediately. There are over seventy men aboard."

"Santos, I knew your Father very well, and he would not be happy at the sight before me right now."

I grew angry at this. I wanted to shout out to him that my father never trusted him, but I held my tongue.

Miguel continued to hiss at me.

"I never would have believed it, but I saw you standing there, covered in Spanish blood, your hand still clutching the armament that you used to take your fellow countrymen's lives. I cannot believe it."

"Miguel, silence your tongue for you know not what you say. The Spanish blood you saw was my own! Can't you see that I am your only hope?" I implored.

"I will see you hang, boy!" he said loudly, "You and your Captain are enemies of Spain!"

I lost my temper at this.

"Miguel, you are a fool, and always have been."

I stomped out of the room, seething with anger and frustration.

Later that evening, after the sun had disappeared, I found myself in Captain Brattock's quarters.

"Please show mercy on these men," I pleaded, "I have known Miguel since I was a child."

It was night and the amber glow of the lantern dimly lit the cabin. The sea was calm and the two small windows were open, letting in the briny air. On the horizon, the bright three quarter moon shone starkly against the dark night sky. I was sitting in the high backed wooden chair, the Captain leaning back in his large one, a bottle of fine Spanish wine in one hand. He was well on his way to drunkenness, but I felt that I had to try.

"Santos, please. I have to be firm here. The *Cristobal* is a great prize. My men are still finding useful treasures on her and have been at it for two days. Your countrymen's employers will probably kill them anyway if they make it back alive!"

He threw his head back in a hilarious laugh at his joke. I did not share his mirth and looked at him severely.

"These men are innocent. Please have mercy and let them go. They are worth nothing to you."

"Santos, we have not abused your friends. Fortunately for them, I do not yet have to resort to torture to find the gold and silver casks. There are many that were not hidden very well, and to tell you the absolute truth, I do not know why they were traveling without an escort. Every good sailor knows that these waters are not safe with so many pirates about!"

He let out another burst of laughter. "The loveliest things we've found are the food, tools, clothing, and medicine they were carrying. And the wine is exquisite. The "Cristobal" is a fine trophy indeed!"

"Your men are so drunk that they can hardly walk, Captain. It's disgraceful. What are your intentions for the prisoners?" I asked.

He looked at me for a moment in a patronizing way, and I knew by the indifferent look in his eyes that he did not care what my opinion was.

"Do you really want to know, Santos?"

"Yes, I do."

"All right. I would like to start with that older one..umm." He stroked his small beard as he tried to remember the name.

"Miguel." I said quickly, "He is the loudest of them, I know."

"Yes, Miguel, that's him. I am going to have my men light torches between his fingers until he screams like a woman and tells me where his private store is. After that, if he and the others are still alive, I will set them adrift in a longboat, left to their own devices."

"That is cruelty! They will surely perish!" I said, my anger rising.

"Yes, I know, Santos. It is a crime indeed. Good longboats are hard to come by!"

At this he threw his head back and laughed again. I could hold my frustration in no longer.

"You, señor, are not an honorable man!" I shouted.

There was a long silence, and he looked directly into my eyes, all the humor leaving him instantly. I saw the anger and calculating resolve take hold. There was a terrible and unnerving coldness in his gaze, and I found it hard to hold.

"I would like to hang every last one of them right now, Santos. As I told you before, I hate the Spanish and the English with equal weight. I quiver in pleasure at a vision of their boots swinging in the breeze from the *Nightingale's* yardarm. I still may fulfill this dream. Let me ask you a question, Santos; when you saw my men in La Habana the day before you were taken, do you recall seeing the man who led them?"

I thought back to that day and remembered the severely beaten older man who had glared defiantly back as the townspeople hurled insults. I recalled that I was in awe of his audacity and bravery.

"Yes, I remember that man. Who was he?" I asked, carefully choosing my words.

"His name was John Culliford, but the men called him "Sea Dog" because that is how he fought. Captain Henry Morgan had him as a sailing master many years ago in the attacks on Portobello, Maricaibo and Panama. "Sea Dog" owned property in Jamaica and had amassed wealth beyond his needs, but he loved the sea and hated Spaniards. Not only was he the quartermaster of the *Nightingale*; he was also the best man I ever met. He was my friend.

Brattock turned his head from me, his voice trembling a bit.

"He not only saved my life three different times during raids, but fought alongside me, helping me to maintain order on this vessel full of malcontents. We had taken a prize off the northern coast of La Florida near the Spanish settlement of St. Augustine. She was a small but fine Portuguese caravel full of silver, and I needed a prize crew to bring her South around Cuba to Jamaica. I chose "Sea Dog" Culliford to lead it because he was the most qualified man aboard. We made fine time sailing due south against the outside of the Bahama Channel for two days, but there was a blow and we lost contact. I got the word later that the Spaniards had taken them in a raid in the Straits. There were twenty-one of them.

"I remember." I blurted out, "They escaped, didn't they?"

He moved his head up and down slowly as he spoke.

"Yes, most of them did. Shortly after you saw my men, the Spanish bastards decided to "make an example" of someone to show what the Spanish Crown thought of the "Brethren of the Sea." Later that same morning, they hung my friend John Culliford, and then had him drawn and quartered. That is why the others fought so bravely to escape. So you see, Santos, La Habana took my friend and gave me you. Believe me when I say this; it was not an even trade. My original plan was to hang you and send what was left of you back there as a message. But, alas, you cast your spell on us and we spared you. Please leave me now, Santos before I regret that decision."

CHAPTER 14
SPANISH REPRISAL

I left the Captain's cabin with great urgency, briskly striding across the deck, my teeth clenched in anger. The night was cool and very dark and the air thick with humidity. I could smell the storm that was brewing and saw that clouds covered the stars from view. Stopping to gaze out across the water, I watched the intermittent flash of silent lightning as it momentarily illuminated the surface of the sea as if it were daylight. Was that a ship's sail that I saw off in the distance?

"How are you, mate?"

The low, calm voice nearly made me jump out of my skin, and I spun around to face its source.

"Who's there?" I demanded.

The lightning flashed one more time, revealing the face of young Calico Jack. He was sitting on a barrel directly behind me.

"What do you want?"

"Santos, I need to tell you something important."

I looked at him and did not reply, so he continued speaking.

"You are the favorite of Captain Brattock. He protects you."

"I have nothing to do with that, Jack. I am a prisoner here." He chuckled softly.

"The men downstairs are prisoners. You are not one of them. They hate you, you know."

"Why are you speaking to me, Jack? I know that you have no love for me."

"You are right, Santos. You are Brattock's little Spanish dog. I think that hounds as a whole are not to be trusted."

I reared back in anger at his words. He continued to speak. "However, I see something different in you. You cannot go home because, if any of those fools below get home safely, you will be seen as a criminal in the eyes of your own people. Captain Brattock has sealed your fate, my friend."

"Why are you telling me this, Jack?" I asked."

"I am warning you, my friend. Changes will be coming soon."

"What do you mean?"

"Mark my words, sir."

With that, Calico Jack got up and moved quickly away.

Frustrated and confused by both the boy's strange manner and his cryptic riddles, I made my way to the hatch. The lightning still flashed periodically, so I looked off into the distance across the turbulent surface of the sea. Again, I could swear that I saw something off in the distance. I shook this thought off and made my way down to my hiding place on the lower storage deck, my thoughts as stormy as the night sky. I laid my head back and listened to the creaking of the ship as she rolled in the growing roughness of the ocean. The wind howled outside as I slowly closed my eyes.

She was there in front of me, her terrible features bathed in that eerie, green light. She was smiling as she moved closer, her black, vacant eyes turned up at the sides like a demon's.

I could feel her foul breath on my chest, and I looked down, too terrified to meet her gaze directly.

"Santos" she whispered, "I am waiting for you. We will be together soon."

I awoke in fear and confusion, and to the sound of a shrill whistle blowing. The dream had been so vivid that I felt that

I had been there, and the woman so real that she seemed to be alive. I saw that it was daylight, and I raised myself to my elbows and looked up at the huge beams that supported the deck above.

Suddenly, there was a terrible blast and a shuddering vibration that seemed to lurch the entire ship. I heard men shriek in fear and pain from the deck above me. There was more shouting, and the rumbling sound of the cannons being rolled into place on the floor above. I looked at the opposite wall and saw three large rats scramble along the surface of the wood and disappear behind a pile of coiled rope. There was another loud explosion, and I felt a huge thud from below and heard the sound of splintering wood as the whole ship seemed to tremble from the impact. I leapt to my feet and ran to the stairs, scrambling up them two at a time. I will never forget the scene before me. The sailors on the gun deck were scrambling madly to load the cannon as their feet slipped and slid on the wet floor. I felt a wave of humid sea breeze and rain hit my face.

I was shocked to find myself looking through a gigantic jagged hole that had been blown through the wall of the hull. I could see the side of a massive Spanish galleon riding very close to us, her cannon aimed point blank at me. There was a huge amount of splintered wood everywhere, and I turned my head toward the opposite wall, seeing the twisted, mangled bodies of two sailors who had been killed in the explosion. I screamed and scrambled up the stairs, springing up through the opening to the main deck. The wind was blowing very hard with rain pelting down, and I could hear what sounded like thunder in the distance. The large Spanish *"buque de guerra"* had lined up parallel to us and was in the process of firing her third broadside into the *Nightingale's* exposed side.

The deck was a mass of confusion as men ran about, madly trying to get some kind of defense organized.

"What has happened?" I cried out at one of the sailors.

"We are done! The Spanish tricked us in the night and came close."

I now remembered the small shape that I had seen off in the distance the night before, and guilt gripped me as I realized that I had not told anyone. I looked to the stern of the ship and saw Captain Brattock frantically shouting orders at his men. There were many of the wounded and dying scattered about the deck, screaming and moaning in pain. It seemed my impressionable mind that the gates of *inferno* itself had opened. The Spaniards were in the process of throwing gaff lines with grappling hooks onto the *Nightingale's* deck in preparation for boarding. I ran to Brattock, shouting to him.

"Captain! How can I assist?"

He turned and glared at me with wild eyes, his saber held high and rain running off the brim of his wide hat, the exertion of battle etched on his face.

"Santos, you must go now! We may have more of a fight here than we planned. There may be danger in this one, boy. You should go and hide!"

The rain began to come down very hard, and I looked around wildly as I ran toward the hatch. I dove headlong into it, tumbling down the stairs to the gun deck below. I heard a sound from below me; men clambering up toward me on the stairway. I found myself face to face with Miguel and the prisoners. He looked at me and screamed with rage, pointing his trembling hand in my face.

"Santos Alvarez! We have prayed to God for our escape and he has granted his salvation! You will hang, boy! I will guarantee it!"

I could not help myself. I swung my fist at him with all of my strength, connecting directly with the side of his bearded face. His head jerked back and he fell to the stairs in a heap, unconscious. The other prisoners stared at me in dumbfounded horror. Trembling with rage, I blurted out the first thing that came to my mind as I looked down at his body sprawled on the stairs.

"I'd sooner be a pirate than a lying swindler like you!"

I turned to face the rest of them. Their looks of helplessness and panic aroused me to even more wrath and resentment toward them. All of a sudden, I was no longer afraid, and I turned to make my way back up the stairs to the main deck. In that moment, I made a decision to try to help Captain Brattock.

"Save yourselves, you fools! It seems that your King has seen fit to spare you!" I bellowed, drawing the saber from the scabbard at my side. I sprung back up to the main deck, emerging back into the melee just in time to witness a large ball split the *Nightingale's* mainmast, the entire top part buckling and wrenching in a twisted maelstrom of ropes and sails. It crashed to the deck with a horrific groan, crushing many men under its massive weight and ripping a gigantic hole in the main deck.

"The ship is lost!" I heard a man scream. I looked everywhere for the Captain. Not seeing him, I then ran all the way across the deck toward the stern, past several injured and dying men covered with blood that had been mangled by flying debris or impaled by huge splinters of wood. There was a great explosion of light and noise, and I felt an impact that lifted me and hurled my body through the air. Then, everything went black.

CHAPTER 15
AT THE MERCY OF THE SEA

Seawater lapped against my face, and my eyes opened to darkness and hard, driving rain. At first, I was confused and had no idea where I was. I bounced on the surface of the sea, up one wave and down the other, my body barely balanced on some large, wooden object. There was a sharp, burning pain in my right thigh and my head pounded with a dull ache. My legs trailed into the water, completely submerged and moving freely up and down with the current. Slowly regaining my senses, I realized the precarious position I was in, so I curled my body, and pulled my feet up onto the waterlogged surface.

I ran my hand over my legs, arms, and fingers to determine that I was in one piece, and found a large, jagged wooden splinter jutting out from my upper leg. I ran my hand over it and tried to assess how bad the injury was. It had gone about two inches into the muscles, causing searing pain.

I slowly started to recall the series of events that had led to my current predicament. I surmised that I was floating on a large section of wooden deck from the ship, and that it had probably saved me from immediate drowning. I could not see a foot in front of my face through the driving rain, and could not move significantly without risking my buoyancy, so I buried my head under my arm and readied myself for the end that was sure to come. The rain pounded down on me and the wind howled over my head. I was completely at the mercy of the elements, and all I could do was wait for either death or deliverance. I reached up to my chest and experienced a small relief as I felt the familiar weight of my father's amulet around my neck. I prayed to God and thought of my darling Dorathea as I drifted across the unforgiving sea.

What had happened to me?

I thought of the fight and the storm, and the great explosion that had sent me flying.

Had I been hit by a cannonball? Why was I still alive?

The wind and rain seemed to gain ferocity with each passing minute, and I held on for dear life. The lonely hours crawled by with aching slowness and many desperate thoughts went through my mind. Night eventually turned into day as the storm gradually dwindled in intensity. The gusting wind decreased and the rain slowed. The sea calmed and my most desperate thoughts waned, only to be replaced by raw exhaustion.

I opened my eyes and saw a lone hawk flying in lazy circles in the brilliant blue sky, gradually climbing as if ascending some magical staircase. The thought came to me, as I admired his freedom and power, that he must be the most wondrous of all creatures and one of the truest miracles of God. My peaceful musings were interrupted by a shout and the bark of a dog from across the field, so I lifted my head from the rough blanket that we had placed on the hillside earlier that afternoon. A short distance away I saw Dorathea running off in the distance through the high weeds, her hands holding up her long skirts to keep them free of traveler burrs. She was giggling lightheartedly as her small terrier ran along with her, yapping and jumping at the folds of her dress as she ran. The sun shone brightly, and I felt that I had never been happier in all my life. She made her way to me, that adorable expression of mock sternness on her beautiful face.

"Santos, how dare you fall asleep when you are with me!"

"*Ahh,*" *I answered, "between the wonderful coolness of this day and the delicious meal you brought for us, I simply could not stay awake.*"

"*The only company I had was my sweet Weasel,*" *she said playfully.*

The little animal ran around her in happy, frantic circles, his eyes glued to her face as he panted relentlessly.

"*Couldn't you think of a more pleasant name for the little thing?*" *I asked.*

"*No. I like it. It fits him and I love it and him.*" *She fell to her knees and grabbed the small dog with both hands, playfully rubbing his sides. As she did this, Weasel's eyes closed halfway and he whimpered with pleasure.*

She laughed again, that girlish titter that sent chills up my spine, and plopped down next to me on the blanket.

"*Do you think I'm pretty?*" *she asked.*

I paused before answering to think of the correct response and just looked into her eyes. Her expression changed to one of indignation at my silence.

"*I asked you a question, you oaf!*" *she said and playfully punched my shoulder.*"

"*Yes, Dorathea, I think you are very pretty.*"

She frowned at this and pushed Weasel over to his side and began scratching his belly. His leg bounced back and forth as she did this as if he were running in place. We both laughed at this, and I again gazed into her eyes.

"*In fact, you are the most beautiful creature I have ever seen,*" *I said, my voice serious.*

She immediately looked away and we both fell into a comfortable silence. I realized that my seriousness had embarrassed her and had probably been a little too much.

"*I'm sorry, Dorathea,*" *I said, "I did not mean to be so forward.*"

She didn't say anything for a few moments, and then turned to me, a knowing smile on her lovely face. She slowly bent her head to mine and kissed me on the lips ever so tenderly. It was the most wonderful moment I had ever experienced. I closed my eyes and became lost in the moment, enjoying the sensation of closeness.

I then sensed that something was wrong. I moved my head back and slowly opened my eyes, and the sight before me caused stark fear to fill my being like an icy river. The woman next to me was not Dorathea at all.

It was her, and her black maw of a mouth was open, laughing hysterically as she stared at me with her terrible, black shining eyes.

"Oh, Santos, your kisses make me swoon!" she said mockingly in that dry, whispering voice.

"YOU WILL DIE SOON, BOY!"

I screamed; opening my eyes as yet another cold, salty wave hit my face. I felt thirst hit me, more powerfully than I had ever felt in my life. I needed water soon, and I knew I could not drink a drop of all that was around me. My exhausted body rose and fell with each wave and it seemed as if every bone in my body ached. I had fallen asleep, but my somnolent mind had been plagued by terrible, vivid dreams. My head pounded worse than ever and the searing pain in my leg burned fiercely.

I knew that the jagged piece of wood had to be removed, so I closed my eyes and clenched my teeth, gripping it as solidly as I could. In one swift motion, I wrenched it free. The pain was nearly unbearable, and I felt warm blood coursing from the wound. I covered it with my hand in an attempt to staunch the bleeding, then painstakingly tore away a large section of my soaked shirt and wrapped it like a bandage around my wounded leg.

Hours passed, and somewhere in my bleary consciousness I noticed that there was a different sound. It was a kind of roar, so I raised my tired head and looked around. At first, my exhausted mind could not process what I saw in the distance. My heart then leapt as I recognized the thin, tan-colored line on the horizon. As I drifted closer, I strained my eyes to catch a better glimpse and soon, a sandy coastline lined with low, green vegetation became visible.

I repositioned myself and doggedly tried to paddle toward it. My efforts were practically futile in my weakened condition, but the wind and waves were favorable and pushed me toward the shoreline. I was soon a short distance from the beach, so I took a chance and rolled off the sodden boards that had been my salvation. Immediately, I became aware of the folly of this decision as I sank below the waves in the deep water. I flailed my arms in useless panic for a time, and then swam for my life in the direction of land. I was so drained, and very close to giving up. I imagined myself drowning, my lifeless body sinking to the bottom.

Miraculously, I brushed the sand of the bottom with my feet, and struggled forward to gain purchase. I soon crawled from the water on my hands and knees onto the soft sand of the shoreline, my body wracked with exhaustion. I inched my way up the beach as far as I could to escape the reach of the advancing and receding waves. I was covered in sand from head to toe and my clothes were rags, but I did not care. I found a large piece of driftwood that jutted up toward the sky and sat back against it, my lungs gasping for air. I looked out at the sea from my new vantage point and felt blackness close over me. I then fell into the deepest sleep I could remember.

PART THREE

LA FLORIDA

CHAPTER 16
CASTAWAY

I awoke to the cry of seagulls. The rain had stopped, replaced by the grayness of a cloudy dawn. The air was chilly on my bare skin, and I winced in pain as I rolled over onto my back. Taking measure of myself, I probed the throbbing wound in my thigh with my fingers. I was relieved to find that the bleeding had stopped and the gash had already begun to scab over, but the searing pain remained steady. Looking down at my arms, I saw that my skin was covered with a deep red rash from exposure to the salt water for so long. My shirt and breeches were torn and barely covered my body and I had lost my shoes. Shifting my weight slightly to relieve the pressure on my wound, I sighed in relief and thanked God that I had survived in one piece.

The wind coming from the ocean was stiff and waves broke on the beach rhythmically, making a gentle roaring sound as they met their end on the sandy beach. Raising my hand to shield my eyes from the rising sun, I searched the horizon in the vain hope that I would see a friendly sail in the distance. There was nothing but an endless line of sand as far as the eye could see. Gulls skimmed along the top of the waves, and I watched absently as they dove to snatch small fish from the shallow surf.

I was so thirsty that I thought I would perish, so I staggered to my feet. The sand was cool around my toes as I walked to the top of the dune line. There were no trees at all, and the vegetation was so thick and bristly that no easy paths were visible through them. I scanned up and down the beach for any change in the landscape that might indicate some source of fresh water or any sort of relief for my swollen tongue and parched throat. Not finding anything, I began to walk to the north. This was the most desolate landscape I had ever seen, and I knew that it must be La Florida.

The sea breeze remained steady as I limped along the beach, staying close to the water because the sand was harder packed and easier to walk on. Small brown and white sandpipers scurried around my wrinkled feet as if I were not there and chased the receding waves down, only to turn and hurriedly run back up the beach as the waves came back in. As I moved along, I looked down at my bloody bare feet and torn breeches and felt that I had never been more miserable in my life. I thought of my father and how much I missed him and his guidance. He would know what to do in this situation. I reached to my chest and clutched the amulet as his face became clear to me in my mind. I began to speak to him out loud as I walked.

"Father, I need you now. I really don't know what to do. You left me alone and I don't know what to do."

"*Santos my boy,*" he answered, "*you will not die here on this beach. I will not allow it.*"

I knew that I was experiencing some sort of delirium, but I welcomed it all the same.

"I am truly lost here, Father. I can only pray for deliverance."

"*Yes, Santos, you must pray to God above and he will provide. Haven't I always told you this?*"

I looked up, and something caught my eye in the surf ahead. There was a ruined wooden structure jutting up from the water about twenty meters out. It appeared to be the remains of a ship that had run aground near the shoreline. As I drew closer, I saw evidence that most of it had been burned.

A pair of broken, charred masts protruded at a sharp angle, with a few remnants of rigging lines hanging from them like broken spider webs. On the beach directly in front of the decayed hulk were a few objects that were only partially buried. I walked as quickly as I could and soon came to what looked like a broken pirogue protruding nearly upright from the sand at a sharp angle. There was a large jagged hole in its side where some large object had smashed into it. I peered inside and was surprised to see a substantial amount of water that had collected in the intact seam of the bow. I dipped my fingers in it and brought them to my lips, and was overjoyed to taste no salt. The front of the boat had filled during last night's rain and had not had time to evaporate or turn salty or rancid. I fell to my knees beside it and thrust my hands into its coolness, cupping my fingers and bringing it up it to my chapped lips. It was the best thing I had ever tasted, but I was careful not to overdo it lest I get sick to my stomach.

I lay down on the beach and closed my eyes, letting the water settle into my body. After a while, I got up and walked to the edge of the beach to get a better look at the ruined ship. Judging by the rot on the remaining wood and the damage by the elements, I surmised that it had been there for a number of years. I figured her to be a square rigged vessel that was known as a "*barque*" back in La Habana. Noticing something on the stern, I waded out into the surf to get a closer look. I pushed my way out until I was nearly up to my chest and craned my neck to see what was inscribed on the title board. It was very faded, but I could barely read the name *REFORMATION* written in script. Underneath, in smaller print was written *Port Royal*.

"An English ship from Jamaica," I said out loud.

Were there any survivors, and if so, what had happened to them?

I spent the rest of that afternoon digging in the sand around the objects on the beach, trying to find anything of value to me. I unearthed a couple of small chests that had been smashed open and were empty and some barrels that were in the same condition. Everything seemed to have been ransacked by some unknown intruders. I found a smooth piece of wood that was almost completely buried, so I dug it up and found it to be a long wooden oar that still had some integrity. It stood higher than me, so I figured I would use it both as a crutch and a weapon should I need it. When I searched higher on the beach near the vegetation, I saw something that looked like some kind of fabric protruding from the sand. I pulled on it and found it to be a fairly large, torn sheet of canvas, presumably from a sail. It took me a good while to unearth it and pull it free. I made slow progress because digging in the coarse sand soon left my fingers raw and sore. I spread the material out on the beach to inspect it and found that, although it was damaged by decay in several spots, most of it was still usable. I sat down on it and massaged my tender hands, trying to come up with some sort of plan for my survival.

My stomach was aching with hunger, and I knew that if I did not nourish myself, I would not last long. The pain of my injury had dulled somewhat, so I made my way to the thick sea grape and palmettos at the top of the beach. I found a small break between them and carefully walked through, taking care not to touch the many sharp leaved cactus plants. I used the oar to bat away some of the thick branches in front of me and to clear the large, intricate spider webs that crisscrossed the path. These had been constructed by golden orb spiders that I recognized from my walks back home. I knew that they were not poisonous to people, but could nevertheless deliver a substantial bite.

The further inland I traveled, the more the landscape changed. I soon found myself in a forest of huge, spreading oak trees with large tendrils of moss hanging almost all the way to the ground. These behemoths were surrounded by a thick undergrowth of sable palm, scrub pine, and bayonet plants. I leaned up against one of them to catch my breath and realized that I was growing weaker from lack of sustenance. I could see nothing that resembled food anywhere around me and did not want to lose my bearing, so I turned to wend my way back to my desolate outpost on the beach near the wrecked ship.

Suddenly, I heard cracking branches from a stand of palmetto trees above the dune line. I could tell that whatever it was had to be large, so I dropped to my knees and froze, my eyes searching the green leaves for a glimpse of whatever it was. I saw a flash of black and became immobilized with fear. I heard a grunting sound, and guessed that the animal lumbering before me was a large black bear. I had read about them in one of Captain Brattock's books, *The Book of Natural History*, and knew how powerful and aggressive they could be. He was only a short distance from me when I saw him raise his great head above the level of the bushes and sniff the air inquisitively. Nearly frantic with fear, I gripped the oar so tightly that my knuckles turned white, not daring to move even one inch. I heard the beast lumber through the bushes near me and began to pray silently, my gaze fixed on the dead brown palmetto boughs covering the ground below me.

Was this how it ended for me? Was I going to die here in this lonely desolate place?

Was it the curse on my family?

Just as I thought that the bear was going to run straight into me, it abruptly changed direction and veered off to the left, wandering deeper into the forest. I felt a wave of relief so great that I saw spots in front of my eyes and felt lightheaded. I was so weakened that I fell to the ground below the bushes and slipped into darkness.

She was there in the darkness, her face wearing an evil, triumphant grin.

It was a younger, beautiful vision of her, and her face bore those familiar stark, white lines.

In another life, she must have been some sort of enchantress. Her eyes were brown and intense, and her hair long, as in all of the other visions.

She then transformed right before my eyes. I watched in horror as she again became the dead thing, her eyes black and fluid, her skin pale gray.

The malevolence of her appearance and the waves of hatred emanating from her were so intense that I knew she must have been sent by the devil himself.

"ARE YOU READY TO GIVE UP, BOY?" she snarled.

I woke with a start and raised my head, looking around wildly for a few disoriented moments. One side of my face covered with bits of leaves, so I brushed them off. The sun had shifted farther to the west and the shadows had grown longer, so I knew that I had been out for a long while. I looked up and saw four pelicans flying overhead, in perfect formation, high in the afternoon sky. I slowly got up and felt my body complain with the sickness of hunger. I bent and picked up the oar and slowly made my way back toward the beach. As I walked, I tried to clear my head of all of the intensely bad thoughts that I knew would do me no good. I resigned myself to the fact that I would never survive if I didn't think clearly and rationally. I hated the cruel woman in my dreams and I would not let her defeat me.

As I approached the edge of the vegetation that led to the beach, I got the strange feeling that something was wrong. I heard something that was the last thing I expected. It was the unmistakable sound of human voices.

CHAPTER 17
VISITORS

I carefully peered over the sea grapes growing along the beach. A short distance from me stood two of the strangest beings I had ever seen. They were very dark skinned, not like Africans, but reddish brown like the *Taino* people from the remote hills of Cuba that I had seen in paintings back home. Their hair was jet black and tied up on their heads in a tight bundle, secured in place with what looked like crisscross pieces of carved bone. Their features were broad and striking, and they spoke with great animation. Both were naked, save for a slight band of woven material encircling their waists and covering their privates. There was a long section of what looked like dried grass that hung from their backsides to below their knees like a horse's tail. They seemed to be having a discussion about the rotted piece of sail that I had earlier pulled from the dune. One of them had a large clay container wrapped in tightly corded rope and slung over his shoulder. I watched as he dropped it to the sand to get a closer look at the piece of canvas.

I watched them from my position behind the large plants, being careful not to make a sound. The kneeling man pulled and poked at the fabric as if assessing its worth and spoke softly to the other. Suddenly, I felt something on my leg, and looked down to see a large golden orb spider creeping slowly up my thigh. In my terrified haste, I had stumbled right into his web. I reflexively reached down and batted it away with my hand, unintentionally shaking the plants in front of me. The man who was standing raised his nose to the air like a dog picking up a scent, then said something to the other man in a sharp, staccato voice. They both turned their heads toward me and began to scan the tree line. One of them pulled a large knife from his side and began to stride toward my position. A flare of panic hit me and I quickly dropped my head behind the broad sea grape leaves, trying to become invisible. In desperation, I gripped the handle of my oar tightly with both hands, drawing it back behind me to deliver a blow, if necessary.

The Indian peered through the leaves and, for one moment, our eyes nearly met. He barked out a command loud enough for the other to hear, and then started to move into the bush, his knife held out menacingly in front of him. I was not sure if he had spotted me or not, so I moved back away from the sea grapes into a more open space. As soon as the Indian emerged into the clearing, I let out an animal scream of rage and swung the oar with all my remaining strength, the stock of it slapping into his right side, catching his arm with a dull thud. He shrieked in terror and pain and dropped the knife to the sand, his eyes wild with shock as he looked me up and down. Turning from me, he ran back toward the beach, wailing and clutching his damaged arm.

I had swung the oar so hard that I lost my balance and fell to the ground, so I lay there for several minutes, afraid to move and sure that I was about to be ambushed and killed. Several minutes passed without hearing anything, so I got up and retrieved my oar. My eyes fell on the knife that the Indian had dropped, so I bent and picked it up. I examined it and found it to be a quality blade of Spanish design and very sharp, so I slid it into the waistband of my breeches. Looking up toward the sun, I slowly began to walk back through the scrub and sharp-leaved bayonet plants toward the beach.

As I drew close to the tree line, I heard someone shout out in fear, so I stood up and peered over the bushes. I could not believe what I saw. Both men were running like madmen up the beach to the north as if being chased by a devil. I was momentarily confused as to how my pitiful attack could inspire such horror. I moved closer to the beach, stopping as I heard another sound that sent a chill up my spine. It was a noise that was familiar, a kind of deep whining grunt. I looked out and instantly knew what had terrified them.

The huge, hulking form of a bear, most likely the same one I had seen earlier, was on the beach, rutting at something with his large paws. I saw that its focus of interest was the clay container that the shorter man had been carrying. The huge animal was having a hard time accessing its contents because the vessel was thinner on the opening side than the bottom. I was upwind, so it could not pick up my scent and was oblivious to my presence. I continued to watch it struggle with the container for several minutes before finally giving up in frustration and tossing it off toward the water. The beast then lumbered back toward the trees.

I thought that it had not noticed me at all until something very strange happened. It paused, and turned its great head toward me. It then looked right into my eyes. The huge, ferocious creature actually held my gaze. It was such a powerful moment that I felt faint. In retrospect, it was possible that a high level of hunger and exhaustion had induced visions in me, but I swear on my father's grave that I saw something so intelligent and knowing in that magnificent animal's eyes that it changed my life forever. It was a look of familiarity that I will never forget as long as I live.

After I had recovered from the shock of this experience, I walked to the discarded clay container that lay on the beach. I picked it up and looked inside. I felt a flood of relief as I discovered that it was full of dried fish. I sat right there on the beach and ate my first meal in "La Florida."

CHAPTER 18
THE CASEEKEY

I had a little more faith in the possibility of my survival, at least for a while. I now had two weapons with which to defend myself; the long ship's oar and the Spanish knife that the Indian had dropped. I quickly devoured the fish that the Indians had left behind, washing it down with a small amount of fresh water from the natural catch basin in the broken boat. Darkness was approaching, and the stiff wind had dwindled to almost nothing. The heat and humidity became stifling, and I started to sweat. I began to feel the bites of a multitude of tiny flies that seemed to converge upon me all at once. Never in my life have I had a more horrible feeling of helplessness. It was as if I were being eaten alive by something that I could not see. It became so unbearable that I fled out into the surf and sat with my head just above the waterline to protect myself from their voracious appetites. After a while, I realized that it would be impossible to sleep in this position, so I slowly made my way back to shore. I located the torn piece of canvas, then crawled a short distance through the dense vegetation, dragging it behind me. I found the most comfortable spot that I could by a large gumbo limbo tree and reclined in its massive branches, wrapped in my canvas and thinking of Dorathea.

As I lay there under the bright moon with the sound of the ocean roaring behind me, I contemplated my dire situation. I knew that no one would be looking for me. I thought of Captain Brattock and his pirates, and the devastation that the ship had endured during the Spanish attack.

Were any of them still alive?

My mind conjured an image of Miguel Mejia's cold stare of contempt before I struck him, and I felt sick to my stomach. How could I have done such a reckless thing? I cursed my anger and the trouble that it had caused me. If any of those men survived the sea battle they would tell my father's friends back home of my supposed treachery, and I would be remembered only as a criminal. I cursed Brattock and his men as my thoughts descended into a dark place.

What was I to do? I knew that I had ended up somewhere on the eastern coast of La Florida, but I had no idea where. The only place that I really knew of was St. Augustine, a place my father had often mentioned. He had a few business acquaintances there, many of whom I had once known by name. I frowned as I tried to remember them, quickly becoming frustrated at my feeble memory. I had always been terrible at recalling details like that, a fault that my father had often chastised me for. I knew that the settlement was located in the northern part of the territory.

I could go there. It might take me weeks, or even months, but I could go there. I surely couldn't stay where I was and wait for the cannibals to return in greater numbers, so I really had no choice. With a little luck, I might even beat the Spanish ship that had rescued Miguel Mejia to the city, and I could properly defend my actions by telling the truth of what had transpired. I had to start walking first thing in the morning. My eyes felt heavy, and I drifted off.

Dorathea and I sat together on the seawall facing the inlet, our legs dangling over the edge. It was one of those magical nights, with countless stars dotting the dark blue sky in a brilliant display, and the soft, ocean breeze blowing in from the north. There had been a gathering at our home that night, and many important dignitaries from La

Habana were in attendance. Our parents were so preoccupied that we had been able to sneak away. I brought her to my favorite place.

"Santos," she said in her playfully flirtatious voice, "how did you find this place? Are you kidnapping me?"

"I stumbled on it in one of my wanderings. Do you like it?" I asked.

She just looked at me, a small smile on her face. "Yes, I like it very much."

I leaned my head to hers and kissed her lips gently, the sensation sending a soft current of pleasure through my body.

"Don't ever leave me, Santos," she said.

I looked past her shoulder and noticed some dark clouds that were moving slowly over the moon's face. For a moment the clouds began to converge and take shape, and I could soon make out an image silhouetted against the orb's celestial brightness. My imagination took over, and it became a huge, billowing monument of smoke. As my eyes focused, a small cluster of lighter clouds above it transformed into the profile of a man standing on top of the murky edifice, his arms stretched out in front of him as if in worship; almost as if offering himself to some great lost God.

"Dorathea, do you see that?" I asked. "The clouds! It's just like when we were children!"

When I got no answer, I turned to her.

She had disappeared.

Panic seized me, and I searched frantically, but she was not to be found.

I looked back at the moon's image and saw that the cloud man on the monument was still there, but he had drifted very close to the edge of the great precipice. The figure then seemed to slowly waver to and fro as if losing its balance. With terrifying slowness, it pitched forward into nothingness, gently disappearing into the night sky.

I heard a woman screaming in the far distance, then the sound of a drum beating methodically. It gradually grew louder and louder, soon becoming so painfully thunderous that I had to cover my ears.

Then, the drumming ceased abruptly, and there she was.

The phantom woman's disembodied face slowly came into view, as if out of nowhere. She smiled at me spitefully, staring at me with her hard, black eyes.

"Santos," she said in a voice that was like wind through whispering, dry grass.

"What do you want? I demanded."

"Do you see the truth in these visions?" she said.

She leaned her head back and let out an evil, hoarse laugh.

I woke with a start, my body drenched in sweat. The nightmare had been terrible; even worse than before. I immediately sensed that something was wrong. The night before, I had wrapped myself in the piece of sail canvas for warmth and protection against the sand flies. I was horrified to realize that there was something large squirming underneath it against my body. I quickly grabbed the edge of the material and pulled it up, peering underneath. My blood ran cold as I found myself looking directly into the beady eyes of a huge snake. Screaming in terror, I somehow leapt to my feet, frantically flailing my hands and trying to unravel the canvas from my body. Thrusting my hand beneath the cloth, I grabbed the writhing creature around its thick torso and pulled it free. The serpent hissed and twisted violently, glaring at me with a menacing look as it reared back to strike. I swung it around my head and flung it at the ground, where it landed with a thud that seemed to shake the sandy earth around my feet. I gasped for breath as I watched it undulate across the sand away from me toward the safety of the thickets. As it fled, I saw that it was red with thick black bands around it. I had always been terrified of snakes, and this one had been in bed with me. I sank to my knees by the large tree, completely exhausted. The fear drained from me, only to be replaced by an overwhelming feeling of sadness. At that moment, I was sure that I was going to die in that lonely place.

I stumbled toward the beach, nearly tripping over a fallen palmetto log. The morning sun was already shining, and a stiff breeze blew in from the east. I emerged onto the sand and was stunned by what I saw. There were at least a dozen natives standing on the beach in front of me, their dark eyes all fixed on mine. Behind them were six long, crudely carved canoes along the shoreline, the paddles lying inside them. I immediately fell into a crouch, pulling the knife from my waist and brandishing it in front of me. I tried my best to appear menacing, while at the same time trying to hide my panic. I recognized the largest of them as the man I had clubbed with my oar the day before. His upper arm was wrapped in a rough bandage, and he glared at me contemptuously. He had painted his body with black and red dye. Many of them leaned on long spears tipped with sharp stone points. They all had dark skin and their hair was tied tightly on their heads around two triangular pieces of bone. They were almost naked except for the grass garment with the horse-like tail.

I noticed that one of the natives was much older than the others. His white hair was very long and fell to his shoulders, and his face was etched with many lines, giving him the appearance of great wisdom. The younger men moved aside as he slowly made his way past them. He stopped about five paces away, looking at me with large, sad eyes. He leaned with one hand on a long, thick walking stick, the very top of which bore an intricate carving of the head of a fierce cat with its mouth open in a menacing growl. Around the old man's neck hung several ornamental necklaces made of multi-colored shells, and a large white pendant made from stone.

The men stood vigilant, but I noticed that several of them glanced nervously toward the vegetation along the top of the beach. The old man walked with a slight limp, and used the stick to steady himself. He and I stood staring at each other for a long moment, the quiet roar of the sea next to us the only sound. After a few moments, he moved a few slow steps closer, and stared directly into my eyes. I could tell that he was doing his best to appear fearless, but I noticed the tremble in his wrinkled hands. He addressed me in a low, quavering voice.

"*Nickaleer?*" he asked.

I was so surprised by this that I jumped back a bit. I did not know what to say, so I answered him in my native Spanish tongue.

"*Mi nombre es Santos Alvarez,*" I said.

The old man breathed a sigh of relief. I could tell that this was good news to him.

His next response rocked me to the core.

"*Ben-va-ne dos,*" he said in a stammering, unsure voice. He pointed his thumb at his chest.

"*Me Ca-no-ba,*" he said.

Had he spoken to me in Spanish? I stared at him in wonder.

"*Canoba,*" I said, pointing at him. "*Donde estoy? Qué es este lugar?*"

His eyes grew large and he backed away from me as if frightened. I realized that if he did understand my language,

it was very little, and probably only a few words. I stepped
away from him, raising my hands in a gesture of supplication
to show that I was no threat. He turned to the others and, in
his own language, barked what sounded like a command. Two
of the natives sprang into motion simultaneously, removing
tightly tied packs of provisions from their backs. They each
approached me slowly, offering me the contents of small clay
containers. The first contained some sort of fresh, darkly
colored berries that oozed juice, and looked so good that my
mouth began to water. I reached in and grabbed one of the
biggest, plumpest ones I could find. I hurriedly bit into it,
quickly discovering the large pit in its center. An unpleasant
bitterness instantly filled my mouth, nearly gagging me. I had
to turn my head away so he would not be offended by my
reaction. It was the worst fruit I had ever tasted. Despite the
foul flavor, I forced several of them down to alleviate my
ravenous hunger, spitting the small pits out onto the sand.
The other Indian offered some dried, raw fish that looked as
though it had been picked up from the beach two or three
days ago. I devoured this as well, ignoring its bad smell. I
noticed that the younger men addressed Canoba as *"Caseekey,"*
and treated him with great respect. I assumed that this was
the old man's title.

We all sat in a circle, there on the beach among the
wreckage of the *Reformation,* and consumed more berries, fish,
and meat so tough that it took several minutes to chew. The
Indians did not look at me, and did not seem to be offended
in any way by my obvious distaste for their food. There was
no attempt at communication, so we all ate and drank in near
silence. I could not figure out why they were showing me such
reverence, but I did not complain.

It was obvious that my new friends were not feeling any sort of urgency, so a long time passed before they made any signs of departure. After what seemed like hours, the old man I now knew of as Canoba raised his head and looked directly at me. He surprised me as his face broke into a toothy grin that looked out of place on his wizened face. It appeared so ridiculous to me that I let out a small laugh. To my surprise, several of them joined in, looking at the old man and chuckling. I had no idea what had happened, but the tenseness in the air left, and I felt safer.

After a while, Canoba raised one bony arm in the air and curtly shouted another order. As if on cue, the two natives on each side of the old man got to their feet to assist him. The rest quickly gathered their things and walked to the canoes, not even acknowledging my presence. I stood there, not knowing what do as they helped him climb into one of the larger boats. Just as I thought they were going to push off and leave me, the old man turned back to me and raised his hand in a beckoning gesture. Having no other recourse, I followed, climbing in and sitting behind him. I made myself as comfortable as possible in the narrow, rough vessel. The canoe was very long and heavy. It was roughly hewn and appeared to have been shaped from a single cypress tree.

As we paddled out into the surf, I remembered Captain Brattock's dire warning of the "Cannibals of La Florida."

CHAPTER 19
THE OFFERING

We paddled all day, moving slowly northward, staying out just beyond the swells in plain sight of the beach. The pain in my leg had mostly subsided, so I was able to focus on my present situation with a reasonably clear head. Despite my sorry condition, I was impressed by the beauty of the windswept, wild coast with its sparse vegetation and tall palm trees waving in the breeze. The formality of our earlier encounter had dissipated, so the Indians chattered amongst themselves in their strange language, occasionally laughing. I was certain that the subject of discussion and humor was me. As the sun began to set, they steered inland and landed their boats in a small cove on the sandy beach. A few of the men ventured off into the palmettos, returning after a short time with pieces of dry dead wood which they laid into a small pile. One of them had a tinder box and a small piece of flint similar to one that any Spanish soldier would carry, and he skillfully used it to light a large fire. They then unrolled small, woven mats across the sand, and they all sat in a row facing the sea. Raising their hands to the east in an act of supplication, they began to chant. They sang together for a long time, their voices rising and falling together, blending with equal rhythm and cadence as if they had been doing the same thing for eternity. After they were finished, they stretched out on their mats to rest.

At first, I found it impossible to sleep over the roar of the sea and the stiff, salty breeze, so I picked up my piece of torn canvas and made my way into the sea grapes to find some quiet cover. I found a comfortable spot underneath a tall palmetto tree and, sitting with my back against it, closed my eyes. I quickly discovered the folly of this, as the unrelenting hunger of the mosquitos and sand flies made rest nearly impossible. I wrapped the material around my face and closed my eyes tightly, willing sleep to come.

We walked along the waterfront, hand in hand, watching the ships coming into the harbor. I noticed a man walking unsteadily along the far side of the street.

"Father, what is wrong with him?" I asked.

"He is sick with drink, son. Look at him and remember what he represents."

As the man stumbled around the corner of a small shop, two other men, filthy and dressed in rough clothing, seemed to materialize from the shadows. They grabbed the intoxicated man and beat him with clenched fists. They then forcibly pulled him into the darkness, out of sight.

"Weakness and unpreparedness have gotten him killed," my father said. "All for a few pieces of silver."

I was shocked by this violent sight, and my father knew it.

Later that night, he took me to his room, sitting me upright in his fine chair. He reached into the great cabinet by the wall and pulled out a long thin object wrapped in bright black satin.

"Santos, I give you this as a father passes his wisdom and word down to his beloved son. You must prepare for the life that you have been born into.

My father looked down at me and smiled as he gently handed me my first sword.

"This is forged from the finest steel in Spain. You must use it to become strong. Superior strength will always be your ally. You must be twice the man of any near you."

I woke abruptly as I felt a hand probing at my chest. I immediately realized that it was searching for my amulet. My arm flew up instinctively and struck it, batting the hand away in one fluid motion. I spun to the left and sprang to my feet, looking into the semi- darkness of the moonlit night. As my eyes grew accustomed to my surroundings, I could see the shape of a man moving toward me. I found myself face to face with the largest of the three natives, the same man I had hit with the oar the day before. He leered at me with contempt. The bandage was gone, and his arm seemed to have miraculously healed.

"Ah, trying to rob me, eh? To take my amulet?" I said.

Before he could think, I let go with a sideways kick, catching his thigh with much force. He let out a small gasp of pain, and I knew that he was surprised at the force of it. He stepped back a few feet and crouched into a fighter's stance. I squared off with him and slowly lowered my hand to the ground, carefully scooping up a small amount of sand. He let out a growl and made a dash at me, quickly closing the distance between us. I swung my fist past his face, flinging the sand directly into his eyes. He screamed in pain, both hands flying to his face. I leapt at him with my full weight, knocking him to the ground, our bodies tumbling together in the darkness. He was very strong, probably more so than myself, but as I wrestled him underneath me something happened in my mind. There was a bloom of red that seemed to blossom behind my eyes, and great rage overtook me. I struck out viciously with my fist and heard the slap of flesh against flesh as I connected, followed by a groan of pain from the Indian. At the same time I pulled my knife from my waistband and swung it down to his throat.

"*Detener o te mataré ahora!*" I said in a hoarse whisper.

I could see his eyes glaring up at me with a mixture of anger and fear. I held him there for a long time until my rage subsided. When I was sure that he would not fight back, I slowly got up, relaxing my grip and carefully pulling the knife away from his throat. He quickly scrambled a short distance away from me on his elbows, and then got to his feet to face me, his eyes still glaring with hatred. I crouched down, ready for more, but the Indian turned to flee. He was immediately met with a sharp blow to the head that sent him sprawling to the ground.

In his place stood old Canoba, his long hair blowing in the breeze and the moonlight glowing on his hair and shoulders. He held his ornate walking staff in front of him, and I realized that it was not just a crutch for the old man but an effective weapon. I could now see in his gleaming eyes the fierce warrior that he had been as a young man. He barked a sharp command at the man, who was sitting on the ground, rubbing his sore head. The Indian slowly got up and slunk off toward the beach.

"*Lo si-en-to,*" he said in a softly apologetic voice. He pointed to the amulet and looked into my eyes, then pointed toward the place where the young warrior had been.

"*Aktil has the sickness of greed,*" he said, shaking his head.

I knew then that Canoba's command of the Spanish language was better than I first suspected. I also knew that I could trust him.

Together we walked back to our crude, beach campsite, and I lay down next to them to sleep.

I woke the next morning to the sounds of the Indians moving about in the pre-dawn grayness. They were already preparing to depart, so I got to my feet and walked into the palmetto scrub to empty my bowels. When I returned, Canoba and his men were sitting on their woven mats, facing each other and chanting some sort of ancient prayer. The one called Aktil emerged from the scrub and walked up to the small group. He carried one of the clay containers, and it was full of fresh blueberries. Canoba looked up at him with a stern expression and engaged him in what sounded to me like a reprimand. Aktil set the container down and looked at me, an expression of sheepish regret on his face. I could see the signs of the beating that I had given him and the swollen lump on his forehead administered by the old man's walking stick.

He walked toward me slowly, at the same time reaching into his waistband. My heart leapt and my hand went directly to my knife, instinctively preparing for another altercation. Seeing this, he raised both of his hands in supplication to show me that he meant no harm. He then held his broad hand out to me. I realized that there was an object on his palm, so I picked it up. He quickly turned and walked back to the others. I looked down and saw that it was a small piece of intricately carved white stone, carved into the shape of a bear.

CHAPTER 20
THE VILLAGE OF AIS

Our strange little party continued paddling for another day until we came to a beautiful inlet that was about one hundred yards across and opened to the sea. We landed the canoes on its southern shore, stepping out into the shallows as the men then dragged them up onto the beach. The water was blue-green in color and so clear and shallow that the sandy bottom was visible from where I stood. As I kneeled down to rinse my face, my eyes saw my reflection. I was startled to see that I had taken on the haggard look of a savage. It seemed that I had aged ten years in the very short time since my abduction by Brattock's men. My cheeks were ruddy with burn from the constant rays of the sun and the relentless sea breeze, and the lower half of my face was covered with the ragged stubble of a beard. My hair was wild and unkempt, hanging down over my shoulders. My bare feet were bloody and swollen from being constantly wet and walking on the hot sand, and my shirt and breeches were in tatters.

I heard a sound and looked up, startled, and saw another dugout canoe with four stout-looking Indian men paddling in unison, gliding quickly toward us across the water from the opposite side of the inlet. Their long boat cut the water like a knife, moving with surprising speed. Looking beyond them, I saw that there were many more coming, and within a few minutes several had landed on the grassy shoreline. As each one slid to a stop in the shallows, the Indians inside jumped out into the water and ran to shore to gawk at me with wide eyes. I felt very nervous as thirty or more formed a group around me, looking at me, chattering as if I were some sort of strange new animal. Unseen hands grabbed at my shirt and breeches, so I covered my amulet with one hand and placed my other on the hilt of my knife as I grew more angry and fearful. I found myself being pushed and taunted mercilessly in a language that I did not understand.

The men wore the same triangular woven straw garment around their privates, with the long, horse-like tail hanging down from their backside. Some of them wore their dark long on their shoulders and decorated with feathers or shells, but most had it bundled on their heads and held in place with crisscrossed pieces of bone. A few had made themselves appear more frightful, wearing varying shades of dark paint or dye that covered their entire bodies, giving them the look of furies. Many of them seemed to be frightened of me and stared intensely from a safe distance. A few were very aggressive, frothing at the mouth and shaking with rage as they pointed at me, shouting unintelligible threats. The effect was so unnerving that I was certain that I would be killed at any moment. I kept hearing the same word over and over; *"Nickaleer? Nickaleer?"* almost as if it were a question. The harassment went on for a few more minutes before the old Canoba raised his staff in the air, bringing them all to a strange, uneasy silence.

"Es-pa-no!" he cried out.

The Indians seemed to pause as one. The anger seemed to magically dissipate and they all moved back slightly, giving me a small amount of breathing room. Canoba began to speak in his native language, and the men grew quiet, listening intently to his words. To my amazement, they started to turn away and make their way back to their canoes. The old man looked at me and smiled as his men pulled their own canoes back into the water. The Indians then helped Canoba get into his. After he sat down, he turned and beckoned me with his hand, so I walked over and climbed in, sitting directly in front of him so that we were facing each other.

"These are my people," he said to me in halting Spanish as we pushed away from the shore.

"Why did they stop?" I asked.

"You *Es-pa-no*," he said, his face growing serious.

"You told them I was Spanish?" I asked, incredulous.

"They fear the Spanish," he said. He then gave me his toothy grin. "You bear man."

I looked at him, my mind full of questions. What had my people done to them to cause such fear?

I was surprised at how numerous the Indians were, and counted more than one hundred men in at least forty pirogues within my immediate view. We rowed past the settlement to the west, heading up what looked to be a river into thick, low forest. I was terrified by the situation I was in, but could not help noticing that the further inland we went, the more beautiful the place became. The river narrowed, becoming more like a stream. I looked from side to side, taking in the splendor of the place with growing admiration. The banks were lined with impenetrably thick white mangroves with spider-like roots that disappeared below the water line. Clusters of short cypress knees protruded above the water between tall shoots of swamp grass and cabbage palm. Massive cypress trees towered high above us, their trunks wide at the water level and thin at the top, their branches draped with long, thick ropes of moss that hung all the way down to the water's surface. Further back from the shore, I could see huge, majestic oak trees with limbs that reached out in all directions, many of them covered with carpets of resurrection fern. Some of the trees were wrapped in the embrace of enormous strangler figs, whose snaking tendrils encircled the oak's massive trunks like an attacker choking the life out of its host. High above my head, the thick canopy formed by interweaving branches and vines allowed only a few beams of sunlight through, giving the place an ancient, cathedral-like atmosphere. A curious raccoon eyed me from his spot on a large chunk of exposed limestone, then quickly lost interest and turned his attention back to the water. A large osprey burst through the high branches, swooping over our heads to the rivers opposite side, eyeing the water for fish that carelessly swam too close to the water's surface. My eyes caught what at first looked like a log floating lazily on the water's surface. Upon closer scrutiny, I was surprised to see a pair of eyes watching me warily. The alligator was at least six feet in length, and watched us approach until sliding soundlessly into the depths.

After traveling for quite some time, we came to an area that was devoid of trees on the north side of the river. I watched as several of the Indians turned their canoes toward the place, sliding into the shallows, and then leaping out to pull them up out onto a small patch of exposed beach. The men rowing our canoe followed suit, and I soon found myself walking into what appeared to be the main village. There was smoke rising from several cook fires, and I could see many people coming out to greet the men. I saw many small, dome-shaped dwellings that were constructed of bent poles with thatched roofs made of palmetto fronds.

The entire place seemed to be covered by vast piles of oyster and clam shells that, in places, rose to more than twenty feet above the ground. I later discovered that these "hills" were actually the remnants of their daily lives. The *Ais* had subsisted on the bountiful shellfish supplied by the rivers clear waters for many generations. After gathering hundreds of whelks from the muddy bottom in large baskets, they then pounded or drilled a large "kill hole" into top of the shell, then pulled the delicious meat out with a long hook. After they ate, they simply discarded the leftover shells on the refuse piles at their feet. Years passed, and the piles became higher and deeper until the whole landscape was altered with these "middens."

The small, domed houses had been built in the area around the shell mounds, while some larger, more elaborate meeting houses had been constructed on top of them. The air was filled with the pungent odor of spoiled fish. The skins of recently killed animals lay strapped to poles to cure, flies buzzing around them as the hot sun dried the raw insides. There were many naked children playing and running about, as thin, scrappy dogs yapped and nipped at their heels. Women sat in small groups around the houses and busied themselves weaving small baskets from saw grass or cleaning fish, the whole time chattering to each other and laughing.

In the center of the village was a long, rectangular structure surrounded by several smaller ones. It was about forty yards in length and ten in width, and open on one side. It was constructed of thick poles lashed together with thongs of animal skin and covered with palmetto thatching. I followed old Canoba as he walked in, making his way slowly through the house's center. There were many men, most of them aged, sitting along the walls and talking softly amongst themselves. When he reached the far side of the long house, he was lifted by two strong, young men onto a raised platform, where he sat on some large, moss-stuffed cushions that had been placed there earlier for him. He crossed his legs and closed his eyes, appearing to fall into some sort of deep meditation. After a few minutes, he raised his head, a crooked, infectious smile on his face as the cheers rose from those who were gathered and waiting.

They love him, I thought. My respect and admiration grew even more for the man.

I pulled myself up the side of the platform and sat with my legs dangling over the side. Smoke wafted through the huge room and the trees around it, as meat and fish cooked over fires on the open side of the longhouse. Old Canoba turned his head and looked at me for a long time, as if sizing me up, and then began to speak to me in his crude Spanish.

"You are not the same as the *Es-pa-no* from the north, I can see this. Their *warriors* come here to us when the winds blow cool. They tell us that they are friends, but they are not. They tell us that they know the one true God in the sky and that we need to find him as they have. In the next breath, they take our men away and abuse our women. That is why the *Ais* fear the *Es-pa-no*," he said, waving his arm toward the people in the room.

I did not say anything, but was slightly shocked at this blasphemy.

His gaze dropped to the amulet hanging on my chest.

"That is old power."

I reached up and clutched the amulet with my hand, feeling its warmth.

The old man stared at it intensely and a small smile came to his face.

"More powerful than the God of the *Es-pa-no.*"

He then turned from me and looked out over the people, beginning a sermon that would end up lasting well over an hour.

As he spoke, I searched the crowd, trying to get a sense of who these people were. What I witnessed, there under the roof of that rough shelter, was absolute devotion. I realized how important Old Canoba was to them. Their eyes were rapt and their mouths silent as he expounded on virtues that I could not understand. He gestured toward me a couple of times, but it was not to inspire hatred or violence. I did begin to worry a bit when, at one point during his talk, he pointed at the amulet hanging around my neck. His voice grew very soft, and all of the people looked toward me, some giving me a look of suspicion and fear.

Something caught my eye on the left side of the room. I was startled to see someone whose features were very different than any of the *Ais*. It was a man who was as black as my friend, Badu, back in La Habana. Why hadn't I seen him before? He was older than I, and dressed in a tattered gray tunic made in European style. Covering his legs were a pair of ragged breeches that were nearly worn away, and his feet were bare. Our eyes met, and he quickly looked away, turning to walk briskly out the side entrance of the building. I felt a jolt of emotion. He was the first person I had seen here that reminded me of world that I knew. I slid down from the platform and hurriedly walked over to where he had been, stepping outside of the longhouse into the cooking area. I searched in every direction, but he had disappeared.

After old Canoba was finished speaking, the women carried in great piles of food in large clay bowls, setting them on the floor in the center of the great hall. All of the men gathered around, and a disorganized feast ensued. As they ate, they threw their food scraps down where they sat, soon creating a large mess. I could see that this was not an uncommon practice, because the floor was cluttered with rotted food scraps from previous feasts. There were soon hundreds of insects and spiders crawling over the discarded remains.

The feast continued for hours until the sun started to go down, and many of the Indians began to wander out of the longhouse. At the west of the village was the entrance of a wide path cut into the trees, and I saw the people walk to it in small groups, disappearing into the forest. Old Canoba's men helped him down from the high platform, and we all left the meeting house together and walked toward the path. The branches and leaves of the trees were so densely intertwined overhead that I felt as though I were passing through a great tunnel. After a few hundred yards, we reached the end where it opened to a sandy beach. I looked to the west and saw that we were on the shore of a barrier island, and a great expanse of water lay before me. I could see land on the distant side that was covered by low trees.

We walked out onto the beach, where a crowd of *Ais* men had formed a great circle around a large pit in which a fire had already been started. Canoba and his men took seats on one of the large palmetto logs that had been placed around the pit. The men were in the process of dragging dried branches from the forest and placing them on the fire, soon transforming it into a huge blaze. One of the women carried a large clay vessel down and placed it on the ground in front of Canoba. The old man reached down beside him and pulled up a medium sized whelk shell that had been cut away on the top. He dipped this into the vessel and, using it as a drinking cup, brought some sort of dark liquid to his lips. He took a large sip of it as the men cheered. He then handed the shell to the man next to him who also took a drink of the strange, black drink. When it came to me, I did the same thing, raising the crude cup to my lips. I grimaced as I tasted its bitterness, but I forced myself to swallow. The ritual continued until all of the men had partaken of it.

I began to feel a strange sensation that started in my toes and traveled up through my body, making me feel numb. The feeling soon went to my head, and objects in front of my eyes became unfocused. One of the warriors got up and stumbled to the edge of the water. My bleary eyes followed him; watching as he fell to his hands and knees and wretched, vomiting on the sand. He then looked up into the sky and started to sing.

Old Canoba joined in; his song sounding strange and new to me. It was more like a lonely-sounding wail and, even though I did not understand its words, it began to stir my soul with is primal message. His song was one of the earth; of humanity; of pain; and of joy. As I listened, I felt a kinship and understanding that I did not know I possessed, and tears came to my eyes. One by one, the people began to sing with him, and there was soon a great howling of cries echoing through the evening air as the sun went down.

Two stout warriors brought a thick, long pole into the center next to the fire pit. It was about eight feet long, and one half of it was painted with a red stripe that wound around its circumference to the halfway point. The lower half of it was painted black. I watched as they planted it deeply into the sand. Then, six men took a position in a wide circle around it. Each of them carried a large rattle in one hand, and they all began shaking them simultaneously and dancing in place. As they did this they began to sing even louder, letting out intermittent yelps that were more like animal sounds than human voices.

I leaned back as a strange euphoria overtook me. The stars in the sky appeared to move around in strange patterns, and the voices of the men became a haunting song that seemed to come from my own soul. I felt as though I were in a dream. The ground around me started to move and undulate, and the songs of the men seemed to blend together in a cacophony of sound that, for some unknown reason, made perfect sense to me. I stood up and began to dance myself, adding my own voice to the wall of sound.

As I hopped back and forth with the others, I stared at the leaping tendrils of the fire. As I gazed into it, the features of a face began to form in the orange and yellow light right in front me. I suddenly felt that old, overwhelming fear rise inside of me. She smiled widely, gazing at me with her black, malevolent eyes.

"*Hello, boy,*" she said in her rustling, hoarse voice. "*You should be careful. I can reach you now! You will soon be mine!*"

CHAPTER 21
THE FIGHT

The feeling of euphoria slowly waned, and my head began to clear. The stiff breeze had all but ceased to blow, and the tiny insects had returned and were feasting on my skin. I got to my feet, still slightly unsteady, and slowly moved away from my place behind Canoba and his men, and walked back toward the village. As I passed a small cluster of domed houses, I heard some men arguing heatedly in that strange, native language. I was curious, so I quietly made my way through a group of tightly clustered trees. In a small clearing, I was surprised to see the black fellow that I had seen earlier at the meeting house. He appeared to be involved in some heated exchange with two large Indian men. I recognized one of the Indians as Aktil, the same one who had attacked me at the *Reformation* wreck a few days earlier. I knew it was him because his forehead was still marked with a dark, purplish bruise where Canoba had struck him with his staff. He leaned in, jabbing his finger into the black man's chest as if threatening him. This seemed to have little effect on the man, who glared back at him defiantly, answering Aktil in even tones that I could barely hear. It looked to me like there was going to be a fight, so I moved in closer, carefully staying out of sight.

In one sudden burst of motion, Aktil brought his hands up and shoved the smaller man roughly, causing him to stumble backwards and fall into the sand. He laughed; a low and cruel sound; and then calmly walked away and disappeared into the scrub, apparently to relieve himself. His partner moved in and started to kick the black man savagely in the legs and sides. I have never been one to stand idly by, especially when the fight was so obviously unfair, so I stealthily ran in and grabbed the Indian's arm, and pulling him around to face me. He was very surprised and swung at me viciously, his hand clenched like a hammer. I easily ducked it and delivered him a swift, powerful blow to the abdomen that doubled him up. Aktil, emerging from the palmettos, saw what had happened and growled in anger like an animal. The black man looked up in astonishment from his place on the ground, as I walked over and offered my hand.

"Wha-why ju do dat?" he asked.

His Spanish was poor, and I detected an accent that I recognized.

"I didn't like the odds, my friend. Are you English, by chance?" I asked.

The sun had not yet set completely, and a crowd of people had gathered to see what was going on.

"Dey going to kill you now!" he said in a fearful voice. He leapt to his feet and sprinted off, disappearing into the scrub. Aktil and his friend started to scream with outrage, pointing fingers at me, accusations and protests pouring from their mouths. Suddenly, old Canoba was there with his guards, leaning on his staff.

Aktil was up now and began to shout out his version of the attack that he and his friend had just endured.

Old Canoba listened patiently, shaking his head, and then turned to me.

"And you?" he asked.

"These men were beating the smaller man and I thought it was unfair."

He looked at me intently, his black eyes liquid with anger as he thought of a response. He then started to speak slowly, choosing his words carefully in his choppy Spanish.

"Caesar is Aktil's slave - stole from *Nickaleer* many winters ago. You have great power-but no say here. I welcome you to our place and you answer with this."

He then turned his attention to Aktil, who was beside himself with frustration and anger.

"You-a warrior who act like child. This second time that you meet the *Es-pa-no* with power and been beaten by him."

Aktil, who obviously spoke no Spanish, glared at me with hatred and sputtered a reply that lasted many minutes, waving his hands in the air for emphasis. Canoba shook his head slowly as Aktil went on and on. He finally finished his ranting, and the old man turned his attention back to me.

"Aktil has no forgiveness. He say you fight him to death. You win, you great warrior."

Aktil gave me a triumphant smile and flashed his dark eyes. He finally had his chance to kill me.

I was placed on one side of the circle around the fire pit; Aktil on the other. He glared at me with malevolence as I realized what I had done to him and why he was so angry at me. I had made him look weak in front of his people. A cheer went up from the crowd as Aktil raised his hands and strutted around as if he had already defeated me. I was led back toward the shoreline a short distance from the fire pit, where I sat down cross-legged on the sand, surrounded by the bodies of the men as they danced wildly and chanted some sort of ancient song over me. It occurred to me that they would, most likely, perform this same ritual over my bloody corpse after Aktil had killed me. For some strange reason, this thought made me smile. I had always possessed a dark sense of humor.

More than an hour passed, and the evening sky was in its twilight phase. The red and yellow tendrils of the fire were beautiful against the azure sky as the stars began to show. The people took their places in a wide circle around the flames. I thought of the impending contest, and decided that I would do my best to defeat Aktil, even though he was much larger and stronger than I was. I had gotten lucky a couple of times, catching him by surprise with some well-placed blows, but how would I do in open combat? I realized that the last chance for a friendly resolution between Aktil and I had passed, so I resigned myself to whatever fate lay ahead.

The dancers became drenched in sweat, eventually surrendering to the heat and sinking to the sand in exhaustion. As if on cue, old Canoba stepped out into the center of the circle near the fire. He raised his hands to the heavens and began to wail. He howled for a full five minutes as he slowly made his way around, making eye contact with everyone there. I then saw Aktil glaring at me from the other side. I was startled by his appearance. He had painted the top half of his face black and the bottom half red with dye, and now resembled some sort of demon. He wore a head dress consisting of a large bundle of wavy sea grass that sprung out wildly on all sides, giving him the menacing appearance of a much larger man. I saw that he was holding a long, thick stick with a heavy whelk shell tied to the end of it with leather thongs. The look in his eyes told me that he wanted blood, and I knew that this was going to be the fight of my life.

The drums started to play a low, rhythmic beat and a hush fell over the crowd as Aktil stood and moved out toward the fire. He walked toward me with slow, prancing steps as if imitating the movements of a heron. He was an intimidating sight, and I began to feel queasy. I got to my feet and walked out a few steps toward him. I knew that it was important to show no fear, so I did my best to hold a look of passive indifference on my face. Aktil's was twisted with anger and hatred, and glistened in the firelight. I suddenly felt overwhelmed and very alone. I think he sensed this as well, like a wolf senses terror in its prey, and seemed to grow in front of me, a predatory smile coming to his lips as he moved in closer.

With a quick burst of motion, he leapt to my right with cat-like speed, swinging his weapon in a short arc, catching me in the shoulder with a stinging whack that sent me sprawling toward the edge of the circle. The blow sent an explosion of pain to my brain and temporarily disabled my thoughts. I fell to one knee, clutching my arm to try to "will away" the throbbing ache as I heard the sounds of cheering from the people. He was much faster than I had anticipated and had beaten me to the punch. It was then that I remembered an incident from a few years earlier.

I had not wanted to practice this day and was sullen and quiet. The day was beautiful and I wanted to be with my friends.

"Santos!" he snapped as he stood near me in the small cleared area near the garden behind our house in La Habana. He held the thick practice stick that we used for training in one hand.

"You must pay attention! Some day you will face an opponent who is much larger than yourself, and you may have to compensate by using other means besides brute strength."

"I don't want to learn to hurt people, father!" I said in protest, "Why must we do this so much?"

Before the words were out of my mouth his stick had flew through the air and cracked against my upper leg. I crumpled to the ground, tears springing from my eyes.

"You see what happens when your mind is not clear, Boy? Do you like that?"

He sat on the ground next to me and put his arm around my heaving shoulders.

"Santos, there will be times in your life when you will have to make decisions. These choices will have to be made without the interference of any feelings. You must clear your head of all thoughts and make up your mind that there is only one way to best certain opponents. You must be prepared to do what is necessary in the coldest, most clear headed way possible."

I got to my feet, grasping my stick, my head much clearer now and held my stick out in front of me as my father readied himself for another attack.

"Remember what I told you. Anticipate the man's next move and you will be ready."

"Victory through honor- you will survive."

My father had prepared me for trials like this. It was all starting to make sense; the years of exercise and hard, repetitious work. My thoughts grew more focused, and I quickly began to dissect my foes tactics and focus on his obvious weaknesses. Aktil had used the weapon of intimidation against me with stunning results. He was very strong, but slow and clumsy. I now knew what I had to do. My father's words rang through my head as I slowly got to my feet, turning to face the gloating warrior. He wore a mockingly superior expression on his face as he slowly moved toward me for another strike. He turned to the crowd and raised one hand in the air, at the same time yelling in a loud voice. I could not speak his language, but I knew what his message was.

"This Es-pa-no has no powers. Where is his friend the bear, now! I will show you how to kill our enemies!"

I felt the stirrings of anger. Remembering my father's wise words, I quickly smothered them with cold, rational thoughts

as my years of training came back to me. I made sure that
Aktil saw my expression of confusion and pain as he moved
closer to me, preparing to deliver another savage blow with
the whelk shell weapon. This time I was ready when he made
his move. He did exactly what I thought he would do and
swung wildly at my head. I parried to the right, the bludgeon
whistling through the air inches from my face, and sprang
straight ahead and around his body, at the same time lashing
out with my foot. I delivered a vicious blow to his leg that
caused him to grunt in pain and drop to one knee. I then
swung hard with my right fist at the side of his head,
connecting with a loud slap as his head dress shook with the
force of the blow. The entire crowd gasped and fell silent as
Aktil slumped and fell to the sand, unconscious. I felt an
overwhelming surge of pent-up energy as I bent down and
picked up his weapon. I raised it over my head as all of the
emotions of the previous days trials came to a head. I let out
an animal shriek from the very depths of my soul.

As my scream died, I heard something that I had not
expected. It was a low chant that seemed to be getting louder
as the seconds ticked by. I looked around at the people in the
circle and saw something different in their eyes. It was a
mixture of approval and anticipation, as if there were
something else that was to happen. I saw old Canoba
approaching me across the cool sand, his great panther-headed
staff steadying his balance. He stood next to me and we both
looked down at the motionless body of Aktil. The chanting
grew louder and louder.

"What do they want?" I asked the old man.

"They want you to finish him. It is our way."

I looked down at Aktil's back and saw that he was
beginning to stir.

"No, I will not," I said, dropping the whelk shell stick to my side.

"The people will not be happy," Canoba said. You must take his life or something of great value from him."

I turned to face him and said, "There is something that I want from Aktil."

"What is it?"

"I want his slave."

CHAPTER 22
CAESAR

The moon was full and air cool as the long fronds of the palm trees swayed in the gentle breeze. I left the fire dance and made my way back toward the longhouse, loping along slowly because I was completely exhausted. My shoulder ached badly and I was feeling a bit melancholy about the fight that had just taken place. I knew that I had proven myself, but at what cost? I just didn't feel as if I had won any great victory. In my eyes, the whole affair had alienated me from the native people even more. I found a comfortable spot in the rounded root of a huge gumbo limbo tree and settled back for a good sleep. I could hear the chanting in the distance and could see the soft glow of the fire. My eyes felt heavy and I began to drift off.

I awoke to a gray, cloudy sky, and stretched my arms out and yawned. As I turned my head, I nearly jumped out of my skin when my eyes met those of Caesar sitting next to me, staring as if he had never seen anything like me before.

"Holy gods, you scared me!" I said.

He said nothing and continued to glower at me.

"At least say something, you fool!" I implored, starting to feel uncomfortable.

At last, he spoke.

"*Quién es usted?*" he asked in his deep voice.

I immediately recognized his accent.

"Aah, I hear it now, from the islands, possibly Jamaica." I said.

I switched languages and began to speak to him in English.

"If we speak this language none of them will know what we are saying," I said.

I smiled at him stupidly and waited for a reply. He asked me the same question again.

"Who ju? What ju want here?"

"Aah, my friend. I have come to procure slaves, and it looks as if this is my lucky day!"

"No," he spat at me, almost angrily. "What place ju come from?"

I looked at him quizzically, truly not understanding what he meant. He continued to speak.

"Ju merchant sailor or son-of-bitch pirate?"

"Ah, you are perceptive, my friend, and I see that you have learned some colorful words from the *Es-pa-no*," I answered. "My secret will die with me."

"Ju are just boy," he said, "Ju die here in this place, I tink."

I looked at him for a long moment without speaking, sizing up this insolent slave. His skin was nearly as black as night and his eyes flashed with intelligence. There were a few gray hairs sprouting through his beard at his temples and on his chin, so I guessed his age at around thirty years.

"Caesar, please listen to me for a few moments. After all, I am your master," I said. "I want you to tell me how you come to be here on this beach with these people."

"Ju talk too fast," he said, giving me an open hand gesture as if I were a child. "Talk slower."

I didn't say anything in reply and he held his gaze. A minute passed and he spoke again.

"Old Canoba, he say ju talk to bears, and dey do what ju want."

I thought of the incident at the *Reformation* wreck site
when the animal had appeared out of the scrub. I remembered
the strange look of intelligence in its eyes.

"Do you believe that?" I asked.

He looked at me skeptically, and then turned his face to
the ground.

"Tell me about yourself first, Caesar."

He hesitated for a few moments, and then spoke in a quiet
voice as if the subject was painful to him.

"I here since I small boy. Come from de water on big boat.
I very jung, boy. Pap belong to Massa Dickinson and his wife
and dey baby. Many white men from Jamaica on de boat
heading for north."

"What kind of people were the Dickinsons?" I asked.

"Dey prayin all de time. All of dem wear black clothes
only," he said.

I pictured a group of piously religious people; possibly
Protestants. My father had told me of people like this who
lived in some of the English islands, especially Jamaica.
According to him, these "Quakers" had dissented from the
Church of England and were deeply critical of all of the
established religions of the day, including Catholicism. It was
always my opinion, in my young, impressionable mind, that
any group like that was destined to burn in hell.

"What happened to their ship?" I asked.

"Bad blow and de boat run up on sand."

"They were shipwrecked?"

He shook his head in affirmation, and then continued to
speak.

"Warriors from *Hoe-Bay* jump on dem and take dere
clothes, even de baby."

"Hoe-Bay?" I asked.

He pointed to the south.

"Dey live dat way two or three days walk. *Ais* men fight dem sometimes, but not since *Es-pan-o* come."

As he spoke, I thought of the wrecked ship back up the beach near where I had landed.

"Caesar, was the name of the ship the *Reformation*?

"Don't 'member. Too much time go by."

He paused then and looked at me, his eyes clouded with painful memories and continued.

"My *Nickaleer* no good. I forget."

I understood this as I remembered Canoba's stumbling Spanish. I figured that Caesar had probably not spoken his native tongue in a great many years.

"Where are the English now?" I asked hopefully.

"I tink dey all die in the sand that way," pointing to the north.

"*Ais* men not good to dem. Beat dem bad and put sand in baby's mouth."

"Why were they so cruel to the English?" I asked.

He looked at me, a grave expression on his face. "*Es-pan-o* soldiers come and tell Casseekey dat if dey see *Nickaleer* dey kill dem fast. *Nickaleer* bad, bad."

"Where did "*Nickaleer*" come from?" I asked.

"*Ais* always call dem "*Nickaleer*. I don't know why, Captain.

I considered the Spanish word "*Ingles*." I could only guess that the *Ais* had corrupted the term to fit their language.

I envisioned the Spanish soldiers coercing these natives with threats of violence. The thought made my stomach queasy. If anyone knew what the Spanish were capable of, I did. The sun had come up now and I could see activity around the village. Smoke began to rise and billow across the palmettos from the morning fires.

"Why are you here with them, Caesar? Why did you not go with the English?"

He looked off toward the scrub, careful not to meet my gaze. I realized that some of the memories that I was asking him to conjure up were most likely not pleasant ones.

"De old Caseekey at Hoe-Bay, he take my Papa and me from Massuh Dickinson and den back to de ship to get tings out he want. He den made us burn it. When we come back he let Papa go, but kept me. He was not a good man. He beat me."

What I was hearing was making me feel sad. As a young boy, Caesar had been pulled from his father to live and be abused as a slave to savages in the wildest place on earth.

"Old Canoba, he take me from de Caseekey at Hoe-Bay and bring me back to Massuh Dickinson," he said.

"Canoba rescued you from the bad Caseekey?" I asked. "What happened when you were returned to the Dickinson party?"

"We all left de *Ais* village together and walk far north," he said. In my mind I pictured a sorry group of half-starved people making their way up the beach toward an unknown destination.

"How many were there, Caesar?"

He stroked his roughly stubbled chin and looked up, a look of concentration on his face.

"Hmm, maybe twenty; twenty-one. I don't remember," he said.

"It must have been awful for them," I said.

"It was very, very bad. De white people, dey not do so well widdout any food. *Ais* men trow rocks at dem de whole way and give dem very hard time. It was de cold time and we all had no clothes at all."

"Why are you still here, Caesar? What happened to the rest?"

"I was wid one white man and two udder slaves; Quenza and Jack. We was so hungry and cold dat we could not go no furder. De white men left us for dead dere on de beach wid the wind blowin' so cold. I knew I was dead for sure. De ones wid me, dey freeze and die right dere in front of me.

"Your friends died? How awful!" I said, feeling pity for him. I had never in my life heard such a harrowing tale. "How did you survive?"

"I pray to Jesus den and knew it was my day. Just as I get ready to go to Jesus, I look up, and dere was Canoba lookin' down at me."

"Canoba found you? He came for you?" I asked, incredulous.

"Jes," he said. "He carried me all de way back here to *Ais* and gave me good medicine."

I didn't speak because I could hardly believe the story I had just heard.

"Why didn't the *Ais* kill me, Caesar? Is it because I am *Es-pa-no?*"

"Many years ago, two *Es-pa-no* holy men come to tell de *Ais* of de only way. Dey say dat de *Ais* shamans not right. The shamans, dey not happy about dis, so dey offer de *Es-pa-no* holy men to de gods in de upper world."

"Offered them to the upper world?" I asked.

"The *Es-pa-no* were nailed to dere cross not far from here, den burned on it, just like dey say happened to dere shaman," he said, his face flat and devoid of emotion.

I tried to swallow a lump that had formed in my throat as I imagined the sight of two Spanish missionaries being burned alive on crosses.

Caesar looked off toward the sea and continued to speak.

"De soldiers come den. Dey take de shaman who burned dem and kill him dead right dere. Dey kill many more *Ais* men, too."

He paused for a moment as if deep in thought. "I see da soldiers kill dere own *Es-pa-no* too, if dey got shine."

"Shine?" I asked. "What is shine, Caesar?"

He looked at me hard for a moment, saying nothing. His face then lightened with his infectious smile.

"I hungry, Captain!" he said.

I looked off toward the village and caught the smell of wood smoke. My stomach rumbled and I realized that I was hungry as well. Caesar got to his feet and extended a hand to me; I took it, pulling myself up. We walked toward the village in the morning light, as unlikely a pair as there had ever been.

Caesar spoke in a lighter voice, friendly and chiding.

"Massuh, ju whoop dat Aktil good, mon."

"Caesar," I said in a calm tone.

"Ja?" he said.

"I am your master now, and you have to obey me."

"Ja," he said.

"You are now a free man."

He stopped and looked at me, a stupefied expression on his face.

"Wha Massa?" he asked

"No! I am not "master.""

We continued to walk, neither of us saying anything. I looked at his face for some kind of reaction to what I had just told him. He was looking straight ahead, shaking his head as if he were trying to figure something out. I then realized that he had never been exposed to the concept of freedom in his entire life, and that the subject was completely foreign to him. He then sensed that I was looking at him and returned my gaze, giving me another wide grin, transforming his whole face.

"Ja, Captain!" he said enthusiastically.

"Why did you call me "Captain?" I asked.

He looked at me, an expression of concentration on his dark face.

"Did you come here on your own boat?" he asked.

I thought about it for a moment.

"Yes, I guess I did."

"Den ju are de Captain!" he said brightly.

We both laughed at my sudden "promotion."

As we walked, I felt the sun's heat on my face, and noticed a flock of large white pelicans flying overhead in perfect formation against the bright blue sky.

CHAPTER 23
THE SECRETS OF THE SLAVE

After the altercation with Aktil, the people of the village treated me differently. This somewhat baffled me because many of the warriors were much larger than I, and some much more formidable than Aktil had been. Strangely, no one provoked me in any way. I was both accepted and avoided. I was welcome in the meeting house, but I could feel the stares from the people who could barely contain their fear and awe at my supposed power over animals. Caesar spent the next few days showing me how to survive among these people. I was very happy to find someone with whom I could communicate and who understood the world from which I had come. My respect was growing daily for his cleverness when it came to living with the *Ais*.

Caesar had been a slave among the natives, but not in the traditional European sense. He was allowed to come and go as he pleased as long as took care of Aktil's meals in the morning and at mid-day. One morning I was with him in the forest, trying to keep up as he nimbly darted through the palmetto scrub. As we made our way along, I asked him a question that I had pondered since I had met him.

"Caesar, why do you not leave? It would be easy for you."

He stopped and looked at me, a serious expression on his face.

"Just follow and try to keep up," he answered.

I knew that we were far from the village because the vegetation was much thicker. Caesar kept such a rapid pace that my gaze had to remain on the ground in front of me so that I didn't step on a sharp bramble or, even worse yet, a rattlesnake. When we paused for a rest, I looked up and stared in astonishment at the beauty of the place. We were in a grove of live oak trees so massive that the limbs were intertwined with each other. Huge swaths of moss cascaded from almost every branch nearly all the way to the ground and shifted lazily in the breeze. Large air plants with pointed, knife-like leaves filled nearly every crook of every branch. I saw movement far to my left and found myself staring across an open area into the eyes of a large buck deer that had been rubbing his antlers on the trunk of a palmetto tree. He held my gaze, almost as if curious about whom I was. I immediately felt a strange connection with the place.

"Come, we almost dere!" Caesar cried. The buck bolted at the noise and bound off, his white tail bobbing up and down as he disappeared into the woods.

We walked into a place free of any thick ground vegetation that was shaded by a thick canopy of vines and serpentine limbs. There was a small, crudely built house in the center of it that had been constructed from vertically placed palmetto logs and rough boards that looked to be planking from the side of a ship. It was about four meters high with a thatched roof of palmetto fronds, and had a small covered area that served as a porch. I stood under it and stared in amazement at the collection of items strewn about. There were sea chests, tools, instruments, and even an old rocking chair.

"Caesar, did you build all of this?" I asked, still in shock at what I was seeing.

"Who ju tink, Captain?" he said, a smile on his face.

The small house was impressive. I bent down under the palmetto awning, stepping into the shelter. It seemed to be very tightly built and strong. I could see, on closer inspection, that it was held together with real ship's nails.

"Where did you find all of this, Caesar?" I asked, incredulous.

"From de wrecks, Captain. Dere are many on the beach, all de time." he said cheerfully.

"Come and see!"

I followed him around to the back of the house and down a short trail that led into the trees. We were soon standing on a small, sandy beach that overlooked a large inlet. I looked up and down the shoreline and saw that it was covered with tall, looming palm trees that stood like massive sentinels, their wide trunks disappearing into the fern covered ground. Red and white mangroves rose several feet out into the water, their tangled roots tenuously gripping the sandy soil below the water's surface.

Gazing across the shimmering water at the far side of the inlet, I saw a cabbage palm forest so thick that the intertwining fronds looked like woven fabric. There was a lofty, dead cypress tree extending high above the palms, its thick, leafless limbs reaching out to the sky; each one draped with long fingers of Spanish moss that swayed gently in the breeze. In its highest branches was a large, sprawling nest that an osprey had built for her young. I heard her distinctive cry and saw her white and black head just above the top of the nest. I realized that she was peering at me, ready to defend her babies should I fly in to attack. At that moment, I experienced a sensation of awe at the simple beauty of the place. I felt like an intruder in some sacred place in which I did not belong.

"It's beautiful here," I said.

"Come, Captain," Caesar said in an eager voice. "I show you my house!"

I followed him up the path that led back to the clearing. As I walked, I spotted something large in the brush that looked out of place. Curious, I stepped off the trail into the trees, stooping to pull away some thick ferns and expose what lie underneath. It appeared to be the lower portion of an ancient, broken wall. It was made of coquina; the same shell rock material that many of the buildings were constructed of back in La Habana. What was this? I looked further, and saw that it was a foundation of some kind. It extended for many meters to the south before disappearing into the undergrowth.

"Captain!" Caesar called to me. "Are ju comin'?"

Making a mental note to investigate my find later, I walked back to the path.

I sat down in the rocking chair and found it to be solidly built and as out of place as anything I'd ever seen. Caesar had placed it on some planks so it would not sink into the sand. I rocked back and forth, enjoying the comfort of it.

"Do the *Ais* know that you have all of this in your possession?" I asked.

"Dis is all of it dey do not want," he answered, "Dey have no use for most tings from de wrecks."

Dark clouds had moved in and it was growing colder. I felt a few drops on my face, so I stood up and walked into the house, my eyes scanning its contents. Caesar had many ceramic jugs and onion bottles made of hand-blown glass, wooden stave barrels, oars, lanterns, and many other items lying all around. There were two small, raised beds placed along opposite walls; one on the left, and one on the right. He sat on the left one, so I followed suit and sat on the other. The beds were fashioned from a framework of poles, with mattresses made from crudely sewn sail cloth stuffed with Spanish moss. As I looked around the place, it began to rain.

The sound of the drops hitting the palmetto roof soothed me, so I lay back on the bed, my eyes admiring the intricate patchwork of the roof. No water leaked through it at all. The coolness of the small, dark place was comforting.

"This is truly amazing, Caesar. How long did this take you to amass all of it?" I asked.

"I come here since I very young, Captain. Dis my place."

Caesar was amazing, I thought to myself. I felt very relaxed, and became aware of how truly exhausted I was. I leaned my head back, and my thoughts drifted. I reflected on of the events of the past few months. I had been through so much that I could barely comprehend it. The incredible thing was that I was still alive. I felt myself drifting off toward sleep, so I let go.

The woman was there, her face twisted in anger, the lips moving as she mouthed her unrecognizable chant. The painted stripes on her cheeks shot down at angles from her temples, giving her the look of a devil. Something was different this time, though. I could understand some of the words that she was saying.

"The time is yours, Santos Alvarez, to leave this place and these people. You are cursed for all time and you will bring ruin to them and anyone else you encounter. You are a dog and will die like one, just as your father did, and his father before him."

"Why?" I screamed, "Why do you torment me so?"

She laughed then, an evil laugh that shook me to my soul.

"You will pay for the crimes of your fathers, boy. You have taken all from me and you will pay."

"I have taken nothing from you, witch! Leave me in peace!"

She was gone, but in her place was something more terrible than ever before.

*Before me, surrounded by inky blackness was the face of my father
and he was screaming in pain, his mouth twisted in a horrible grimace.*

I was being shaken, and I came out of my dream abruptly.
It was Caesar.

"Captain, ju all right? Captain!"

He continued to shake me as I reached full consciousness.

"Caesar! What, what do you want?"

"Captain, ju screaming out! Ju been dreaming!"

"Oh, yes Caesar. Pay me no heed. It is just me."

"Ju got bad spirits in ju, mon," he said, a concerned
expression on his face.

After a short while, the sun's rays replaced the grayness
outside.

"De rain stop, Captain. Come, come, I show you."

We left the small clearing and ventured down another
small path cut through the trees and bushes, this one heading
off toward the east. I could hear the waves crashing far off in
the distance, so I knew that we were near the ocean. It was
very hot, and small insects flew around my head as I followed.

"Here," he said, and pointed to a raised area in the trees.
It looked like the other mounds I had seen back at the village
of the *Ais*. There were four tall oak trees growing out of the
top in a tight circle. By the ancient look of the place, I
guessed that this one had probably been abandoned many years
prior.

"Captain, dis a sacred place. Dere are many of the old
ones buried here from long ago," he said.

"There are people buried here, Caesar?" I asked, looking
at the raised area of the mound.

"Jes, Captain. Dey lay dem down and place all of dere favorite tings around dem, den cover dem with fine black sand from de bottom of de river."

"Doesn't it bother you at all that they are here?" I asked.

The *Ais* will not come," he said. "Dat is why I make my place near here."

Caesar walked along its perimeter for a few moments, and then seemed to recognize something. He cleared some loose branches out of the way and reached in with his hand, grabbing and pulling out something heavy, dragging it into the open. I saw that it was a large trunk, much like the one that passengers use on a long sea voyage. He knelt next to it and unfastened the large hasp on the front. He paused and looked up at me, his face set with an expression of seriousness.

"If you tell Canoba of dis, I am dead." he said.

"Show me," I said, my curiosity piqued.

He lifted the old lid of the chest and showed me its contents, and I nearly fell over from shock. It was two-thirds filled with Spanish coins. They shone brilliantly in the sunlight, and I could only stare. The gold *doblones* were round and the silver *cabos* had irregular cut edges, and all bore stamped markings. There must have been hundreds of them.

"My God!" I exclaimed, and he smiled at me mischievously. "You're a rich man, Caesar!"

He reached into the pile and pulled out a handful of the coins.

"Here, these are yours," he said quietly, "for being so good to me."

He placed five gold doubloons into my outstretched hands.

"Ju like shine, don't ju, Captain," he said, shaking his head and smiling.

Why do you say that, Caesar?"

He smiled and pointed at the amulet hanging around my neck.

"Oh, that," I said dismissively, waving my hand. "It was a gift from my father."

"Can I touch it, Captain?" he asked as he gazed at it.

"I suppose you can," I said.

He picked it up from my chest, hefting its weight in his palm, its chain hanging between his fingers. The smile left his face and he dropped it. The medallion bounced lightly against my chest.

"We go back now, Captain," he said, averting his gaze.

"What's wrong Caesar? Don't you like it?" I asked.

He turned and looked at me, a serious expression on his face.

"Captain, dere is big magic in dat piece."

"Why do you say that?"

"It told me, Captain," he said.

We were soon making our way along the thin trail back toward the camp.

"Caesar, do you like your life here among the *Ais*?" I asked.

He pondered this for a few moments before he answered.

"I tink I was born to live here, Captain. When my papa had to leave me with the Caseekey, I remember dat he told me to act like a man and do what I had to do, and he would come back for me soon. He walked up da beach wit Massuh Dickinson and de Quaker people. None of dem had any clothes on because de *Ais* took dem. I knew dat he wouldn't come back because de same ting happened to my Mama back in Jamaica. De slave traders took her from us, just like dat. Papa say to be strong and dat I would be all right. I didn't say no words for a long time, but late at night after the village was asleep, I cried and cried. I cried for years, but it didn't change, and after a while my tears dried up. I knew what I had to do and I did it. I learned the *Ais* ways and how to make myself one of dem. I don't do everything dey do, but I do enough to make dem let me be."

I felt sad as I listened to him; sad for the small boy who had been left to the mercy of the savage natives and their hostile environment. But it soon dawned on me that I had not heard any sorrow in his voice during his tragic account. Caesar's story was one of survival against impossible odds, and he had emerged the victor. He had done the best with what he was presented, and I knew that he was the toughest man I had ever met. I was rapidly growing to love and respect my new friend.

"De best ting I learn, Captain, is how to trade wid de *Es-pa-no*," he said, his eyes narrowing as if he were sharing some great, hidden secret.

"You trade with the Spanish, Caesar?"

"Jes, Captain, when dey come every once in a while."

"I thought you told me that the Spanish would kill you if they found "shine" here?"

"Not all of dem, Captain. Dey don't want de *Ais* or *Calusa* to have it, but dey know to come to Caesar!"

"*Calusa*? Who are the *Calusa*? I asked.

"Ooh, mon, de *Calusa* are de bad ones from the west," he said, letting out a low whistle for emphasis.

"Are they different Indians than the *Ais*?" I asked.

"Dey kill *Ais* men, and *Es-pa-no*. Dey stronger dan anyone," he said. "Dey come to de *Ais* village to trade, but de Caseekey pay dem in shine like in my chest."

"Canoba pays the *Calusa*? What for?"

"*Ais* men very scared of de *Calusa*. Don't want war wid dem. Dats why he pay."

I grew quiet as I tried to imagine these fierce people.

"What else do the Spanish traders want from you, Caesar?"

"Dey want de ambergris dat wash up on da beach," he said.

"Ambergris? I asked."

"Jes, Captain, from de whale. It made inside of de whale, and it come out way out trew his mouth into da sea, den it wash up on de beach in clumps. Da *Es-pa-no* want it for dere women. I show you some when we get back."

"For their women?" I asked, surprised.

"Dey use it for the stink water, Captain. Dey pay me in silver!"

"Stink water?" I asked, and then I understood.

"You mean perfume," I said.

"Jes, Captain, jes!" he said excitedly, shaking his head up and down enthusiastically.

"You are a remarkable man, Caesar," I said.

As we walked back toward camp, I remembered something.

"Caesar, do you know about the history of this place?"

I don't think he understood the question, because he did not answer, looking at me quizzically.

"I found something down by the water. Was there another house here before you came?" I asked.

He gave me that same confused look again, and then smiled, as if a lost memory had returned to him.

"Ah, Captain!" he said cheerfully. "Ju find de wall!"

"Yes, I did. What was it from?" I asked eagerly.

"De *Es-pa-no* build one of dere forts here many, many years ago, even before Old Canoba was born. Dis is where de *Ais* burned de two *Es-pa-no* holy men. De *Ais* do not like it here. Dey tink it is full of bad spirits."

"Were all of the Spaniards that were here killed, Caesar?" I asked, incredulous.

"Not all of dem were like you, Captain. De *Ais* legend say dat de men here were prisoners of de *Es-pa-no* and speak a different tongue. De *Es-pa-no* chief leave dem here to die."

"Were they English, Caesar? *Nickaleer?*"

He shook his side to side. "No, Captain. De *Ais* Caseekey wanted to help de *Es-pa-no* chief, so he let dem build dere fort here. After de great *Es-pa-no* chief left, de prisoners got out and steal from de *Ais*. Dey also took dere women. De *Ais* men want revenge, and kill dem all."

Later that day as Caesar took his midday nap, I returned to the broken wall in the trees. I followed it through the thick growth, pushing away long palmetto fronds and spider webs as I went. A few meters down, the wall turned sharply to the west. I could now see how large the fortification originally was. I noticed an unusual object a short distance from the foundation that was covered with moss and vines. Walking around it, my curiosity grew. It reminded me of an ancient headstone in a graveyard. Digging my fingers in, I pulled some of the moss away. It was made of granite, and I was shocked to see crude letters inscribed on it. I spent the next few minutes clearing a large area on the stone's flat surface. The words were written in French, and I now thanked my father for forcing me to learn it. This is what was written there.

WE ARE THE REMAINING FRENCH SUBJECTS OF
KING CHARLES LEFT HERE TO DIE BY THE EVIL
SPANIARD
PEDRO MENENDEZ DE AVILES
MAY GOD SEEK JUSTICE FOR OUR SUFFERINGS

SANTA LUCIA
DECEMBRE 13 1565

I was stunned by these words. What had happened here? This was not a gravestone in the true sense, but it had the same meaning. I remembered a story that my father had told about many French Huguenot sailors that were taken prisoner on the Florida coast one hundred-fifty years earlier by the hero Menendez. Was this the place where some of those men had ended up?

I knew of the Catholic Saint Lucie. She was one of seven women, apart from the Blessed Virgin Mary, commemorated by name in the Canon of the Mass. Her feast day back in La Habana was the thirteenth of December. I sat for a long time, staring at the stark words that had been crudely carved in granite. They seemed to cry out to me in anguish and loss. I now realized I was standing upon the graves of Christian men, and that my countrymen had preceded me to this place many years before.

As night began to fall, I walked back to the camp. He was there by the fire, roasting some fresh fish.

"Caesar," I said to my new friend, "Your fine home needs a name. I hereby christen it *Santa Lucia*!

CHAPTER 24
CHERA AND THE CALUSA

It was late afternoon and the sun descended toward the western horizon, its rays casting great shadows across the sand, and I could see the nearly transparent form of the rising moon far out at sea. The sky was turning twilight blue, and the thin, high clouds were barely visible, floating like wisps of white smoke. The meeting house was full to capacity, and the people were chattering constantly like a flock of birds. Old Canoba sat on his platform at the very eastern end of the room looking balefully concerned, as was his manner. Caesar and I took our usual place near him so we could hear what the old wise man had to say. My new friend had been training me in the native tongue, but I was still far from comprehending the simplest utterances of it. The Caseekey was struggling to be heard over the chattering crowd, so he stretched his bony arms out wide in front of him until everyone took notice, and then very slowly lowered them. The people understood the gesture and a hush fell over the room.

He settled back, raised his head, and began to sing his song. It seemed to me to be a very sad story filled with the inflections of a long and painful life, and it reminded me of my own loneliness. I watched him, fascinated by the way his voice rose and fell, feeling the hair stand up on my arms and shoulders as I got caught up in the emotion of it. When I first heard him sing a few days earlier, I did not understand it at all, but the more I listened, the more I understood the raw feelings that the songs conveyed. It was the song of his life; of his years of wisdom; the story of his people.

When he finished I wanted to clap, as I would have done
in La Habana when a talented street entertainer finished a
performance, but I knew that I could possibly be killed if I
did so here. No one spoke or made a sound. A few moments
passed, and one man let out a low, mournful wail. Another
joined in; then more and more, until everyone was singing his
or her own song.

I was startled by a commotion at the west side of the great
house. There was a hush, and the crowd parted as five people,
four men and one woman, walked toward the center of the
room. I knew at once that these were not people of the *Ais*,
but visitors from somewhere else. They were physically larger
and more imposing than the *Ais* men, with painted bodies and
elaborate tattoos on their powerful arms and legs. They had
the lean, hard features of warriors, and two of them carried
long, taut bows. Their clothing consisted of deerskin
breechcloths so small that they barely covered their privates.
They wore their hair long, with a few osprey feathers jutting
out at sharp angles from the tops of their heads. The skin
around their eyes was painted with thick, black circles, giving
them the appearance of phantoms.

They were adorned with various articles of jewelry crafted
from small shells and sharks teeth. I guessed that the man in
front was the leader. He was older than the rest, and his arms,
legs and chest bore tattoos that were much more elaborate
than those of the other men. He had a stately manner, but his
movements were like those of a cat, and he exuded a calm
confidence as he slowly approached the platform where old
Canoba sat. I was thinking about how intimidating he was
when I noticed the woman who was with him.

There was something different about her. She was young and lean, and had very dark skin. Her cheekbones were high, giving her a regal appearance. Her black hair was tied up on top of her head in a bundle, the excess spilling down her back and shoulders. It occurred to me that she was an exotic beauty, especially when compared to the squat women of the *Ais*. As I looked closer, I noticed a thick leather collar tied around her neck with a long, rawhide thong attached to it on one side. My eyes followed it down, and I was shocked to see that its other end was secured to the waistband of one of the warriors. She was a prisoner!

Her dress was dirty and worn, but I could see that it was very colorful and appeared to be of European design. She wore so many bracelets of colorful beads around her neck that they looked like woven fabric. I saw no fear on her face, only an expression that could be construed as something between stoicism and weariness. She looked up and met my eyes, and something very strange happened. She smiled at me, and I felt a flood of recognition and familiarity that struck me to my soul. Her gaze shifted to the amulet around my neck, and the smile left her face. She quickly broke the connection, looking down at the ground self-consciously.

No one had noticed the exchange between us because every eye was on the imposing hunter, who had begun to talk to old Canoba in a different language than that of the *Ais*. He soon became animated, raising his voice up and down as he explained something, waving his huge arms for emphasis. He frequently turned, gesturing back toward the girl. The Caseekey sat and listened patiently, every once in a while nodding his head in agreement and periodically interjecting short comments. The two men exchanged words for a very long time and then paused, speaking in lowered voices. It seemed to me that they were trying to strike some sort of agreement. After a while, old Canoba raised his hands in front of him and shook his head back and forth as if saying "no" to something. The large warrior gave the old man a snort of disdain, then turned and strode off toward the open side of the long house, tugging the leash that was around the girl's neck. I experienced an unexplainable feeling of desperation as I watched them disappear into the night, the girl running behind to keep up. I pulled Caesar away from the others.

"Who are they?" I asked him in a hoarse whisper.

"*Calusa* hunters," he said, "come to trade. The leader is Soco."

"These men are *Calusa*?" I asked.

"Jes, Captain, dey come from far to the west. Like I tell you before, dey very strong and kill many *Ais* warriors in de past. De old Cassekey pay dem when dey come so dey don't kill. Very powerful spirits dey have."

"Who was that woman with them? Did you understand what they said?"

I realized that I was badgering Caesar, but I had to know more about the woman. It was as if she immediately understood me, or at least knew something about me.

"Soco is de big one. He is very good trader and comes to de *Ais* village with slaves. She is a prisoner taken in a raid by *Calusa*. Her people are the *Hitchiti* from the north land. Soco wants to trade her to Canoba, but de old man say no, Soco want too much for her."

On impulse, I turned to my friend, a wide smile on my face.

I got to my feet and took off in pursuit of the warriors.

"Wait!" Caesar cried and ran after me. "What are you doing?"

"I'm going to buy her!" I shouted.

"Dat is a bad idea, Captain!" Caesar warned.

I was amazed at the amount of ground that the hunters could cover in such a short time, but I soon saw their forms ahead of me in the pale moonlight. As I drew closer to them, I did my best to keep quiet so as not to startle them. They soon disappeared like ghosts, so I paused to listen closely, straining my ears to catch a sound that would betray their position.

Suddenly, everything exploded, and I felt a crushing pain and saw millions of tiny lights as I was struck with a long, blunt object. I fell backwards on the path, my hands flying to my face. I had not seen the warrior hiding in the darkness, and the well-placed blow from his war club sent me sprawling. They were all four standing around me now, glaring down at me, their eyes filled with malevolence. I could not see the woman because my head was reeling from the blow, and there was blood running down my forehead, into my eyes. One of the powerful warriors grabbed my tunic and pulled me up to a standing position. I saw Soco, looking down at me as if I were an insignificant rabbit he had caught and was about to skin.

"Wait!" I heard someone yell.

It was the familiar voice of Caesar, approaching us in the dim light of the torches. He spoke to them in their native tongue and sounded as if he were begging for my forgiveness. One of the *Calusa* warriors spat out an oath, and Caesar quickly answered. They paused, as if thinking over what to do with me, and then slowly began to move back. Soco stepped directly in front of Caesar and talked to him for a long while, his voice sounding even and serious. He then turned and walked down the path, the other warriors falling into step with him.

Caesar pulled me aside by my shoulder, whispering hotly into my ear.

"Ju very foolish, Captain. Ju never run up on a *Calusa* hunting party in de night like dat. Dey kill you right here in dis place and take your head. Dey like it."

"I need to talk to them, Caesar. That is all I want."

"I told dem dat ju want to trade and dat ju have money. Soco say you like de crazy man. He say for us to follow dem to where dey camp."

We made our way down the narrow path, trying our best to keep up with the fast moving hunters, who moved like graceful cats through the pale night. We soon came to a small clearing several yards higher than the ground around it and encircled by sprawling oak trees with Spanish moss hanging from every branch. This was a wise choice for a campsite because it not only concealed the hunters, but afforded an excellent vantage point from which to spot any coming intruders. In what seemed like no time at all, they had built a small fire in the center of the clearing and had each taken a place around it, all sitting with their legs crossed. The woman was behind the warrior that had her tethered, her head down, her long hair undone and hiding her face. Caesar and I stood by, unsure what to do, both of us very leery of angering these dangerous men yet again. Soco looked up and signaled us to sit across from him.

The dancing firelight made the warriors look like evil fiends from some other world as they sat staring into the flames. Soco began to speak to Caesar in his deep, severe voice. He went on for a long time, Caesar periodically responding to him by shaking his head in agreement or making a brief statement. Soco casually looked at me as he spoke, and I watched his gaze fall to the amulet around my neck. This gave me an uneasy feeling as I sensed his interest in it. An hour passed as the two men nattered back and forth. Even though I could not understand a word, the tone seemed to remain friendly. Caesar leaned over to me and whispered in my ear.

"Soco is willing to deal wid you. He wants to be rid of de woman because she is slowing dem down and making it hard to hunt. He is considering de price."

I felt nervous and looked over to where the woman sat. Her face was now visible and I could see that her eyes seemed to be rimmed with tears. Soco pretended to be pensive for a few moments, making a dramatic show of staring up at the sky as if he were making some great decision, then looked down at Caesar and barked out his final offer. His large hand came up and pointed at my amulet. I instinctively covered it and felt the warmth radiating from its surface.

"No," I said in a firm voice, shaking my head.

Soco burst into harsh laughter and jumped to his feet. He dismissed me with a wave of his hand, and then walked away nonchalantly, disappearing into the trees behind him, apparently to relieve himself.

"Oh, dey kill us now. What de matter, Captain? I tought you want de woman?" Caesar asked.

"The amulet stays with me," I said, "It was a gift from my father."

"We can bury it wid you," he said.

I turned my head and saw that she was now looking at me. She smiled softly, and then returned her gaze to the ground in front of her. I cursed myself for being so headstrong. Something inside of my head reminded me that I had to

protect my father's amulet at all costs. I also knew that these
men would not take the woman with them for long. She
would be sold as a slave to someone else or simply killed in the
forest.

There was a cry of shock and pain from the woods,
surprising all of us. The warriors leapt to their feet, one of
them grabbing a long stick from the fire with its end burning
brightly, and leapt off into the darkness of the palmettos.
Caesar and I followed them as they made their way down the
dark path toward the screams. There was a rustle in the
bushes off to the right of the trail, and I heard a sound that
made my hair stand on end. It started with a low, rumbling
growl and then grew into a screeching scream that chilled me
to my very soul. My heart leapt with fear as I saw it there in
the darkness, its fierce eyes glinting in the reflection of the
torch. It was huge; its body long and sinewy, its golden fur
glistening in the moonlight.

"A panther!" Caesar exclaimed, "A huge one, and it has
Soco!"

The animal was standing over Soco, who was lying on the
ground and appeared to be injured. The proud, insolent *Calusa*
warrior had been reduced to a terrified creature afraid of
making the slightest move. The panther did not appear to be
intimidated at all by the warriors and growled threateningly,
as if daring them to come nearer. The man with the torch
stabbed it toward the cat in an attempt to scare it off, but the
animal stood its ground, moving back only a few inches and
thrusting out savagely at the flame with its huge paw, snarling
viciously and showing its huge mouth and long fangs. I
frantically tried to think of a way to distract it and save the
man's life.

All at once, I began to experience a strange numbing sensation, and felt the amulet around my neck start to grow warm against my breast. I shook my head to clear my thoughts, but the feeling only grew with intensity. In the corner of my eye, I saw something move close to me. I glanced over and saw the *Hitchiti* woman standing there. She did not seem fearful at all, but wore a look of calm on her face. She swayed back and forth gently, her eyes tightly closed. Her lips moved, mouthing words that seemed to be only for her own ears. I looked back at the panther, and saw that its demeanor had changed. It stared at me silently, its amber-eyed gaze locked on mine, and an overwhelming familiarity pervaded my thoughts. I felt admiration and wonder as I watched its sleek curves and muscled body. The woman suddenly shouted.

"*Nakuma!*"

All other sounds ceased abruptly, except for the soft moans of the wounded man. The panther stood still for a moment, then slowly turned its great body and plodded toward the woman, leaving its wounded prey lying in the sandy scrub. It rubbed its huge flank against my leg as it walked slowly past me, and I heard the woman speak. It was a soothing tone in a language that I did not understand, and the panther nodded his great head to her as if it understood.

The warriors stared in stunned disbelief, momentarily forgetting their wounded leader bleeding on the ground. The panther calmly walked to her, and she reached down to gently caress its golden fur with her open hand. It then made a circle and plodded back to me, rubbing its side against my thigh like a common housecat. I looked at the woman and saw that same gaze of absolute serenity and peace.

I knew then that I was in no danger, and that she possessed something very powerful that was beyond my understanding. The panther sat on the ground at her feet and seemed to contemplate me, narrowing its eyes with affection. It then turned toward the terrified warriors and emitted a barely detectable growl. I walked over and bent down, gently scratching its great head behind the ears. The animal closed its eyes with pleasure and purred loudly.

I then stood and took a couple of steps toward the huddled band of hunters.

"Tend to him," I said in a calm, but firm voice.

There was a flurry of action as they rushed to the wounded Soco. I saw that he had been bitten on the upper arm and was bleeding profusely. It was a substantial wound, but not fatal, and his men set about dressing it. Soco turned and stared, first at me and then at the panther, a look of disbelief and shock on his ashen face. It was so strange; I could not believe what had happened, but the events felt natural. I looked at the woman and saw that she was still in that strange trance, her body swaying almost imperceptibly.

"Captain Santos!" Caesar cried.

It was if some sort of spell were broken. The woman opened her eyes and looked at me with an expression of surprise. The panther, startled by Caesar's voice, jumped up and bound off into the forest. I suddenly regained all of my senses. The *Calusa* men sensed the change and, quickly helping Soco to his feet, disappeared down the trail.

"Caesar, what is it?" I asked.

"You all right, Captain?"

"Yes, Caesar. It's all right now.

My body was trembling with chills that made me feel drained and weak, as I tried to rationalize what had happened. Caesar stood next to me and spoke softly into my ear.

"I don't know, Captain, but I get bad feelin' from dat *Hitchiti* woman. I tink she a witch, mon. She *Shanga*'"

I felt a flare of anger and spun around, looking him directly in the face.

"She saved our lives. Can't you see that the warriors wanted to kill us? Couldn't you sense that about them?"

Caesar gave me a look of frustration and shook his head.

"She cast some sort of *ju-ju* on you. What about dat animal, Captain? I tink dere another reason you want her," he said.

Caesar knew me better than I thought. Somewhere deep in my mind I knew that I had found someone with powers that I could not comprehend. I walked over to where she stood and looked into her dark eyes.

"What is your name?" I asked.

She shook her head slightly. I realized that she didn't understand, so I tried again in Spanish. Her eyes brightened a little and she answered me.

"Chera."

"Chera," I said, "my name is Santos, and this is Caesar."

She gave me a smile, and I realized that her Spanish was very limited. I turned to my friend.

"Caesar, I will be back. Please guard our new friend."

"I don't tink she need no guardin', Captain," he said, shooting a nervous glance at Chera, and then at the beast at her feet. "I come wid ju."

We strode off in the direction the warriors had fled.

They were a short distance up the path, tending to their leader's wounds. When they saw us coming, they shrank back, as if some sort of evil spirit had come to kill them.

"No reason to be frightened," I said in an even voice, "I come in peace."

As I spoke, Caesar translated my words. Soco was sitting on the ground, his back against a gumbo limbo tree. His shoulder had been bandaged and he still looked badly scared. He gazed up at me with the closest thing to a brave expression that he could summon.

Caesar translated our words.

"What do you want, shaman? Are you here to finish us with your panther?" he asked, his voice quavering.

"No," I answered. "I want to be fair with the mighty *Calusa* people. I will not steal the *Hitchiti* woman from you."

Soco watched warily as I reached into my breeches and pulled something out. I opened my palm to him. In it were the five shiny gold doubloons that Caesar had given me.

CHAPTER 25
SHAMAN

The night air was cooler and I could hear the humming drone of the insects and the lonely cries of night hawks and herons as they hunted the small creatures of the scrub. Caesar, Chera, and I walked together to Santa Lucia, where he quickly kindled a large fire. For some reason I felt very tired, and could barely find enough energy to help him gather dried wood for it. My mind was racing with questions. Who was this strange woman, Chera, and why had she been delivered to me? I sat in my usual place and pulled my blanket tighter around my shoulders to keep out the slight chill, and looked across the leaping tendrils of fire at her. She was waif-like in appearance and stared into the flames as if somewhere else, far off from where we were. She was beautiful, but not in the same way Dorathea was. Chera's beauty was exotic and raw, especially when she looked at me and flashed her shy smile. I met her gaze and held it, and saw in her eyes an understanding that nearly unnerved me. After a while, my eyelids grew heavy with fatigue and I lay back on my blanket on the sandy ground. As I beheld the myriad of stars in the dark blue sky, I felt her lie down next to me. It felt awkward and part of me wanted to protest and pull away from her, but I was so tired that it didn't matter. I let my mind relax as she burrowed under the blanket into the space by my side.

It was a dark, quarter-moon evening and we were together barefoot on the beach, our toes in the cool sand. We walked arm in arm, and I felt so close to her that we were one. Our fathers would have been furious with us for leaving our rooms in the night, but we loved the forbidden excitement of our secret meeting. Dorry was giggling, telling me a story of how a boy in town had made a fool of himself to get her attention. I laughed, but deep inside I knew how that poor devil felt. She pulled loose from me and laughed louder, running ahead of me on the dark surface of the sand.

"I want go swimming!" she shouted.

"No, Dorry. We have no dry clothes. Your father will kill me!"

"Too late, Santos!" she said cheerfully, and unfastened the buttons on her long, flowing nightshirt.

I thought I was going to faint as I beheld the outline of her naked form, her long hair flowing in the briny breeze.

She ran into the surf, the waves washing around her calves. I pulled at my breeches, the buttons stubbornly holding as I pawed at them with my clumsy fingers. As I pulled them off, I lost my balance, stumbling to the sand. After what seemed like forever, I finally finished removing my clothes. I looked down the beach toward Dorry. I could not see her.

"Dorry! Where are you?"

There was still no answer. I ran down the beach a ways, looking into the surf for any kind of movement, fear starting to crawl into my mind.

"Dorry?"

I saw her on the beach a short distance ahead of me, facing away and standing still, as if looking at something.

"Dorry, wait for me!" I shouted and ran toward her. I stopped, and then slowly walked the few remaining feet to her, savoring the sight of her long hair flowing in the gentle ocean wind. I touched her shoulder and she turned to face me.

A scream formed on my mouth but no sound came. It was not the beautiful countenance of my Dorathea. What I saw in front of me was the terrible woman from my dreams. Her pale grimace was even more terrible than I remembered, and her eyes were black, vacant holes. She smiled widely and spoke to me, her voice a dry rattling croak.

"SHE CAN'T HELP YOU, BOY."

I opened my eyes just as the scream died in my throat. It was still night, and I found myself looking into Chera's soft, concerned eyes.

"Estoy aquí. No la tema!" she was saying over and over.

I instinctively reached up and embraced her, scared out of my wits. She held me, reassuring me in a low, soothing voice that I should not be afraid, and that the woman could not harm me. I could feel the heat of the amulet on my chest and sensed the power surging through it into my body. She embraced me for a long time, gently stroking my back until the panic subsided. When my mind returned to me I pulled back from her, looking deeply into her dark eyes.

"Who are you, Chera?" I said in Spanish.

She said nothing, and gazed at me; a warm, reassuring smile on her face.

I felt the warmth of the sun's first rays on my face and opened my eyes. It took a few moments to remember the terrifying dream from the night before, but it soon came back to me. I turned over to look at Chera and saw that she gone. I smelled something cooking, so I raised my head toward the fire. She was there, tending to a large piece of meat as it roasted on a spit. Caesar walked in from the trees carrying some fresh fish that he had speared from the river. I got up from the ground, dusting myself off, and walked over to the fire, sitting down on a palmetto log near Chera. Neither of us spoke. I found myself lost in deep thought as I tried to figure this quiet woman out.

"Good morning, Captain," Caesar said cheerfully. "Chera get up early to cook. I like dis!"

I looked at her, and she turned her head toward me. Our eyes met, but we said nothing, as some innate understanding passed between us. I felt so strange. What was happening to me?

Caesar sat down next to me on the log, his face wearing a wide grin.

He reached behind his back and picked something up, hiding it from me.

"I have a gift for ju, Captain."

He held the object out. It was a medium sized sword sheathed in a worn, leather scabbard.

"Ju need this here, Captain."

I let out a low whistle and slowly pulled the blade out, admiring its gleam. I carefully touched the blade with my thumb to check its sharpness.

"Thank you, Caesar. Where did you find this?" I asked.

"De *Es-pa-no* soldier I got it from won't be needin' it, Captain," he said nonchalantly as he absently looked at his fingernails.

"Dis Chera, She really sumpting, Captain," he said. "I try to talk to her dis morning while you sleep. I learn a little 'bout her."

"What did you learn?" I asked, a little sarcastically.

"Dis woman amazing. She speak de old language of her people, but she know a little *Nickaleer* and *Es-pa-no*, and even some *Calusa*, just from being wid dem," he said.

"All she want to talk about is ju, Captain. She very worried for ju."

"Why is she worried about me?" I asked.

"She say you haunted man. Bad tings in ju. She say you been cursed."

I grew angry at this and shot him a hard look.

"I don't believe in curses or ghosts, or fairies. Tell her she is wrong."

Caesar looked back at me, his eyes wide and serious.

"Captain, dere are ghosts all around us all de time here. Ju got to believe. She powerful, mon. Don't forget de big cat in de forest!"

This was too much for me. Was I supposed to accept as true that this woman had some kind of supernatural ability to communicate with beasts?

"Caesar, do you really think she conjured that animal to attack Soco with some kind of magic?" I said, louder than I had intended.

He started to move toward me. Chera turned her head to me, a look of fear on her face.

"Captain, she has powerful magic. Ju need to listen to her!"

I felt the heat rise in my face as I started to grow angry. I wanted to hit him.

"Enough of this nonsense!" I screamed.

I leapt up and sprinted off into the woods, not even noticing the brambles that bit into my legs. I ran until I was far to the west side of the *Ais* village. The vegetation was thick, but I carefully made my way through some mangroves until I was on the edge of the great lake. The water glimmered like diamonds as the sun's rays hit the small waves. A few yards in front of me, a large fish shot up out of the depths and flew through the air, slapping back into its surface a short distance away. On far side of the lake I could see the sand beach topped by trees that seemed to go on for miles in either direction. Swiping at a mosquito on my neck, I drew in a deep breath and took in the forbidding beauty of the place. I then realized that I was crying. Tears streamed down my cheeks as I peered out through the thick branches at the water.

All of my life I had been plagued by rumors of family curses and bad magic. I had grown to hate the mention of anything even remotely spiritual, including my father's devout Catholicism. His great religion had not helped him in the end, had it? Life was what it was, and that was that. I just could not accept anything else. I believed that all men were truly alone in the world, and that their destiny was of their own making.

But what of the dreams? What of the terrible Indian woman who seemed to hate me so much?

I felt like I was on the verge of madness. What was I thinking? Who was this woman; this Chera? Then one thought occurred to me, louder than a cathedral bell. .

Could she help me?

A cloud of remorse settled over me, and I slowly made my way back toward the camp, feeling like a fool. When I walked into the clearing I saw Caesar and Chera embracing by the front door of the house. I walked up to them, stopping a few feet away. Caesar glared at me, an angry expression clouding his dark features. I looked at Chera's face and my heart sank. Her eyes were wet, and I could see that that she had been crying.

"Ju hurt her feelin's Captain. She say she love ju."

"Caesar, how can she love me? I only met her last night," I said in a low voice.

"She say she love ju forever, Captain, way before now."

She looked vulnerable now; more so than I had seen her yet, and I knew that my actions had hurt her deeply. I felt a wave of shame, and without thinking, extended my hand out to her. She looked at me with pleading, red-rimmed eyes.

"I'm sorry, Chera," I said.

She hesitated for a moment, and then slowly reached out and took it. I gently pulled her to me, and she suddenly threw her arms around my neck, sobbing. I looked over her shoulder at Caesar, who was now smiling. My eyes narrowed at him, and he shrugged his shoulders, his smile growing even wider.

We walked into the trees together, hand in hand, not speaking. After a while we came to a raised area crowned with a tight grove of live oak trees. I knew from what Caesar had taught me that this was a burial mound of the *Ais* people and considered very sacred. Chera seemed to become distracted, releasing my hand so she could examine the mound closely. After walking around it slowly three times, she took my hand and pulled me along until we found a comfortable place to sit beside it. We sat for a long time across from each other, our legs folded beneath us just gazing into each other's eyes. For some strange reason I felt more comfortable with her than I had with any person in my life.

"Chera," I said softly, "I know that you cannot understand my language that well."

She smiled and nodded her head.

"Did you tell Caesar things about me? Something about a curse?" I asked.

She looked momentarily apprehensive, and turned away.

"Come now, you can tell me. You have to tell me what you feel."

She looked at me shyly, appearing unsure of what to say, and then started to speak.

"I have seen you in my dreams," she said in a very quiet voice.

These were the first words she had said to me since I had met her, and they were as clear as any I had ever heard.

"Really?" I asked; my curiosity now triggered.

"You are cursed by the woman," she said.

At these words, I felt my head grow light and saw spots in front of my eyes. I had to steady myself on the ground with my hand because I nearly passed out. She saw this and placed her hand on my knee to steady me. I had never told anyone about my dreams, and I was instantly stunned.

"She was hurt by your blood. I see her pain and anger as brightly as the stars," she said.

"Why me?" I blurted out, louder than I intended.

"Not you, your blood. You carry the curse inside of you."

She pointed at the amulet hanging around my neck.

"This belongs to her."

I felt the anger rising again.

"No," I said sharply, "This was the last gift from my father."

She shook her head back and forth slowly.

"May I see?" she asked, holding her hand out.

I pulled the chain over my head and handed it to her. She took it and rubbed it with her thumb and forefinger, feeling its weight and texture.

"This is old. Very powerful," she said.

"Chera, I believe that it is my duty to protect this with all my power. It has been in my family for generations and was cherished by my father. I also believe that it has protected me. An *Ais* warrior tried to steal it from me."

She looked down at the amulet, shaking her head. "This is ancient magic."

We sat there in silence for a long moment. After a short time she reached into the pouch that hung from her side and pulled out a small piece of ornately designed cloth which she unfolded and laid out on the ground. It was bright yellow with blue and green stripes crisscrossing it. She then placed two small objects on it that looked like they had been fashioned some sort of white stone. One was a figurine carved in the shape of a leaping panther. Each of its eye sockets were inset with a tiny, green gemstone that twinkled in the sunlight. The other object was a long, worn looking arrowhead.

"The panther is my totem animal, Santos. He guides me and helps me to make decisions every day. The arrowhead represents not only the battles that are fought throughout our lives, but the battles of the past. These both have great power."

She placed her hands on her knees, then closed her eyes and drew in a deep breath as if praying.

"I have seen a vision, and this is how it must be. These people, the *Ais*, have lived here since the early times and believe what their gods tell them, Santos. They believe that there are three worlds; the upper one being the sun and moon; the main world being the one we all live in with the plants and animals, and the lower world which is filled with demons and ghosts. We can choose the one we want to live in by our actions. The woman of your nightmares is of the lower world, and it is from there that she gains her power. You can defeat her, Santos; you have the power inside of you. I was raised in the *Chukotalgi*, or Panther Clan of my people by wise men who taught me the ways of the Great Spirit. I ask for his guidance through the panther totem, and he helps me to make decisions every day. I speak to the animals through him, and he tells me what is wrong and what is right. When I was very young, I had a vision that I would one day meet a man haunted by an ancient demon. The Great Spirit told me that if I were to guide this man, using love and the powers within myself, I would be greatly rewarded. When I first saw you, I knew that you were the one, and that there was great power within you."

I looked into her beautiful, dark eyes and saw a welcoming familiarity that was at first disarming. I then allowed myself to trust her, and became lost in their richness. There was something ancient in them, and for the first time in my young life I felt safe. Until this point in my life I had shunned all spiritual things, but I could not help feeling that this woman was in some way sacred. I felt a wave of relief that I had never experienced, and pulled her to me. We embraced for a long time, not saying anything, as the giant cypress and oak trees looked on with ageless stoicism.

CHAPTER 26
THE WRECK

The storm had come exactly as Caesar had forewarned. The worst of it had blown through during the night and had been, at times, quite frightening as the howling wind and driving rain made sleep nearly impossible. Sometime during the turbulent night I was able to drift off.

A few hours later, I opened my eyes to gray daylight, and quickly sensed the thickness of the early morning air. I rose and walked outside into the briny wind, immediately feeling the heavy dampness on my bare skin. All along the beach, the fronds of the high palm trees bent in unison as strong gusts continued to blow in from the sea. The sky was a leaden gray and the clouds were moving very fast to the west. The ground was littered with branches and fronds that had been torn off by the howling wind.

"It was a good one, Captain," Caesar said, wearing a wide grin. "Not the worst, but pretty good."

He had an uncanny ability to sense approaching storms, and had predicted this one's arrival with alarming accuracy. A few days earlier, I had noticed a change in his carefree attitude, and had seen him sniffing at the air like some sort of animal. He wore a concerned expression on his face as he warned us all about the coming change. Even though the weather had been close to perfect, we diligently made preparations to the camp by securing the roof of his shelter by tying it down between two palmetto trees with thick ropes.

Chera was terrified and had spent the entire night huddled in a corner of the shelter, softly chanting some strange incantation over and over again. She now crept out into the daylight, a look of relief on her face. I walked to her and embraced her, my hands gently caressing her back.

"It's all right, Chera. The foulest part of the storm has passed," I said in a soothing voice.

My cheek was chafed from the coarseness of the woven blanket that Caesar had given me to sleep on. It was folded twice and stuffed with Spanish moss, but it afforded little comfort from the roughly hewn raised platform. According to Caesar, sleeping on this would prevent snakes from crawling in with me during the night. As he told me this, my mind went back to that lonely night on the beach when that very thing had happened, so I gladly complied with his advice. He was now packing some rough hand tools into a canvas pouch.

"We must go, Captain, de time is right."

With that he strode off toward the beach, leaving me behind. I hastily snatched up my shirt, blade, and scabbard and started after him. I paused and turned to look at Chera.

"We'll be back. I'm not quite sure what is going on, but I'm going to find out." I said.

I caught up with him on the path and stayed close behind as he scrambled down it toward the ocean. As we moved, I clumsily attempted to tie the leather scabbard of the sword to my side.

"Caesar, what is the hurry?" I complained as he scrambled through the scrub.

There was a shout from the beach, so he darted off the path, bolting through a thick patch of thick sea grape plants. I did my best to keep up, and soon emerged onto the sandy expanse of the beach just as he was about to disappear from view. I was surprised at the speed and agility of my friend as he sprinted ahead of me. We were moving so fast that we soon overtook three *Ais* men running in the same direction.

Caesar shouted something to them that I could not hear, and they answered, not slowing their pace. Caesar turned his head back to me, his face alive with a wide smile.

"Captain, there is a wreck a short distance to the north of us!"

I was panting heavily, and my legs soon grew tired from the exertion of running in the soft sand. Still somewhat confused at the urgency of our mission, I doggedly followed him. I could soon see our destination on the beach ahead. The great hulk of a ship leaned haphazardly to one side in the short surf. There were a large number of people on the beach around her, and I quickly realized that she was a casualty of last night's storm. As we got closer, I could see the masts of the ship cocked at an unnatural angle and the tattered sails flapping in the stiff wind, making a loud, whipping sound. The violent winds of the storm had driven her right up onto the beach. The sternposts and rudder were visible in the shallow water, and the deck was facing out to sea. There were at least fifty *Ais* men there, and I could see that a few of them appeared to be standing guard behind several white men dressed in European style clothes kneeling in a line on the beach. There was something very wrong here, and I felt a strange apprehension as I slowed my pace. It was the first time I had seen my own kind since I had been on Brattock's ship, and my mind quickly jumped to an irrational conclusion.

Would this be the point of my rescue from this place?

Memories of the angry looks of betrayal that I had received from Miguel Mejia and Carlos Anguiano back on the *Nightingale* came to me and made me wary. I had no way of knowing if word had spread about my supposed "treachery" with the pirates, or what the repercussions of such a thing would be. I thought of my long wild hair and ragged clothes and knew that I would most likely be viewed as a criminal or vagabond.

There were many *Ais* men climbing all over the doomed ship, and I saw them carrying many assorted items up the beach, depositing them in piles before returning for more. There were olive bottles, chests, clothes that I knew they treasured greatly, and much more. I looked at the men being held prisoner on the beach and knew by their dress that they were merchant seamen, most likely from one of the many ports in the Caribbean. One of them let out a loud plea for mercy, and I immediately surmised that they were English.

My old nemesis, Aktil, was there, and it was obvious that he had assumed the role of leader among the *Ais* raiders. He screamed violently at the poor devils, and I heard the same word that I had grown so familiar with during my early encounters with the *Ais* people: "*Nickaleer.*" I now realized that these poor British souls were not my rescuers and that they would probably all be killed. Caesar told me that the *Ais* were under strict orders from the Spanish soldiers who visited them to kill any English sailors who were unfortunate enough to wash up on their shores.

The soldiers also spread rumors among the islands about the supposed acts of cannibalism among the natives. I had seen some strange bones in the fire pits back at the village and suspected that the *Ais* men sometimes consumed the flesh of their enemies. Caesar had denied that they participated in this act of barbarity, but he went to great length to defend the practice as one of ceremony rather than necessity. It is my own theory that the *Ais* may have believed that if they consumed the flesh of a powerful enemy they would absorb his power.

I slowly walked up to the line of men being held there. They were a sorry looking lot, with many of them suffering from the ravages of scurvy, their teeth a mass of rotting gray. Several had red patches of skin on their exposed parts that were burnt and peeling from the effects of the sun. One of them, a scrawny seaman with a shock of blazing red hair, saw me and tried to catch my eye. He spoke to me in a voice as creaky as an un-oiled door hinge.

"Aye, mate. Can you help us 'ere? These savages don't seem to want to."

"I cannot, for I am a prisoner as well," I said.

At the sound of my voice, Aktil spun his head around to look at me, a sneer of contempt on his face. He spat out a declaration at Caesar that I didn't understand. Caesar ran over to my side and looked at me warily.

"Aktil wants to know if ju want to kill these *Nickaleer* ju self, Captain."

Out of the corner of my eye I caught some movement from the wrecked vessel. On the stern deck above the Captain's cabin was a sailor, clinging onto the railing for balance and holding something in one hand. There was a loud booming sound that I recognized as a gunshot, and one of the *Ais* men near me shrieked in pain, his chest erupting in a fountain of blood. He tried to cover the wound with his hand, and then spun around in a circle before collapsing to the sand. I looked up in horror and saw that the sailor was fumbling to load another round. A very strong young warrior strode past me, at the same time expertly sliding a short spear into a curved device that he had been carrying on his shoulder. He ran a few steps forward for momentum and slung his arm out ferociously in a wide arc, releasing the spear with terrific force. It sang through the air with deadly accuracy, striking the sailor directly in the chest with a thud. The blow was so shocking to the man that he didn't make a sound. He looked directly at me, an expression of confusion on his face, and slowly crumpled, his lifeless body sliding down the deck and splashing into the sea.

Aktil shrieked with rage and raised his war club high into the air. The man kneeling in front of him was older, with silver hair and leathery skin. Aktil savagely brought the club down on his head, killing him instantly. The remaining prisoners, quickly realizing that the same fate awaited them, leapt to their feet and began fighting back at their captors in an act of savage desperation. One large fellow with a red stocking hat on his head and a great black beard bellowed with insane rage and leapt at Caesar, who happened to be standing close to him. Alas, my friend was too slow to react and was bowled over by the huge man. They both tumbled to the sand, spitting and fighting. The sailor rolled to the top on his knees and grabbed Caesar around the throat with both hands, choking him. Not knowing what else to do, I pulled the knife at my side from its scabbard and leapt onto the giants back. I reached around and grabbed his beard, pulling it up and forcing his massive head back.

"Let him go, you fool!" I screamed at him.

"Never!" he bellowed. "I may die 'ere, but I'll take this darkie savage wit' me!"

I drew my arm back and, with all the strength I could gather, smashed the silver hilt of the rapier up against the side of his broad face. The blow made a dull crunching sound, and the sailor's body immediately relaxed, slumping over into the sand. Caesar bellowed an oath as he sat up and gasped for breath, massaging his sore neck with his fingers.

I got to my feet and looked down the beach, just in time to see three of the Englishmen disappearing into the distance.

"They escaped!" Caesar cried.

"What does it matter?" I asked. "They will die on the beach in a few days. They do not know how to survive here!"

Caesar looked at me gravely.

"If they do live they will bring more men back for revenge," he said in a low tone.

Behind him I watched as the *Ais* men fought the remaining sailors. Caesar sprang to his feet and ran toward the wreck, splashing through the water.

"Hurry, Captain! There isn't much time!" he shouted.

I followed him, and together we waded around the ship to where the deck was exposed to the incoming waves. From that angle, we were obscured from the view of everyone on the beach. Caesar found a good section of railing that he could reach, and grabbed onto it, tugging it sharply to make sure that it was sturdy. He swung himself up onto the deck, holding onto it for balance. He held his hand out to help me, and we were both soon making our way across the lopsided deck toward the main hatch. When we reached it, he dropped down through it, disappearing into the darkness below. I arrived at it a few moments later and looked down into the inky darkness, not nearly as eager to plunge down into it as he had been.

"Caesar! What are you looking for?" I called out in a hoarse whisper.

I got no reply, so I waited. I was definitely not anxious to join him in that dark hold. I worked my way up to the railing of the ship and carefully looked down at the beach. The slaughter was still going on, so I quickly ducked back down. I heard a sound from below, so I moved back to the main hatchway. Caesar's head emerged from the darkness, his face drenched in sweat. He gave me a broad smile and let out a grunt of exertion as he swung a large canvas bag up through the hatch. I heard the telltale clinking sound of coins inside it, so I grabbed the top and pulled it open, peering inside at its contents. The bag was full of silver coins that were roughly cut and stamped. There were so many inside that the bag was hard to lift.

"Captain," he said, "we cannot let the *Ais* know what is in here."

"How do you propose to hide it?" I asked, incredulous.

Caesar said nothing, but grabbed the loose top of the bag, and quickly tying it into a tight knot. He grabbed a large piece of sail that had torn loose from the rigging and, producing a small sharp knife from his breeches, cut a long, thin strip from it. He then wrapped it around the knot he had made and secured it. Clutching the bag in one hand, he got to his feet and, in one quick motion, tossed it into the ocean beside the wreck. He looked at me and smiled.

"Dose fools on de beach rather fight dan come and get de silver. We come back later and find our bag, Captain!"

We then climbed down from the wreck and made our way back to the beach. All of the outnumbered sailors had been killed, and the *Ais* men were now stripping the clothes from their bodies. Caesar and I quickly made our way back toward Santa Lucia.

CHAPTER 27
NIGHTWATCH

Chera smiled at me from her place across the red and yellow flames of the campfire. I could hear the ocean's faint roar in the distance and smell its brininess in the cool evening air. I gazed back into her beautiful eyes as the logs shifted in the fire, letting out an intermittent sputter and crackle and sending a line of sparks straight up toward the leaves of the palmettos. Caesar was sitting on a log on the far side of us and was lost in concentration, fashioning a tool from a long branch with his knife.

"Caesar," I said, "can I ask you question?"

"Yes, Captain, of course," he said.

"Why do you have to hide your treasures from the *Ais*?"

He looked up at me with a sardonic look on his face. His skin glistened with sweat and appeared to be made of glass in the flickering firelight.

"Because, Captain," he said, "dey would kill me for it."

There was a pause, and then he continued.

"De *Es-pa-no* come too. Dey search de *Ais* men for de shine. If dey find any shine dey kill de *Ais* men or take dem away."

"Why do the Spaniards kill the *Ais* if they have "shine" as you call it?" I asked.

"I tink it because de *Es-pa-no* don't want dem wreckin' any ships, Captain. Dey want it all for dem selves," he said.

He paused for a moment and stared off toward the swaying palm trees.

"De *Es-pa-no* very bad, Captain," he said.

He then shook his head as if to rid himself of an unpleasant thought and sprang to his feet.

"It is time, Captain. The moon is out."

With that he walked to the doorway of his rough cabin and picked up his large canvas bag, slipping the long handle over his head. He then stepped to the roaring fire and bent to pick up a long stick that had cloth wrapped tightly around the end and appeared to have been dipped in something. He stuck it into the licking flames for a few moments, and then pulled it out, the torch end burning brightly. He gave me a sidelong glance, and then strode off toward the tree line. I jumped up and hurriedly found my small sack and scabbard and took off after him.

It was not hard to see where he was going because the torch blazed brightly as he quickly made his way along the trail, the light of it reflecting off the huge oak and palmetto trees around it. We soon emerged onto the beach and began to walk swiftly in the direction of the wreck site. The beach looked completely different at night. The moon hung low over the trees and was huge, full and clear, casting a near daylight brightness over the landscape. There was a cool breeze blowing in from the sea and the waves were beating their tranquil, never-ending rhythm against the sand. As I walked briskly to keep up with Caesar, I noticed that there were none of the minute biting insects that plagued the earlier hours of the day. The night birds and seagulls cried as they flew low over the short surf, hunting for small fish that ventured too close to the surface of the water.

I looked to the north and saw the silhouettes of palm trees as they leaned toward the ocean, their fronds swaying in the gentle wind. It was no wonder that the native people found this place so sacred. During the day, the heat was blistering and hostile, but during the nocturnal hours the moon seemed friendly and all knowing. I saw Caesar pause and gaze toward its roundness, and I heard him quietly recite some ancient chant that I supposed he had learned from the *Ais*. I did not understand the words, but I thought the cadence of it beautiful, so I tried to retain it, like an old melody.

After a short rest we continued north, Caesar's torch lighting the way. Ahead I saw several large shapes moving very slowly and methodically up the beach toward the sea grapes. As we drew closer, I could see that they were great sea turtles that had crawled up on the beach to lay their eggs. I was amazed at the agility and determination of these huge creatures, and stopped for a while to watch their progress. Several were as long as a man and three times as wide. I noticed that they seemed to turn their great heads slowly toward Caesar's torch as if they were drawn to the light like moths. Their fins acted as paddles in the sand and propelled them across the cool surface of the beach, creating strange wide tracks that looked like no other I had ever seen.

"Captain, we come back later and gather de eggs. Dey very good eatin'!" he said.

Every day I was gaining more and more respect for my new friend. He was proving to be one of the smartest and most resourceful people I had ever met. It seemed that he knew everything that there was to know about this place. He knew all the names of the plants and which could be eaten, and which would poison you. He knew the traits and characteristics of all of the animals of the scrub and could name all of the fish that were taken from the sea. Having to endure a very hostile environment for nearly his entire life, he had grown into a shrewd survivor. He also knew how to influence people and could cajole them into seeing things his way. I had come to the realization that his years of servitude to the *Ais* had not been as unbearable and cruel as I had first imagined it. His was the existence of a man who was more free than any I had ever known because he had adjusted himself to the spare way of life and had gleaned from it all of the advantages he could.

We were soon approaching the wreck site. Through the darkness, I could see movement on the beach, so I gripped the handle of my scabbard in readiness for another fight. I soon realized that what I was seeing were vultures that had come to pick at the few remaining dead bodies that the natives hadn't dragged off. As we drew closer, they flew off to a safe distance and waited impatiently for us to leave. The smell of decay was awful, so I moved to a position upwind of the naked corpses.

"Tank the Lord dey did not burn it yet!" Caesar said in a hoarse whisper.

He handed me the torch and walked to the far side of the vessel. I heard him splash into the water, then dive under and swim out into the surf. I looked around at the scene there on the shore and recalled the violent events that I had witnessed. The ship had an ethereal, strange look in the yellow reflected light of the torch and reminded me of a great wounded sea animal that had wandered too close to shore. I thought of the men whom I had seen die there earlier that day and a wave of sadness hit me. I held the torch higher and looked at the stern leaning at a sharp angle in the sand and saw a name scribed on it. It was faded, but I could still make it out. It read "*AGAMEMNON.*" I knew that the sailors were British, but they had been rougher looking than the merchant seamen that I had seen in La Habana. As I contemplated the memory of them lined up on the beach, I began to suspect them of being pirates.

I was startled by a sound behind me, and I whirled around. I recognized it as a groan of pain, and my eyes searched wildly for its source. I saw a large form lying in the sand a few feet away, so I carefully approached it. It was one of the bodies that we had passed as we came in. The sound came again and I saw that it was indeed coming from the naked corpse. My heart leapt with fear, and I felt as if I were experiencing another one of my terrible dreams. This was a very large man and I could see that there was dry, crusted blood all over his head. One of his arms moved and I once more heard the groan. All of a sudden, I knew who he was. This was the huge man that had attacked Caesar, and the same one that I had been forced to dispatch with the hilt of my scabbard. I took a step nearer to him, taking care not to get too close.

"You there," I said, "are you awake?"

He groaned again and he shifted his large body, rolling over on his side. He looked at me with the dazed eyes of a man just regaining consciousness.

"Oo' are you?" he asked in a thick English accent.

"I am Captain Santos, currently of the *Ais* people," I said.

His hand went to the wound on the side of his head and he groaned in pain again.

"Wot 'appened to me?" he asked in a voice that sounded like an overgrown child.

"You attacked my partner, so I dealt a blow to your skull that should have killed you," I said.

His eyes regained a bit of clarity and I saw fear enter them as he remembered what had happened.

"Where are the men? Do you 'ave any water?" he asked in that same confused voice, and I sensed his growing panic.

I pulled my sword from its scabbard and pointed it at him.

"Your men are dead because one of them killed an *Ais* warrior with his musket. If you attack me, I will finish the job that they didn't."

He looked at the ruined ship, then down at his nakedness and tears formed in his eyes as the hopelessness of his situation hit him all at once.

"Cap'n, I am at your bloomin' mercy 'ere. 'Oo am I going to attack?" he said, his voice breaking. "Just save me from those bleedin' savages!"

I felt a wave of pity for him and lowered my sack from my shoulder and reached inside, pulling a torn rag from it and handing it to him. From behind me I heard Caesar emerging from the surf, carrying the bag of coins that he had earlier marked with the long piece of sailcloth in his hand.

"What is going on, Captain?" he asked as he looked at the miserable, naked man lying there, crying like a child.

"This is the crazed giant who attacked you today, Caesar," I said, "It seems that I didn't hit him hard enough."

"Kill him now, Captain. The *Ais* will come back tomorrow and do it anyway," he said in a flat voice.

"No, please Cap'n! Don't be doin' that! Oi'll do whatever you say, just spare me." he wailed.

I could not help it, and I burst into laughter at the ridiculous appearance of this huge, bearded man crying there in the sand. I looked over at Caesar and he began to laugh as well.

"What is your name, sailor?" I asked him.

"Shadwell Wallingsworth, sir, but me men call me Shad," he said, a glimmer of hope in his tone.

I thought for a few moments about the unexpected development.

"Caesar, can I have a moment with you?" I asked.

I placed my hand on his shoulder and we walked a short distance away.

"We can't just leave him here, Caesar. Aktil will come back tomorrow and find him. He can't survive out here alone," I said.

"Captain, dis man try to kill me today," he said in a low voice.

"I would say that he was under a bit of stress at the time, wouldn't you, Caesar?" I asked.

Caesar thought long and hard for a few moments, his face screwed in a frown of concentration.

"If de *Ais* men find him wid us, they will kill us all," he said.

"I don't think so, Caesar. The *Calusa* hunters have most likely warned them of Chera's power. I think that they are too frightened to come near us," I said.

"Captain, we can take him wid us, but if he try to kill me again I will give him to de *Ais* to eat," he said, a solemn expression on his face.

We walked back over to the hulk of a man. He looked up at us with large, terrified eyes.

"Shad, my partner and I have discussed this matter, and the way I see it, you have two choices. You can decide to go it on your own and take your chances with the *Ais*, or you can come with us as a servant. If I were a prudent man, I would kill you now, but unfortunately, and luckily for you, I do not have it in me. The first thing I would like you to do is apologize to Caesar here for trying to take his life earlier today."

He stared dumbly at me for a moment, and then spoke.

"Oi' am very sorry, sir, for tryin' to strangle your slave in such a violent manner."

"Shad, my huge friend, we need to get something straight. If anyone is a slave here, it is you. Caesar is no man's property. He is your Captain, and you will answer to him at all times."

"Oi' won't bend to a bleedin' scrub!" he bellowed, temporarily forgetting himself.

"Come along, Caesar. We must go and leave this fool to make his way back to wherever it is he came from." I said, turning to walk away.

"Wait!" Shad yelled. "Oi' am sorry, sir. Oi' will do as you say. The scrub, umm, I mean Cap'n Caesar, will be treated with the utmost respect."

"All right, I guess we will let you live."

I whispered to Caesar. "Did you hear that!" I said, laughing, "Captain Caesar! I love it."

Caesar smiled broadly.

Shad got up from the sand and I saw how large he truly was. He stood three to four hands taller than me and twice as wide.

"We need to find you some clothes," I said.

We spent the next few hours clamoring around and through the ship in search of things that the *Ais* wreckers had missed. Caesar gathered some dry wood and lit a small fire on the beach for light, his crude torch long since extinguished. Shad proved to be a valuable asset because he was so familiar with the ship's layout. He found a trunk that had been under the care of the ship's quartermaster containing enough clothing for ten men. I could not believe that the *Ais* wreckers had missed it, but there it was. He pulled the largest pair of breeches and blouse that he could find and put them on, blessedly covering his nakedness. He also found a crossbow with a quiver of arrows, and a musket with a full supply of powder and shot.

We were able to salvage several other useful items from the hold of the *Agamemnon* that the *Ais* had either left behind, or had no use for. This included blankets, shovels, navigational charts, and a chest full of clothing and firearms that would prove invaluable to us. There was also a round shaped object that I had seen Captain Brattock use many times aboard the *Nightingale*. I explained to Caesar that it was called an astrolabe; an instrument used for celestial guidance by navigators and ship's captains.

The night went by quickly, and as the blues turned to gray, Caesar started to periodically look up at the sky.

"We need to go," he said, "morning come soon."

"Wait!" Shad said, startling both of us. "Oi' need to sneak below one more time for jiffy!"

Caesar and I glanced at each other. Should we trust the giant?

"Go ahead, Shad, but if you try anything sly, we will leave you here for the *Ais*."

"Got it." he said as he took the torch from Caesar's hand and clamored up the side of the ship and disappeared down through the main hatch.

After a few minutes we saw the glow of the torch and the figure of Shad emerging onto the upper deck. He made his way down the side of the ship quickly and nimbly for such a large man. He walked up to us, a huge grin on his bearded face.

"'Ere you are!"

He handed me a small box. I took it from him and immediately noticed the fine craftsmanship of the item. It looked like a travel chest, but was small enough to hold with one hand. Caesar held the torch, as I carefully opened it. I sucked in my breath in amazement at what I saw. The box was lined with red velvet, and in it lay an ornately crafted cross made of solid gold. Each of the four points of it was encrusted with green emeralds, and mounted on the center of the intersection of it was the largest jewel of all: a white diamond. It was hung with a long hand- crafted gold chain that must have taken months to construct.

"Where did you get this, Shad? It must be worth a fortune!" I exclaimed.

He smiled at me widely, his bad teeth showing.

"Why, I acquired this fine item from the Queen of Spain 'erself!" he said.

Caesar and I both laughed out loud, and together the three of us made our way back up the beach toward Santa Lucia, lugging our newly found prizes on our backs.

CHAPTER 28
A LIGHT IN THE DARKNESS

I ran as fast as I could through the night along the road that ran past our house, my face covered in sweat and my clothes in disarray. I was experiencing a feeling of fear and panic like never before. The sense of urgency was overwhelming as I ran toward the place where I had grown up and where I knew my father waited for me. The night was thick and suffocating with moisture and the sound of the insects buzzing in the trees was nearly overwhelming. Only a few moments earlier I had been at my place on the wall by the great waterway, and had felt the strongest premonition of danger ever. Tears streamed down my face as I swiftly made my way toward the house. Soon I could see its familiar silhouette in the distance, rising out of the gloom as I approached. The sight of its familiar contours calmed me at first, and then increased my unexplained sense of foreboding.

Wait.. was someone there?

In one of the lit side windows of the house I could see her, and even from that great distance I could tell that it was my Dorathea.

She was waving to me!

I tried to shout, but my voice would not make any sound, so I ran toward the house with all of the speed that I could muster. I finally reached the door and grabbed the latch. It held fast, locked from the inside.

Where was she? Where was my Dorry?

I flew into a panicked rage and began to pound on the heavy, wooden door with both fists. It suddenly gave way, slowly swinging open to pitch black emptiness. Dorathea was gone and my father was nowhere in sight. Then I saw her: that terrible woman from my nightmares. She was floating; unnaturally suspended in mid-air; a dull, yellow light barely illuminating her against the houses black interior. *The grimace of hatred was gone, having been replaced by an expression of calm serenity. I could see how beautiful she had been in life, and how regal she must have looked to her followers. Her mouth did not move, but I could hear her speak to me in a hollow-sounding voice that seemed to originate from far away.*

"Our time is coming, boy. I have been waiting for you to come to me."

With that, she smiled. The smile widened, slowly contorting into a hideous grimace that stretched out too wide for her face. Her skin took on that gray, pallid color of rot, and her eyes transformed to a shiny, jet-black color and sank back into her head as if she were decaying before my horrified eyes. Her beautiful, raven hair seemed to quiver as if the earth beneath her were shaking and lost its shiny hue, becoming straw-like and streaked with gray. I heard her scream out; a terrible wail of hundreds of years of pain.

"No, witch!" I shouted out in fear. "You cannot do this to me! I have done nothing to you!"

I felt something happen, as if a change in the air had occurred, such as when a storm from the sea approached. I became aware of another presence there, in the same space. The phantom woman seemed to sense it as well.

She became quiet, and the awful smile left her face, replaced by an expression that I had never seen before. She began to scream again, but this time it was different. It was as if she were not directing her malice at me. Her form began to writhe wildly, and her fingers clutched at the air as if in pain. She began to slowly fade away, gradually becoming transparent before fading into total blackness.

"Captain! Captain!"

I awoke to someone shaking me. I was in my place on the platform inside the shelter and Caesar was looking down at me, both hands on my shoulders.

"Captain! Ju was dreamin' again! I could hear ju moaning and I woke!" he said.

I shook my head to rid myself of the terrible, realistic vision that I had just seen.

"Where is Chera?" I croaked.

"Chera? I do not know, Captain. She was by the fire last night, but she did not come in," he said.

"I know where she is," I said, rising from the bed. I walked out through the doorway into the pre-dawn grayness and looked around in all directions at the surrounding trees. Quickly moving across the camp and into the trees on the far side, I made my way down the narrow, seldom used trail. I was soon standing next to the ancient burial mound and the cluster of huge oak trees that Caesar had shown me when I first came.

"Chera!" I shouted, "Where are you?"

I walked around to the far side of the mound and I saw her small form lying on one of Caesar's salvaged blankets. Dropping to my knees next to her, I gently shook her shoulders.

"Chera, are you all right?" I said to her.

She was awake but entranced; her eyes rolled back in her head. I didn't know what else to do, so I embraced her, holding her close to my breast and kissing her face gently.

"Chera, I know it was you in my dream. I know it. Please come back to me," I said.

She woke then, and looked up into my eyes. I saw a look of pure love there, so honest and good that tears came to me. I got down on the blanket next to her lean body and kissed her again, feeling a raw wave of emotion that seemed to have been building up inside of me since I had met her. A flood of feelings ripped through me that were so new that I felt flushed and confused, but Chera's reassuring smile soon relaxed me. My senses were on fire as I first removed her clothes, then my own. She was stunning, and I remember feeling that she was the most beautiful woman I had ever seen. We made love for the first time right there underneath the spreading live oaks that crowned the burial mound.

Chera and I spent that whole day together laughing and talking. Even though she struggled with many words, I found that I could understand her perfectly. In this way, I was able to penetrate the shield of stoicism that she maintained when there were others around. She opened up to me completely, and I saw in her animated face the beautiful, impetuous little girl she had once been. She told me a story of how, as a child, she had rescued a panther kitten from a large red wolf. She took it back to her village and hid it in a wicker basket for months until it simply got too large and unruly to keep. One day, it simply bounded off into the forest. Broken-hearted, she had cried for days.

She later saw the animal again, gazing at her from the trees when she was alone. It was her belief that the panther had followed her through her young life and protected her, and that the animal had told its brothers and sisters all over the natural world to do the same. This story would have been fantastic to me if I had not seen it with my own eyes.

Chera had long been considered a shaman with special powers by her people in the far north ever since she was very young. When vicious tribal warfare started, she fled with her parents and the rest of her people into Spanish Florida. During their journey south they had encountered a mighty *Calusa* war party, and a great fight had ensued. The *Calusa* warriors had killed her parents and the other members of her party, and taken her prisoner. Although she grieved, she had never been frightened because she knew deep inside that her animal friends were watching from the forests.

"Are they watching now?" I asked.

"They have been watching you for a long time, Santos." she said.

"What do you mean, Chera?" I asked.

"Santos, I have something to tell you," she said, "and you may be surprised."

"Go on." I said.

"I have known of you for a very long time. I have seen you in my dreams for many years. We were destined to be together by entities that are much higher than either one of us."

"Is that what you believe, Chera?" I asked, smiling broadly but not taking her seriously.

She frowned at me. "You don't understand. "

"It's not that, Chera. How could you have known me before our first meeting?"

What she said next absolutely stunned me.

"The Indian woman means you great harm, Santos."

We did not return to the camp until that evening. Shad and Caesar were sitting by the fire eating some freshly caught fish, so we joined them. We were both starving after our long day of wandering, so the food was delicious. When the fish was gone, we roasted chunks of succulent rabbit meat on long sticks held over the fire. It was a beautiful, balmy night, and Caesar had set up several tall torches at various spots around the clearing, illuminating the entire camp in a soft, amber light. Shad sat on a large log at the far end of the fire wrapped in a blanket, a despondent look on his face.

"What is the matter, my huge friend?" I said brightly, trying to cheer him.

"I don't rightly know, Captain. 'Oi've lost everything," he said.

He was so large that the blanket he wore barely covered his broad back. His head was wrapped with a wide piece of cloth, giving him the appearance of a Turkish Prince.

"Oh, I don't know about that, Shad." I said "You have us!"

A few moments passed as we became lost in our own thoughts, both of us entranced by the flames.

"Shad," I asked the hulking man, "where were you and your men headed?"

"Oh," he said almost dismissively, "nowhere for certain."

"What does that mean?" I asked.

"We was eyeing for merchant vessels, chiefly Spanish ones, sir," he said.

"Ah, so you are a pirate!" I said.

"No, not a pirate, Captain," he said a tad defensively. "The *Barsheba* 'ad Letters of Marque from England to protect 'er interests on the high seas, sir,".

"*Barsheba*?" Your ship was the *Agememnon*, I said. "Who was your Captain? Was he Greek?"

"The Captain's name is Henry Jennings, and 'is ship is the *Barsheba*. We was a prize crew aboard the "*Agamemnon*," which we took in the Straits of La Florida a few days ago. Our sailin' Master, 'ees name was Longfellow. You saw 'im get 'is head stove in by that savage on the beach."

"Ah," I said, "such is the way of the *Ais*, my friend. They don't have much use for outsiders."

Shad's eyes went narrow and his face took on a frightening edge.

"I remember the one 'oo done it to John Longfellow. There was ne'er a finer man. If I ever meet the red bastard again 'eel wish 'is mum were 'ere," he said.

"Well, if I were you, Shad, I would stay clear of the *Ais* warriors," I said. At this, Caesar let out a loud laugh, surprising the both of us.

There was a commotion at the edge of the clearing, like someone running through the thick vegetation, and a figure burst through into the clearing. I was surprised to see that it was a young *Ais* boy. He was totally out of breath from running, so much so that he could not speak. Caesar stood up and walked toward him, speaking a few clipped phrases in the native language. The boy finally caught his breath and answered him in excited gasps. Even though I could not understand a word of what was being said, I recognized the gravity of the words by the expression of shocked dismay on Caesar's face. After the dark-skinned boy had delivered his message, he looked at us with frightened eyes, and then turned and fled back through the trees and toward the beach.

"What is it, Caesar?" I asked.

"De *Es-pa-no* come from de north outpost. Dey are in de village, and dey are beating old Canoba!"

CHAPTER 29
THE SINS OF MY OWN

The night sky was darker than usual because huge, slow moving cloud banks had blocked out the stars, and the low sound of thunder could be heard in the distance out over the sea. There were far off lightning flashes that illuminated their majestic caverns and hills on the horizon, momentarily exposing their immense size and beauty. The salty night air was so wet that a light sprinkling was falling on my skin. We ran along the hard sand of the beach until we reached the trail that led to the *Ais* village; our bodies covered with the sweat of exertion; our faces set with expressions of angry determination.

There were two longboats of European design pulled up high on the beach, and many footprints of booted men could be seen in the sand. We stealthily made our way up the trail, taking care to be very quiet. Caesar thought that we should take a more direct route than usual, so we cut through the thick bushes as fast as we could, slowing warily as we approached the outskirts of the village. We soon saw the low shapes of the houses in the near darkness. The buildings appeared to be deserted, so we moved closer to the meeting house. Something was not right. There was no light from the fire that usually burned just outside the great longhouse. Carefully creeping up to the outside wall of the structure, we heard low conversation and the recognizable jargon of Spanish men.

"*Sargento*, where should we look next?" a voice said.

"*Silencid* Do you want to wake the whole village? It has to be here somewhere," a man with a gruff voice answered.

"The old medicine man wasn't much help." The first man said.

There was low laughter, then a creaking sound.

"He won't lie to me again."

Had these men beaten the old man? I felt a surge of anger building inside of me.

"We wouldn't even have known of the wreck if it hadn't been for the *Inglés pirata*. He didn't want to talk, but we convinced him otherwise!"

There was more laughter and I heard a third man.

"Yes, he died like a weak *Inglés* always does; crying and whining like a woman."

"He died like a pirate should; at an appointment with the hangman!"

They all laughed at this, and from their voices I was able to discern that there were five men in the longhouse. This did not include the old man, Canoba, who was probably badly injured. I remembered the three Englishmen that I had watched escape up the beach the night before, and now knew what had become of at least one of them. They must have arrived at the Spanish outpost to the north hoping for mercy, only to be tortured by these cruel soldiers. I thought of the terror of being shipwrecked on this beach, and was now reminded of how truly lucky I had been in my own experiences.

"The savages looted the ship and took everything of value from it. I want to find what they did with all of it, especially the gold and silver," said the *Sargento*, whom I took for their leader.

"We've been through many of the houses and found nothing, *Sargento*," one of the others said.

"Keep searching!" was the gruff response. "If I have to, I'll kill every one of these beasts."

"I'd like to find an *Indio* wench to desecrate!" one of them said, a lascivious tone in his voice.

I immediately took a darker dislike to this one. Turning to Caesar, I pointed back toward the beach, and together we crept back in the direction we had come. After a short time, we emerged onto the sand where the longboats were. I had formulated a plan, so I signaled to Caesar to help me. Each of us grabbing one end, we quickly carried the boats into the trees a good distance away, hurriedly covering them with loose, dry palmetto fronds.

We then began to make our way back toward the village, moving slowly so as not to be detected. From somewhere in the cluster of low, round houses, I heard a woman let out a yelp. We made a dead run toward the source of the sound. The small round shelter made from bent poles and palm fronds was a short distance from the others, and it was from here that we heard the sounds of a struggle. The noises from inside told us that a woman was being attacked against her will. It was very dark, but our eyes were accustomed to it, so I had no trouble seeing one of the booted feet of the attacker sticking out through the shelter's opening. I kicked it lightly.

"Hey, it's my turn," I said in Spanish, making my voice sound low and rough.

"Go away! This one's mine!" The attacker said. I continued my ruse.

"Come out here for a moment. I want to see her."

"Oh, for God's sake in Heaven!" he said, highly exasperated as he clumsily climbed out into the darkness.

As soon as he did this, Caesar attacked from behind, clamping his hand over the would-be rapist's mouth. I

approached him and pointed my sword at his stomach, poking
his skin with its sharp tip.

"If you scream out, my friend, you will die here in the
sand," I said.

He looked at me with surprise and fear, his eyes glazed
over and the smell of alcohol permeating the air around him.
He was of middle age and had dark, wavy hair and a pointed
beard and mustache. His clothes were worn, probably from his
long journey from St. Augustine or wherever he came from,
and he was drenched in sweat. A very young *Ais* woman
poked her head out of the opening of the house and looked up
at us. Seeing what had happened, she scrambled out into the
night and ran away. I could hear her crying softly as she fled.

"So, how long have you been defiling young and helpless
native women?" I asked him.

He grunted at me and jerked around, trying his best to
break the grip Caesar had on his arms.

Suddenly, from the darkness there was a "*whooshing*" sound
and a "*thuk*," and the rapist's head jerked back, his body going
slack. I looked at him and saw, to my horror that a long arrow
was protruding from his right eye socket. I spun my head
around to see where it had come from, scanning the trees
behind us. He then stepped out from the trees, a young *Ais*
warrior whom I recognized, wearing a look of frightful rage. I
glanced down at his side and saw the atlatl that he gripped in
his right hand. This was the same fierce weapon that I had
seen him use earlier on the beach with deadly effectiveness.
Caesar and I glanced at each other, a deep understanding
instantly communicated between us. These atrocious acts were
being committed by my own countrymen.

We dropped the dead man to the ground and ran back
toward the village. No matter what had transpired, we

needed to help the old man. We ran into the longhouse and stopped short, stunned by the sight before us. Canoba was swinging to and fro in the breeze, the rope around his neck tightly bound to the large support pole that ran across the meeting house. His eyes were open and sightless, and his long white hair whipped in the breeze. His body looked very thin and frail as it moved slowly back and forth like a pendulum. The young warrior who was with us flew into a fit of despair and anger and let out a wail that was so loud that it woke the entire village. More men were soon running toward the longhouse to see what had happened, and great cries of rage filled the night air. There was soon an angry mob racing down the trail to the beach carrying hastily lit torches. I pulled Caesar aside to speak with him, but he spoke first, his face taut with anger.

"De *Es-pa-no* tink dat dey make an example of Canoba to the *Ais* people. Dey will die tonight from what dey do," he said, tears running down his shining face.

CHAPTER 30
RECKONING

The large throng of enraged natives burst from the trail onto the beach in search of the Spaniards. Caesar and I ran to where we had hidden the boats and found them where we had left them. We then checked the sand by the trailhead for footprints to determine which direction the men had gone. I lowered the torch I was carrying and saw the tell-tale swishes in the sand heading up the beach.

"They are headed north, Caesar, toward Chera!"

He moved closer to me and bent his head toward mine, as if whispering a secret.

"We be careful, Captain. We do not want de *Ais* knowing where our place is! You and I will separate from dis mob a ways up de beach."

"What about the boy who came to the camp?" I asked. "He knows where you live."

"Dat boy is different. I know him since he very young. He is my friend, and he helped me build de house. He don't tell de *Ais* no-ting."

We ran with the others for a good distance, gradually moving away and drifting off into the palmetto scrub toward the secret trail. As we ran, I hoped that Chera had not ventured too far from the camp. I was genuinely worried for her safety, and I now realized the extent of my new found love for her and her strange powers.

My thoughts shifted to Canoba, and how friendly and protective of me he had been. I recalled being in awe of his wonderful singing, and felt my eyes start to water with sorrow. How could a man of such vast life experience and wisdom have his life torn away so suddenly? And what of

these awful, evil Spanish men? I was appalled at how they
could so callously kill an old man like Canoba for the love of
gold or silver. They were my own people; my own heritage
and blood! I started to wonder if my Spanish brethren had
always been this brutal and uncaring to the native people of
La Florida. My mind went back to Captain Brattock's ship
and the look of contempt that Miguel had given me, and how
much I had enjoyed clouting him in his rat-like face. Was I
starting to doubt the sanctity of my own heritage?

Just before we reached the camp, we heard a scream of
pain from the direction of the beach to the east. We moved
into the trees and made a beeline toward what we thought
was the source of the sound.

"*Ah, ella es muy delgada!* This will be a good night indeed"

I recognized the voice as belonging to one of the Spaniards
back in the longhouse. I raised my hand into the air, signaling
for Caesar to stop, and bent my head to the breeze. Not
hearing anything, I crept closer and found myself near an
opening in the thick, spreading leaves. I saw that we were
adjacent to a small clearing, so I carefully pulled some
palmetto fronds aside for a better look. The sight that greeted
me left me frozen with terror. Next to a huge spreading live
oak tree that was illuminated only by the light of a single
torch, was my darling Chera. She appeared to be struggling,
and I saw that behind her was a large man with his arm around
her neck. I then saw the glint of a cold, steel knife in his hand.
The soldier had a desperate look, and appeared exhausted and
filthy, with very long hair that was tied on the back of his
head.

What was Chera doing here? How had this happened? My
mind raced uncontrollably.

"Don't move!" The low voice came from directly behind us, and I felt the end of something pointed push into my back, biting into my flesh.

"Walk into the light," the voice commanded.

I was roughly pushed out into the clearing, nearly stumbling over a cypress root that had grown above the sand.

There were four of them and they were a rough looking bunch indeed. Swarthy and leather skinned, they all wore mustaches and beards and had the look of desperate men. Their uniforms were worn and dirty, and they were armed to the teeth with pistols and swords. Two of them were wearing rough leather sandals on their feet and the other two wore leather boots that came up to their knees. I seethed with frustration and could barely contain myself. Chera looked at me with surprise and sadness, and slowly shook her head at me before dropping her eyes to the ground.

"You murderers. You will not leave this beach alive!" I spat at them.

"Ah what have we here, a fellow countryman? We have not seen you here before," said the man holding Chera tightly, the knife blade poised at her throat. I recognized his voice as the one belonging to the "*Sargento*." He was larger than the others, and had a rough, handsome face with cruel, black eyes.

"I am nothing like you," I said defiantly. "You are dead men."

The man behind me pulled my hands behind my back roughly, and quickly tied them with a coarse piece of rope.

"Are you the filth who stole our longboats?" he asked.

"No, de *Ais* are very smart. Dey do it," Caesar said.

The man with the knife flicked his wrist slightly, and an unseen Spaniard materialized out of the darkness behind Caesar, swiftly whacking him in the back of the head with a small leather club. He immediately fell to the ground and sprawled out on the sand face first; unconscious.

"If there's anything I can't stand it's a slave who speaks out of turn," the *Sargento* said with a chuckle, a sardonic leer on his face.

A dark rage spread through me, and I struggled futilely against my bonds.

The man with the knife continued to speak in his mocking tone.

"We have heard tales for a long time about these people here, and the treasures they collect from the wrecks. We didn't find much at the village where the savages live, so it must be you who knows where it is all hidden. Judging by how angry you are, I figure that this beautiful woman here means a good deal to you. I was getting ready to have some private fun with her, and I think I'll let you watch to loosen your tongue a little about the location of your hidden hoard."

He then dragged the still struggling Chera over to a spot where a dirty, tattered blanket had been spread on the ground, and threw her down roughly. I felt that I would go insane with anger. The *Sargento* laughed, and started to unbuckle his breeches. "She is a fine looking woman, señor. I will let you know my opinión of her in a few minutes!"

Just as I thought that all was lost, there came a high-pitched, unnatural sound from the trees. The *Sargento* jerked his head up toward it and scanned the jungle with his eyes. It came from no animal that I knew of, and sent chills up every man's spine, including my own.

"What was that?" the man with the knife behind me said. I could hear the fear in his voice, so I pounced on the opportunity.

"That woman there, she is a powerful witch. She can summon animals to do her bidding. That was the cry of the largest golden panther that you have ever seen, and he is going to kill all of you," I said. "The *Ais* warriors will be here soon. They will descend upon this place with screams of black-hearted vengeance on their lips. You have no boats and they are many. They will roast what is left of you on their cook fires and consume you for what you have done! You will be dead just like your friend back at the village."

"Ricardo? Where is he?" one of them demanded.

"Dead," I said. "Killed by an angry warrior. You will be joining him in *infierno* very soon."

I could see that these words, spoken in their own language, had the desired effect, as two of the Spaniards by the trees looked at each other, fear in their eyes. The man behind me suddenly struck me viciously across the head, sending a whirl of stars and blinding pain through my brain and causing me to stumble to one knee.

I heard Chera scream, and something huge passed before my eyes, momentarily blocking my view. The next few seconds were like a blur. I heard the *Sargento* let out a grunt of pain and he seemed to straighten, and his hands flew to his neck as he desperately clutched at something around it. Suddenly, his entire body lurched toward the trees as if pulled by some brutal, unseen force. He was then dragged by the neck across the sand and through the fire, the burning logs falling away and sending a mass of sparks flying into the night air. He disappeared into the darkness just beyond the firelight by a huge, spreading oak tree. I could hear him choking and sputtering, and there was the sound of a struggle. His body then came back into view by the poor light of the scattered fire, suspended in the air as if some invisible demon had plucked him from the earth, his booted feet kicking wildly as he swung back and forth a few feet above the ground. It happened so fast that the two Spaniards by the trees stood in stunned silence. As they realized what had happened they glanced at each other with panic in their eyes, and then fled into the trees.

My head was still swimming from the thump I had received, but I remember turning to my left and seeing a huge man hunched down next to me. He was raising his arm again and again, delivering violent punches to a squirming figure lying on the ground. Each blow made a slapping sound as it connected, and the man on the ground soon stopped resisting. I looked over at Chera, who had stood up and was looking at me anxiously across the fire.

"Did he hurt you?" I shouted.

She shook her head and took a couple of steps toward me.

"Stay back!" I yelled, raising my hand.

The giant leaned back and grinned, and I found myself looking into the childlike face of Shad. With a theatrical wave of his hand, he presented the broken man on the ground to me.

"Would you fancy a go at 'im, Cap'n?" he said in an impish way.

The front of his shirt was covered in blood. Realizing that the danger had passed, I rubbed my temple with two fingers, trying to relieve my aching head.

"No, Shad. I think you've done quite enough," I said. I still felt dizzy and disoriented.

Managing a weak smile, I reached out and took his meaty hand. "Thank you for saving us."

"Tweren't nothing, Cap'n. A good sailor takes care of 'ees own."

I got to my unsteady feet and stumbled over to Chera, falling into her arms in a wide embrace, my eyes streaming with tears of relief.

"Why didn't you wait for me at the camp? Why did you come looking for us?" I asked.

"I was worried about you. You are my man," she said in a strangely calm voice, as if the answer were as obvious as the rising sun.

Caesar had awakened from the blow he had received and was sitting on the ground rubbing his sore neck.

"Why do everyone have to beat de slave?" he said in a loud voice.

We all laughed at this. After all of the tension and mayhem of the last few hours, this seemed like the funniest thing we had ever heard. I walked over to Caesar and plunked down next to him, placing my arm around his shoulder and pulling him toward me.

"Whatever you do, Caesar my friend, don't ever make our friend Shad angry." I said, as we contemplated the ruined man lying on the ground. He laid on the sand moaning quietly, his face a mass of blood from Shad's pounding. I looked up at *Sargento's* lifeless body swinging slowly back and forth in the breeze. It was the same way Canoba's frail body had looked hours earlier.

There was a sound from the darkness, and two men whom I had never seen before stepped out of the trees into the dim light of the torch. At first, I thought that the two remaining Spaniards had returned to resume the fight, so I tensed up and reached for my empty scabbard.

"Cap'n," Shad said, "these men are 'ere for me. They are the ones what escaped from the *Agamemnon* on the beach when the *Ais* attacked us. They came upon the camp after you left.

They was in a very bad way, so I fed 'em. They are so
grateful that they want to join us. They need our 'elp, sir.
Remember, they are the ones what killed theses Spanish
bastards 'ere."

He gestured toward the hanging man.

"What of the other two Spaniards?" I asked. "Where do
you think they went?"

Shad smiled. "They ran off toward the beach, Sir, right to
where the savage's war party is waiting for them. I'll reckon
that they are not very happy souls about now."

The first man stepped forward and spoke up in a high,
reedy voice. He was very thin, like a skeleton, his clothes
hanging from his bony structure like loose rags. His disheveled
appearance made it hard to determine his age. My guess was
anywhere from thirty to fifty years. His face had a pinched
look and his eyes seemed very close together.

"I am Michael Storm, sir. 'Oym obliged to 'ave dispatched
this foul vermin for you," he said, gesturing up toward the
unfortunate Sargento.

"Stormy don't look like much" Shad said from behind me,
"but 'ee can fight like a demon and he's very strong despite 'is
'ungry look. And 'ees very good with a rope."

"I can see that," I said as I looked up at the hanging
corpse.

The other man stepped forward. He was shorter and
younger than Storm and had a stocky build. He had dark hair
and a wavy, thin beard on his chin that seemed to have a hard
time growing. When he smiled at me I could see that his teeth
were in very bad shape, with several missing.

"My names Fly, sir. Obliged to make yer acquaintance."

"Fly?" I asked, incredulous, "What sort of name is that?"

"I can explain," Fly said, "Me and the Stormy 'ere, we've been livin' on the sea most of our lives. We was both orphans when we signed on to our first sea voyage, so our Christian names didn't much matter. Our Captain wanted something easy to remember, so we just sort of kept the names that 'ee called us."

"Are you men buccaneers working under this Captain Jennings, like Shad, here?" I asked.

"Well, that would depend on your definition of the word, sir," Fly said. "Would you find it rude of me to ask 'ow you arrived 'ere at this god-forsaken place?"

"If you would like to know, I was taken prisoner by Captain Brattock, the pirate. I spent months aboard his vessel, the *Nightingale*."

"The *Nightingale*?" they both said aloud.

"You've heard of her?" I asked excitedly.

"Well, yes, we 'ave, as a matter of fact. Captain Brattock and the *Nightingale* was a legend of sorts among the Brethren," Stormy said. "We 'eard that she was blown to bits a few months ago by the Spanish right off this coast somewhere."

"What became of Captain Brattock?" I asked warily.

"Well," he said, looking down at the sand as he spoke. "This is how we 'eard it. Captain Brattock was taken prisoner aboard the *Marguerita*. He was tried for piracy right there on the ship and then.."

"Yes," I said eagerly. "then what?"

"Rumor 'as it that the Spanish put a bounty of two hundred pieces of eight for any bloke 'oo could bring in Brattock's 'ead. The Spanish bastards hung him high from the mainmast of their ship, then lopped 'ees noggin off and mounted it on the *Marguerita's* bowsprit. It stayed there all the way back to the Spanish Main. The Spanish reveled after that victory, I'll buy ya. Brattock plundered many of their galleons."

I was stunned at this news. My friend, Captain Brattock, had been good to me, and the Spanish had viciously murdered him at sea without a proper trial. I was now convinced that my life had taken a turn in a new direction.

CHAPTER 31
RITE OF PASSAGE

The *Ais* people were hurt deeply by the loss of their beloved Caseekey. Caesar and I followed the entire funeral procession in our own pirogue to witness the somber ceremony. This is the way I remember it.

Canoba's remains, along with several stacks of woven baskets, were carried to the west shore of the island. His body was gently placed inside a brightly painted ceremonial canoe by two warriors. A shaman followed, carrying the old man's long hunting bow and worn, leather quiver of arrows. A large procession consisting of most of the villagers, including men, women, and children, filled the other canoes and pushed out into the river, rowing southwest in a seeming mass migration. As they moved over the water, the shaman prayed loudly over the body. The women sang Canoba's death song in unison, their voices reflecting the pain of a thousand years. We soon came to a small, secluded beach on the mainland side of the river. After we had gotten out of the canoes and pulled them up onto the shore, the people, young and old, each took a single basket from the large stack and walked into the water a few feet. They fell to their knees and began to scoop large handfuls of dark, wet sand into the baskets.

When all of the people had a full basket of sand in front of them, the shaman walked directly to a thick, vine covered area at the tree line. One of the young men from the village stepped forward and stood by the shaman's side. The holy man then dropped Canoba's bow from his shoulder and removed one of the long hunting arrows from the quiver. He placed it in the bow and pulled the taut string back, pointing the arrow up toward the tops of the trees to the west. The people were silent as he let an arrow loose with a "whoosh." As it sailed high over the forest, the people cried out a great cheer, and raised their hands toward the sky. The young man then sprinted off in the direction of the arrow, quickly disappearing into the thick growth.

Canoba's body was lifted from the canoe by the same two strong warriors as the people began to solemnly march, single file and heavy baskets in hand, into the forest. After a short time, there came a shrill whistle from somewhere ahead. The shaman stopped, and then turned to face the people. He raised him arms into the air, at the same time letting out a great cry of triumph.

"De boy find Canoba's arrow," Caesar said to me in a low voice.

I didn't understand the meaning, but I said nothing. The whistle came again, and the line moved slowly toward it. We soon came upon the young man, who stood in a beautiful clearing surrounded by huge oak trees with long, creeping branches that were so thick that they blocked the sunlight. He solemnly handed the arrow to the shaman.

The women and children of the group never ceased their wailing songs as they carried their baskets of sand to the center of the clearing and dumped their contents on the ground. There was soon a small hill growing as more and more sand was added. The women then walked back in the direction of the river to refill their baskets. As they did this, the men gathered dead branches from the surrounding forest, throwing them into a large pile a short distance from the mound. They then used flints to light a large fire, onto which sacred herbs were thrown. This formed a ghostly haze and filled the air with the pungent smell of burning red mangrove and cypress twigs. The men then joined the women in the basket filling and emptying, which went on for several hours until the mound was as high as a man's knees.

The women then formed into two rows facing each other, creating a gauntlet that ended at the mound. Canoba's body was carried between these two rows, the women reaching out and stroking his cold skin lovingly as he passed. The two warriors gently laid the body down on the side of the mound in a sitting position, his head back against the sandy surface, his unseeing eyes looking toward the sky. Several baskets full of broken pottery fragments were then brought up, their contents gently spilled around the body. These were the remains of Canoba's favorite possessions, buried with him to ensure a comfortable journey to the upper world. More baskets full of sand from the river were then brought. One by one, each member of the tribe poured the contents over the dead Caseekey's body. This continued until he was completely buried. The shaman then produced the quiver of the old man's hunting arrows and proceeded to drive them, one by one, into the ground at even intervals all the way around the perimeter of the mound. He then reached into a deerskin pouch hanging from his side, pulling a white object from it. I looked closer and saw that it was a large whelk shell with the top cut away to form a vessel. This was Canoba's drinking cup, which the shaman perched on top of the mound. Many long prayers and incantations followed, and the grieving, shouting, and dancing lasted well into the night. The celebration of Canoba's death would go on for three full days and nights until the people were totally exhausted. Only then would they make their way back to the canoes.

Later, as Caesar and I rowed back to the eastern shoreline in the darkness, I could see the red glow of a flame far off in the vicinity of the *Ais* village.

"What is that, Caesar? Is there a fire in the village?" I asked.

"Jes, Captain. De *Ais* burn Canoba's house. It has always been dere way," he said.

I shook my head as I thought of the old Caseekey, and how much his sudden, violent passing had damaged these doomed people. I vowed to myself that night that the Spanish would pay for his death.

CHAPTER 32
PANTERA DE FLORIDA

Many months passed without incident after the attack of the Spanish soldiers. In that time, we made great strides in improving our lives in the hostile new world in which we found ourselves. We had enlarged Caesar's main house, with two additional rooms for sleeping quarters and storage. Since the attack by the Spanish, the *Ais* had learned the whereabouts of our camp, but stayed away out of fear and respect. Many mornings we woke from sleep and found offerings of food and articles from shipwrecks that they had scavenged and had no use for. This included ships bells, trunks and chests, trinkets and china, some remnants of clothing, navigational equipment, and most notably, wine and other spirits. The *Ais* had no use for alcohol, and could not understand why anyone would need it, but they knew that it was our custom. On the occasion that these deliveries were made, the celebrations of the men would last all through the night, with raucous laughter and singing.

I had no idea what the future held for my ragtag band of outcasts on the desolate beaches of La Florida, but I knew that I could not go back to the civilization I once knew without facing retribution for my supposed crimes. Nevertheless, Dorathea and my home in La Habana constantly permeated my thoughts. Our relationship with the *Ais* had developed into one of mutual respect. This was mostly due to their fear of Chera's seemingly supernatural influence over the beasts of the forest. Tales of a pirate captain and a powerful witch with a cutthroat crew who wreaked terrible vengeance on helpless castaways were now being told over the campfires of the mighty *Calusa* tribe to the west and among the Spanish soldiers who manned the remote outposts to the north.

The storm had raged for nearly two full days before it had passed inland to the southwest. We spent the duration of it huddled inside the sturdy house, which Caesar had reinforced with thick ropes tied to the surrounding trees. Hour after hour, the howling wind gusts and driving rain bent the tall palmettos and surrounding vegetation nearly to the ground. We had more or less grown accustomed to gales of this intensity in the summer months and had prepared ourselves for their occurrence. Caesar predicted this storm's arrival with his usual uncanny accuracy by "a feeling in his ears." This one had been bad, but not the worst we had seen, so the camp had survived without major damage.

Having been through many hurricanes during my childhood in La Habana, I knew that even the smallest one could have great potential for devastation. I found them to be amazing in their ferocity, and admired the strength and power they exerted on the land. The destruction was not surprising to me because, as a child growing up, I had seen many hurricanes wreak havoc on both buildings and ships alike. When I was nine years old a sea tempest raged through our area, destroying the ramshackle homes of the poor and killing many with its fierce winds and flooding rains.

Many storms had come ashore since I had come to Caesar's camp, but like the natives, we had grown accustomed to their arrival, simply hunkering down until they passed. The most worrisome problems for the *Ais* occurred when the water came up and flooded their coastal villages, often catching them unprepared and wiping out their dwellings. Caesar had been wise in his choice of a camp, having picked the highest area available on which to build his shelters. Despite this fact, he often warned that if the right storm came along there would be no safe place.

I ventured outside to see a sky so blue and clear that it seemed that the storm had never happened. The air seemed very pure and fresh, as if the gale had cleansed the earth by giving it a good scrubbing. I made my way through the clearing and beheld a landscape covered with hundreds of torn and broken palm fronds and branches that had blown free in the fierce wind. Several large trees had been uprooted, and were now lying in haphazard angles all over the sandy ground. Out of the corner of my eye, I saw a flash of movement, and I turned to see Caesar running toward me from the trees at the south edge of the clearing. He was out of breath and very excited.

"Captain! I find someting! Come see!" he said, placing his hands on his knees and gasping for air from his long run.

Stormy, Shad, and Fly, hurriedly ran to the edge of the water where we stored our pirogues, and we were soon making our way across the inlet, paddling furiously, each of us realizing that time was of the essence. I soon saw what it was that my friend was so excited about. There, a short distance before us and leaning heavily to one side, was a ship. Caesar explained that he had spotted it as he was searching for wrecked vessels. It was abandoned, and had run aground in the storm very close to the shoreline near the mouth of the inlet. According to what he had seen, it was not badly damaged and had not yet been found by the *Ais* wreckers. We soon reached its side, quickly tying off our pirogue and climbing aboard. I did a quick inspection of the listing vessel, finding her to be a small sloop of somewhere between fifty to seventy -five tons with a low draft that had a suffered a large tear in her mainsail and drifted off course. The crew was mysteriously gone; vanished into the furious winds of the hurricane for whatever reason.

We descended the short stairway to the lower deck, and I was surprised and happy to see six nine-pound cannons with shot and charges still fit for service. Below decks, we found many useful things. Fly was delighted at the discovery of an old fiddle in a worn case complete with a bow and resin. He was familiar with the instrument and knew a few tunes from his youth. He immediately began to play a melodic jig that made us all smile.

Caesar, ever the enterprising soul, came up with an idea to free the sloop from the sandbar where she had become lodged. I stayed with the ship as he and the others returned to camp to get more supplies to implement his plan. Within an hour's time of his leaving, I spotted three *Ais* men approaching in a dug-out canoe from the opposite shore. They came very close to us before they saw me, and I made sure they could see me waving at them. They returned the gesture, but I could see the looks of frustration on their faces at the loss of this valuable prize. They turned around and continued paddling west, scouring the shore for other treasures. It seemed that they were still terrified of me from the stories that they had heard.

As I waited for the men, I stayed busy by cutting away the damaged mainsail from the rigging that held it. Caesar soon returned with Fly, Shad, and Stormy and several long handled shovels that we had salvaged from a wrecked Dutch Flute a few months earlier. Luckily, the tide was very low so we took turns swimming out and digging around the grounded section of the sloops hull. After a few hours of this we were ready to give up, convinced that freeing her was a hopeless endeavor. We loaded the damaged sail into our boats and paddled back to camp to rest.

Later, as we sat around the fire, the Englishmen were laughing and pushing each other jovially as Chera worked busily repairing the torn sail. This was a huge undertaking because it had to be done one stitch at a time. A very intoxicated Stormy and Shad danced a hornpipe in the sand by firelight as Fly scratched out an ancient Celtic jig on his fiddle. The men and I laughed at this sight and happily clapped along in time. Caesar seemed to be lost in a trance of concentration. Suddenly, his face brightened as he seemed to have some sort of revelation.

"Captain, I have an idea!" he said.

"What is it, Caesar? I answered.

"We get de *Ais* to help us."

"Why would they help us, Caesar? What do they have to gain?" I asked.

Caesar gave me a look that I had grown very familiar with during the time I had known him; one of seriousness involving calculation and intense concentration. It was very hard to argue with him when he had made his mind up about something.

"We can use de ship to fight de *Es-pa-no* dat come to hurt us. What we take from dem we can give some to de *Ais*. Dey like treasure from wrecks, Captain," he said.

"You mean we pay them?" I asked.

"Jes, Captain. Dey fear de Spanish more dan us. We should help dem," he said.

I let out a sigh, betraying my doubt at his idea.

"We can try, Caesar, we can try," I said resignedly.

The very next day we ventured into the *Ais* village. We were immediately greeted by four tall warriors led by my old nemesis, Aktil who had recently taken over as Caseekey of the tribe since the murder of Canoba. Unlike the old man, Aktil did not speak Spanish, so Caesar had to communicate with him using the old language, thus leaving me out of the conversation. The two men exchanged words for a long time as I tried to read their expressions. I knew that Aktil hated me for making him appear weak in front of his people. He kept glancing toward me, an expression of contempt on his face. From what I could see Caesar was giving a fairly convincing argument based on the looks of thoughtful consideration from the native men. Suddenly they turned and walked away from us, heading toward their communal meeting house.

"What did they say?" I asked.

"Dey need to consult dere gods, Captain. Dey don't trust us much. Aktil say many of de people been getting sick from bad spirits. He say dere is a place in de trees where dey go to die," he said, an expression of concern expression on his face. I was very surprised at this.

"Caesar, let's go there and see if we can help."

He asked an old woman where the sick place was, and she gave him directions, pointing to the north into a thick hammock of oaks. We walked down the path a good distance until we came to a place where there were many people gathered near a large, crudely constructed lean-to that looked as though it had been hastily put together. Underneath it were several mats upon which lay people in various stages of sickness. The smell was awful, and I knew that there was something very wrong. I covered my mouth with my hand and knelt down to view an older man, who lay in a curled up position. There was something familiar to me about his wasted condition. His entire body was covered in small red sores that appeared to be inflamed, causing the man great pain. Then realization and horror hit me all at once– this was smallpox. I had seen many epidemics rip through La Habana as I was growing up, and had even contracted the disease myself as a young child.

I had miraculously escaped its mostly fatal clutches, but it had left its signature on me in the form of blotchy pock marks that remain on my face even to this day. I looked up and saw other sufferers of the disease moaning in pain all around me. I also saw their wives, children and husbands, many of them not yet affected, leaning over them in deep, hopeful prayer. I saw that they were clinging to the hope that their gods would deliver their loved ones from the terrible scourge. I leapt to my feet and ran among them, shouting and pulling them away from the mats.

"No, get away!" I said, "You must get away!"

In their grief, they did not understand and stared at me in shock and anger. My efforts proved fruitless and I began to cry, tears of frustration rolling down my cheeks.

"Don't they see?" I implored.

Caesar just looked at me, not understanding what I was saying. I then remembered that he had been with these people for most of his young life, and did not understand what a plague was.

"Come Captain," he said as he clutched my arm, "we must go."

"Caesar, you have to make them understand. They must leave this place. The sick ones will die and the disease will spread," I said.

"Captain, dey do not want your help. Let us leave dem in peace. Let dem pray to dere gods."

We walked back to the village slowly, both of us in a dark, pensive mood. Aktil and his men were waiting for us. He and Caesar conversed for a short time then both nodded their heads as if agreeing about something, then the delegation turned and walked away.

"Dey will help us," he said, "if we pay dem like you say. Dey will use de great canoe wid the *Es-pa-no* sail."

We waited for several days until the conditions were just right, with a hard north-eastern breeze coming in, and then went back to the grounded sloop. Chera and Fly had miraculously managed to repair the mainsail, so we set about rigging it; first attaching it to the top spar and to the mast on its foremost edge, then to the long boom below. We set it out, and it billowed beautifully against the eastern breeze. I could see the tension on the masts as the sails tried to pull the ship free from the sand, but she held fast. I looked to the west and was surprised to see another sail approaching us from the river. As it drew closer I saw that it was the largest pirogue I had ever seen. It had a high mast and its own billowing sail, and carried what looked to be close to twenty men. It slid across the water at an amazing speed and was soon abreast of us. I waved a rope to the man in the very front of the pirogue, a huge fellow with bursting forearms. He expertly guided the canoe in toward us, and I threw the rope out to him. He secured it tightly to the canoe's masthead, and I tied mine to the sternpost. He then sat back down and barked out a sharp command. All of the *Ais* men, ten on each side, began to paddle furiously. The rope tightened, and we turned our sail to meet the east wind full on. Nothing happened. It was as if the ship was frozen into a great iceberg, and doubt began to creep in. It seemed to be an impossible task. Then, almost imperceptibly, I felt the smallest shift of movement. I watched as the *Ais* men valiantly strained at their paddles, suddenly feeling a strong gust of wind from the east. Miraculously, the hull slipped free all at once, and the sloop righted, and I felt the familiar swell of buoyancy underneath her. We all let out a great cheer, raising our fists in victory toward the *Ais* men, who answered with their own wailing cry. It was one of the finest moments of my entire life. We had all joined together; two groups of men from completely different worlds and accomplished a common goal: we had freed that ship. The thought crossed my mind that the vessel was indeed blessed, and deserved a fine name. The first thing that came into my mind was Chera and her miraculous powers.

"*Mis amigos!*" I shouted; my voice loud and triumphant; "I christen this ship the *Pantera De Florida!*"

CHAPTER 33
THE HIGH PLACE

The summer drew to a close and cooler winds moved in, bringing respite from the heavy, moisture laden air and clouds of mosquitoes. The days were splendid and perfect, but the nights were often so cold that we had to wear more clothing and sit huddled around the fire for warmth. Taking advantage of the mild weather, we all worked hard to repair and restore the *Pantera* to seaworthiness. This was not an easy task with the limited resources available, but Caesar had collected many useful items in his years of wrecking that proved invaluable to the effort. We were able to patch together all of the damaged sails and rigging, and did our best to free the hull of barnacles and sea growth that had formed over time. We simply did not have the manpower to do a proper careening and breaming as I had seen done in *el Puerto* at La Habana many times as a child.

I was determined to become a better sailor, so I tried to focus on learning everything I could about all of the ship's parts and inner workings. Shad taught me well, and I could soon name all of the masts, sails, and rigging, as well as each of their purposes. The *Pantera's* design was simple: she had three masts with six sails consisting of a jib topsail, a jib sail, a stay sail, a mainsail, a top sail, and one "course" sail that remained furled most of the time. Her hull was constructed of Bermuda cedar, which was very hard and resistant to rot and water damage. The best advantage she had was the low draft of her hull which could allow us to easily maneuver her through the shallow waters of the inlet, unlike the huge galleons and war ships that traveled through *El Estrecho de la Florida.*

When Shad deemed her ready, we launched her out into the river to see how she performed and what we would need to make her our weapon. It was not an easy thing to do at first, because the mainsail was so large and difficult to sheet that we nearly capsized more than once when the wind caught hold. The ship was unwieldy and difficult to maneuver, but flew when pushed by a stiff wind. We practiced "sailing windward;" a maneuver that the more experienced sailors had mastered on other vessels. Shad explained to me that this would allow the *Pantera* to escape from certain situations speedily, while leaving other ships foundering in her wake. This action required a steady hand and a lot of repetition to master because the sails had to be held at a precise angle to the wind. Too close to the wind and the sails would "luff," or lose the direct wind; too far from it and they would "stall," or lose forward momentum, even though the sail appeared to be full. I was determined to gain a complete understanding of techniques like these, so I listened intently and tried again and again to master them. Within a few months' time, Shad had made us experts at maneuvering her in and out of the shallow inlet.

I knew that we would need an advantage if we were going to be successful in our new venture, so I scouted the entire area around Santa Lucia for ideas. Canoba had once told me of a sacred lookout from which the *Ais* wreckers could see for miles. I spied it from the beach on the west side of the river a short distance away, so I found one of Caesar's dugout canoes and paddled across to the other side. I then made my way through the dense jungle, using my saber to whack the vines and branches out of my way as I went. I soon felt myself gradually climbing upward, my feet sometimes slipping under me on the broad sea grape leaves and causing me to stumble to one knee. I discovered the remnants of an old trail that had become nearly obscured by undergrowth, clearing it as I went.

In a short time I arrived at my destination and was very pleased at what I found. It was indeed a peak; a natural formation of the land that was much higher than anything else around it. It was level at the top, and there was plenty of room to build a small shelter with more to spare. There was a slight depression in the center of it, and when I looked closer I found the remains of an old fire pit. As I gently kicked at the charred wood with my toe, I tried to imagine the conversations that had taken place over it for a thousand years.

No one had been there for some time and the vegetation had grown quite high, so I spent the next hour or so clearing it away, periodically drinking water from a leather canteen that Caesar had given me. When I was finished, I was drenched in sweat. I gazed out through the opening I had made, and what I saw took my breath away. I could see far out across the ocean, much farther than I could ever see from the ocean shoreline near the camp. I looked to the north and south, discovering that I could see far up the beach in either direction. A wave of weariness came over me, so I stretched out on a loose pile of cut sea grape leaves and let the cool breeze blow over my face. It felt wonderful, and I closed my eyes for a moment, enjoying the magnificent solitude of my new hideaway.

I was in a long hallway with very high ceilings that appeared to be a temple of some kind. I slowly drifted along its length, my body gliding as if my feet did not touch the floor. There was a tall doorway to my right with a soft light emanating from its interior. The sound of sweet music came to me from inside, giving me a feeling of calmness and serenity. I came to the doorway and saw a large bed covered with a beautifully decorated blanket. The entire inside of the room was bathed in the amber light. I looked up and noticed that I was not alone. On the corner of the bed sat a thin woman dressed in white; her face buried in her hands. Her hair was fiery red and very long, falling down around her heaving shoulders. I realized that she was crying. This saddened me and I moved closer, sitting next to her on the bed.

"What is it?" I asked, "Why are you so sad?"

She looked up at me and I could see that she was very beautiful, despite her swollen, red eyes. I did not recognize her, but there was something familiar in the shape of her face and the set of her eyes.

"Do I know you?" I asked.

It took a moment, but the beautiful woman answered me.

"Do you not recognize me at all?" she asked, her eyes pleading.

"No, I do not. Why have you come to me?" I asked.

"Santos," she said, taking my hand and staring straight into my eyes, "I am your mother."

I was stunned and could not say a word.

"My mother is dead," I said to her, "She died when I was very young."

She placed her hand on my cheek tenderly and her touch felt warm, and she smiled resignedly.

"Santos, I am sorry for leaving you. I could not help it."

I felt a great swelling inside of me and my eyes started to water.

"Mother? Is it really you?" I said.

"I cannot stay long, Santos. I have a message for you, so you must listen."

I stared at her, dumbfounded. I knew it was her because I could see it in her face; the same familiar features that I had seen my whole life in the mirror.

"I will listen," I said. I looked away from her as she spoke so she would not see the tears.

"I know of the terrible dreams you have, my son. I loved your father very much and he was plagued by the same demons. I tried to help him but he was far too headstrong to listen, and for that he paid with his life. The execration is real, Santos, and its origin will become clear to you in due time."

I turned my head to look at her, and was immediately gripped by terror. It was not my mother at all. It was the Indian woman, and she was beaming at me with her hideous gaping mouth and her black, shining eyes and rotted teeth.

"YES, IT WILL COME VERY CLEAR INDEED, BOY."

My eyes flew open, and I momentarily had no idea where I was. There was a sharp sound from above, and I recognized it as the cry of a hawk flying overhead, in search of mice or squirrels to snatch in its talons. I sat up and shook my head, trying to rid myself of the vivid dream. This one was different than any I had ever experienced and, although it terrified me, part of me wanted to go back to talk to the mother whom I had never known. I had actually seen her! The cruelest of tricks had been played on me by the angry spirit. It was like having a precious gift abruptly snatched from my hands. This dream made my hatred and fear of the phantom woman more intense than ever.

The twilight hour was nigh, so I gathered some dried sticks and lit a small fire in the ancient pit with my flint and steel. I sat cross-legged on the ground in front of it and watched the tendrils of flame, gradually becoming absorbed by their fluid movements as they reached for the heavens. I felt very small and insignificant in this magnificent wilderness, and once again thought of the countless native hunters who had sat in this very place over hundreds; maybe thousands of years. Had they reflected on their own lives as I was doing now? I got up and walked to the edge of the clearing and took in the blueness of the ocean in the waning light of evening. The fronds on the many palm trees below waved gently in the soft sea breeze. The stars were starting to show themselves, and I gazed up at them and thought of how beautiful and forbidding this place was. They always reminded me of Dorathea, and she entered my thoughts now. Was she alive and safe? Was she happy? I knew that no matter what happened I would always love her, and that there would eternally be a place in my heart that only she could fill.

My thoughts then turned to Chera, my passionate lover and companion with the knowing smile. For some reason, I had the feeling that she was my protector and had been sent to me from some higher place. She knew of my love for Dorathea, and had accepted it, even showing pity at the pain I endured at her loss. She knew me better than anyone ever had in my life. I had never met anyone like Chera.

I thought a great deal about my future and where I was headed. What was my purpose for being here? Why had I been placed in the position of leader of a ragtag band of outcasts on a desolate beach hundreds of miles from home? My thoughts turned dark when I thought of the Spanish men and their cruelty toward the *Ais*. I thought of the Spanish soldiers and the way they had brutally crashed into my life, and how they had callously taken the life of the innocent Canoba. The wrinkled, smiling face of the old man came to me, and I felt a helpless wave of sadness. It was no wonder that the natives were terrified of their retribution. I knew that the reign of the *Ais* in this area was doomed, and that the Spaniards would come more and more frequently down the coast in pursuit of treasure.

I was disconcerted by the sick people I had seen earlier that day and how vulnerable they were. These people needed help combatting the abuses of these greedy Spanish fools. I thought hard, trying to find some way to make them pay for their cruelty. I knew that they loved gold and silver more than life itself, and treasured it above everything. I remembered the feeling of astonishment I had experienced at the sight of Caesar's horde of silver and gold back at the burial mound. What did riches mean to me? I had never worried about money because my father had always made sure that we were comfortable. I realized now how foolish and naïve I had been. If I was ever to make it away from this place and back to civilized society, I would need money to survive. Shad and his men talked about "prize booty" all the time, as if it were the most important thing in the world. The best revenge I could take against my Spanish brethren would be to hit them as hard as I could where it hurt the most, while making myself rich in the process.

I extinguished my small fire and started down the hill back toward my canoe. As I walked away from my secret place, a thought occurred to me, so I paused and turned to look back at it. I breathed in deep at its beauty and spoke out loud to no one but myself.

"I hereby name you *"El Lugar Alto*, The High Place."

I turned and began my journey back to Santa Lucia, thinking of my mother's face and her dire warning.

CHAPTER 34
OUR FIRST PRIZE

I heard the cry from the edge of the river and instantly recognized the voice of "Dunkirk," the *Ais* boy of about fourteen years whose dark face I could now see poking out through some thick mangroves. Some weeks earlier, Shad had given him that ridiculous name while in a drunken stupor as we sat around the evening fire. Upon hearing his new moniker, the boy had simply stared back at the pirate and smiled eagerly, not comprehending anything the inebriated sailor was saying. He had the curiosity of youth, and saw everything we were doing as a great adventure. The elders of the tribe had not objected to the boy spending time with us, so he had been there all through our preparation, enthusiastically performing many of the mundane chores that Shad and the boys did not want to do. He did not seem daunted by the superstitious tales that the holy men had been weaving about strange powers and evil rituals that supposedly happened at our camp, and had been there every morning ready to begin the day's work. He proved to be very intelligent indeed and was a valuable asset to our new family. I could only wish that there were more like him.

Dunkirk had a special talent. He had the uncanny ability to perfectly mimic any bird in the jungle. The *Ais* held birds in very high spiritual regard, so the boy had taken it upon himself to learn everything about them. When he accompanied me on my long walks through the forest, he would often startle me by letting loose with the cry of a nighthawk or the halting call of an owl. I grew to like and respect him very much.

He ran into the camp and straight to Caesar, who was rinsing his face with water from a dark, clay bowl on the low table by his house. They spoke back and forth in the native *Ais* language, the boy waving his arms excitedly as he spoke. Caesar turned to me, a smile across his face.

"Captain! Dunkirk spotted a vessel this morning from *El Lugar*! Ship east!" he bellowed.

I had shown the boy the lookout a few days before, and he had taken to spending his time diligently watching the ocean from there with his young, sharp eyes. I now ran to him, giving him a quick pat on the shoulder.

"Excellent!" I shouted, and he responded with a wide, toothy grin. He did not understand a word of our language, but knew that I was very happy.

Snatching up the last of our meal, we ran down the trail to the river where the *Pantera* was moored a short distance from shore. After rowing out in our canoes, we quickly boarded her and snapped into action, hurriedly unfurling the sails and pulling up the anchor. Shad and Stormy ran the lines out and quickly raised the mainsail, putting us directly in the southwest wind. The *Pantera* started to move slowly at first, and then slid along more quickly as her sails billowed with the force of the wind.

"Captain," Shad yelled from his position on the bow, his gruff voice booming, "I 'ope the prize is Spanish!"

"No way of telling till we see her colors," I answered. "She'll see ours first, mind you! Remember, men, we number only six, but we have to give the illusion of a full crew.

"Remember our lessons, mates!" Shad bellowed. "The hour's upon us!"

He then let out a howl of laughter as the sloop started to glide rapidly toward the inlet. The ship was moving slowly as the crew painstakingly maneuvered her through the shallows toward the open sea. The men and I were soon able to stabilize the sails, and we started to gain more ground, soon cutting the waves on a clean southeast course. I used the small spyglass Caesar had given me to scour the horizon, soon catching sight of the prize ship's sails as they billowed in the distance. She had covered a considerable amount of water in the time it had taken us to get out, but I knew that the lighter, nimbler *Pantera* would soon overtake her.

Caesar climbed up the mast and balanced himself on the brace that held the main sail, one hand gripping the upper portion of the mast for balance. He looked down at me with a wide grin on his face. It felt good to me that my friend was enjoying our new business venture so completely. As we drew closer to the vessel, I could see that she was an aged looking Dutch flute that was much larger than us. I looked toward the top of her long mast and saw that she flew the colors of *Madre Espana*. I turned my head toward our own flag and compared the two, finding them to be almost identical; even though ours had been in one of Caesar's trunks for years and was faded and slightly torn on the edges.

Caesar stood on the brace grinning like a child, gazing eagerly at our impending prize.

"The first thing I'll take is that flag," I shouted up at him. "Yours is worn out!"

I felt a wave of nervousness inside as we approached the vessel. I could make out the figures of three men standing on deck by the rail. On the stern was her name: *El Guerrero*.

"Well, at least the odds are with us," I said in a low voice to Shad as he took his place next to me on the deck. "They appear to have a very small crew."

"Cap'n, maybe we should 'old off on using the guns. She's much larger than us," he said.

I waved to the men on the deck of the prize. They seemed to hesitate for a moment, and then one of them waved back at me. For a brief moment, I felt a pang of unease and actually considered turning away and searching for another prize. I then remembered the Spaniards who had killed Canoba and attacked us on the beach, and my resolve strengthened. I turned and strode to the hatch, quickly descending down the stairs to the lower deck, where Fly and Dunkirk were manning the guns. They both looked at me anxiously.

"Fly, I have an idea that you will probably think is insane, but hear me out," I said. "There is something not quite right here and I think that we should approach this cautiously. You and Dunkirk man the sails. You needn't worry, we won't be long."

"Aye Cap'n, as you wish," he said rather dejectedly, obviously disappointed that he wouldn't be accompanying us. I walked up to him and pulled him aside, speaking low, as if in great trust and secrecy.

"Fly, I need you to man the ship. I consider you the most able seamen we have. The fate of the *Pantera* is in your reliable hands," I said, staring into his eyes with a look of grave seriousness. His face brightened noticeably as he realized the importance of the task.

"Cap'n, I will defend 'er to me death!" he said, showing his rotted teeth in a broad smile.

"That is what it takes, sir!" I said, grinning back at him.

As we turned directly into the wind and cut sail, and the sea rolled us high, then low. Shad, Stormy, Caesar and I moved to the long canoe we had stowed aboard, hastily untying it and sliding it over the side where it splashed into the water. One by one we climbed down and got into it, and were soon paddling toward the merchant vessel.

"Do your best to conceal your scabbards!" I said as we bounced on the waves, moving closer to the Flute. As we drew alongside her, I looked directly at Caesar.

"Remember, you are my slave," I said.

"Jes, Captain. I remember," he answered.

"Shad," I said to the huge bearded man, "don't say anything at all!"

Taking my lead, he just nodded his head.

As we drew up to the very side of the ship, her rope ladder was unrolled down to us, the wooden rungs clattering against the hull of the ship. I reached out, caught it with one hand, and pulled myself out of the canoe, temporarily swaying back and forth in the wind. My foot found the rung below, and I climbed up the ladder one at a time. I came over the top railing, my feet landing solidly on the wooden deck. I steadied myself and looked around. The men of the *El Guerrero* were standing near me, the largest of them a man of thick build dressed in a dingy gray overcoat that looked as though it had been on him for a very long time. He wore a beard that was tied into a tight, long braid that hung to his broad chest. His complexion was bronze and wrinkled from the sun. On his head was a broad black hat held on by a leather chin strap. I warily inspected the two other men standing near him and immediately sensed that something was not right. They did not look at all like the merchant sailors I had seen back in La Habana, but were filthy and had the appearance of *criminales*.

"*Buenos dias, mi amigo!*" he said, extending a broad hand and smiling, showing his decayed teeth.

"*Sí, cómo estás? Mi nombre es Santos Alvarez,*" I answered, taking his hand and squeezing it.

He continued speaking, shaking my hand vigorously.

"It is good to see fellow Spaniards out here! What can we do for you?"

By this time Shad, Stormy and Caesar had climbed up the ladder and were now standing on the deck behind me.

"Ah," the man said as he looked them over. "You've brought others. My, he is a big one! I see you've brought *el negro. Es que su esclavo?*"

"Yes, he belongs to me. He accompanies me wherever I go," I said, glancing at Caesar, whose hand was on his scabbard.

"There is nothing better than a well-trained slave," the man said. "Makes life so much easier. But Captain, I must ask. Is it prudent to arm him?"

I spoke up, hoping that Caesar would not.

"We were wondering if you wanted to trade for some items we have procured on the coast here. From where do you hail?" I asked.

He paused for a moment before speaking, his steady gaze fixed on me.

"We hail from *la costa africana* and are making way for Cartegena," he said. "We are simple merchants. What do you have to trade?"

He was a little too eager and had a wolfish look in his eye, and I grew more suspicious. I chose to play along.

"Yes, we have five large chunks of ambergris, and this slave here that we procured from the natives," I said, sweeping my hand back toward Caesar. "We would like to trade for supplies that we need."

His eyes grew large at this.

"Ambergris? Where is it so I can appraise it?" he asked. Out of the corner of my eye, I noticed the two men slowly moving closer to Shad and Caesar. My instincts flared, and I gave the ever vigilant Shad the signal, flicking my fingers out at an angle. Shad's meaty hand slowly moved behind his back, so I spoke to create a distraction.

"What was your name, Captain? I didn't catch it."

"I am Captain Luis Ricaurte from Cartegena," he said, and I saw his hand move quickly to his side. "And you are all dead men!" He grabbed the hilt of his short sword and quickly pulled it from his scabbard.

Fortunately, I anticipated this move and already had my blade out. He whirled his at me viciously and I ducked, easily avoiding it. I swung my leg out and kicked his shin hard, and he dropped to one knee, letting out a howl of pain. Behind me, I heard one of the other men scream, and I turned just in time to see Caesar pitch him over the railing, his body hitting the water below with a loud splash. Shad was now working on two men at once, swinging his fists wildly like an angry bear, connecting with loud slaps. Captain Ricaurte stood up and swung at me wildly, missing with his blade, but catching my forehead with the hilt of his sword. He was very strong for his age and the blow was effective. My head snapped back with the force of it and stars flashed before me, and I staggered backward. Through bleary eyes, I saw Shad's opponent go sliding across the deck on his side and crash into several barrels that had been stacked to one side. They all came down, two of them rolling directly across the man's upper body. He shrieked in pain, his body twisting and convulsing in agony. My head cleared quickly, but not soon enough. I turned to face Ricaurte and saw a glint of sadistic pleasure in his eyes as he drew his arm back to deliver the killing lunge at my chest. From out of nowhere, something hard smashed into the side of his head, causing his whole body to lurch to the side. He spun around and fell to his knees, wavering for a moment before crashing to the deck on his face. I turned to look into the eyes of Caesar, who held a long marlinespike in both hands, his face boiling with rage as he stared down at the motionless body.

"Well trained slave indeed." he said in a low tone that under any other circumstances would have frightened me.

We tended to the two badly injured men as best we could, but we could not save them. Every one of *El Guerrero's* small crew, except for the unconscious Captain Ricaurte, perished in the fight. We set ourselves to the grim task of disposing of the bodies and scavenging whatever valuables that we could. I made my way to the stern where the main cabin was. I had to find out what it was that these men were willing to die for. As I stepped through the doorway, I heard Stormy let out a yell.

"Cap'n, you'd best see this!"

I hurriedly made my way toward the main hatch, and saw him waving at me from it, his skinny upper body visible. In his other hand was a burning torch.

"Look, sir," he said.

I peered down into the blackness and at first saw nothing, and then Stormy lowered the torch, illuminating the interior. I sucked in my breath as I saw many dark, frightened faces looking up at me.

"*El Guerrero*" is a slaver, sir," Stormy said.

CHAPTER 35
ABRAHAM

I walked over to Captain Ricaurte, who lay motionless on the deck. Pulling my blade from its scabbard, I bent down over him and clutched a leather thong that I had seen earlier hanging around his neck. With one motion I sliced it and pulled a ring of heavy black keys from inside his filthy tunic. I walked back over to the hatch and offered them to Stormy, who took them from me and disappeared into the darkness of the hold. I heard the sounds of chains falling to the wooden deck, and one by one, the bewildered people timidly walked up the stairs out of the darkness. The men were half-naked and the women clad only in rags, and most were bent over from being cramped. As they emerged from the darkness, they raised their hands to shield their eyes from the bright sun, and looked around in every direction as if experiencing a new world for the first time. I counted seven men and five women, all adults save for one boy and two young girls who were still in their teen years. I looked at Caesar and noticed that he was acting a bit strange, staying clear of the group and looking out to sea. I walked over to where he stood by the railing on the far side of the deck.

"Caesar, are you feeling well?" I asked.

"I'm fine, Captain. I was not ready for dis, sir." It was then that I saw the small tears running down his face.

"Caesar, we have to take care of them. We will take them with us."

He looked at me intensely, then wiped his face with the back of his hand and walked back over to the group of people.

"Is dat all of ju?" he asked them.

They simply stared back at him as if not comprehending anything he had said. There was an awkward silence as they gaped at each other as if they were all trying to understand what they were seeing. The moment was broken by the sound of heavy footsteps on the rough stairs inside the hatch. A man's large head emerged into the sunlight. His movements were cat-like as he ascended the stairs and stepped onto the deck, rising to his full height. We all stared at him in astonishment. He was at least a foot taller than any other man I had ever seen. His skin was so black that it gleamed in the sun, his rippling muscles like coils of rope underneath its surface. The breeches and torn shirt that he wore were so tight that they seemed close to tearing. Unlike the others he had an angry, defiant look in his eyes and glared at me suspiciously.

"Saints preserve us look at the size of 'eem!" Shad said with wonder.

The man looked around the deck and spotted Luis Ricaurte, now shaking his bloody head and getting up from the deck, having just regained consciousness. The giant's face transformed immediately into an expression of dark rage and he flew into motion, surprising all of us by running straight at Ricaurte with unnatural speed. The slaver's Captain looked at him and screamed in terror, turning to escape. Quickly realizing that there was nowhere to run, he fell to his knees and raised his hands in front of him in a cowering gesture. The giant was on him swiftly, picking him up from the deck into the air by his collar. Ricaurte's feet swung wildly as he struggled for breath and futilely tried to kick at his attacker. The giant paused for a few moments and pulled the man's head close as if whispering to him. He then held him an arms-length away, and with one short, savage punch to the face, sent Ricaurte flailing backwards over the side of the railing into the sea below. We ran to the giant's side and saw Ricaurte thrashing about wildly in the water, his heavy clothes quickly weighing him down. The ocean current was moving swiftly, so the distance between him and the ship grew rapidly, and it was not long before we could barely see him in the waves.

"I'd say he's a might angry, wouldn't you Captain?" Shad said.

The giant stood there in the same spot, staring out at the waves like a statue for a long time, as we tended to the others. After a while I walked up to him, carefully measuring my distance.

"You there, do you speak English or Spanish?" I asked in as calm a voice as I could. He turned and looked at me with the same defiant, angry expression. There was a long pause, and I thought that he hadn't understood me. Then he began to speak.

"My name is Abraham. I was taken against my will by the trash that you saw me discard into the sea. Any other questions?" he asked.

I was so astounded that I could hardly speak. His was a very deep, resonant voice, and he had just answered me in perfect English.

"Um..My name is Santos Alvarez. I am pleased to make your acquaintance," I managed to stammer.

"I suppose you'll take us to the nearest port to be sold," he said. "Isn't that what pirates do with contraband?"

"I assure you that this is not my intention at all, señor Abraham. I am not a slave trader."

"Then why did you attack this ship if not to gain contraband?" he asked, insolence in his voice.

"My men and I had no idea that this was a slaver," I said. "We are in search of riches from my Spanish friends."

He stared at me again and I could see his mind working as if trying to figure me out.

"What do you intend to do with us?" he asked in a voice that had lost some of its edge.

"I know one thing I won't do," I said as I peered over the railing. "I'm not going to anger you."

"That man threw a woman and her child overboard a few days back. He did this because they were sick."

"Oh my God," I said.

"Your God did not help her," he said. "I pray for their souls every day."

I could see the sickness of rage as I watched tears form in his eyes. He averted his gaze, looking out to sea as he continued to speak.

"I sat down in that stinking hole and swore that if I ever got the chance I would kill him myself," he said.

"That is understandable," I said. "I am very sorry for your loss."

He smiled at me now, a twisted expression of barely contained fury on his face.

"Do you know what I said to him before I sent him over?" he asked.

I did not answer.

"I told him that mine was the last face he would ever see on this earth, and that I would chase him to hell," he said.

"Abraham, is it?" I asked, changing the subject.

He shook his head slowly.

"Please help us with this vessel and I will help your people back at our camp."

He thought about this for a few moments, and his demeanor began to soften. I was then surprised to see tears flooding his eyes.

"I am grateful, Captain Santos, for your help in delivering us from the hands of these men. I am forever in your debt."

With that he dropped to one knee and bowed his head in a gesture of supplication.

"Please do not do that," I said. "You owe me nothing. I need your help as you need mine, Abraham. Please help my crew."

It was much easier to manage the ships with more men, even though they were inexperienced seamen. We soon arrived at our inlet without incident. We rowed our canoes from the ships, now anchored safely in the river, to our makeshift landing. When we walked into camp, Chera was already preparing a meal of fish for our return. I embraced her and buried my face in her long, fresh smelling hair.

"We will need a lot more fish," I whispered to her.

Later, as we sat around the fire, I marveled at how our group had grown in such a short time. I watched the Africans as they whispered quietly to each other. They had been fed the first real food that they had seen in a very long time and kept looking over at me, their eyes full of gratitude. Abraham stayed clear of the group, sitting off by himself on the far side of the fire pit and staring into the flames. I got up and walked over to him and sat on the ground next to him.

"Abraham, please tell me your story. I am quite interested," I said.

He said nothing and continued to stare into the fire. I did not say anything and patiently waited. When he realized that I would not leave, he began to speak.

"I was born in Northern England near the Tweed River. My mother was owned by a planter named Block who grew oats and raised cattle. I never knew my father because he had been sold when I was very young. Master Block was different than most in that he was very kind to us. He was a man who liked his gin more than working with his hands, so he took me into his home and encouraged me to learn about the proper way to run a farm. He did everything for me, including teaching me how to read and write. These skills were absolutely forbidden to our people, so I secretly studied and worked as hard as I could. Due to my size, I was greatly sought by other yeoman around the area, so Master Block knew he had a good investment. He was a good man, but the drink took hold of him and he made a mistake. I caught him trying to take advantage of my mother."

"I guess he didn't look at you the same way after that," I said.

"I threw him from the second story window," he said in a soft, flat voice.

Abraham continued to stare into the fire, a sad expression on his face, and continued speaking.

"Master Block was badly injured from the fall, so his overseer came after me with revenge in his heart. I ran away and hid in an old abandoned house a short distance away, but the slave catchers had dogs, and I was soon caught. My bold actions proved to be a grave mistake because I was severely punished; I received a beating with cat o' nine tails so severe that it nearly killed me. The only reason I wasn't put to death was that I was worth more alive at auction. I nearly died from infection, so Block sold me to an investor who was headed for Hanover, Jamaica to head up a sugar plantation. I was put on a ship south and never saw my mother again."

I found his story so compelling that I could only stare. "Please continue," I said.

"Jamaica was hell on earth for me because I was not used to the heat and desolation of the place. There was an Irish overseer there who was very abusive to the slaves, despite the terrible working conditions. He had a special hatred for me because of my lack of fear of him. He whipped me whenever he could, for any reason he could think of. One day, I decided that I had taken enough from him, so I told him that he was a worthless, sick fool who would die in the cane fields with nothing. He had me dragged into a sugar shack where his men tied my hands behind my back. He then ordered the other men to leave so they couldn't see what he was going to do to me. While he was talking to them, I slipped a small blade from a pocket in my breeches and cut the ropes that held my hands. I pretended that my hands were still bound and waited for him to start. He drew his arm back and delivered me a hard crack of the whip, but I reached out and grabbed it and held tight. Before he knew what was happening I pulled him toward me and wrapped it around his neck. He won't be whipping anyone again."

He paused for a moment and took a sip of water from an onion shaped bottle.

"So, how did you end up here?" I asked him.

"I had to run then. I made my way to Port Royal, hiding in buildings during the day and running at night. I knew what would happen to me if I were caught so I was very careful. When I got to the docks there was a great deal of commotion because of a large slave auction that was being held. I didn't know what else to do, so I slipped into the line with these people you see here. We were all purchased by Captain Ricaurte to be taken to a tobacco plantation in Virginia colony in America. On that terrible journey, there was a woman and her small boy chained next to me in that stinking hold. The boy had a terrible, wracking cough that would not stop. The poor woman was very frightened for her son, so I talked to her and held her hand through the night. As the days went on, she also got sick. The rotten food and bad water we were given added to her misery. She asked me to pray for her as she got thinner and her cough grew worse. One day Ricaurte and his man came down into the hold and looked at them. He ordered his men to bring her and the boy up to the deck. I attacked one of the sailors but was beaten with a heavy stick until I was out. That's the last I ever saw of that poor woman and her child. I swore then that I would kill Ricaurte or die trying."

We sat in silence for a long time and looked at the flames before I spoke.

"Abraham, I would like you and the others to stay here with me."

CHAPTER 36
THE ANCIENT MARINER

The next few months were spent learning how to work with the slave ship survivors. The biggest challenge I had was learning their language, but Abraham proved to be a valuable asset in this. He did not speak their strange tongue flawlessly, but knew enough to communicate with them. He was a natural leader, and the strongest man I had ever seen. Abraham could drive a whale harpoon into a thick tree from fifty yards away. His skill with a cutlass was devastating. This weapon was a short, curved-blade sword that had a rounded, brass guard around the handle to protect the wrist. When it was wildly swung through the air in a distinct pattern, it was nearly impossible to defend against in a close fight. Abraham schooled all of the men in its proper use.

They all listened to him and followed his directions obediently, except for Fly and Stormy, who preferred to take their orders from Shad or myself. This was an acceptable arrangement for everyone, and there was no trouble. There seemed to be an underlying knowledge that we were all in this together, and that survival meant harmony within our ranks. We gave the Africans clothes that Caesar had hidden from the *Ais* and stowed in his hidden sea chests. They made quite a sight stumbling around the ship's deck trying to learn how to control the ship dressed in their ill-fitting European coats and breeches.

I gradually got to know them individually, and found that each of them had his own strengths and weaknesses. I did not know their real names and probably could not have pronounced them correctly if I did, but I learned the names that they had been given by their previous owners or the

slavers. There was, of course, Abraham, then Benjamin; a man
of indeterminate age who always kept a broad smile on his
face, Joseph; a man of about thirty years who was excellent
with his hands, Samuel and Simeon; two brothers who had
somehow managed to remain together through their captivity,
Matthew; an older man who was an excellent singer, Elias; a
young man who was a very diligent worker, and a slow-
minded teenage boy named George who possessed a great
sense of humor that I enjoyed immensely. George also had a
great affinity for the animals in the forest, and had already
adopted a young raccoon who had ventured near our campfire.
The women were Betsy; the oldest of them and an excellent
cook, Elizah, Mercy, and two teenage girls named Lydia and
Charity.

Every now and then, I would catch a glimpse of a native
face spying at us through the leaves and branches. I knew they
were there, watching everything that we were doing. There
was only one time that we had trouble with the *Ais*. It was a
humid day in the middle of summer, and Caesar was off on
one of his exploring excursions to find ambergris on the beach.
He was quite a distance to the north, on the ocean side of the
island near a small stream that cut through the saw grass.
Looking down at the sand as he walked along, he spotted a
large gray clump entangled with seaweed sticking up though
the sand. On further inspection, he was delighted to find that
it was the largest piece of ambergris that he had ever come
across. He knew that one of the harmless Spanish traders who
occasionally came by would pay handsomely for it, so he
began to work it free. Just as he pulled it loose from the sand,
he heard a noise behind him. He whirled around and found
himself face to face with two large *Ais* men. He recognized
the larger of the two as none other than his old friend, Aktil.

"What do you have there, Caesar?" Aktil asked in the native tongue.

Caesar realized that they had followed him that morning with the intention of robbing him if he found anything of value. He cradled the piece of ambergris under his right arm and raised his hand in a submissive gesture.

"Aktil, you must know that Captain Santos is near. He will not be happy that you followed me here."

"Ah yes, Captain Santos. I don't think he is near. I think you are by yourself as you always are when you hunt. Is that the whale gold I see? You always were good at finding it," Aktil said, wearing a wide smile as he lifted the long, heavy stick that he always carried at his side and began to move closer. Thinking quickly and trying not to panic, Caesar threw the large chunk at the two approaching men. They both moved to dodge it, and he sprinted off toward the trees. He ran wildly down the trail, never looking back as the old fear came back to him. As he fled, memories of the regular beatings he had received from the sadistic Indian during his early captivity came flooding back.

Abraham and I were gathering wood with two of the new men, Joseph and Samuel, when he reached the short trail that led to the camp. I could immediately tell that something bad had happened to him.

"What is it, Caesar?" I asked.

He was so angry that he could barely speak, but he managed to give a rambling account of what had happened. I listened patiently, my expression growing darker as he recounted the details.

"This is not good. The *Ais* have to be taught that they cannot do this to us," I said.

Abraham said nothing, but signaled to his men, and together they vanished into the woods. Caesar and I started up the trail and I tried to calm him down as we walked back to camp.

"You have to bring quiet to your mind. I want you to rest for a while, and later on we will go to the *Ais* village together to protest this. We cannot live together in peace if they rob us whenever they like," I said. "I long for the days when Canoba was alive. He would have never allowed Aktil to do these things."

As the afternoon sun started its descent to the west and the shadows grew long, Caesar and I walked toward the *Ais* village together. As we approached its outskirts, three small children ran across the trail in front of us, laughing as they played in the tall weeds. We soon saw the familiar lines of smoke rising into the sky from the fire pits, and our noses caught the scent of cooking meat. Just before we emerged from the trees that marked the edge of the village, I heard a sound coming from the woods behind us. It was a high pitched, shrill whistle that we often used as a signal out on the water. I had taught Abraham how to do it using the two longest fingers of his hand.

"Wait; something's not right," I said.

We turned around and headed toward the sound. After a short time, we emerged into a small clearing between some tall saw palmetto and pine trees, and what I saw there astounded me. Abraham was there, sitting on the sandy ground facing a large oak tree with branches draped with long tendrils of moss hanging all the way to the ground. Next to him was a large stake driven into the ground on which a thick rope was tied. My eyes followed it up to the largest branch of the tree. Then I saw him. Aktil was hanging by his feet at least fifteen yards above the ground. He was alive, but his face had been badly beaten and bruised. He appeared to be sobbing, tears streaming down his forehead into his hair. His mouth was covered by a tight, cloth gag, through which he whimpered in fear.

"Is this the man who robbed you?" Abraham asked.

Caesar looked up at his old master.

"Yes, it is," he said in a low voice. Abraham continued to speak.

"I want you to tell him something, Caesar. I want you to tell him that I am a devil giant from the west, and that if he attempts to harm anyone in this party again I will come for his soul. I will not stop with him but will take all of his people. It will be his doing and his alone."

Caesar looked at me, and I could see a smile forming on his face. He turned his head up and gave Aktil Abraham's message in a loud, clear voice.

"Caesar," Abraham said, "Also tell him that if he tells anyone of our chat here today, I will hear of it and will come for him. If I have to do this, he will be right back where he is now, and I will leave him for the mosquitoes and vultures."

Caesar delivered this message to the terrified Aktil, who could only grunt his consent in between sobs. Abraham then took hold of the rope and untied it, lowering the man slowly to the ground. Aktil lay there in a pitiful position as I untied his bruised feet. As soon as I had finished and was clear of him, he leapt to his feet and stumbled off into the weeds, disappearing quickly from view. That was the last time we ever had any trouble with him.

That night as I lay in bed next to Chera, I told her what had happened. She didn't say anything, and I thought for a moment that she did not approve of Abraham's actions. There was a long pause before she finally spoke.

"Fear is the only thing Aktil understands. Most of the *Ais* are not like him."

She hesitated, and I knew that another thought had come to her.

"What is it Chera?" I asked.

"They are sick, Santos, and the disease is spreading."

I saw them," I said. "I visited the shelter in the forest."

"There are many more now, Santos. I am frightened for them," she said.

"What can we do?" I asked. "I have seen sickness like that back in La Habana. There is nothing they can do but wait for it to pass. I lost many friends and relatives to it."

"I am going to them, Santos. I have to help in some way," she said.

"Chera, you can't help them. You need to be here with us."

"Santos, there are five women here now to cook and do the work. I am going to help them."

I said nothing and stared up at the crude ceiling of our shelter.

"Please, Santos, they have no one."

"All right, Chera. I know you have to follow your heart."

She held me close and I kissed her gently, and I could feel her heat as never before. I picked up a small, rolled-up blanket, and together we walked out of the shelter and down the trail in the direction of the *Ais* village. We soon came to the place where I had first seen the true splendor and wisdom of this woman next to me. This was the most beautiful place I knew; the burial mound of the ancient ones. Quickly gathering some small branches, I lit a small fire, then found a comfortable place nearby between two large oak trees and spread the blanket out on the ground. We sat together and I gazed at her, the amber light of the fire accentuating the beautiful lines of her features. I took her into my arms and kissed her so softly that our lips barely touched, at the same time pulling her body close to mine. We both knew what we wanted, so we stood back from each other and slowly removed our clothes. I looked at the silhouette of her naked, lithe form in the moonlight and felt warmth that I had never experienced before. I gazed into her smiling face and knew that she felt it as well. We fell into each other under the pale moonlight.

With our passions spent and our desires fulfilled, we fell blissfully asleep in one another's arms. I woke a short time later, and watched her peaceful form as she slept, her shoulders rising and falling gently with her breath. It was strangely quiet, and the fire had burned down to a pile of bright red hot coals that glowed in sharp contrast to the darkness of the night. I rose and walked down the trail, enjoying the cool evening air. As I walked, I looked up into the sky at the countless stars that brilliantly emblazoned the night sky. There was a hunter's moon, so it was very bright, and the landscape and all of its features were in plain view as if the entire world were different shades of blue.

I made my way toward the intersecting trail that led to the sea. All around me were the glowing insects of the night, but they did not light or pester me at my ears. The nocturnal world seemed more alive and enchanted than I could ever remember, and I felt a peace in my soul like I had never known before. The silhouettes of the oak and palmetto trees against the night sky looked like ancient sentinels with their arms outstretched. I saw the opening in the trail ahead that marked the entrance to the beach, and I could hear the crashing waves of the sea. As I emerged onto the cool sand, I saw the vastness of the ocean spread out before me and felt the salty wind blow through my hair. The moon was huge and bright in the clear sky, and there was a single, thin patch of cloud just behind it.

I looked to my left and saw something unusual. It was a light of some kind that seemed to be moving toward me a good distance down the beach. It had the swaying movement of someone walking; back and forth, back and forth. I waited, straining my eyes to see who it could be. Was it Caesar or Abraham? A shipwrecked castaway? As it came closer, I could see that the source of light was a ships lantern with a single candle in it. The man who carried it walked toward me, stopping about ten yards away. He held the lantern in front of him at chest level. I could not see his face in the dim light beneath his large, weather-beaten hat, but I noticed that he was bone thin, and wore a tattered old Spanish sailor's uniform complete with white breeches and a blue waist coat that looked as though it had been on his body for a hundred years. He had very long, white hair and a wispy white beard that streamed out over his shoulders and blew about in the strong sea gusts. The strangest thing about him was that he did not seem to be in any kind of urgency or distress.

"Who are you, old man?" I asked out loud. I still had not seen his face.

"*I am you,*" he said in a hollow voice.

I was stunned by his answer and didn't quite know how to respond.

"You speak nonsense," I said sharply, fear causing my voice to quaver. "What are you doing out here in this desolate place?"

"*I am you, you stupid boy. You need to heed me,*" he said.

I became angry at this impertinence. He held the lantern higher, blocking his face.

"Who are you to talk to me in this manner?" I said, my voice growing sharper. "I will knock you to the ground, old man."

"*Be silent, boy!*" he said, his voice deeper and very forceful.

I was truly alarmed by this reaction and stepped back in fear. The voice continued as I looked into the smoky amber light of the ancient lantern.

"*I am you, boy. Like you, I am cursed by an ageless execration that commandeth me to roam this beach for eternity. I am the spirit of all who have perished here. I have come to warn you that you must atone for the sins of your blood, boy!*"

I stepped backward away from him and tripped on a high spot of sand, falling to my rear end on the beach. I was now petrified as I realized what this was.

"*You look at me now and know that you and I are the same. You have no hope in this world or the hereafter, Santos Alvarez!*" he shrieked.

From the lower angle of my sitting position, I could now see his countenance, or should I say the lack of one. His face was not there, just the raw, dry white features of a skull grinning at me from below the battered hat. A pair of eyes that were bulging and watery with brown pupils filled the empty sockets, staring at me with burning intensity. I screamed louder than I ever had in my life. I turned and scrambled away on all fours from the terrible apparition. Somehow getting to my feet, I stumbled back toward the trail at the top of the beach. I looked back only once, and saw the figure standing where I had left it, its profile dark against the sea, the dull light of the lantern burning and the long beard and hair blowing sideways in the briny wind. I ran up the trail and heard something very familiar: it was the laughter of the Indian woman from my childhood, and I knew that she haunted me still, and that she always would.

A hand gripped my shoulder and shook it gently. I opened my eyes and looked into the face of my darling Chera. I looked around and saw that I was still by the mound where we had been the night before. My body was covered in sweat.

"Santos," she said firmly, "you were dreaming again."

I looked at her with wild, fearful eyes.

"I hate her, Chera. Why does she torture me so?" I said.

She looked at me intensely for a moment, and then spoke.

"She is a malevolent spirit, my love. It is a primal magic that she uses; very, very old. I will try to help you, Santos, but it will be hard. She is of another world, one in which I have little power. My strength is with the living creatures."

I threw my arms around her, never wanting to let her go.

CHAPTER 37
THE ARTICLES OF CONDUCT

Shad and the other English sailors continued to work with the new men to improve their sailing skills. They had been eating fish, meat, and fresh fruit for months now, and their state of health had improved dramatically, in contrast to the sickly bent people I had discovered in the hold of the *Guerrero*. Abraham had assumed the role of leader, and was doing well, both in training and in administering fair discipline when they did wrong. He was also involved in their spiritual lives, often taking part in their nightly rituals of singing and dancing around the fire under the moon and stars. It is my belief that these people were overjoyed to have truly found a place to live where they were not beaten, chained, and constantly on guard for the hated slave catchers and overseers. They looked at me with genuine affection and gratitude, and acted like men and women who had been given another chance. The men not only received lessons in sailing, but also in how to fight. We taught them how to defend themselves when under attack, and how to handle a blade. Abraham and I made it clear to them that, even though we were attacking ships, we were not murderers, and that we were only to take what was necessary to sustain us.

It was a fine day, and a cool breeze blew through the camp. The smell of the campfire smoke blended with the aroma of fresh fish that was cooking on flat rocks near its flames. Over by the south edge of the clearing were several raccoon and bear skins that had been stretched and mounted on racks made of cypress poles, their white linings showing brightly in the noonday sun as they cured. Chera and I were taking a well-deserved rest. I was sitting on a comfortable oaken bench that Caesar had built, as Chera stood behind it, massaging my shoulders with her skillful hands. The men had gone off in the Dutch prize ship with Abraham, and the women had gone into the forest to forage for berries. Santa Lucia was unusually quiet.

"Santos, you have grown so strong," Chera said as she gently kneaded my tight muscles. "You have become a good man."

"I wish I felt more like "a good man." Sometimes I truly detest the fact that I can never go home, even though I know that I will face the gallows should I dare it. I feel as though I am responsible for every man here. I want to help these people, but I fear that many of them will die. They are not accustomed to the brutality of warfare at sea, and I worry what they will do under real circumstances that prove to be dire," I said.

"You have helped them already, my love," she said. "They will go to the ends of the earth for you. Give them a chance," she said.

"I don't even know what I will do with gold and silver if I get it. I hate the Spanish and do not want to trade with them," I said.

"Caesar has already told you; you can go to Jamaica and exchange it. You do not have to deal with the Spanish at all," she said in a gentle voice. Her hands felt so wonderful on my tired neck.

"Santos," she said, "I have something to tell you."

"Go on," I said.

"Like you, I want to help people. I am going to the village to help the sick ones."

"Chera, we have discussed this. Your place is here with me," I said.

"I must go, my love. They have no one who understands sickness. I went there yesterday to see them, and five people perished in one afternoon. It seems as if their gods have turned away from them. I am going to stay with them for a while, Santos. I have no choice in this," she said.

"What if you get sick like them?" I asked.

"I will be fine," she said, a hint of defiance in her voice. "I have endured sickness before with my own people. I will pray for them, Santos. I cannot watch children die, while I do nothing."

I knew it was hopeless, so I relented. The very next morning, Chera was gone.

Later that afternoon, I was staring into the fire, feeling very melancholy. It seemed that part of me had gone with her. I was confused and angry that I didn't understand her obsession with helping the *Ais*. This was selfishness on my part, and the realization of it made me even more sad and ashamed.

Suddenly, there was a great commotion as Abraham and Caesar burst from the trailhead, each of them wearing a broad smile.

"Captain Santos! We have taken another fine prize!" They announced proudly.

"Really? What did you take?" I asked with growing enthusiasm.

"She's a fine pink, Cap'n!" Shad said as he walked up behind Caesar and Abraham. A pink was a style of merchant ship that had both a very shallow draft and a narrow stern. I had seen them in the harbor back at La Habana many times. I noticed that Shad was carrying a large canvas bag under his broad arm that clanked awkwardly as he walked.

"She was loaded to the rails with thirty-five hogs, food, barrels of water, and something else that you're going to find very useful indeed," he said.

He lowered the bag to the sandy ground and pulled it open. Out of it fell three navigational rulers, a sounding lead, and a ring dial that could be used as a compass. I felt my heart leap with excitement as I saw the largest item. It was a book with a cover that was embossed with large gold letters. I picked it up and read the title: "*Howard's Book of Navigational Principles.*" This was the first book I had seen since I was a prisoner on Brattock's ship years before.

"There's more there, Cap'n," Shad said, his voice full of pride. "There are maps, charts, and more books. It's a bloomin' treasure trove for a man o' words like yerself, sir!"

He and Stormy laughed out loud at this, and the faint smell of alcohol hit my nose. I quickly realized that they were half drunk.

"There was something else on board as well, wasn't there Shad?" I said, even though I already knew the answer.

"Yes, sir. There were many fine spirits aboard. The men are very happy for this, sir!"

I knew that life had been hard for them here at the camp, so I did not protest their intoxication. I knew that some of them may never see their true homes again.

"Let me see this fine vessel," I said, getting up to my feet. "What of the crew?"

"Spaniards," Shad said. "They were very stubborn at first, but we brought them around."

Abraham gave me a hard look and motioned me to come with him as the Shad and the others headed back toward the shoreline.

"Captain, we need to talk," he said in a low voice.

"What is it? I asked, as we walked away from the others.

"It's the English sailors, sir. They have a taste for torture and murder."

I paused and looked off into the distance, stroking my small beard as he spoke.

"Tell me," I said.

"We were running toward the inlet when we spotted the pink on our lee side, running with the wind to the south, so we took up the chase and soon overtook her. She had a Spanish crew made up of six sailors and two merchants who were plenty fearful of us, and practically gave her up. Shad and the other Englishmen stormed aboard and commenced to beating the old Captain hard and demanding where the valuable ships stores were held. When the old man refused to cooperate, Shad ordered him to be lashed to the main mast, where he was thrashed with a burning log on his bare back. He eventually broke down and told them where the money was hidden, but he was in very bad shape, and I don't think he made it. One of the other Spaniards tried to go for a spade and attack Stormy, but he was run through with a blade and his body tossed over the side. I did my best to stop them, Captain, but they had the fever. I think that they have done this kind of thing before, sir."

"What did you do with the rest of the crew after looting the ship?" I asked.

"We did what you asked, sir. We let them go in their longboats," he said.

"Well, the Spaniards will either stay away for good or come back with a vengeance, Abraham."

I thought about this for a long time. Shad and the other Englishmen had been through a good deal on the high seas, and understood what it meant to intimidate the crew of a captured prize. Brattock had done the same thing many times during his career in the Caribbean. I knew that word would spread quickly about this incident, and that there would be repercussions. I could not condemn Shad for what I perceived as reckless behavior, but I could do something else.

The very next morning the men were sitting around the smoky fire, many of them nursing the sickness of excess from the night before. The women were busily preparing food by the shelters and chattering softly to each other. I wore my shirt and jacket, as well as a pair of fine leather boots that Caesar had procured from one of the wrecks he had scavenged, and walked out into the open area west of the fire pit.

"Men," I said in a loud voice, "there is something I would like to say."

They all focused their attention on me.

"I want to congratulate you on capturing your prize. I understand that it went well."

There was a low murmur of approval as they congratulated each other once again. Abraham had taken a position in front of the African men and was doing his best to translate what I was saying in a low voice as I spoke.

"I feel that it is time to make some decisions regarding the organization of our crew. As many of you know, it is customary to have a man be responsible for many decisions that are to be made that may affect the future of our very lives. It is for this reason that I think that we should choose one man of our party to be Captain."

The men all looked at each other, surprised at my words, and there was a general silence. After a short time, Caesar spoke up.

"Captain, ju de only one can do dat."

"Oh, oi' don't know, sir." Shad said with a mischievous smile on his face. "Oi' think that our man, Dunkirk over there, would be a right fine cap'n indeed."

The English sailors burst into laughter, and everyone looked at the *Ais* boy, who was grinning widely, not comprehending a word Shad had said.

"The truth is," I said in a loud voice to quiet them, "that we never had a vote to decide it. I am not a dictator. If you men want me to be your Captain, I will require certain things from you as well."

Shad looked at me suspiciously.

"What are you saying?" he asked.

"If you want me to lead you then you will have to abide by my rules. These will be obeyed with no exceptions."

There was another silence except for the low voice of Abraham as he interpreted my words to the Africans.

"If you men would like me to be your Captain on this day, then say "Aye."

It took a few moments, but the tension was broken by Caesar's voice as he stood and shouted out.

"Aye! I can tink of no other man to do it!"

He was soon joined by all three of the Englishmen, and then the Africans shouted out their approval. All of them leapt to their feet and crowded around me, cheering together.

"All right, all right, men!" I shouted, laughing as I tried to restore order.

After a few minutes they calmed down and returned to their seats.

"If I am to be Captain, we must agree on certain rules of conduct. These will be written down and signed by every man here. If we do this properly, there will be no room for quarrels or disagreements among us. If we are to be a successful prize crew we must be a single unit."

They were cheering boisterously now. I signaled to Caesar to come to my side, and I whispered my instructions into his ear. He returned a short time later with a rolled up piece of parchment paper, a feather quill, and an ink bottle that he had taken from the *Guerrero*. We made a makeshift table from some old deck planks, and for the next two hours I wrote up our articles. They read as follows:

On this, the 20th day of the sixth month of the year of our Savior seventeen hundred fourteen, we of sound mind the crew of the Pantera de Florida construct these articles of conduct of which we will all abide and agree upon. We understand that to deny these articles will be punishable by death or banishment from the crew.

   I.   *Every man has a vote in affairs of the moment.*

   II.   *The elected Captain receives two shares of a prize, the Officers receive one and a half, the First Mate and any other officers receive one share, all others receive one half share. The women and children will be taken care of by what is left.*

   III. *Anyone caught holding out or deceiving the others regarding his share will be punished by marooning or exile from the camp.*

   IV. *No person to game at cards or dice for money.*

   V.   *Keep pistols, piece, and cutlass clean and ready for service.*

VI. *Deserting your ship or post during battle is punishable by death.*

VII. *If any man is injured or loses a limb during battle he will receive the sum of eight hundred silver pieces.*

VIII. *No man will take the life of a prize ship crew unless under threat of life or limb.*

IX. *Undeserved torture will not be tolerated and will be punishable by exile or marooning.*

After we had finished all of the men gave a resounding cheer and raised their hands in unity. I took advantage of this happy moment to make my point, my gaze leveled at Shad. He had been uncharacteristically quiet during the formation of the articles and had avoided meeting my eyes.

"Remember men, I am the Captain and I will enforce these articles with my very life. This means that there will be no more indecencies committed during our hunting."

CHAPTER 38
SECRET OF THE SANTIAGO

It was a beautiful, cloudless day on the water, and the brilliant light of the sun glistened on the rippling waves as we caught the east wind and made our way out of our inlet into the open stretches of the Atlantic. I looked off the port side of the *Pantera* and saw several porpoises playfully leaping through the water at her hull and in her wake, acting as if they thought that the sloop was one of their own. Caesar was at his post high up in the rigging, acting as lookout. He was wearing a large slouch hat with a wide brim to block the sun's rays from his eyes. It was secured by a long, leather thong around his neck to keep it from blowing away in the strong wind. Shad was at the stern of the ship shouting orders to Mike Storm and Fly as they ran about the deck tending to the sails and making adjustments. The rest of the men were below decks preparing for any action by tending to the powder, weapons and shot.

Abraham was at my side near the bow, both of us looking out toward the sea. We had dressed for the hunt. I wore my finest black jacket and hat, my high leather boots and breeches, and had two braces of pistols hanging from my shoulders, crisscrossing my chest in the middle. Abraham had painted his face with streaks of white war paint, and had asked one of the women to braid his hair into long, tightly woven ropes that hung down from beneath the red bandana wrapped around his broad head. He wore no shirt, and the muscles under his skin glistened in the sun like black granite. A long scabbard and sword hung from his wide leather belt. He looked like the largest, most menacing pirate I had ever seen. This was part of my strategy of intimidation and fear that would, in my opinion, ultimately save both time and lives. The men and I had planned our strategy carefully. We hoped that we could successfully implement it and test our talents.

Caesar suddenly howled above the roar of the waves and wind, sending a jolt of excitement through all of us.

"*Ship ho to starboard!*"

Abraham and I looked off to the right, and soon located the tell-tale white dot on the horizon.

"Due south by southeast, men! Remember that we have to use the element of total surprise and speed to achieve success!" I shouted.

We turned with the wind and made our way swiftly across the waves toward the prize in the distance. The ship was soon in view, and I perceived her to be a small galleon of Spanish origin. I had the men run up the Spanish colors, and we closed in on her quickly as she bounced up and down in the rough seas. I signaled to Abraham to go below decks and get ready. I thought it strange that such a vessel was traveling so close to the coast alone, and felt a pang of apprehension. It would be an audacious move for our small ship to attack a galleon of any size. We closed the distance between us quickly, and I could see her crew members peering at us from the bulwarks. We waved to them, trying to appear friendly.

"Careful of those guns, men," I said in a low voice as we came up on her.

We were fully exposed now, so it was more important than ever to seem amiable. She was a handsome galleon with about thirty guns, and if she wanted to, she could have ended us swiftly. I had seen the vessel's name on her stern as we came up on her: she was the *Santiago*. A short bearded man wearing a stocking cap poked his head out over the railing and shouted to me across the waves.

"What is your business with us, señor? Make it quick or we will fire on you."

"I am a loyal subject of *Madre España!*" I shouted in Spanish. "We are a ship in distress and need assistance!"

I could see the suspicious look on his face and how he hesitated. I continued my plea.

"We have had an altercation with a very vicious band of pirates and have injured men on board. Please see through God's eyes that we need help from our *compatriotas!*"

He then disappeared from view. I turned and saw Abraham peering at me from the hatch, so I gave him the "thumbs up" signal. He ducked back down, and I felt the rumbling vibrations below me as the gun hatches were opened and the sixteen pound cannons rolled into place. I silently prayed for the men to hurry before the Spaniards could get time to react. The bearded man appeared at the railing again.

"Señor," he shouted across the water, "we cannot help you. You must take your vessel away now or we will fire on your ship."

I responded to this with a shout of my own.

"Fire at will, men!"

A "knipple" shot is two cannonballs that are connected with a short length of chain that, when shot from the barrel of a cannon at close range, has a devastating effect. There was a thunderous boom and a shuddering vibration from below as two of the mighty guns fired simultaneously. The knipple shots spiraled wildly through the air, careening into the forward and rear masts simultaneously. The tops of both split off and fell in a mass of wood splinters and twisted ropes, instantly rendering the ship helpless and immobile. There was a cacophony of screams from the galleon as injured men were hit by falling objects and jagged sections of the masts.

"*Rápid!* Get us out of the range of those guns!" I shouted.

The men scrambled around the deck pulling and adjusting the sails and rigging, and we were soon gliding past the galleon's starboard side, out of range of the fifteen guns that were hastily being rolled into place. We let out a great cheer as the smoke cleared and we were able to see the extent of the damage we had afflicted on the *Santiago*. There was a huge explosion of sound and smoke as ten of the Spanish guns fired at the same time in a futile attempt at retaliation. Several men appeared on the ship's forecastle with musketoones and began firing at us, but the distance was too great for the inaccurate weapons, the shots falling either short or veering wildly off to our side.

"Ready the grenadoes!" I shouted.

On my command, we turned the *Pantera* to the wind and veered closer to the bowsprit of the galleon in what seemed like a suicidal distance to the crippled, but still heavily manned and armed vessel. As we did this, I signaled the men to begin their assault. They lined up along our own bulwarks, each carrying a basket of small, round glass bottles stuffed with black powder, a short fuse sticking out of one end. George, the teenage boy, carried a small, burning torch and walked along behind the men, lighting fuses as he went. They began hurling them across the water onto the deck of the stricken vessel, daringly exposing themselves despite the heavy fire from the Spanish guns. The *grenadoes* exploded on contact, creating even more smoke and confusion on the galleon's weather deck. Men screamed in panic, and I saw a few of them jump over the side and into the water. I heard a familiar cry from the galleon's deck.

"*El fuego!*"

Red flames leaped up on the deck, and I saw black smoke billow up toward the sky. The men on board collapsed into panicked mayhem and soon abandoned the fight, concentrating their efforts on putting out the fire. To my shock and dismay, I watched as one of our own took a musket ball to the head, instantly falling to the deck in a lifeless heap. It was Benjamin. He had been one of my favorites, because he always had a smile and a good word for everyone. I instantly flew in a wild rage.

"Bring up the guns and make ready with boarding hooks!" I screamed, and we pointed all of our fire power at the burning ship.

We brought the *Pantera* around for another swing at the galleons broadside, this time moving in even closer. The bearded Spaniard appeared at the railing, a wild look of panic on his pale face.

"Are you the *Capitan* of this ship?" I bawled.

He nodded his head up and down at me. "I am Captain General Suarez of *Marina Real de Su Majestad!*" he shouted, his voice barely audible above the mayhem of battle.

"Your ship is doomed! If you fire on us now, I will leave you here to be burned alive, or drown like rats! Do you capitulate to me?" I asked.

He looked over his shoulder at the wreckage of his ship and turned back to me.

"Yes. .yes, we capitulate! Please help us!" he answered.

"Throw the hooks!" I cried, and the men sprang into action, swinging each one in a wide arc and expertly pitching them to the galleon's deck. We pulled the *Pantera* close to the mortally injured ship and prepared to board her.

I shouted across the water. "Captain Suarez, have your men drop their weapons and move them back toward the stern. If you do not do this you will all die!"

One by one, my men leapt over the railing onto the wooden deck, each armed to the teeth, wielding flintlock pistols and boarding axes. Our appearance was intimidating, with our brightly colored clothes and rough manner. Abraham and I stepped onto the deck and looked around, surveying the damage we had inflicted. The Spanish sailors had done what I commanded, and the deck was littered with cutlasses, knives, musketoones and other articles of war. There were at least thirty men on board the *Santiago*, and they had all moved to the rear of the deck, looking at us with expressions of fear and panic. We walked to them, doing our best to appear fearless and in control, even though we were secretly intimidated by their superior numbers. The Spanish sailors gawked at Abraham and me as if we were phantoms from another world. We both knew that if the attack had gone any other way, they could have easily overpowered us. We scrutinized them deliberately, looking each man in the eye to show that we were in control. When we came to the bearded Captain, he slowly stepped up to me, stocking cap in his hand. He looked small and very tired.

"Captain," I said to him, "I hereby take control of this vessel. I want your men to deal with that fire right now."

He instantly barked some orders, and several men flew into action, running toward the burning section of deck. He then turned back to me, his eyes locking on mine.

"You are Captain Santos, the fearsome *pirata*, are you not?" he asked, his voice quavering slightly.

I was taken aback by this. He had not only recognized me, but had identified me by name.

"Do I know you?" I asked.

"Everyone knows of you," he said, avoiding my direct gaze.

"What have you heard about me and my men?" I asked.

"It is said that you have joined forces with the cannibals of La Florida, and that you hate the Spanish. It is also known that you feed your prisoners to the cannibals," he said.

I looked at Abraham in surprise, and we both nearly burst into laughter. I then saw the gravity of the situation and quickly capitalized on it. I now understood how a force the size of ours had been able to overtake so large a crew.

"What else have you heard about us?" I asked him.

"It is said that you have a great stronghold in the jungle where you keep stolen slaves that you train to be ruthless killers, and that you have mountains of hidden treasure. It is all that is talked about in St. Augustine and La Habana."

I flashed Abraham another look, and he responded with a broad smile.

"Why are you out here by yourself, *Capitán*?" I asked. "I thought it customary to for the *galeones placa* to travel in packs?" I asked.

His eyes widened at this and I could tell that this was a sore subject for him.

"We were separated from the rest during bad weather," he said. "I will probably lose my head over this."

"Such is the revenge of the bloodthirsty *Realeza española*," I said.

The fire was soon brought under control, and I instructed the Captain to take all of his men into the hold below.

"I am warning you, sir, if you resist or fight my men in any way, I will unleash a horde of Indian warriors on your crew. They will be tomorrow's morning meal," I said.

Needless to say, the Spaniards complied and the entire crew was soon secured below decks. My men searched the rest of the ship and found it packed with all that they could have hoped for: fresh fruit from Venezuela and Columbia, clothing, medicine, and another fine violin for Fly, still in its case. Most importantly, Shad found wooden cases full of hundreds of freshly minted gold and silver bars and coins. I could not believe our good fortune. It took us many hours to load the booty from the galleon onto the *Pantera*. We were careful to treat our Spanish prisoners compassionately, allowing them plenty of food and water from the stores.

We paused our looting for a short somber ceremony of remembrance, as we consigned our friend Benjamin's remains to the sea. I gave a short speech in which I praised the sacrifice that he had made for us and the bravery and selflessness of his actions. Matthew, the singer, began a sad, African song in his low, quavering voice. One by one, all joined in, and the air was soon filled with a chorus of voices. As they sang, my thoughts went back to the day I had first seen young Benjamin on the slaver; the day we had released him from that hellish prison. I thought of how proud I had become as I watched him gain back his strength. My eyes filled with tears, knowing that I had lost a friend and a family member. I turned to look at Abraham and saw the tears streaming down his face as well, smearing the white war paint on his cheeks.

After we had loaded everything we could onto the *Pantera*, I had the men spike the fuse holes of every one of the cannons on board. I then had Captain Suarez brought up to the deck. He stood before us, a look of hopeless sadness on his face. I addressed him formally and respectfully as Caesar, Abraham, and Shad all stood with me at attention.

"*Capitán*, I have brought you here to tell you that I have finished with your vessel. I will be turning it back over to you now, and you are free. This is a very busy shipping route, and you should see another vessel within a few days to assist you and your men with the broken masts. My men have incapacitated all of your weapons. If I see you again I will not be so charitable."

After I had finished, the man broke into tears. It was embarrassing, so I turned to look at the others for support.

"All is lost, Captain Santos," he said, his voice quavering. "I will be hung for allowing this to happen."

"The officers will understand, *Capitán* Suarez. Piracy is common in these waters," I said.

"No, you do not understand. I have already lost one vessel in the Azores," he moaned. "My ship became a victim of the shallow reefs. Please hear my one request, senor."

I felt myself losing my patience.

"What is it then, *Capitán* Suarez?"

"Take some of us with you. We have discussed it during our time in the hold. Your attack on us happened to coincide with an impending mutiny. There are five of us who want to join you. If you leave me here, the savage criminals of this vessel will hang me and many others here. I feel that I cannot control them any longer. I have nothing back home now."

I did not know what to think of this request, so I pulled the others away for a private meeting. "What do you think?" I asked them.

Abraham spoke first.

"It seems very unnatural that an *El capitán del barco* in service of the *español rey* would surrender his command for a life of piracy," he said.

~ 307 ~

"I agree," Shad interjected. "Never trust a Spaniard, that's what 'oi say. He'll cut yer bleedin' stomach open if he thought there be a doubloon inside."

"Shad," I said, "let me remind you that I am Spanish."

He broke my gaze and looked down at the ground as I continued.

"Let me also remind you that I saved you from a similar fate at the hands of the *Ais* warriors. What if I had left you on that beach by your wrecked ship? None of us chose to be here in our present position, but here we are. If there is one thing that I have learned, it is that a little compassion may go a very long way. Some of these men may have skills that could prove to be of great use to us. I, for one, cannot leave them here to be slaughtered by their own crew of malcontents. Something has gone terribly wrong on this ship, and I fear that there will be no good outcome."

"But Cap'n," Shad said, his eyes wide with concern, "what if they are assassins sent by the Spanish to kill us?"

"Shad, does that even make sense after the battle we just had with them?" I asked.

He did not answer as the ludicrousness of his idea sunk in.

After a few minutes of discussion, we made our decision, so we returned to Captain Suarez. I stepped out in front and looked directly at the man.

"We have taken a vote, *Capitán* Suarez, and we have come to a decision. If you and your men are willing to disavow the *Realeza española* and be branded as traitors in your own world, as well as swear to and sign our articles of conduct, you will be allowed to join. In order to save face for you in front of your crew, we will make it appear that we are taking you and your men prisoner." All of them slowly shook their heads in compliance.

We then cut a small contingent of the *Santiago's* crew away from the others and informed them that we would be holding Captain Suarez and his men for ransom, and that the rest of them were free to go. There was one man who did all of the talking among them, a young firebrand named Manuel, whom I guessed to be the chief instigator of the impending treachery.

"The Spanish will not pay a ransom for *Capitán* Suarez. He is a coward and a *Jonás*," he sneered. "He is *mala suerte*." The men behind him grumbled their agreement.

"Let me inform you, señor Manuel, that King Philip's soldiers do not take kindly to treason and mutiny. I would lay very low if I were you," I said.

"Bah!" he snorted. "These men are my witnesses. We are all united in the face of a fool who would soon lead us to our deaths!"

As we walked away from the group, I held my saber at Captain Suarez's back to complete our ruse.

The "prisoners" we had taken consisted of the ship's carpenter, the sail maker, the cook, and the cooper, along with his young assistant. We then readied the *Pantera* for sail and released the wounded *Santiago* into the hands of the remaining sailors to limp her along until some ship came by. As we made our way back to our inlet, we reflected on what had happened. Not only did we have a fine haul of booty; our crew had grown in number significantly. I looked at Captain Suarez, who wore a sad, pensive expression.

"They will hang young Manuel an hour after they land," I said.

"Yes, I know," he said. "The *estúpido* does not understand that the investors and soldiers do not care about the crew, especially ones involved in an incident such as this. The gold and silver is gone, and Manuel's "friends" will not be loyal to him under the duress of the inquisitors. The crown will hang anyone directly involved, starting with him."

He was silent for a time as the reality of what had taken place seemed to sink in.

"I don't know," he said in a sad voice, "perhaps I am the *Jonás* that Manuel sees."

"Captain Suarez, Manuel's luck is about to run out. As you know, there are no more superstitious men than sailors on the high seas," I said, "and I am not one of them. I am offering you a chance to restore your luck, but it will be on the other side of the law."

"I realize this, *mi capitán,* and I thank you. I will swear my allegiance to you," he said.

CHAPTER 39
<u>SAVIOR OF THE AIS</u>

We arrived back at Santa Lucia in very high spirits with our boats laden with gold, silver, and other treasures. The women had prepared a delicious feast for our homecoming. All along the roughly hewn tables were large clay bowls of muscadine and blackberries freshly picked in the forest, and large platters loaded with chunks of fish and turtle meat roasted over the fire on long spits. The men were happier than I had ever seen them, and it was good to see them smiling and laughing with one another. To me, the victory was bittersweet due to the absence of my sweet Chera, who was still with the *Ais*. The selfish part of me was angry with her for not being there to share in the celebration, but the sensible part understood that this was where she had to be. One small solace was that there were more men of Spanish heritage in the party now with whom to talk about events back home.

After large amounts of wine had been consumed and all of our bellies filled, I learned from Captain Suarez and his men the exact nature of the trouble on board the Santiago and the near mutiny that had occurred as a result. From the personal accounts that these men gave me of their various experiences, life on a Spanish treasure galleon was not one to be envied. There was very limited space on board, and as many as two hundred men were expected to share sleeping quarters cramped into a very small area on the lower deck. There was always the problem of cleanliness with no proper privies or methods of removing human waste. The bilge holds often stank so badly that the smell would carry over the entire ship. This resulted in other problems, such as chronic rat plagues, during which the vermin got into the ship's food stores and water supply, and even ate through spare rigging. The meals were also difficult because cooking fires could only be used during fair weather. Fire was always a threat, especially in the high winds of the open ocean.

Captain Suarez had once been one of the most promising young officers in the *armada española*. Always under pressure to move faster, he often struggled with the task of administering firm and fierce discipline to his crew. A gentle soul at heart, he often let things go that he shouldn't have. He had already been involved in an incident under his previous command in which he had placed a young and inexperienced boy in the important position of lookout from the crow's nest on the center mast. The boy was the son of the high ranking *Capitán General* Salmon of *Marina de Su Majestad*. The job entailed keeping watch from nearly one hundred feet above the deck, and the lad had badgered Captain Suarez for days to allow him to do it. It was a very important task that consisted of watching for other ships or hazards and conditions in the water ahead, and Captain Suarez had resisted because he considered the young man arrogant and immature. He eventually relented under the pressure of the lad's threats.

A week later the young man fell asleep at watch and failed to alert Captain Suarez of a shoal, so the ship ran aground and was nearly lost. There was a long, painful investigation of the incident in the high maritime court in Spain. Captain Suarez was eventually cleared, but it had proven very difficult to recover from the stigma of this event in such a competitive field, especially with an enemy like *Capitán General* Salmon, who had stubbornly insisted on his son's innocence throughout the hearing. Suarez had been very fortunate to find the command aboard the *Santiago*, so he began to carefully scrutinize every decision he made.

Sailing a vessel the size of a galleon involves much responsibility because they are very top heavy and generally have three or more masts with a multitude of sails. As I had learned myself, ships riggings are very complicated and require great skill from each sailor. Every man has to know the name and locations of all the ropes and sails, as well as the tools needed to repair them should they tear or be damaged in an accident. Many of the *Santiago's* seamen were pressed into service by force and did not know the difference between port and starboard, nor did they understand many of the terms and commands used by the boatswains mate. When Captain Suarez ordered the ship to change tack and sail into the wind, confusion often ensued and tempers flew, with blows soon following. There were so many green sailors on board that resentment and anger soon spread among the entire crew.

Then the worst thing imaginable happened; thirty-seven men perished in an outbreak of sickness, their wasted bodies hastily flung overboard. This prompted more bad feelings and talk of superstitious entities at work to undermine their mission and kill them all. The situation grew so desperate that Captain Suarez, at one very low point, actually considered suicide as a possible solution. It seemed that the attack of the *Pantera* could not have come at a better time.

He leaned back against a tree, the strong wine loosening up his stiff demeanor.

"Captain Santos, I admire you so much," he said, slurring his words slightly. "I guarantee you that those miserable men on the Santiago started killing each other the minute we left them. They were a cursed lot."

I gazed into the fire and tried not to look distressed at his choice of words. He stared at my face for a long time, and then continued to speak.

"You know, there is another story that I heard about you. Do you mind if I indulge?"

My heart skipped a beat.

"Be my guest, señor," I answered, slightly wary.

"There is a silly story about you that involves some sort of curse. I generally dismiss such things as children's fantasy."

"That is wise, Captain Suarez. Such tales can be dangerous with sea going men."

"Ah yes, I know this to be true. But still, it seems to add to your legend back home. Makes you kind of a tragic figure, you know," he said.

I got up from the ground and dusted the bits of leaf and sand from my breeches.

"I think I shall retire, Captain. It is a pleasure to have you with us," I said.

"I hope I have not offended you Captain," he said, obviously flustered.

"Not at all, señor. Rest well."

I strode off toward my quarters. I missed my darling Chera more than ever.

The next morning I was awakened by someone clutching my arm, shaking me. I looked up into the face of Dunkirk, the *Ais* boy. He stared into my eyes, wildly frustrated and trying to speak, but the words would not come. I sat up and grabbed his shoulders.

"What is it, Dunkirk? What is wrong?" I demanded angrily. I was still half asleep.

He gestured wildly toward the door of the shelter. I heard the sound of raindrops hitting the thatched roof and could smell the wetness of the air.

"Is it Chera?" I said with dread.

The boy shook his head up and down, and my heart sank. I leapt up from the mat and hastily dressed, together we raced off toward the *Ais* village. We did not stop at the cluster of shelters and the longhouse, but continued past them down the trail to where I knew I would find her. I ran into the clearing where the sick ones were, my eyes frantically scanning the rows of sick under the shabbily constructed shelters. I saw that there were many more people now than before. Three more crude shelters had been constructed, each filled with coughing, vomiting, and emaciated souls. I saw a group of women clustered around one bed on the far side, and tears sprang to my eyes. As I walked between the wretched and dying, I knew I would find her there.

The women around her looked up at me with pity in their eyes, and slowly moved back. It only took one look and I knew what had happened. She was there, but not in the way I remembered her. I got down on my knees, my eyes now nearly blind with tears, and looked at her. She gazed up at me with eyes that were bloodshot and damp. A smile came to her dry, chapped lips and she took my hand in hers. Her skin was covered with red blotches that were oozing, and she looked withered and haggard. Her fingers felt fragile and weak, like the bones of a bird. I lost all composure and fell to her, taking her into my arms and pulling her close.

"Why, Chera, why didn't you tell me sooner?"

She answered in a whispery voice that was as dry and soft as leaves in the fall.

"Santos, my love, you have made me so happy," she said.

"Please don't leave me," I said, raising myself up and looking into her eyes, my voice hysterical.

"I will never leave you, my love," she said. "I am going to the high place."

There was a whelk shell cup half full of water next to her on the ground, so I picked it up and held it to her lips.

"Drink, Chera. Be still and drink." I said.

"Santos, you must listen. Follow your heart and you will find your way," she whispered.

I stayed with her until darkness came, and all through the night until the next day. I could see that she was growing weaker as the minutes passed, and I tried to keep her comfortable. Just before midday, the time came. I stared into her eyes and watched her slip away into the upper world that she always spoke of. I was past crying, and felt a strange sense of relief that she was beyond the pain and suffering. I stayed with her until late into the night. Sleep did come to me, despite the moans of the dying all around me. In the morning, I wrapped her in the rough blanket in which she had died and carried her back toward Santa Lucia.

I soon came to the place I knew she would want to go. Looking up at the burial mound, I recognized the spot where we had first made love on that wonderful, moonlit night. With tears streaming down my face, I laid her gently on the soft ground. I spent the next hour or so clearing the place of debris all the way down to the bare sand. When I finished, I walked the short distance to the nearby lagoon. I found a basket that Caesar had left there and waded out into the shallow, brackish water. I bent down and dug my hand into the black sand of the river, bringing up a large handful and dropping it into the basket. I repeated this time after time until it was full. I brought it back to the mound and carefully poured it over her. I repeated this for hours and hours until night came and I was too tired to do any more. I fell to the ground, completely exhausted, and went to sleep.

"Santos, wake up!" she said. "Come see! We have to go to the ocean!"

I dragged myself from the bed still groggy with sleep.

"What is it that is so important?" I said.

"Just come, I have something to show you!"

She ran from the shelter toward the trail. I grabbed a still-burning torch from the ground and followed her down the trail that led to the beach. The sea grapes were thick and it was like walking through a twisting tunnel. I could soon hear the soft crashing of the waves ahead and soon emerged onto the cool sand. It was a beautiful night with a full moon so bright and vivid that I could see the features of its rough surface. Countless stars shone brightly against the dark sky with such brilliance that I stood for a moment, in awe of such beauty. I looked down the beach and saw her a short distance ahead of me; her hand beckoning me to come to where she stood next to a large pile of driftwood. I could hear the rhythmic beat of drums as I made my way toward her. There were other figures moving there and I strained my eyes to see who they were. I heard the sound of voices singing. This was not ordinary singing, but a sound of joy so profound that I felt an overwhelming rush of emotion. There was a sudden flash of red and yellow light as the driftwood burst into flames. The fire took hold almost immediately, and soon became a huge pyre that must have been visible for miles. As I approached it, I saw that the shapes around it were people; natives, and that there were a lot of them. Some of them were dancing wildly around the fire, huge smiles of joy on their faces. I saw that they ranged in age from old to very young, but they all were singing and grinning, even the oldest and most decrepit. I felt that I recognized some, but couldn't remember where I had seen them. They clapped their hands in time with the drums and seemed oblivious to me.

Then I saw her. She moved into the firelight in a seductive dance. The terrible ravages of sickness were gone, and her radiant beauty beamed brilliantly in the firelight. She dressed in a scant, flowing dress that I had never seen her wear before. Her movements were so fluid that she seemed to move with the waves of the ocean, rising and falling gently as she made her way around the fire. Our eyes met, and I looked into her dark, mystical eyes and saw pure happiness as the soft ocean breeze blew her long, lustrous hair around her face. She turned away and looked up toward the top of the beach, raising her arm in a slow wave of greeting. I turned to look and was completely stunned by what I saw.

There were animals there. Bears, panthers, raccoons, turtles, birds of all kinds flying overhead and standing on the ground, in a large group, just sitting there as docile as anything I had ever seen. They made noises; grunting, squawking, growling, but they were not aggressive and none of them attacked each other. They simply gazed at Chera with what looked like admiration. I was overcome and began to wail her name.

"Chera, my Chera, please return to me. Please don't leave me!" I moaned.

She came to me then and placed her finger over my mouth.

"Santos, can't you see? This is not the time for sorrow. This is the time for joy and happiness like you have never known. This is the upper world that I told you of! I am giving you a glimpse of what life really means! It's about love and happiness and the great creatures of the forest and the earth and all of its bounty! Come, dance with me."

She took my hand and pulled me toward the fire. A sound came to my ears, and I felt a wave of emotion that was nearly overwhelming. It was old Canoba's song. I turned my head to the crowd of people, and there he was, grinning widely and singing loudly. The tears streamed down my face as I looked into his wise old eyes. They seemed to be so calm and reassuring that I was sure that he was where he had always wanted to be. I had never danced in my life, but I could not resist. I held Chera close as our bodies slowly moved in perfect unison. I felt such a sensation of pleasure and well-being that I never wanted to leave. The happiness that I had always felt when I was near her seemed to have multiplied. We moved slowly together for what seemed like hours with our strange audience watching. She then looked into my eyes and spoke.

"Santos, you must never let the terrible woman of your dreams overcome you. There is no curse that cannot be broken."

"But what will I do without you?" I said, my voice choking with raw emotion.

"You will always have me," she said.

I opened my eyes suddenly and felt the sun on my face. I shook my head and got up to my elbows as I tried to wake up. I turned and looked at the fresh pile of dark, wet sand that I had put there the night before.

How long had I slept?

I had the strangest feeling that someone was looking at me so I turned my head. I found myself looking straight into the face of Aktil. I was so startled that I scrambled away in a wild search for a weapon.

"No Captain, dey not come for fight."

I looked up and saw that Caesar was with him. I thought it odd that these two were together, but both men looked at me with the same strange light in their eyes. I looked behind them and saw that they were not alone. There must have been fifty of them there; women, children, old people, and young warriors all lined up on the trail. They each carried something in their hands; flowers, shells, necklaces, beads, plants, and a vast array of sacrificial items.

"What do they want, Caesar?" I asked.

"Dey come to honor Chera," he said.

I felt the tears well up again in my eyes as I realized what this was.

"She is here," I said, pointing to the mound I had made. One by one, the *Ais* filed by and left their gifts, each saying a few words that I did not understand. There was soon a huge pile of offerings on the mound.

"Caesar, who are these people?"

"Captain, do ju remember when you came to see Chera for de last time?" he asked.

"Yes, even though I would rather forget," I said, looking down at the ground as I felt the tears coming again.

"Do you remember de sick ones?" he asked.

"How could I ever forget, Caesar. There were so many."

"Captain Santos, look at dem. Dese are dose people," he said.

"How can that be?" I said.

"Dey are well now. She took de sickness wid her," he said. All of a sudden the dream of the night before made perfect sense. A flood of tears filled my eyes, and I had to turn away as a flood of realization and grief overwhelmed me.

CHAPTER 40
STORM

Caesar had sensed a drastic change in the weather approaching, constantly looking at the sky with a worried frown on his face. I had learned to trust his "feelings" regarding these matters, so I made the trip to *El Lugar* to get a better perspective. The clouds overhead had become solid and were moving methodically across the sky in one great mass. The warm wind was acting strangely. It seemed at first to drop off to almost nothing, and then began to move erratically; first blowing southeast, then northwest, rifling through the sparse saw grass of the hill down below me. I opened my mouth, flexing my jaw so my ears would pop from the change of pressure in the air. A small flock of seagulls flew inland over my head in perfect formation as if running from something. My best guess was that the storm would be here in a few hours.

I could barely hear the rhythmic sound of the *Ais* drums on the wind and knew that the ceremony to appease the storm gods had begun. I gathered my tools and started down the slope of *El Lugar* and back to Santa Lucia. As I walked down the steep slope toward the sea, I caught the fragrant aroma of a rosemary bush that grew along the ridge. This scent brought thoughts of Chera. It had been one full year since she had passed into the higher world, but it often seemed much longer. I missed her as much as I had the day she died. If I concentrated very hard I could sometimes feel her presence around me. I swear that on some occasions, I could even smell her hair in the soft breezes from the sea. The *Ais* people had raised her to the level of deity after what had happened. The terrible disease had not left the stricken tribe completely, but every person she had personally tended to was now free of it. If I ever questioned the existence of her powers, that experience erased any doubt.

It was late July in the year of our Lord Seventeen-Fifteen; nearly five years to the day since I had washed up on the beach far to the south. Since that time, my life had taken many very strange turns. I had become a larger-than-life outlaw of the high seas with the formidable reputation of wreaking havoc on Spanish efforts to control the east coast. I was feared in all of the northern Spanish settlements, and tales of my conquests had reached mythically exaggerated proportions. The reality of my situation was that I was a man without a home in the civilized world. Shad and his men often sailed to the pirate havens of Jamaica and New Providence to cash in some of the treasure that we had accumulated, but I would never join them. I knew that if the Spanish caught me, I would suffer greatly and be made an "example." I had seen Spanish justice involving pirates in La Habana and was horrified at its brutality.

One memory that stuck in my mind was impossible to forget. A pirate captain had been scheduled to be hung in the square, and it seemed that everyone in the city came to witness it. He was a swarthy, angry man who showed his contempt for his Spanish captors all the way up to the scaffold. He cursed and spat at the crowd, who jeered back at him and threw stones until the soldiers stopped them. When he saw that the hangman had not tied the noose correctly, the pirate berated the man for being a fool. He then snatched the rope away and handily tied a perfect noose, thrusting it back into the hands of the embarrassed and furious hangmen. I remember feeling sick as I watched the poor devil dancing in the air with his face turning purple and his tongue sticking out. I turned and ran from the place, not wanting to see any more. I later learned that his corpse had been enclosed in a steel gibbet and suspended from the *Castille* wall at the mouth of the harbor as a warning to other pirates. It had remained there for two years, and every time I saw it I felt that same queasiness.

I did not consider myself a coward in this respect, but I was not a foolish man, either. The reason I was reluctant to leave the safety of our coastal hideout was that I was now responsible for the safety and well-being of every man and woman there. Unlike the English sailors, I had no strong desire to travel to the rough and tumble ports of the English islands to carouse in their thatch-roofed taverns with drunken, boastful pirates or to lay with women of ill repute. I had no plan for my accumulated wealth, which was indeed staggering. I had spent very little of it over the years, only using it to procure needed supplies brought back by Shad and the others. This was not true for them; I had seen them squander almost everything they had earned over the years. It was true that I was not driven by the same mad lust for money as they were, because I had grown up in a wealthy house and knew that it would not always bring happiness. I suppose that I just wanted to accumulate as much of it as I could with the improbable hope that I would someday be able to live a normal existence.

I had retained the childhood desire to be by myself in the wilderness. I grew to love the unexplored areas around Santa Lucia, becoming intimate with its terrain and hidden treasures. I also became familiar with all of the plants and animals and their individual characteristics.

As for the spoils of my labor, I kept my share well hidden in a small cavern that I had dug into one of the many ancient burial mounds a short distance from camp. I stumbled across this particular mound two years earlier, during one of my wandering excursions. It was easily recognizable because it had a tight cluster of six live oak trees growing from the top of it, creating a canopy of wide branches. The mound was at least eight feet higher than anything else around it. As I was digging my cave into the side of it, I uncovered the skeleton of one of its inhabitants. It struck me as very strange because this warrior had been buried in a sitting up position, and his skull was facing backwards toward the north, as if the man had been decapitated and his head intentionally put on his corpse in this fashion. Caesar had once told me that the *Ais* would sometimes do this to an enemy who had been slain in battle. His head would be placed facing the direction that he had originally come from, as if he should have reconsidered the journey. I knew that this was an excellent place for my treasure because the *Ais* would not come to pay respects to a slain adversary.

As I walked into Santa Lucia, I saw that the men were already making the necessary preparations for the approaching gale by tying the roof supports and reinforcing the walls of the main house. It was the largest building in our place and would have to protect us all when the high winds arrived. Juan, the Spanish carpenter from the *Santiago*, shared his expertise by showing us good ways to anchor the buildings. There was a general feeling of apprehension among us because we could never guess at the intensity of the approaching storm and would be at its mercy. The clouds in the overcast sky were moving faster as the wind gained strength. I moved about the camp assisting the men and women, eventually making my way to the south side where Shad and the other

English sailors were driving long poles into the sand around their shelters.

"Shad," I said, "you and the others will join us in the main house. It is the sturdiest one we have. I have a bad feeling about this storm. All of the conditions are right for a bad one."

He was on his knees pounding on a large stake with a mallet. He paused and looked up at me.

"Cap'n, the men and I will stay in our shelter 'ere. The Spanish men keep to themselves, and we will do the same. We built 'er strong, sir," he said.

I looked over toward the small structure that Captain Suarez and his men had built for themselves. It had the appearance of sturdiness, but unlike Caesars house, it was out in the open without the benefit of surrounding trees.

"Shad, you know that the main building is the strongest. God will protect us if we all stay together.

"I beg to differ, sir, but we'll take our chances 'ere," he said obstinately.

"It's the Africans, isn't it," I said. "You hate them."

"I don't 'ate them, Cap'n. I just don't want to live with them all the time. We can take care of ourselves."

"Do as you wish," I said, my frustration barely concealed. I knew of the underlying tension that existed between the English pirates, the Spanish, and the slaves, and felt helpless to do anything about it. When they were sailing together on the *Pantera* they got along fine because there were so many tasks to be completed. It was when back on land during long periods of inactivity that the animosity grew and festered. It usually began with a disagreement over some insignificant item such as a weapon of some kind, and then grew into a scuffle. The English and Spanish sailors had all been raised with slavery and felt that the Africans were beneath them. I did my best to unite them all, but my efforts were not always successful.

A few hours later, we sat huddled in Caesar's house as the winds came and began to howl through the trees around the camp. Caesar and Abraham were positioned on either side of me as we listened to the groaning of the rafters and wall supports as they were pushed and pulled by the powerful gusts. We were in complete darkness because we had sealed the entrance of the house solidly with long planks. We listened to the repetitive, unintelligible prayers of the African women as they sat in fear with closed eyes and joined hands. The driving rains came next and pelted against the side of the house with such fury that it sounded like the great roar of some wild animal.

"This is very bad," I said in a low voice as the storm progressed. "The gale is stronger than I have ever seen."

"Jes, Captain," Caesar said, "I have seen it dis bad only once before when I was very young. De wind destroyed de *Ais* village completely. Many died dat day."

"Let us pray together," I said. I began to recite the Lord's Prayer. I had taught it to Caesar a few years earlier, and Abraham already knew it, so they both joined in.

I could feel the wall behind me bending and groaning as the howl of the wind reached a feverish pitch. Our prayers were interrupted by a tearing sound and a great crash from outside, as if something had been pulled apart. Something large smashed into the wall, and we all jumped with fear. The wind raged on, and at times I felt the entire house start to vibrate and creak as if it were bending and twisting. We sat in the darkness for many more hours, unable to do anything but listen to the wailing of the wind outside.

Then, as quickly as they had started, the winds abated to almost perfect stillness. We sat for a while, afraid to move. I then climbed to my feet and dusted the sand from my breeches. Caesar grabbed my arm and tried to pull me back down.

"Captain, it is not a good idea to go out now. We are in de center of de storm. Dere is more coming very, very soon."

"I know, Caesar, but I must check on the shelters. They are all we have."

Reluctantly, both of them got up and helped me pull the planks away from the doorway. I looked up at the sky and saw that it was almost yellow in color with small areas of blue sky peering through. The air was unnaturally still and thick with moisture. I was not surprised by the sight before me, but I felt relief that it was not worse. There were palmetto fronds strewn everywhere and I could see many uprooted trees in the surrounding forest. There was a large amount of debris strewn throughout the camp consisting of contents of the smaller storage buildings that had not survived the crushing winds. Both the English and Spanish buildings had survived, but were badly damaged. Part of the roof had torn loose on Shad's house, and the Englishmen were feverishly trying to repair it. Captain Suarez and his men crawled out of their building and were walking around it, inspecting it for damage.

"Men, please listen to me." I said in a pleading voice. "This storm is very bad, and I fear that it is not over. Please let good sense prevail and come into Caesar's house."

"I beg yer pardon, Cap'n, but I believe me and me mates will take our chances 'ere," he said. "We've already survived the first 'alf."

"As you wish," I said. I walked over to Captain Suarez, who was directing his men in repairing a wall that had been torn loose on their small shelter.

"Are you well?" I asked.

"Yes, Captain. I think that it will be all right for us," he answered.

"Captain Suarez, I have been through many storms before and have learned that the second part is often times worse than the first."

"I appreciate your wisdom sir, but I have full faith in Juan, my carpenter. We will be fine. I can't say as much for your English friends. Their house is looking a little rough." he said.

I felt my frustration mounting at the attitudes of both men. I had a very bad feeling about the storm. I went back to the main house and went inside, securing the planks over the door. Less than an hour later the second half of the *huracán* hit with a vengeance. The winds were now going in the opposite direction and seemed to be more furious. As we sat huddled in the dark house, the driving rain pounded against the outer walls with the same roar as before, but with a new intensity not there in the first half. I then heard a tearing, splintering sound from outside and the piercing scream of a man.

"I have to go out!" I screamed at Caesar.

"No Captain! It is madness!" he said.

Ignoring him, I pulled one of the long planks loose from the bottom of the door. I heard the sounds of debris whacking into the side of the building.

"I'll be back! I can't leave them to die!"

I crawled on my belly out into the storm through the small space I had made. The wind was so strong that I felt as if it would carry me away, but I got to my feet and somehow managed to stumble to Shad's shelter. Several palm fronds slapped into me with frightening force, causing me to shout out in pain as I slowly made my way. As I struggled to see the shelter through the driving rain, I realized that it was gone. It had completely vanished, leaving only broken stumps where the support posts had been.

"Shad!" I screamed at the top of my lungs.

I heard a sound that was different from any of the others. It was a low rumbling that seemed to shake the very ground. I turned my head toward the east and screamed in terror at what I saw. I was then hit by a wall of water nearly as high as my head. It came so fast that I had no time to react, so I went head over heels with it. The deluge swept me away from the camp as I struggled to keep my head above its surface. My legs bounced over small trees and roots, and I felt my knee turn painfully as it struck something very hard. I was completely at the mercy of the torrent and flailed around impotently as I was carried further and further away from camp.

"I will die here," was my first thought as I struggled for breath. I had no time for rational thought. "This is how I end."

It was then that I saw the upper half of an oak tree ahead of me with a very thick trunk and wide, spreading branches. If I could only grab one and hold on, I may be able to gain some sort of control. I was approaching it very rapidly and did not have much time to react, so I threw my arm out wildly, grabbing at anything. The current was too fast for me and I failed to see the large trunk of the tree right in front of me. My head smashed into it and everything went black.

CHAPTER 41
AFTERMATH

She smiled at me from across the fire. Her beautiful brown eyes gazed at me, drawing me in completely. The moon was full and the stars were brilliant against the night sky.

"My darling Chera, I have come to you. We can be together forever now!" I said.

Her smile faded, her look turning to one of reproach.

"Santos, it is not your time. You have more to do. You cannot decide when it is your time. The Great Spirit is the only one who can do that."

I felt sadness as I looked at her. Her image began to grow blurry and to transform. I recoiled in horror as Chera was replaced by the thing that I feared most; the face of the native woman of my nightmares. I felt cool wetness around my breeches and shoes and saw that the ground was flooding with fast moving water. Panic suddenly overtook me as the water rose around me, quickly submerging my body all the way to my shoulders. She was still there, laughing at me. Just before I was completely overcome by the rising water, I heard her awful words.

"Santos, I will decide when it is your time, just as I did with your weak father! You are MINE!"

I heard the terrible laughter echoing through my brain.

My eyes opened and I had a terrifying sensation of displacement. It was night time and very dark, and water was dripping on my forehead and into my eyes. My first instinct was to reach up and wipe my face with my hand, but my balance was off, and I soon realized that my body was entangled in a tree; my torso wrapped around the trunk and my legs intertwined with some of the branches. Looking down, I was horrified to see the ground far below me in the moonlight. My senses came back to me and I remembered the storm and the raging water. I shifted my weight and tried to straighten my legs a bit, moving my arms and legs to test the extent of my injuries. Aside from a terrible headache from the blow I had received and a sharp, aching sensation in my right knee, I appeared to be intact. I moved slowly toward the center of the tree and wrapped my arms around the trunk, freeing my legs and pulling myself upward to a more comfortable position. The branch I was on was massive, so I got to my feet and stood on it. I looked down, and all I could see was the dull whiteness of sand in the pale moonlight. I began to climb down slowly, carefully descending from limb to limb. I swung down from the lowest branch and landed on the soft sandy ground with a thud, wincing at the pain in my knee. My tunic was hanging from my body in tatters and my breeches were split and ruined. My boots were still on but filled with water and sand. I sat down on the ground and pulled them off one at a time, turning them upside down to empty them. I was exhausted, so I lay back on the sand and closed my eyes.

I awoke in the gray of the morning dawn. The sun was low in the east, and the coolness of night had not yet surrendered to the beating rays of the sun. Getting to my feet, I tried to ignore the now familiar twinge of pain in my knee. The landscape had changed so much that I did not know where I was. The few trees that had stubbornly withstood the water and wind were bent over as if they had been pounded into submission by some massive force. Looking to the west, I could see the lagoon a short distance away and a small island that I recognized, and I slowly began to get a sense of my location. I found it hard to believe that I could have been carried that far from Santa Lucia. Judging the direction from the position of the sun, I began to slowly limp toward where I thought it might be.

After a short time I heard voices, and soon emerged from the trees into the clearing that held the remains of our camp. I was relieved to see Caesar, Abraham, and several of the others huddled around a small fire, deeply engaged in conversation. Looking around, I was shocked at the extent of the damage to our home. The landscape was entirely altered. The trees had been either torn up by their roots and thrown asunder, or stripped of all their fronds and bent over nearly to the ground. The walls of Caesar's house were still there, but the roof was gone. There was no sign of Shad's house, and the Spaniard's shelter lay in ruins.

"Yo, men!" I called out.

"Captain, you're alive!" Caesar shouted, as they all got up to embrace me.

"Yes, thanks to the branches of a great oak tree," I said.

"The others?" I asked apprehensively.

"No sign of Shad and the other English, except for him," Abraham said, pointing off to one side of the fire. Stormy sat on a stump, his clothes filthy and soaked and his face in his hands.

I noticed Capitan Suarez sitting to my right; a look of exhaustion on his face and his clothes torn and ruined. There was a large bloody bandage on the side of his head, and I could see dried blood on his neck.

"Are you well?" I asked.

"Yes, thank you, Captain Santos. It is a minor wound. The wind was too much for the building. We would have been safe, if not for the water. Benito is missing. This storm must have been sent directly from hell," he said, looking away.

"We heard the terrible screams of the English sailors as they were swept away. It is my belief that they had to leave the shelter before it was destroyed. This is very, very bad."

Our camp was completely decimated. The water had swept away all we had. We spent the rest of the morning gathering broken materials to erect a temporary shelter from the pounding sun, while the women did their best to prepare a meal with the meager supplies that remained. After we had eaten, we organized three search parties to look for survivors and lost property. My group, consisting of George, Matthew and myself, walked to the west, searching every place we could for any sign of injured or lost men.

As we came close to the mouth of a small creek that emptied into the lagoon, I experienced a feeling of dread as I became aware of the familiar smell of death. We were soon greeted with a terrible sight. All around us lay the bodies of animals that had drowned in the deluge, their bodies swept toward the water and deposited where a bottleneck had formed at the creek's narrow outlet. The twisted remains of raccoons, armadillos, and squirrels lay everywhere, their corpses beginning to swell in the morning heat. There were at least a hundred snakes there, their twisted bodies intertwined in clumps. As we stared at the bizarre sight in stunned silence, George heard a soft groan from behind a clump of palmetto roots. Pulling away the top layer, we saw the sand-covered figure of a large man lying there.

"Shad? Is that you?" I asked.

I saw a large arm rise and wipe the sand from his face.

"Cap'n," he said.

The men quickly gathered around and pulled the smallest of the roots away. His body was wrapped around a stubborn sea grape, so George and Matthew each took an arm and pulled him free, dragging him across the sand. He was very heavy, and they grunted with exertion. He had been knocked unconscious during the flood, but miraculously seemed to be uninjured.

"Captain," he said in a quavering voice, "I guess we should 'ave come into your shelter."

For some strange reason we all laughed at this. It was a light moment in an otherwise tragic day. We were not so lucky with the other men. We soon located the twisted remains of our friends, Fly and Benito on the edge of the lagoon among a large stand of mangroves. They had drowned in the deluge, their bodies face down in the water.

"This is terrible," Abraham said as we pulled them from the water. "How could any God be so cruel?"

We brought the bodies back home where we cleaned them up as well as we could. They were then solemnly carried to an area near the stone monument by the river. I chose this place because it was my belief that it was the graveyard of the original European inhabitants of Santa Lucia. Samuel and Simeon dug the graves, and Abraham did a fine job of carving their names into two short pieces of cedar planking. Elias and I drove the markers deep into the soft earth at the head of each of their resting places. Before we covered them, everyone turned to me. I was distraught, but I managed to say a few choking words.

"Here lie two of the finest men I have ever known. They were both searching for a purpose when they came to this wild place, and they understood the dangers of life here. It is my belief that the last days of their lives were spent as free and happy men. They will be sorely missed by all of us. I pray that God will accept them into his kingdom as his children for all eternity."

Shad stepped out from the rest and slowly walked to the side of the grave, holding something behind his back. He dropped to his knees and leaned over the body of his friend. He slowly pulled the small fiddle from behind his back and gently placed it on Fly's shoulder.

"E're you go, mate," he said, his deep voice choked with emotion. "You'll be needin' this where you're goin'. You can play for me any time, and I'll 'ear you."

It was one of the most moving things I have ever witnessed, and my eyes filled with tears. There was a long silence, and we began to somberly fill the graves with sugary sand.

Captain Suarez was crushed at the loss of Benito. The man had been his friend and crew member.

"I failed that poor boy," he said to me, a sad expression of sorrow on his face. "I have made yet another bad decision that has resulted in tragedy. I am considering walking north to St. Augustine to surrender myself and accept my fate."

I found myself getting angry at his words.

"Captain Suarez, you are my friend, but I have to tell you that right now I would like to beat you senseless."

He was taken aback, and stepped away from me as I spoke.

"You once told me that you were one of the most promising young officers in the *armada española*. I know that you have had a degree of bad luck in your career, but you must remember that the events that have befallen us have had a dire effect on all, not just you. When will you realize that your men need you more than ever?"

We both looked around at the pitiful state of our devastated camp. The remaining Spanish sailors were standing in a group by the graves, glancing at us apprehensively and speaking to each other in low voices.

"What of them?" I asked him. "What would Benito say at your thoughts of cowardice?"

I regretted the words as soon as I said them, but I was so disappointed with him that I could not stop. His expression changed, taking on a hard look, and his hand instinctively reached for his scabbard. He then paused as his mind worked. He turned away from me, and walked to a fallen palmetto that lay across the sand, sitting on it and burying his face in his hands. I realized that he was crying. All of his pent up sadness came flooding out with his tears. I sat next to him and placed my hand on his back.

"Captain Suarez, we are men saddled with the monumental task of responsibility for the lives of others. I need you now more than ever. We will survive, and we will see that these men are cared for. I am appealing to the sense of duty to your friends and countrymen that I know still lives inside of you."

He looked at me with red-rimmed eyes. The anger was gone from his face, replaced by an expression of resignation.

"Yes Captain, I am with you," he said in a small voice.

Just as we were throwing the last few shovelfuls over the graves, we heard a man running toward us through the undergrowth. It was Dunkirk, the *Ais* boy, and he had a look of panic on his face. He was out of breath and jabbering unintelligibly in his native tongue.

"What's he saying, Caesar?" I asked.

He tried to calm the frantic boy down, speaking with him for a long time. They frequently pointed toward the east, nodding their heads.

"Captain," Caesar finally said, "he says that we need to come with him now. Something very, very bad has happened!"

What could be worse than the tragedy that had already befallen us?

PART FOUR

SHIPWRECK- 1715

CHAPTER 42
DISASTER IN THE WAVES

Abraham, Caesar and I ran along behind the young *Ais* boy, trying to keep up as he dashed nimbly through the mire of torn and ripped trees and bushes. It was a longer journey than I had anticipated, but I soon heard the familiar roar of the ocean just ahead. The intense rays of the afternoon sun were upon us, so we were drenched in sweat. We paused to rest, and I took a swallow of water from the small leather canteen that hung from my side. After batting hoards of mosquitoes away from our faces, we walked out onto the beach. I shaded my eyes with my hand to cut the glare of the sun, and heard many voices. As my eyes grew accustomed to the brilliance, the sight before me was unbelievable.

There were dozens of people on the beach. They were in various stages of distress and were huddled in groups around what appeared to be injured members of their party. A short distance off shore, the front half of a wrecked ship was visible, her bowsprit jutting up at an awkward angle, the waves pounding her in the short surf. There were soldiers, sailors, women, and even children wandering the beach in a confused and disorganized throng. A feeling of dread came over me as I saw many bodies floating motionless in the surf, drifting in and out with the pounding waves. I knew then that this was a tragedy of epic proportions.

"What in God's name happened here?" Abraham asked.

"Can't you see? The storm has claimed them!" I said.

"We have to help dem," Caesar said.

"Wait!" I said. "Let us not forget who we are!"

There was a moment of silence as we looked at each other.

"Who might we be then?" Abraham asked.

My mind raced for a suitable identity.

"My name is Pedro De Silva and you two are my servants. We were shipwrecked further down the beach, agreed?" I asked.

Caesar nodded his head.

"Pedro De Silva?" Abraham asked with a skeptical look on his broad face.

"He was a childhood friend of mine in La Habana. He won't mind if I borrow his name for a while."

With that, we started out onto the beach.

"Follow me, and don't speak," I said as we walked, "and try to act like slaves!" I hissed, looking back at them.

"We won't have no trouble wid dat, Captain," Caesar said, giving Abraham a smile.

With that, we all walked to a large group of people. Many of them turned to stare at us, especially the women, and shrank away in fear as if we were going to attack them. I didn't understand this, because our clothes were as torn and disheveled as their own, until I thought clearly for a moment and considered our appearance. Here I was, a long haired and bearded vagabond, roaming the beach with two men who were most likely perceived as slaves, one of them a giant. These people had just survived the most harrowing experience of their lives, and were understandably fearful. I was in the lead, so I raised my palms in a gesture of friendship and called out in Spanish.

"*Estamos aquí para ayudar!* Who is the commander here?" I asked.

There was no answer, just a general turning of heads toward the center of the crowd, where a man in uniform lie stretched out on a filthy blanket. He was obviously badly injured, and was being attended to by two other officers. I made my way through the crowd toward him until I was stopped by two soldiers.

"What do you want?" the larger of the two demanded.

"My men and I are here to help. You have many injured here. I am very familiar with this place."

The two soldiers eyed Caesar and Abraham suspiciously.

"Are these your slaves?" The shorter one asked.

"Yes," I said, giving Caesar a quick look, "I have brought them to assist me."

The larger man let out a grunt and turned, walking toward the injured commander. He knelt in the sand and gave him a few words, then got up and walked back.

"*Maestre* Gomez will speak to you. This will be a short conversation because he is exhausted," he said.

The three of us started toward the man, only to be stopped again by the soldiers.

"Only you. Your slaves stay with us. We need manpower to help the wounded," the large soldier said.

Abraham started to protest, but I gave him a sharp look. As if reading my thoughts, he backed down and said nothing. I walked to the officer who had raised himself up to his elbows. He was a man of middle age with a small beard cut around his mouth and with dark hair that stuck out wildly from his head. He was very distraught, and looked to me as if he would break down in tears at any moment. His uniform was in disarray and covered in sand.

"Who are you, sir?" he asked me abruptly.

"My name is Pedro De Silva, sir," I said. "I am a merchant sailor from La Habana. My men and I were shipwrecked further up the beach. We have come to help."

He looked at me suspiciously before speaking.

"As you can see, this is a terrible disaster. The gale was the worst I have ever seen in all my years on the sea. The *Nuestra Las Nieves* is lost there, along with my *Capitan*, General de Echeverz," he said, pointing out at the wrecked ship. "He is drowned with at least a hundred others, and I have been left in command. The damned storm pitched us like a child's toy. I have had men out all day trying to survey the entirety of this disaster. I pray to God in all of his mercy that the other ships got through and will be here soon to assist us."

"I am here to help," I said.

"You have no choice, Señor De Silva. *Madre España* is in need of your service here and you will obey," he said dismissively.

The taller soldier stepped forward. "*Maestre* Gomez needs to rest," he said in a curt voice. I looked around for Abraham and Caesar. There were moans of pain and despair everywhere, and the desperateness of the situation was quickly reaching hysteria. I spotted Caesar tending to a group of injured people who were lying in a row at the top of the beach near the dune line. A helmeted soldier armed with a long pike was standing guard. As I walked toward them, I frantically tried to think of a plan to get them away. I strode directly up to the soldier, doing my best to display a manner of importance and rank.

"Soldier!" I barked. "I need these slaves to find food and fresh water for these poor souls. I will be taking them with me."

"I have orders to keep them here," he said sharply.

He, too, looked exhausted, thirsty, and ready to fall to the ground. I looked at the people he was guarding and noticed a child among them. She was a beautiful young blonde-haired girl who appeared to be semi-conscious, her hysterical mother clutching her tightly. The woman leaned over the girl, crying and stroking her hair, unable to do anything else. I strode to them and fell to my knees by her.

"What can I do to help, señora?" I asked.

"It's the terrible heat!" she said in a pleading voice. "We have no water and she has passed out. It is too much for her! She is only a child!"

I said nothing in response, but pulled my leather canteen from under my shirt and handed it to her.

"This is all I have, but it will help her. You need to get her to some shade from the sun in the trees further back off the beach," I said.

The woman lifted the child's head and helped her to drink.

"Not too much at once, little one," I said, "you may not have water for a while. Make it last," I said in my most reassuring voice.

The child opened her tear filled eyes and looked at me, the water having revived her.

"God bless you señor," her mother said.

I leapt to my feet and strode back to the guard.

"Do I have to summon *Maestre* Gomez, you fool? He is not a patient man right now!" I screamed, doing my best to sound like an insolent Spanish officer.

"No sir," he said, more than a little flustered by my tone. "They are yours."

I gestured impatiently to Caesar and Abraham, who followed me as I strode up the beach. When we were a good distance away from the wreck, Caesar ran up alongside me.

"Captain Santos, why ju pull us away?" he asked. "Dey need our help."

"Can't you see, Caesar, that this is a trap for you?" I said. "There are too many to help them all, and the Spanish bastards see you and Abraham as animals that they can commandeer and work to death. The *alto mando* cares nothing for you," I said, my frustration showing.

"That is a plate galleon back there. It is full of gold and silver from the Caribbean, probably from La Habana. I saw many like it growing up there as a boy. They will want to protect it, and it is my belief that there will be more of them further up the beach. The galleons always travel together for safety against pirate attacks."

"Captain, what does this mean for us?" Abraham asked.

"We must travel most stealthily up the beach and see the extent of this disaster. This may be a very bad day indeed for King Philip."

We made our way north, walking near the top of the beach in case it became necessary to flee inland. There was much more devastation than we could have ever imagined. The further we traveled, the more ships and wreckage we encountered. There were hundreds of people on the beach, both dead and alive, so we did our best, helping everyone we could by doing such things as hastily erecting shelters from drifting pieces of wreckage or pulling victims from the surf. Abraham estimated that there were one thousand to fifteen hundred survivors cast onto that lonely, long stretch of beach in the hottest part of summer, most of them having no provisions whatsoever.

CHAPTER 43
IN THE HANDS OF GOD

The long, blisteringly hot day gradually passed into evening, and we could see the light of several fires ahead of us on the beach, each one glowing in the bluish twilight like sentinels every few hundred yards apart. We stopped by one large blaze where a group of soldiers had gathered. None of them seemed to notice us or care who we were, so we settled in for the night. Many destitute people gravitated toward us and sat as close to the fires warmth as they could for protection against the biting insects that always came out and feasted at the end of the day. Caesar, Abraham and I continued to disguise our true identities and tried to offer any kind of solace or assistance to the newcomers we could.

The soldiers were actually laughing amongst themselves despite the misery surrounding them. I soon discovered why. Sitting right next to me was an officer, who I soon found out was the commander of one of the stricken vessels. He was an older man with short gray hair, and had tired eyes with wide, dark circles under them. He was sitting on a small barrel with several of his men, an onion shaped bottle in one hand that he periodically raised to his lips. As we talked, I learned that his name was *Capitan* Lavioes of the Urca De Lima. He seemed to be more civil and respectful than most of the Spanish officers I had met in the past. His crew had salvaged many cases of wine from the stricken ship's hold and, with nothing else to do, were imbibing to excess. The wine was having its effect, so it was from him that I chose to try and get the truth about what had happened on this dark day.

"Capitan Lavioes," I asked in a nonchalant manner as I absently poked the flames with a stick, "you seem to be a very learned man. What is the news from *Madre España*? I have been away a long time and have heard nothing of the war's progress."

"Señor De Silva, this is the story of what happened as far as I know. I do not know how long you have been at sea, but I fear that Spain has changed for the worst during these many years of war with the *Gran Alianza*. As you may know, the conflict finally came to a close with the signing of the Treaty of Utrecht one year ago. This guaranteed that *Su Majestad Philip* would rule Spain without question, and give up his right to eventually claim the throne of France. England, Austria, and the Dutch no longer have to fear the power imbalance that this would cause, so they have been ordered to stop fighting and sinking our galleons at every opportunity. His Majesty has ordered the treasure *flotillas* from La Habana to resume immediately. The royal coffers are nearly empty because the treasure ships from New Spain have been under siege by English and Dutch pirate bastards."

He paused for a moment to take a long draw from the bottle.

"Tell him about the dowry, Captain," one of his men said with a laugh from the other side of the fire.

"Silence!" Captain Lavioes snarled back at him. "Don't ever disrespect *Su Majestad*!"

I watched as his anger brewed for a moment. He was very intoxicated, so he soon relaxed and continued to speak.

"King Philip lost his Queen, Maria Luisa of Savoy, to consumption just a year ago. This was a crushing blow to him, I fear, because he loved her very much. A new marriage was quickly arranged to the fiery new Queen; Elizabeth Farnese of Parma."

I remembered my father speaking of Queen Luisa affectionately.

"Yes, Captain, I remember the Queen," I said. "I don't mean to be rude, but what do these events have to do with those which what have taken place here?"

His temper flared at this, and I could see the combined effects of the alcohol and fatigue taking its toll on the man.

"Señor De Silva, I assure you that the reason we are sitting on this beach watching my countrymen die is a direct result of the events I am telling you of now, so please do not interrupt me again," he said.

"I apologize, Captain. Please excuse my impudence," I said, lowering my gaze.

"Her highness, Elizabeth, is no lilting flower, be assured of that," Captain Lavioes continued with a sarcastic tone. "She is a ball of fire who will not take no for an answer. It is widely believed that she told His Majesty that the Royal marriage would not be "consummated" until her family received an immense dowry."

I could not believe what I was hearing, and I heard some of the drunken soldiers snicker.

"That is scandalous," I said.

"Yes it is, my friend," he said, then took another long gulp from the wine bottle.

"Two and a half years ago I was commissioned as Capitan of the *Santissima Trindidad* by her owner, Don Miguel De Lima. The old mariners called her the *Urca De Lima*, and she was one of five proud ships of the *Plata Flotilla*. All of us were under the command of *Capitán General* Don Juan Esteban de Ubilla of His Excellency's naval force, a very capable and honorable man. All of the ships met in Vera Cruz, and we all anticipated a quick and safe journey home. We soon discovered that we had to wait for overland shipments of silver, gold, from Peru and china, silks, and spices from the Orient to arrive. This was all being carried over the mountains on mules from el Puerto de Acapulco to the trade vessels waiting at Veracruz, so the wait was long and agonizing. To make things even worse, there were many shipments from the mint in Ciudad de México that came trailing in at the last minute.

After months of waiting, we were finally able to depart, at long last sailing to el puerto de La Habana. When we arrived, we found another fleet of galleons awaiting our arrival to accompany us on the long journey home. These were the six ships of the *Squadron de Terra Firma* fleet under the command of *Capitán General* Don Antonio de Echeverz y Zubiza. The ships had recently arrived from Cartagena, and their men were as impatient as we were to depart.

Both Capitáns were very anxious to get underway because of the lateness of the season, but there proved to be even more delays. Private investors had left mountains of cargo on the docks of puerto de La Habana for us to load into our already full holds for the trip back to the mother country. There was also a French vessel, the *Grifon*, which El Gobernar de La Habana commissioned to sail with us for protection against pirates. This was against the wishes the Admirals of both fleets who vehemently protested. This dispute cost us even more time as the month of July rapidly flew by.

Capitán General Ubilla was apprehensive of the danger of Atlantic storms in the summer season, but he was also anxious to get underway. We were already months behind when we learned of the addition of the Queen's dowry, which had not even arrived at La Habana. This was a maddening hindrance that, in the end may have proved to be our undoing. I am not exactly sure, but I heard that this treasure consisted of an unimaginable collection of pearls, emeralds, and gold packed in several sturdy chests. When it finally arrived, it was stored in Capitán General Ubilla's personal cabin. It was only six days ago that we were finally able to start our journey toward the homeland after a wait of nearly twenty months."

"Yes, I know La Habana well! I grew up under its shadow," I said a little too eagerly. "I used to watch the soldiers load the treasure ships as a boy."

This was the first news I had heard from my former home and I was ravenous to hear all of it. The Capitan paused and stared into the fire, shaking his head slowly before continuing. He began to speak again, completely lost in his story.

"We were a majestic, invincible armada; a true symbol of Spain's power and wealth moving slowly northward toward the straits of La Florida along the Nuevo Canal de Bahamas. I knew that we had overburdened the *Urca De Lima* so completely that her load lines were submerged, but the weather was fair and the spirits of the men so high that I believed providence was with us. We made good headway at a slow, but steady, six knots on a careful course that our navigators had pre-planned to avoid any hazards. They all took pains to keep us on a roundabout route, sailing slightly east past Punto Ycaco, then north past Cayo Sal, Hombre muerto Clave, and then back west-northwest across to Cayo Tavona. We now had to turn north to start the demanding task of tacking our way through the El Estrecho de la Florida. The first three days were heavenly, and we made great headway. It seemed as though we were headed for successful accomplishment of our mission.

On Tuesday at about mid-day, the wind suddenly died down to almost nothing. The sweltering heat was nearly unbearable in the still air. I looked up at the high, thin clouds off the starboard bow and sensed that something was different, but I couldn't place what it was. It then dawned on me that the sea birds that usually lined our rigging were gone. The silence that was left without their chattering and squawking was unnerving and strange to me. The seas were calm, but there was a low, heavy swell coming in from the southeast that grew more pronounced as the day passed.

As night fell, a thin haze began to move in, making visibility poor. Capitán General Ubilla's ship, the *Regla*, signaled to us to light all of the lanterns so that all of the ships could stay in sight of each other. I remember their soft glow in the distance, barely visible as they rose and fell through the milky vale of fog like ghostly spirits in the night. Tension seemed to grow among the crew as the old seamen and mariners started to mutter about aches and pains caused by impending weather. There was an overall feeling of dread, and the night was very long and sleepless for all of us.

The next day proved no better, with the haze thicker yet, and the swells growing higher and even more pronounced. I heard great sliding crashes from below decks as the weight of packing crates shifted, so I sent some sailors down to tie off and secure them. I then ordered all of the hatches to be closed and locked down, and all sails shortened and reefed in preparation of a blow. It was so dark that we were forced to light all of the lanterns in the early afternoon. We then anxiously waited for night to fall. My crew tried to urge the *Urca* on faster, but she was doing all she could in the erratic wind. As soon as darkness fell, the wind started to blow at about forty knots, and we began to pitch violently. The driving rains started, drenching everything on deck, and we soon had trouble spotting the other ships through the darkness. We held on and tried to maintain our course, but the wind and rain worsened, making navigation impossible as we lost sight of the shoreline.

There was general panic on board as the priests started to wail out prayers that could barely be heard over the constant roar of the intensifying gale. The wind soon reached what must have been seventy-five knots and the colossal waves increased to twenty feet or better. Then, the worst of my fears were realized."

There was silence as all of the men sat spellbound by the man's story. He paused, and gazed up at the night sky, for a moment lost in his own thoughts. After a short time, he continued.

"I looked up as the main mast splintered and bent to a bizarre angle, the rigging growing slack and becoming entangled into a great mess. All we could do was hold on for dear life and pray to God for our safe deliverance. I watched in horror as many of my men were swept overboard as the giant waves surged over the railings, engulfing everything in their path. I will never forget their screams as long as I live."

The Capitan paused again, and no one made a sound. The images that he brought up were so painful that there was nothing to say. I saw that there were tears streaming down his wind-burned face.

"Below decks, the men tried to pump the water out as it came in. This effort proved futile because of the huge volume pouring in from the deck. We were forcibly turned dead west and driven toward this godforsaken shoreline, and I knew that we were done for. As God's luck would have it, we found ourselves in a small inlet with outcroppings of rock on each side. My men were able to keep us upright as the hull slid into its shallow sand, and we frantically dropped anchor. We sat there for hours, unable to do anything but wait, as the storm relentlessly pounded us. Finally, the fiercest winds began to abate and the men began to cheer for the Lord's mercy on our souls.

Our main mast was snapped off and hanging over the side, held only by a few splinters and the tangled rigging, but the *Urca De Lima* was intact. There were two small skiffs on board that we hurriedly used to get some of the crew to the northern shore. We were in the process of getting as many survivors over when the second half of the storm hit us with a vengeance. We realized that the weather's abrupt calmness was only the hurricane's eye. Scrambling into the ruined ship, we huddled inside as the howling wind pushed us against the rocks with great force. Then the most terrible thing happened; our broken mast that was still hanging from the ship became jammed between the *Urca's* hull and the rocks. The screaming wind and waves continued to push us, and the mast acted as a lever, breaching the hull at the point of contact. The whining shriek of the splintering wood caused everyone on board to panic, so many people jumped off the deck, trying to swim ashore in a desperate attempt to escape as the ship lurched and began to sink. Thirty-five souls drowned in the roaring mayhem of the hurricane and the *Urca* sunk where she was stuck, with only portions of her deck left visible above the waterline."

"Captain Lavioes, I am very sorry for the misfortune that has befallen you," I said. "Remember that God has a reason for everything. He often grants us deliverance if we have faith."

He smiled weakly at this and looked away. "What about them?" he asked, as he turned his gaze toward the sea. "I only hope that he has mercy on these people, because these wild beaches of La Florida will not. The people have no food or water, and their ears have been filled with endless tales of hostile cannibals that inhabit these shores."

As he said these words, I thought of the *Ais*, and wondered how they would react to this disaster.

CHAPTER 44
<u>GHOSTS OF THE SEA</u>

I awoke to the sight of millions of stars spattered across the dark blueness of the sky, and the gentle roar of the waves as they lapped onto the beach in their never ending rhythm. The salty heaviness of the ocean's scent came to me, and the sand was cool and damp against my skin. I turned my head to look for Caesar and Abraham, and saw only a vast expanse of empty beach. Startled, I quickly looked back to the south and found the same desolate sight. Gone were both of my friends, the hundreds of people, the wreckage, the burning fires, and the screams of the wounded and dying.

I was alone. I got to my feet and aimlessly walked a few yards in each direction, feeling totally bewildered.

Where was everyone?

In the distance I saw a stand of palmettos on the horizon, their trunks leaning toward the sea and their fronds bouncing lazily in the mild gusts of wind. I looked out into the dark blue of the ocean, and could barely make out the white crests of breaking waves. I thought it very strange that there were no sea birds diving into the short surf or noisily carousing on the beach. I began walking slowly north. I had gone only a short distance when I heard a strange sound on the very cusp of the gentle ocean breeze.

Could it have been a voice?

I cocked my head toward the ocean and tried to detect the faint sound again. It was definitely there, and I realized that it was the whispery moan of a woman or child. Straining my eyes to see its source, I at first saw nothing. Then, a short distance out from shore, I glimpsed a shadowy form that was barely discernible in the darkness. I stared at it intently, and soon noticed a soft, pale light surrounding it. It was gauzy in appearance, like a bank of sea mist, and I realized that it was slowly moving toward me. I blinked my eyes because the image made no sense to me. Could it be...floating across the surface of the water? I felt a cold fear, as if someone had poured cool water over my head and stood completely still, afraid to move. I then saw another shape to the right of it, then another to the left.

What in hell was going on?

The noises in my ears grew louder and became more jumbled as more ghostly figures appeared. My fear transformed to terror as the strange words took form and became vaguely recognizable to me. It was my name they were calling.

"Santos."

I heard the name like a delicate murmur from the wind itself.

I could now see many forms on the water; hundreds it seemed, and they were now moving slowly toward me, gliding across the waves as if carried by some unseen force. I began to panic and backed up, wildly turning my head in both directions, in search of an avenue of escape. My eyes met more shapes on the beach itself. I was soon surrounded by the apparitions, and I stood frozen in horror, a soundless scream on my lips. As they drew even closer to me, I could make out definite features on the shadowy forms, and I nearly fainted from fright at what I was seeing. They were people, or what was left of them, moving toward me on that lonely beach. I could see the ghastly spirits of men, women, and even children bathed in that unnatural pale light; their features calm and knowing as they gazed at me with dead black eyes that had no pupils. They were wearing the same rumpled, torn clothes that they had perished in, and appeared to be soaking wet. Many of these ghouls were covered in seaweed, and some were dragging broken and twisted limbs behind them as they slowly moved toward me across the sand.

"Santos," they whispered with no movement from their lips, as if they were sending the message from inside themselves.

Then I saw her. Her body was bathed in that same eerie, greenish light that shone out in all directions. She moved toward me across that

lonely expanse of beach in that terrifyingly slow, unnatural way, her
loose clothes waving and pulsating out in all directions. Her hands
shifted through the air, back and forth with slow, graceful movements,
and the shrouds of her ancient dress hung down like moss from an oak
tree. The shapeless forms on the water slowly drifted into the area
behind her, forming a terrible legion of phantoms from a nightmare. As
the woman moved closer, I could see the expression of mocking
triumph, and I knew that she was pleased with the death and
devastation that had so recently occurred on that beach. A seething
anger that I had never felt before rose in me, and I began to tremble,
pointing an accusatory finger at her terrible form.

"You devil witch!" I shrieked at the top of my lungs. "I will see
you back to hell where you belong!

She tilted her head and began to howl with horrifying laughter.

Abraham shook me violently, his massive hands on my
shoulders.

"Captain, Wake up!"

I looked up to see his worried face in the early morning
grayness.

"Wha, what's wrong?" I asked.

"You were screaming, Captain, in your sleep!"

I turned away from him and got to my feet, nearly
stumbling on the sandy embankment on which we had made
camp.

"I. . I'm fine, Abraham. It seems like good weather this
morning," I stammered, doing my best to feign normalcy.

"Ju worry me, Captain," Caesar said from his blanket a
few feet away. "Dem demons got ju."

Despite the terrible nightmare, my stomach growled with hunger. We had gathered our food along the way in the hammocks along the coast. Our meals consisted of sea grapes and hearts of saw palmetto, acorns from the live oak trees, and small animals that Caesar trapped with his clever snares. We had found this place on some high ground the night before. It was a safe distance from the tide line, and the thick sea grape trees afforded some protection against the elements. The last two days had been a long tour through the death and devastation of many shipwrecks, and the experience had taken its toll on us. We were exhausted and depressed from witnessing so much suffering. After eating a meal of roasted squirrel, we continued our progress up the beach.

We were anxious to get back to camp to start dealing with our own losses, but felt that it was important to see the full extent of the treasure ship disaster. Stretched out before us were what remained of the once mighty, proud ships; now trapped in the surf like mortally wounded animals trying to make it to shore. As we strode along, we talked about the millions of gold and silver pieces that were now scattered across the ocean floor just beyond the shoreline. The Captain of the *Urca De Lima* had said that all of the treasures of *Nueva España* were on those ships. There was enough booty there to make any man fantastically rich for the rest of his days. This subject helped us to pass the hours as we talked of what we would do with such wealth.

As midday approached, I spotted something far ahead, and could soon make out the shapes of people on the beach. All of us fell silent, each knowing that we would soon be witnessing more carnage. We then came upon a cluster of makeshift shelters that looked like a strange little village. These were the crude dwellings of destitute souls who had been unwillingly deposited in a lonely, savage place during the most inhospitable season of the year. As we made our way between them, the moans and wails of the injured and dying filled our ears. A few provisions had been salvaged, but the people were near total desperation. Many of the more pale-skinned men and women were already suffering from the effects of sunburn, and bore large crimson patches of skin on their bare shoulders and faces. Fresh water was incredibly scarce, and many people were showing the symptoms of extreme thirst, especially the children. There were more than a few that had survived the storm and all of its ravages, only to die from exposure to the elements. They huddled in small groups under pieces of wreckage and flotsam as if waiting to be rescued at any moment; an event that I knew would take a very long time indeed. As we sat down to rest, a woman ran up to us with an expression of grinning, sunburned madness, her wild red hair flying in all directions, and asked us when the next ship out would be leaving. I took her arm and led her to the shade of a huge gumbo limbo just past the dune line and gently reassured her that rescue would be imminent. I knew that she would most likely not make it through the night.

A short time later, Abraham touched my shoulder and pointed to a man crouched down near the water line, directly in front of a wrecked ship that was on her side, the waves bathing her deck. He appeared to be running his fingers through the sand as if searching for a lost item, and I saw him pick something up and stuff it into his pocket. We walked over and stood around him in a circle. He seemed oblivious to us and continued his work without looking up.

"What are you doing, señor?" I asked.

"Mind your business and leave me alone," he said in a gruff voice.

One of the objects fell from his pocket onto the sand. It was a large silver coin with irregular edges that I instantly recognized as a Spanish reale.

"Profiting from disaster?" I asked sarcastically.

"These are mine. I found them here in the sand," he said.

"The soldiers may not agree with you," I said.

The man looked up at me in anger, and then jumped to his feet, striding off toward the others. I looked at Caesar with a knowing look, my gaze then trailing off toward the waves that were rolling in.

"These waves will be full of treasure, you know."

They both shook their heads in agreement. We all looked up at the sound of sporadic splashes and commotion in the water around the wreck. There was a large swirl on the surface, and I saw a sleek, black fin slowly descend below the waves.

"What is that?" Abraham asked.

"Dat is not de only ting the ocean is full of," Caesar said in a soft voice. "Dey are cleaning the sea of the *Es-pa-no* dead."

I will never forget the sight of those menacing fins cutting through the surface of the water as long as I live.

CHAPTER 45
SALVAGE CAMP

We walked for many miles in the blazing hot sun, encountering hundreds more desperate survivors along the way. As we passed, we had the opportunity to witness both the best and the worst qualities of mankind and the ways they reacted to the direst of circumstances. There were the reserved, silent types, both men and women, who simply put themselves to work with thin-lipped resolve and determination by constructing shelters, digging holes in the high dune line in search of fresh water, helping the sick and wounded, or tending to the children and elderly. Then there were the weak, sitting idly by and wallowing in their own misery, crying out to us for help that was simply not there, or wailing out of resigned apathy. It was my own opinion that the latter type would not survive long here on the beach. There was a third kind that was the worst of all. These were the men and women who, so intent in their goal of self-preservation, would stop at nothing to protect their own interests. We experienced one of these that same afternoon.

Near one of the wrecks we saw two young women sitting huddled together, wrapped in a torn piece of sail cloth that was their only protection against the relentless sun. They were sharing a small loaf of bread that they had received from a recently salvaged food chest. As we passed, they smiled and said hello. This bright greeting took me so off guard that I stopped and looked at their young faces. One of them was a very pretty girl of mixed race with green eyes and olive skin, and the other a fair-haired beauty with large blue eyes who was obviously suffering from sunburn. I saw that her face and shoulders were crimson, but she smiled at me despite her obvious discomfort.

"Is there anything we can do for you, señoritas?" I asked.

"No, señor," the dark skinned girl said. "There are many people who need more help than us. We are just happy to be alive."

"Ah, señorita, you have discovered the secret to dealing with misery; even during a tragedy of this horrendous scale."

"Yes, we are praying together for deliverance, and the Lord will grant it," the darker girl said as she squeezed her companion's shoulder reassuringly.

"Well, *buena suerte*, ladies. Please be careful," I said.

"Gracias, señors," they said. "We will make due until the rescue ships come."

"I wish they all were so strong and brave as those girls," I told Caesar as we walked away.

For a brief moment, I saw in them the same compassion that had always been part of my darling Chera, and I once again felt the pang of loss.

From behind us came a scream, and I whirled around to see what it was. A tall, broad shouldered man with long, gray hair and dressed in the torn remains of fine clothing was involved in a struggle with the two girls. I saw him snatch the small loaf of bread from them and abruptly stride away up toward the dune line despite their crying protests. As if on cue, Abraham took off like a shot toward the man, covering the distance between them in a matter of seconds. Lowering his shoulder, he slammed into the man's side with his full body weight, sending him sprawling across the beach. The man looked up, his sand covered face red in pain and astonishment.

"You stupid animal! I'll kill you for your insolence!" he stammered as he got to his feet, wincing with pain. I could see that he was reaching toward a leather scabbard strapped to his belt, so I ran as fast as I could to Abraham's side.

"Is this how a man acts?" I said to him in a firm voice, "robbing innocent girls of their bread?

"Is this how a man controls his slaves?" he shouted, an insolent sneer on his face. "Do you know who I am? I'll have you flogged and your feral slave here hobbled."

"I don't know you, but I assure you that I can see the kind of man you are. You'll hand over the bread now or I'll have Abraham here throw you to the sharks."

"If ju pull dat knife on your side, mon, ju best be ready to use it," Caesar chimed in, a smile on his bearded face.

The man looked at me and hesitated for a moment, turning his attention first to Caesar, then to Abraham, who was an intimidating sight to behold. The giant stared at him with an angry stare, his face clouded with rage. He opened and closed his large hands in readiness, his huge, rippling muscles taut as a ship's rigging. He breathed steadily, as if waiting to strike, and you could almost hear him growling, as if he were a great lion waiting to make a kill.

The man seemed to consider the odds, and soon enough his sense of reason prevailed. His expression turned to one of disgusted resignation and he hurled the bread at us, immediately turning to stride off across the sand. I bent to picked it up from the ground, brushing the sand from it with my fingers. I handed it to my giant friend and smiled.

"All right, sir. It's obvious that chivalry is not dead, so take your spoils of battle to the maiden."

Abraham looked at me, the anger slowly melting from his face.

"I'm sorry Captain, but I cannot tolerate that sort of thing. I was very poor when I was young, and grew to hate the aristocrats. I'm afraid I've used bad judgment here."

I laughed at this. "I don't think that you are the one failing to use prudence in decision-making," I said, looking off after the man.

The three of us walked to the young girls, who were now standing up. The dark skinned girl smiled widely and reached her hand out to Abraham. He took it and looked down, avoiding her direct gaze.

"You are a brave man sir," she said in a voice that was almost playful. "My giant knight in armor! This is Gabriela Juarez of Trinidad, and I am her servant, Adelena."

"I, I am. . Abraham," my normally eloquent friend stammered.

Both girls looked at each other and giggled at this as Abraham nearly shrank with embarrassment.

"My name is Pedro De Silva and these are my servants. Which of the ships were you on?" I asked.

"We were on the *Almirante*," Gabriela said. There was a pause, and her demeanor changed to one of sadness, her eyes filling with tears at the terrible memory.

"My family lives in a small village on the south side of Cuba. My father ordered that I go to the mother country to be married. Adelena is my servant and companion, and Rafael. ." she trailed off and began to sob uncontrollably.

Adelena spoke up. "Rafael is the soldier to whom our care was entrusted by Gabriela's father. When the storm hit with its full fury, he put us on one of the only small boats on board and pushed us off toward shore in the blinding rain. We had to watch as the ship then hit the rocks and disintegrated. We never saw brave Rafael after that. He saved our lives."

Both girls were crying, the despair that they had been concealing now rising to the surface. Adelena suddenly fell into Abrahams arms, sobbing with deep breaths. Completely embarrassed by the girl's forwardness and not knowing what else to do, he stood there like a statue as the girl let out all of her fear and sadness. After a few minutes had passed, I spoke up.

"Gabriela, have you heard of any other places where you might be able to go?"

"There is talk from some of the men that there is a camp to the north where there are many soldiers," she said.

"You girls will come with us now so we can protect you. There are bad men here who are showing their true colors. We will deliver you to a safer place," I said.

We turned to resume our journey up the beach. The girls looked at us as if unsure, then joined hands and fell in behind us. As we walked, Caesar moved closer to me and spoke in a low voice so they could not hear.

"We must be careful, Captain. Many *Es-pan-no* know of us to de north. We may be recognized if dere are a lot of soldiers in one place."

"Yes, Caesar, that is good advice. Why don't you go ahead and scout this camp from the trees," I said. As the sun started to set, we found a comfortable place to light a fire and rest. The mosquitoes had come out and were swarming around our heads, so I threw some saw grass on the fire to make more smoke. The girls were miserable, so I covered them up from head to toe with the sail cloth to afford them some relief. After some time they fell asleep. It grew very quiet, with only the sound of the waves gently breaking on the shore, as Abraham and I sat staring into the flames.

Suddenly, Caesar emerged from the brush covered with sweat.

"Welcome back, my friend," I said. "What did you see?" He sat next to me by the fire.

"Captain, de girl was correct. De Spaniards make camp to de north. Dere are many of dem and dey are already trying to get de shine from de water wid dere boats. We must be careful," he said.

"Hmm," I said, stroking my beard, "I'll go with you tomorrow to have a look."

The next morning, Caesar and I were crouched in the tall sea grass just to the south of a large makeshift camp. It had been roughly constructed on a raised section of land that was very narrow, with the river on one side and the ocean on the other. Caesar gave me his small spyglass to help me see what was going on. I placed it to my eye and observed the activity in the camp. As he had said, there were many soldiers there as well as women and a few children. They were in the process of erecting walls from scraps of lumber salvaged from the wrecks as a protective barrier. I spotted a few tall *Ais* men there carrying crates and performing menial tasks.

"Caesar, I doubt that they are there by choice," I said in a low voice.

"Captain, ju know dat some of de *Ais* are friendly wid dem," he said.

I continued to look through the small glass until my eyes fell on a figure that looked out of place. It was a woman, but there was something different about her. She wearing a dirty white dress, and I could see that she had very dark hair. I couldn't place it, but I felt an odd familiarity in her movements.

"Caesar," I said, "I want to go in there."

"Captain, are ju sure?" he asked, unable to disguise the worry in his voice.

"Yes, I am. Remember that this is our place. We have the advantage."

He rolled his eyes at me in frustration as I got to my feet and started toward the camp.

I walked briskly through the crudely built gate, acting as though I was supposed to be there. There was so much bustle and activity going on that I was barely noticed by the large throng of soldiers and sailors that were working doggedly in the sun. The men wore remnants of their uniforms, many of them wearing rags tied around their heads to keep the sweat from running into their eyes. I saw that there were several large crates stacked in the center of the camp and assumed that they were full of salvaged items from the wrecks.

There was a commotion on the far side of the camp. I saw a small boy with a rope in one hand struggling with a medium size boar that was nearly pulling him to the ground. He shouted for help and was soon assisted by a tall *Ais* man clad only in his woven waist garment and long necklace. Together they tied the struggling pig to a stout palmetto tree. The cooking fire had been lit, and there was an older woman stirring the contents of large steel cauldron with a long stick. I looked around for the woman in the white dress, but she was nowhere in sight.

"You there," came a rough voice from behind me. I turned to see an older man dressed in a worn uniform walking toward me across the cleared ground.

"Where do you come from? What is your business here?" he demanded.

"My name is Pedro De Silva. My small vessel was wrecked in the storm. I am here to offer help and maybe procure some food."

The man laughed sarcastically when I said this. "You and everyone else here, *mi amigo*."

He looked at me suspiciously. "I have been all the way down the beach here on my damage assessment, señor, and I do not remember seeing you or your ship."

"I fear that it was destroyed completely sir. I come here out of a sense of duty for *Su Majestad* and the Spanish Crown," I said.

At the far side of the camp, I saw the woman walk from the trees into the open. I could see her clearly now, and was overwhelmed with a flood of shock and recognition. I grew dizzy and nearly passed out as the blood instantly drained from my face.

The woman was none other than my lost love, Dorathea. She met my gaze, and her eyes grew wide with surprise. Everything stopped for me. It was as if that moment were suspended in time. She was older, and her dress was covered with the dirt of survival, but she was still more beautiful than I remembered.

I was then aware of a shout from behind me that seemed as if it had come from some other world.

"It is Santos Alvarez! There is a pirate among us!"

CHAPTER 46
SPANISH JUSTICE

I felt a wave of panic and looked around wildly for some means of escape, but before I could react I was grabbed by strong arms and thrown to the ground. There was a shocking sensation of pain and loss of breath as a leather-booted foot delivered a crushing blow to my ribs. A man walloped me in the face, the surprising sting of pain igniting bright lights in my head. Everything became lost in a blur and I found myself completely disoriented. I heard the simultaneous cries of men shouting as I was lifted up by the shoulders and dragged to an area to the north end of the camp. My hands were tied behind my back and I was blindfolded. Several men screamed oaths and names of all kinds at me, and then dealt me a vicious beating with countless blows to my head and body. The only thought I had before I lost consciousness was the hope that Caesar and Abraham were safe.

I awoke sometime later to the cold splash of water on my face. It was night and I could see the glow of fires through the wet cloth, but my eyes were so puffed and swollen that nothing was clear. I noticed that my hands were now free, so they instinctively rose to my neck in search of my amulet. My heart sank as I realized that it was missing.

"Santos Alvarez. What a surprise."

The voice sounded vaguely familiar, but I could not place it, nor did I care.

"Do you remember me? My name is Allejandro," the voice said.

Then it came to me. This was Allejandro Ruiz from my childhood back in La Habana.

"Allejandro," I said in a weak voice, "How are you?"

"Ahh, you remember me, Santos. Do you remember everything?" he said.

Then I remembered.

"Dorathea. Is she here?" I asked hopefully.

"Santos, such things do not matter anymore. You will not have to worry about them," he said.

"Allejandro, I can explain everything," I said.

"Well, I hope so, because you will have to convince the hangman tomorrow. You are famous, you know?"

"What are you saying, Allejandro."

"You are a famous pirate, sir, just like you always wanted to be when we were children in the schoolyard. They talk about you all the time like you are some kind of devil. They say you only prey on Spanish ships and that you hate your own people with a passion. They also say that you torture your prisoners and turn them over to the cannibals. A great tale, isn't it?" he said.

I let out a sad laugh. "And you believe all of that?"

"Who am I to argue?" he said.

There was a pause as we both contemplated the situation we were in after all those years had passed.

"You know, Santos, I was not surprised by the stories that I heard about you," he said.

"What do you mean?" I asked.

"My father never liked your father. He used to say that Reinaldo Alvarez was an arrogant man who only cared for himself. I always knew that your family was made up of traitors at heart."

I fell silent at these words. I had not seen his face yet, but I could remember the cold, mean-spirited eyes of his youth. I knew that things never really changed with some people, and that he was trying to goad me into a fight. I felt anger rising uncontrollably and knew that I had to contain it. I tried to change the subject.

"Dorathea. Is she here?" I stubbornly asked again.

"Ah yes, Dorathea," he said. "After you left she was so sad. I felt that it was my duty to restore her happiness, so we have made a wonderful couple since. We are set to be married, you know, when we get to Spain."

"I want to talk to her," I said.

"I'm afraid not, Santos. She does not consort with scum like you who prey on their own kind."

I could control my anger no longer.

"Allejandro, you and I will meet again," I said with a low, trembling voice.

He then kicked me hard in the ribs, the pain making me feel nauseous. I heard him stride away through the saw grass, leaving me to my own misery.

Hours passed and I drifted off, hearing men snoring in the distance and the loud night-time chorus of the cicadas in the trees. I shifted slightly and felt the dull ache of my bruised ribs. There were tiny insects biting the exposed skin on my face, so I tried to lift my shoulder to rub my cheek on my filthy shirt. It was no use, so I gave up and slumped back down against the rough surface of the palmetto tree. I heard a sound, very faint, to my right.

"Santos? Is it really you?" whispered a female voice, one that I instantly recognized.

"Dorry. I knew you would come," I said, my voice reflecting the relief I felt.

"Please keep your voice down as low as you can! I am taking a great risk coming here!" she said in that same hoarse whisper.

"I, I don't know what to say," she stammered. "I had to see if it was really you."

"Dorry, I have so much to tell you," I said.

"Why did you leave me?" she said.

"I was kidnapped by pirates that very night, Dorry, you have to believe me," I pleaded.

"Allejandro saw you that night, Santos," she said in a voice that was mildly accusatory.

"What did he tell you, Dorry?" I demanded.

"He said that he witnessed you dealing with the escaped pirates, and that you willingly joined them."

"And you believed that nonsense?" I said incredulously.

"What else was there to believe?" she said. "You were gone."

"Allejandro is a liar and a fraud," I said.

"Don't say that, Santos! He has been very good to me," she said.

"And you are going to marry him," I said, finishing her sentence for her.

"How did you know that?" she asked.

"Because he was here, taunting me about it right before he kicked me. He is still a stinking coward."

"I have heard enough," she said. "I know that you joined the pirates because Miguel Mejia not only saw you, but was attacked and beaten."

I remembered the thin faced man whom I knocked to the floor of Brattock's burning ship.

"Yes, I did hit him. The ferret deserved it, Dorry," I said.

"You have no right to speak like that. I am leaving now," she said.

"Dorry," I said, "Wait. I have one more thing to say."

I heard her pause at this, saying nothing.

"I am so happy that you survived this great disaster. God was smiling on us," I said.

She turned and walked away, and I heard sobbing.

The next morning, there was a great bustle of activity all around me as men continued to build the crude walls of the camp. I was no longer the center of attention, so they left me alone for the time being. The sun was blazing and I was very thirsty, but I did not cry out. After a few hours had passed, I heard the sound of men in front of me.

"Ho, pirate, what have you to say for yourself?" a man with a gruff voice asked.

"I am innocent of these accusations," I said, my voice cracking from thirst.

"Lift him to his feet," the man said. I was pulled roughly to a standing position.

The rag that covered my eyes was snatched from my face, the sun's rays blinding me and causing me to wince and groan with pain. I slowly peered up and caught a glimpse of my captors. The man who spoke first was a large soldier with a filthy, bearded face. I looked around and saw that all of the men were very rough in appearance. They stank of sweat and had pinched, angry looks on their faces.

"Hang him now. Let's be done with him," one man said.

"No. I have orders from *Capitan General* Salmon that he will be used as a slave to work the salvage boats. We need every man we can get to retrieve the King's treasure. When he is of no use to us any more, then we will hang him."

CHAPTER 47
TREASURE UNDER THE SEA

It was the hottest time of year, and the warm breeze blew
in stiffly from the sea, often bringing rain storms in the latter
part of the afternoon. Many days had passed in the miserable
camp, during which I was treated like a caged animal. I only
saw glimpses of Dorathea as she busied herself with various
tasks around the shelters. She was careful not to meet my
eyes, and I began to believe that she had truly become a
stranger to me. The man in charge was *Capitán General* Salmon,
who had taken it upon himself to act as the personal *enlace* of
the Royal Governor of St. Augustine and the Spanish crown.
Within a short time of the disaster, he had organized the
soldiers to build a crude barricade around the makeshift fort,
and had sent the pilot and navigator north by canoe to St.
Augustine for provisions and assistance. The *Capitán* was an
older man, with long gray hair tied back on his head and a
small, well-manicured beard that grew to his chest. He was
strong, despite his advanced years, and had maintained the
physique of a much younger man. A strict disciplinarian, he
tolerated no thievery or bad conduct of any kind. He had an
explosive temper, and I saw him berate a good many men for
minor infractions, even striking them on occasion.

I witnessed the worsening conditions of the camp with
each passing day. Scores of people perished from thirst or
exposure, while many died of any number of unknown
maladies or afflictions. More ravaged survivors drifted into the
camp daily from the south every day, each attempting to enter
the overcrowded ground inside of the palmetto log barrier,
only to be turned away by the soldiers. The entire area around

the camp became littered with haphazardly built shelters and people in various stages of suffering with nothing to do but wait for rescue. The mosquitoes and other small, biting insects were, at times, so unbearable that men would bury their wives and children up to their necks in the sand so they could sleep in peace. The roughly hewn crosses along the high dune line marking hastily dug graves were terrible reminders of what was to come for many of them.

I was held in a crude stockade that had been built from thin logs in the southwestern corner of the camp, and was constantly under the scrutiny of Salmon and his guards. There were a few *Ais* men who lumbered about the place who toiled at different tasks, all prisoners of the Spanish. They were the tallest people there, towering almost a foot above the diminutive soldiers. I often caught them staring at me. I knew that they recognized me as someone possessing divine powers, and probably expected me to burst free of my bonds and kill every Spaniard there. I owed this reputation to my beloved Chera, whom they looked at as a Goddess, and whose passing they still mourned. They feared me, but they were even more fearful of the iron hand of the Spanish. Their people had been brutalized by these men for nearly two centuries, and their docile servitude to them was a contradiction that I never quite understood.

The men and I were forced to dig several deep wells in an attempt to hit fresh water below, and actually experienced some success, even though the water was sandy and brown and had to be filtered several times through large pieces of rough cloth. Luckily, it was the rainy season, and the wind brought small storms ashore at almost the same time every day. Every available container was utilized to catch water, including the *morion* helmets of the soldiers.

One hot afternoon, I watched two large sailors drag someone in through the makeshift gate. The man was vaguely familiar to me, so I strained to get a look at his features. They threw him in with me, and I soon realized who he was. It was the same man whom we had caught picking up gold and silver pieces from the beach a few days earlier. It seemed that the soldiers had caught him with the coins he had salvaged. They were very rough with him, and kicked him like a dog many times. He cried out in pain, and wantonly pleaded his innocence; a sickening performance that made me think even less of him than I already did. They tied him in a standing position to a tree near me, so that he faced my direction. Capitán Salmon walked out in front of him and made a bold speech that everyone in the area could hear.

"Everyone listen! We have been fortunate enough to have been delivered by God from death in the angry sea. Rescue ships from the north will be arriving soon, and will take the stricken people away from this cursed place. This wretch has been caught thieving the King's property. This is not the way true Spaniards should behave in the eyes of God, especially under these direst of circumstances. To show that I am a true man of God, I will leave his fate to Padre Padilla."

He stepped back, and swept his hand in a flourish.

A small man clothed in the traditional brown dress walked forward, the water damaged book of prayers under his arm. He was an older man with a thin strip of graying hair ringing his bald head and large, dark circles under his eyes. The sun was not his friend. There were blotches of red, inflamed skin on his pale face and head. He looked around at the crowd; his beady, grey eyes cruel and accusatory. Raising his hand, he pointed at the thief with a long, bony finger.

"This man here is an example of what is wrong with us at the very base of our existence, if we allow Satan to control our actions!" he said in a high, reedy voice. He paused for a moment, drawing a collective gasp from the gathering crowd.

"We are, even in this hostile place, emissaries of the Crown and King Philip himself. To steal this rightfully bestowed wealth is a sin against God himself. This man here has consciously made the choice to steal here on the beach, as his countrymen die around him. He must be made an example!"

He paused and looked over the crowd, glaring with wide, fanatical eyes.

"He can no longer be trusted in the eyes of the Lord!"

The crowd muttered its agreement.

"I have consulted with God on this matter, and I rule that he be punished severely for his crime." God Bless and save us all!" he said, turning to look at *Capitán* Salmon.

The crowd paused, waiting for Salmon to speak.

"God sentences him to fifty lashes," he said loudly, glaring at the thief with contempt.

With that, Salmon waved his arm at the crowd with another dramatic gesture, and then turned and walked away. The thief shrieked as the two large soldiers fell upon him, untying his hands and dragging him off to a spot on the outside of the log barrier. They then tied him to a large fallen log, chest down. For close to half an hour's time they proceeded to whip him mercilessly with the full number of murderous blows. His screams were so terrible that I put my hands over my ears in an attempt to block out the sound. When the cruel sentence had been fully administered, his motionless form was dragged across the sand and thrown into the rough stockade with me. I grimaced as I looked at the bloody, gnarled mess of his back. I couldn't endure the grisly sight for long and turned away, only to meet the eyes of Dorathea, who was standing near the gate. I thought, for a moment, that I saw regret and emotion in them, but she quickly broke our gaze and turned to walk away.

"This is not right!" I yelled at her as she left.

Two days later, soldiers were at the gate of my little prison. The thief, whose name I had still not learned, was barely coherent, having fallen into a state of delirium as a result of the pain and infection from his wounds. He now sat leaning on his side against what was left of a small cabbage palm tree, moaning softly.

One of the soldiers barked at me. "You men get up. We have much work to do."

We were both pulled from our jail and pushed through the camp, past the cook fires and shelters and out onto the beach. There were three small skiffs lined up, each one large enough for fifteen men and rigged with oars, a crude manual rudder, and a small sail. Each was also loaded with coils of rope and several large baskets. The *Capitán* was there, marching up and down the beach shouting out orders, his eyes anxiously looking out at the waves. Allejandro was also present, barefoot and dressed only in breeches and a shirt. I was now able to get a good look at him. The years had not changed his features that much, but he had grown strong. I could see the mean-spirited child that I remembered, despite the scrawny beard that he was attempting to grow. He now glared at me with contempt. I knew then that he wanted me dead, and would have killed me already, if not for Salmon's need for an expendable labor force.

"You men have been assigned a very important and brave mission," the *Capitán General* said. "The rescue boats will soon arrive from St. Augustine, but a tragedy even greater than the loss of life has befallen us. We must recover the King's treasures from the clutches of the Devil's wet hands, and we must start now. His Excellency will be pleased knowing that we have established this effort so soon after the disaster. Each of you will be assigned to a boat for the salvage effort. This will be an enormous task, but your sacrifice will be made for King and country. God be with you all."

"Are you mad? I shouted out loud. "You'll kill all of these men! Those waters are infested with sharks!"

Allejandro immediately leapt forward and slapped my face hard with his open hand, knocking me backwards.

"Get back in line!" he screamed. "How dare you speak to the *Capitan General!*"

Salmon nodded his approval at him and turned away, stroking his beard as he inspected all of the "divers."

Allejandro waited until he was out of range of hearing, and then moved close to me, looking directly into my watery eyes, an expression of mirth on his face. He spoke in a low voice, nearly laughing.

"I hope those sharks have a taste for pirate!"

I saw then that he had grown up to be the monster that I knew he always would be. I remembered the beatings he had given me on the playground when I was very small. These had continued until I was able to defend myself and show him up, which I had done at every opportunity. His hatred was as raw as ever, and I made a promise to myself to be ready at all times.

"Get aboard!" a loud, boisterous sergeant bellowed at us.

Most of the men were in no shape to swim, let alone search for lost treasures, but had no choice in the matter. We silently walked to whatever boat was closest, several of the men grumbling below their breath. After pushing the boats out into the deeper water, we all climbed inside. I looked toward the bow and saw that Allejandro had made sure that he was on my boat. He made himself comfortable, leather whip in hand. We all positioned ourselves on the crude wooden seats, and the men who had been assigned to the oars begrudgingly began to row backwards into the gentle surf. The boats were soon a few hundred yards out, near the spot where the twisted hull of the *Capitana* lay exposed just above the water's surface. As the small boat rocked back and forth, I turned to my right and for the first time noticed that there was a young boy next to me. He was dark skinned, with handsome features and a sturdy look about him, but the stricken look on his face betrayed his fear. I watched his eyes move over the surface of the water carefully, as if searching for the tell-tale fin.

"Hello, friend," I said in a calm voice.

"*Buenos dias*," he said, his eyes never leaving the water.

"What is a boy so young doing here on this fool's mission?" I asked him.

"I was chosen by the soldiers to do the King's important work," he said, a hint of false bravado in his voice.

"Hmm," I said, stroking my beard, "What is your name, son?"

"Jose," he said.

"Jose, I would like you to do me a favor. If you do this, I will reward you with a gold piece when we get back," I said.

He smiled at me. "You have no gold piece, señor. You are the pirate prisoner. The soldiers have taken everything of yours."

"Aah, you are a smart one, Jose. But pirates always have a trick up their sleeve," I said, smiling.

He stared at me intently, as if weighing my words in his mind.

"What do you want me to do?" he said.

"Simple," I said. I want you to dive with me only. When I go down, I will be able to help you," I said.

He looked at me skeptically, and then smiled.

"*Bien señor*," he said. I saw a look of relief on his young face.

"All right, men," Allejandro bellowed, "who'll be the first to dive? The treasure is below decks in wooden trunks, but the water is fairly shallow."

I looked around and saw no volunteers among the ragged men. As if on cue, Allejandro's eyes landed on Jose.

"You there," he said, "We need someone small and agile to get in there. It will be you."

"I'll go first," I shouted, hoping Allejandro would turn his attention from the boy. "I know treasure better than any man here."

"*Perfecto!* The hero of the day," he said, his cruel eyes shifting to mine.

I got up from my seat and quickly slipped over the gunnel into the water, at the same time trying not to think about sharks. One of the men bent over and lifted a large ballast stone from the bottom of the boat and held it over the side just above me. I gripped the side of the boat with one hand and looked up at him, at the same time sucking in a large breath of air. In one motion, I reached my hand up and took the stone from him, lowering it into the water and cradling it in my arm. I let go of the boat with my other hand and let the weight of the stone take me down into the depths quickly.

I could see nothing, and quickly dropped the stone when I felt my feet hit the sandy bottom. I reached out in front of me, my hands flailing wildly, and soon felt the wooden surface of the ship's deck where it lay sideways on the bottom. Fumbling my way upward, I found the splintered remains of the mainmast where it had been torn asunder, and near it the main hatchway. I felt my lungs starting to burn, so I made for the surface, kicking my feet and breaking the surface of the water seconds later. I gasped for breaths as I trod water in one place. My vision cleared and I looked toward the boat.

"Did you locate the hatch, pirate?" Allejandro shouted.

"Yes," I managed, sucking in air in ragged breaths, "I'm going back down."

"You'll take him with you!" Allejandro said, and I saw him grab Jose's arm and pull him toward the side of the boat. "You tell him where to swim, and he will go in the small areas," he bellowed.

"No!" I screamed. "He's just a boy! It is too dangerous!"

Allejandro roughly pushed Jose over the side, the boy's body making a small splash as he went below the surface of the water.

I swam to Jose and pulled him to me, as he struggled to keep his head above the water. He kicked furiously with fear.

"Relax, son, and be a man." I said, speaking as calmly as I could. "Save your energy. Just do as I say."

"*Si*, I will try, señor!" he said, attempting to relax a bit and taking deep breaths as I held his quivering body.

Pulling him along, I swam over to the exposed part of the hull sticking out above the water. I braced myself against it with one arm and rested. Jose was very frightened, his eyes frantically scanning the surface of the water around us.

"Jose, I have found the hatch. We need to get in there and pull something up to make these fools happy. I'm going to go down and do some exploring, so just put your head below the surface and pretend that you're following me."

He said nothing, but looked at me with wide eyes. After a few seconds he nodded his head in agreement.

I took in a huge breath of air and plunged down into the murky seawater. I soon located the hatch and quickly swam into it. A sharp pang of fear hit me as I realized how easily I could become lost in this inky blackness, so I turned and looked behind me, the saltwater burning my eyes. I could make out the dull light of the entrance, so I continued deeper into the ship. I swam down toward the bottom where I thought the boxes and chests would fall, and put my hands out in front of me. A wave of relief swept me as I came into contact with a wooden crate that had broken apart and was lying asunder in a pile. I reached down below it and desperately groped through the silt until my fingers found a smooth surface which I recognized as a plate. On further inspection I realized that there were more, so I hurriedly grabbed two of them and stuffed them in my shirt. I turned and frantically made for the dull light of the hatchway, swimming through it as I felt my lungs burning like they were on fire. I swam furiously toward the hazy daylight, my head soon breaking the surface. I sucked in huge, desperate gasps of air.

I looked toward Jose and was immediately alarmed by what I saw. He was screaming and pointing at something in the water a short distance away. I turned to look and felt my blood run cold with fear as I recognized the fin sticking above the surface of the water, gliding toward our position with purposeful menace.

"Jose! Make for the boat!" I screamed.

I grabbed the boy by the back of his breeches and tried to pull him alongside me as I frantically thrashed the water with powerful strokes. I then realized that Jose had grabbed the exposed railing of the sunken ship and was holding me back. The boy was frozen with fear, and could not move. I quickly pried his hands from the railing and yanked his small frame away, stroking with one hand as best I could toward the salvage boat. I heard the men cheering us on as I struggled through the water. I had never been so afraid, and expected at any time to have my legs savagely grabbed by the predator. I could see the boat in front of me, but Jose's trembling, rigid body slowed me down so much that it seemed I was not moving at all.

The next few moments were a blur. I felt the boy's weight removed from me as the men in the boat lifted Jose to safety. I grabbed the edge of the gunnel and pulled myself up, scrambling over the side and collapsing into the bottom of the boat. The men cheered for me, and I felt the wake from the large shark rock the boat as it swerved past, mere seconds after my escape. I lay there for a few moments, unable to move.

"Well, what did you bring up, pirate. We don't have all day."

It was the snide voice of Allejandro. I felt the familiar plume of anger grow in my head, and looked up into bright sunlight, seeing only his dark silhouette in the brilliance. Trembling with barely contained rage, I slowly got to my feet and carefully stepped between the men to a position in front of him. He was glaring at me, an insolent look on his face. Slowly reaching into my shirt, I pulled one of the small white plates from it and held it in my hand, holding it up for him to see. It was beautifully painted with richly colorful flowers and exquisitely detailed green vines all along its edges.

"Ah, Santos," Allejandro said, his face brightening, "You have found part of the Queen's dowry! This is China from the

Orient, and it can mean only one thing: You have found the treasure!"

I calmly drew my hand back; the plate still clasped in my fingers, and smiled back at him.

"Yes, Allejandro," I said in a calm voice. "This one is for you only."

I then swung it as hard as I could against the side of his head, the plate smashing into countless pieces on impact. Blood immediately spurted from a small wound on his cheek, and he cried out in pain and outrage, stumbling backward. He then tripped, falling over the side of the boat into the water below.

"Some things never change," I said as the astonished prisoners gaped at me.

CHAPTER 48
ESCAPE

The sun was slowly descending into the western sky, the gray-blue phase of twilight signaling the approach of starlit darkness. I was on my stomach with my hands tied behind my back, my cheek resting against the damp sandy floor of my cage. I was in more pain and exhaustion than I had ever felt, and only wanted the peaceful escape of sleep. I could hear men arguing outside, but their words hardly mattered. Insects that were so small they could barely be seen were mercilessly feasting on the exposed skin of my arms and legs. Hours earlier I had been dragged back to shore by an enraged and bloody Allejandro, who after securely rendering me helpless with bonds, had proceeded to beat and kick me mercilessly for a full hour.

"Please, *Capitán General*, let me kill him. The bastard struck me in front of the salvage crew! He needs to be made an example of to the others!"

I could hear the rage and frustration in his voice.

"No, Allejandro, he is a pirate and must stand trial. He will be hung, but only by the laws of *la Corona española*. My word is final," the old man said.

"You'll soon be mine, Santos," she said. "The Spaniards will kill you and feed you to the sharks. The prophecy will have been fulfilled. You are worthless to anyone and you will spend eternity paying for the crimes committed against me."

"Leave me alone, Spirit," I said groggily through swollen and bloody lips.

She laughed and glared at me with those empty black eyes.

"Come, my son," she cooed, *and extended a hand out to mine through the darkness, "I will be your guide through the underworld. You were meant to be here."*

"No!" I said, "I will never go with you!"

"But your father," she said.

"What of my father?" I sputtered.

"He is here, with me, Santos."

"Santos!"

It was a hoarse whisper, and it had come from outside the cage. I lifted my head dazedly, looking through swollen eyes off toward an orange glow that illuminated the blackness of the night.

"Who. . who's there?" I asked.

"Shhh," the voice whispered. "I don't want to be heard."

"Dorry?" I asked dazedly.

"Yes Santos. I have come to talk to you," she said.

Her face came into focus in the light of the small torch that she held. Gone was the hard look that I had grown so accustomed to, and in its place one of fear and concern. I saw that she was still as naturally beautiful as she had ever been, and my heart leapt with joy and relief.

"You came to talk to me?" I asked.

"Oh, Santos, you are such a fool. I saw what Allejandro did to you today, and I could not bear it. You had no chance. Santos, I am so confused!" she said.

"Allejandro has not changed at all," I said, laughing bitterly, "In fact, he's gotten worse."

"Santos, I have come to warn you. Allejandro is wild with thoughts of revenge on you. He wanted to kill you today, but Salmon forbade it," she said.

"I almost wish he had succeeded," I said, bitterness in my voice.

"Salmon thinks that you have located the chests containing the Queen's dowry. They are going to send you back down there as soon as the sun rises tomorrow," she said with sadness in her voice, her words choked with tears.

"They are on a fool's mission," I said flatly. "The water is still full of sharks feeding on the dead of the wrecks."

"Santos," she said, "I'm so sorry. I was thrilled to see that you were alive. All those years I heard the stories and. ."

"Stop," I interrupted. "Don't say anything. I love you, Dorry, and I always have."

"I brought you something, Santos."

She thrust her hand through the bars and slipped the object into my hand.

"You brought it back to me!" I said, gazing at my father's amulet. I knew then that Dorathea was truly back.

"Allejandro had it with his things. He gloated over the fact that he had stolen it from the most infamous pirate in the seas. It made me sick, because I knew where it belonged."

I took her hand in mine and pulled it to my face, kissing her fingers gently as I listened to her words.

"I'm going to get you out of here!" she said, pulling her hand back.

"Dorry, no, the risk is too great. I'll do the best I can," I said.

She was already on the move, and I heard what sounded like a knife cutting at the leather thong that held the crudely fashioned door of the cage closed.

"Hurry!" she said as she pulled it open, the edge of it catching on the sandy ground.

At first I was paralyzed with fear and could not move, but I quickly realized that the situation had suddenly changed and that there was no turning back. I got to my feet and scrambled through the opening. I found myself face to face with her. This was the woman I had never stopped loving, and I was nearly overcome with emotion. I hesitated for just a moment and looked into her large brown eyes, noticing that they were brimming with tears.

"Come, Santos. It's time for us to go," she said urgently.

I looked down and saw her hand reaching out to me. It was a vision that will stay with me for eternity. I took it, and together we hurried off into the safety of the trees.

The low hanging clouds made it a very dark night. We had to take care as we moved through the palmetto scrub with only the dim light of the torch. We could see the glow of a few small fires on the beach where a number of the remaining shipwreck survivors had made camp, so we were careful to hide ourselves in the trees. A few days earlier, I had overheard the soldiers speaking of the growing threat of hostile attacks by the *Ais* from the south. For this reason, most of the survivors had moved north to be near the main salvage camp where the rescue ships from St. Augustine would soon be arriving. I was once again amazed at the enormity of the disaster, and hoped that salvation would come quickly for the unfortunate souls marooned at *"Palmar De Ayes,"* as the Spaniards called it.

We paused to rest, and she turned to face me. We looked at each other for a moment, and then fell into a deep embrace. I held her close, and made a promise to myself that I would never again let her go. A thought occurred to me, so I gently pushed her away to see her face.

"Dorry, what will you do? I have nothing for you here. My home was destroyed in the storm," I said.

"Shhh, Santos. Do not worry about me. I have no fear as long as I am with you. When you first disappeared, I was lost. I never realized how much I depended on you. It was like I had lost my best friend and brother. I was plagued by a great black sadness for a whole year. Allejandro was always there, walking with me every day, consoling me in my anguish, filling my head with tales of your treachery. At first I resisted his advances, still hoping that you would return and make it all go away. As time passed, I grew to depend on the comforting tone of his voice and the reassurance of his constant presence. I really believed that he loved me; so much so that I eventually agreed to marry him. Soon after I made the commitment to become his betrothed, he changed. His temper grew short and he began to speak sharply to me. I soon began to see the real person, but it was too late to change my plans because my father had already invested the huge dowry. I began to resent Allejandro and his childish arrogance. He does not love me; he loves having me at his side like some sort of prize he has won. He always hated you, Santos, and was the driving force behind all of the vicious rumors about you."

"I don't care about any of that, Dorry. I have you with me; that's the only thing I care about. I have learned to love this place, and have many friends that I want you to meet," I said.

I took her into my arms again and kissed her face all over, gently stroking her body. That moment was among the most memorable of my life. I had found it again, the love that was so cruelly and unexpectedly taken away in my youth. I then thought of Chera, and I felt a momentary pang of guilt.

Had I not loved her more than anything?

I then remembered the words that she said to me.

"You must be happy, Santos. Life is too uncertain. Live your life always, even if I am gone."

I looked up into the night sky and felt tears of love streaming down my face. My darling Chera had sent me a message.

"What is it, Santos?" Dorry asked with concern as she saw the wetness on my face.

"Nothing is wrong, my love. I have seen divinity and love in its truest form and it has touched my life," I said as I clutched her hand in mine.

We walked to the south all that night until our tired, sand-chafed feet were too sore to continue. As darkness transformed to the gray of early morning, we passed three more of the wreck sites. Eventually, the first orange rays of the sun appeared across the ocean's far horizon. All along the beach head were huge, black fire pits and areas where crudely fashioned crosses marked the hastily dug graves of those who had perished. I saw that, in sharp contrast to a week before, there was almost no one on the beach, save for a few stragglers around the abandoned shelters. These ragged men were digging in the sand along the shoreline. We rested for a few moments, watching as they picked through the loose debris from the wrecks that littered the shallows, occasionally finding silver pieces of eight and stuffing them into their pockets. I thought of warning them of Admiral Salmon's harsh treatment of thieves, but decided against it, leaving them to learn the lesson the hard way.

These were either foolishly greedy or extremely brave men, because the *Ais* were now appearing on the beach to claim whatever salvage they could get. The Indian salvagers feared the Spanish, but a lone man did not stand a chance against them.

We were both exhausted, but I insisted we travel along the dunes at the top of the beach, clinging to the safety of the sea grapes. The further south we walked the more confident I became, because I recognized many trees and landmarks that pointed the way home. As night approached, I found a comfortable depression in the sand among some long sea oats, and we both lay down in each other's arms, soon dozing off.

My sleep was blissfully dreamless, and I woke as the rays of the early morning sun hit my eyelids. I was alarmed to hear the sound of approaching footsteps through the sea oats, and instinct kicked in. In one fluid motion, I rolled out of my sand bed and rose to a crouch, at the same time pulling the small knife from my breeches. Peering through the thin reeds, I tried to catch a glimpse of who the intruder was. I then heard a sound that I instantly recognized. It was the cry of an osprey.

CHAPTER 49
DELIVERANCE

I felt a wave of relief and slowly rose to my feet. I then answered the osprey's cry with one of my own. Just as I expected, I was looking at the smiling face of Dunkirk. A few yards behind him stood my old *Ais* nemesis, Aktil.

"*Hola mis amigos!*" I shouted, walking toward them through the tall grass. We greeted one another with smiles and hard slaps on the shoulders. I was so glad to see them that I momentarily forgot about Dorry, who still lay in the sea oats a few yards away, too terrified to move.

"Dorathea!" I shouted, "These men are friends!"

She slowly got up, staring at the Indians with fear in her eyes. I quickly realized that they must have been an unexpected and intimidating sight to her, since the only natives she had ever seen were those who had been whipped into submission by the soldiers. Aktil was adorned in full war regalia, and had dyed his entire body black except for a large, inverted triangle of blood red on his chest. He wore nothing but the small grass-woven garment around his privates, its tail hanging down in the rear. In one hand he held a long bow that stood nearly as tall as he was, with a quiver of arrows slung at an angle across his back. His black hair was tied on top of his head, bundled and secured with long thin bones. Dunkirk was completely different in appearance, wearing a blue Spanish-style shirt that hung below his waist and ragged, filthy white breeches. His hair was covered by an English sailor's cap, and he carried a short, curved cutlass, giving him a distinctly savage appearance. Realizing how these men must have looked to her, I immediately made the necessary introductions.

"Dorry, these men are my friends from the *Ais* village. They will help us. This is Aktil and Dunkirk."

Aktil looked at the beautiful white woman with suspicion.

"She. ..like Chera?" he asked in broken Spanish, and I knew that he was asking if Dorry was another powerful medicine woman.

"No," I said, shaking my head. "She is my woman."

About two hours later, we walked onto the path that led to Santa Lucia. As we emerged into the clearing, I looked around and was surprised at the progress they had made in rebuilding. No one was about, so Dorry and I walked to the center of the camp.

"This is your home?" Dorathea asked.

"Yes, it is. This is Santa Lucia, Dorry, and I've had many happy years in this place," I said.

The main house had been re-fitted with new planks and palmetto fronds, and several new shelters had been built around the camp's northern perimeter. Suddenly, a cry broke the tranquil silence.

"Captain Santos!" Caesar had emerged from the door way of his house and seen us. He ran with his arms open wide, colliding with me in an embrace that nearly sent us tumbling to the sandy ground.

"You're alive!" he exclaimed as he pushed me back and looked me up and down.

The commotion drew more attention, and my people began to appear from the shelters.

"Captain Santos Alvarez!"

Shad and Mike Storm emerged from the trees, each carrying a string of large fish. They walked quickly to us, slapping me on the back in warm greeting.

"And 'oo is this beautiful maiden?" Shad said as he looked Dorathea up and down.

"You'll never believe it, even if I tell you," I said. "All that matters is that she is here to stay."

I looked across at the entrance to the western trailhead and saw Abraham walking toward us, a wide smile on his face. As he drew closer, I noticed that he wasn't alone. I soon recognized Adelena, the girl we had met on the beach, at his side.

"Ah, Captain. It is very good to see you," he said in his deep, resonant voice. "When you ventured into that Spanish salvage camp, I feared the worse."

"You were correct, Abraham, in questioning the wisdom of that move. Love will make men do the most foolish of things," I laughed.

"I know what you mean, Captain" the giant man said as he looked toward Adelena, who stood next to him, her face beaming. "I had to build a bigger house."

All of the men erupted in laughter at this. More people heard the commotion and came out of the buildings, all of them cheering at the sight of us.

"Dorathea saved my life. She helped me to escape in the night," I said, squeezing her tightly to my side.

I looked at her, secretly trying to gauge her reaction to these people. She was wide eyed and speechless, and looked slightly dumbfounded by all of the attention. They gathered around us, all of them cheering and chattering excitedly.

"*Buenos Dias*, Captain Santos!"

I turned to look, and saw that Captain Suarez and his men had also joined the fray. I walked to him and shook his hand warmly.

"Dorathea, this is Captain Suarez, formerly of the *Santiago*. He is our brother."

She stared at him in shock.

"I have heard of you!" She said. "They say that you were taken prisoner by the pirates and killed in the jungle. There was a long trial for the crew, during which a mutiny was uncovered. They hung several of the corrupt crew members in La Habana. It was very scandalous," she said. "*Capitán General* Salmon told us the whole story."

Captain Suarez's eyes narrowed. "What was that name?" he asked as the smile left his face.

Dorathea seemed surprised. "*Capitán General* Salmon. He was our escort on the trip back to Spain."

"He is here? In La Florida?" Captain Suarez asked, his face turning ashen.

All of a sudden I remembered the story he had told me many months before. I hadn't made the connection while imprisoned at the camp. Salmon was the same man who had persecuted my friend in *Madre Espana* many years before.

"I am a dead man," he said. "They have found me."

I shook my head. "Captain, you are mistaken. They have been shipwrecked here. They are in a very sorry state and will not be coming here."

The man turned away and walked off into the trees.

"I will be back, my dear," I said to Dorry.

I found him sitting on a large palmetto log. His head was bent down, his face buried in his hands.

"I must go," he said in a choked voice. "If I stay here I will be endangering all of you. Captain Santos, if Salmon learns that I am here, his men will kill us all."

I walked over to him, placing my hand gently on his shoulder.

"Captain Suarez, remember what we have here," I said. "You are our brother, and we will fight together. We are stronger than those fools."

He looked up at me, and I could see the pain in his eyes.

"I am a disgrace to my people, sir. Sometimes I wonder if I deserve to live," he said.

I grew angry at his words. "Captain, we have discussed this before! I need you to help me lead these people. Stop acting like a coward!"

He stared at me, dumbfounded. I returned his gaze, and eventually his expression changed to one of dull acceptance. He stood up and brushed himself off with his hands.

"I am sorry, Captain Santos. You are correct. It is very easy to forget myself."

The festivities continued into the night around the blazing fire. Caesar uncorked two bottles of Spanish wine that he had stowed away and passed it around. The African women danced wildly, the orange light of the fire glistening on their skin as the men kept a rhythm on their crude drums. Stormy pulled out an old fiddle and placed it under his chin.

"Mike, I thought we buried that instrument with Fly?" I asked, incredulous.

"This 'ees the one we found on the *Agememnon*, Captain. 'Oi been savin' it all this time," he said in his high, scratchy voice.

"Well, when did you learn to play it?" I asked.

"Well, Captain, when the storm took' my friend Fly, I thought it would behoove me to learn 'ees trade, you know?"

He gave me his toothless, infectious grin. "I'm not as good as 'ee were on it, but 'oi can 'old me own."

With that, he began to scratch out a barely recognizable Irish melody. It didn't sound very good, but it was better than anything else we had. He began to stomp his leg up and down in time to it, and I laughed so hard that I nearly fell to the ground. To everyone's delight, Shad got to his feet and began to cavort about in a strange, jerking hornpipe that sent the men to howling. My own eyes glistened with hilarity at this ridiculous sight, and I looked at Dorathea to see her reaction. She was laughing too, and it was clear that she was having a wonderful time, clapping her hands in time to the music and moving her shoulders in time with the rhythm. I knew that our little group of misfits had just gained another member.

CHAPTER 50
VENGEANCE

The next few months were spent rebuilding our lives. We constructed strong houses raised up on stilts to prevent flood waters from again claiming us, and our camp became better fortified than before. The men then worked at re-fitting the *Pantera* and making repairs from the storm's damage. Sails were sewn together, planks were reinforced, and ropes were spliced and rolled into neat piles on the deck as we prepared to resume our pirating activities. As time passed, my thoughts seldom went to the unpleasant memories of the disaster on the beach, as if it were an event that was better forgotten.

As the time for the *Ais* migration inland drew nearer, I told the men that I had to visit the village to procure certain supplies and get news of any shipwrecks. My real purpose was hidden from everyone but Dorry. In fact, I was worried about them. Sickness had returned to the natives with a vengeance, and it seemed that their numbers were growing fewer with each passing month. Several of the young men had defied the staunch rules of the older members of the tribe by experimenting with, then falling prey to alcohol that they had procured from the Spanish shipwrecks. The natives seemed to be more vulnerable to the adverse effects of the demon rum than any people I had ever seen. It is my belief that these poor, primitive souls were so pure in their physical makeup that the alcohol attacked them with a virgin's vengeance. I saw many of them die from its affects in a very short time. When I was on the beach alone, I could sometimes hear the soft crying of my darling Chera on the night breezes mourning them.

It was not only the sickness and alcohol that were wreaking havoc on their numbers, but something else over which they had no control. The men were simply disappearing in the night. A woman and her children would often wake up to find their man gone. I had a notion of what was going on, but I could not prove it.

I told Abraham and Caesar of my suspicions. On a cool, clear moonlit night in late September, we walked down to the beach near the *Ais* village and concealed ourselves in the sea grapes along the shore. Just as I suspected, there was a light visible a few hundred yards out on the sea. As it moved closer to shore, we could soon make out the shape of a boat. Its hull slid into the shoreline in the calm night air and six men clumsily climbed out, trying their best to remain very quiet. They were Spaniards from the salvage camp, and I could see that they carried pistols and ropes. They quickly located the path that led to the village, indicating that they had been there before. It was at least one quarter of a mile to the village, and the path meandered around trees and hammocks. We quickly followed Caesar's alternate path through the jungle to gain an ambush point. We could hear them whispering amongst themselves as they moved past.

We then heard a loud, shrill wail that sent the men running backward in panicked disarray. The Spaniards abruptly stopped moving and frantically looked around in confusion for the source of it. The sound was so terrible and piercing in the still air of the night that it even scared me. I heard a commotion in the trees on the other side of the path, and then a scream of pain as one of the Spaniards was hit by a spear.

"It's the *Ais*!" Caesar whispered hoarsely. "They are attacking!"

Like us, the warriors had been waiting and were now exacting retribution on the slavers. They had been pushed to the edge and were now fighting back against their enemy as they had done for thousands of years. The night erupted with the sounds of men locked in close fighting. I could hear weapons whirling through the air and making contact with flesh.

"*No, no, por favor no me maten!*" one of them cried just before an *Ais* war club crushed his skull. I heard another of the Spaniards trip and fall very close to me. He seemed to be uninjured and leapt to his feet, tearing off down the trail toward the boat. I went after him. I experienced a thrill that I cannot describe as I pursued this man, whom I knew to be scared out of his wits. Just as he burst onto the beach I caught him, jumping at his legs and taking him down face first into the sand.

"I've got you, slaver!" I said triumphantly.

"Let me go, you filthy savage!" the man bellowed.

There was something familiar about that voice, so I spun him around to see his face. I found myself staring into the moonlit face of Allejandro Ruiz. He was as shocked as I was, and we simply stared at each other for a moment. I was then consumed by the same familiar black plume of rage that has haunted me since my youth.

"You!" I screamed.

His face went pallid as he saw the severity of my anger and he closed his eyes, his lips quivering.

I drew my fist back and delivered such a blow to his face that it caused his entire body to shudder. He let out a grunt of pain, and I hit him with another. All of the frustration and anger that had been building inside of me came out in a flood of violence that I could not contain. I pounded and pummeled him, delivering so many blows that I lost count. I then became aware of a man shouting in my ear.

"Captain, stop! You'll kill him!"

It was Caesar, and I saw that he was standing directly in front of me, staring into my eyes with a look of worried disapproval.

"What do I care for this son of a dog!" I shouted, my sight still partially blinded by anger.

I wiped my hand across my face in an attempt to remove the sweat from my eyes and found it covered with blood. Looking down, I felt my anger wane as I saw what I had done to Allejandro's face. He was alive, but he would carry those scars the rest of his life.

"Captain, I don't care about 'dere miserable lives either, but dis not right!!"

"What do you mean?" I shot back.

"We must let dem go, Captain. We not murderers like dem!" he said.

I looked off into the distant, dark ocean and let my mind assess his words, soon realizing the wisdom in them. I got to my feet and walked toward the sea, panting heavily with exertion, reeling with spent rage. Looking down at my hands, I saw that my fingers were glistening with blood. A thought then crossed my mind.

I had meant to kill him. Was I now a complete savage?

CHAPTER 51
THE VISION ON THE BEACH

It had been nearly a month since our encounter with
Allejandro and his men from the salvage camp, and the slave
hunting attacks on the *Ais* village had all but ceased.
Gathering information from several reliable *Ais* scouts, I
learned that most survivors of the wrecks had been taken away
by rescue ships, and that the salvage operations were
continuing up and down the coast. I also learned that a huge
part of their efforts involved forced labor, a fact that
explained the disappearance of so many native men from their
villages. I had even gone to spy on their progress, peering out
at their operation from the cover of the sea oats.

I was amazed at both the tenacity and ingenuity of the
Spanish salvage crews in retrieving the King's treasure from
the ocean's forbidding depths. I watched as two large vessels
dragged long chains that measured from three to four hundred
feet in length back and forth in wide sweeps across the ocean
floor. There was a wooden buoy suspended on the surface of
the water marking the chain's exact center so the crew could
see where it was and prevent it from becoming tangled.
Following closely were two smaller rowboats carrying men
who constantly measured the water's depth with long
sounding leads. When the chains snagged something on the
bottom, the sailors lowered large grappling hooks to try to
discern whether it was one of the lost ships or a piece of rock
or coral. If the object did indeed prove to be what they were
looking for, the salvage divers were summoned. These men
were a rough collection of *Arawak* and *Carib* slaves who had
been brought from the south because they were excellent deep

water swimmers and could endure the depths longer than anyone else. Their Spanish captors often made them use diving bells that trapped air inside, enabling the diver to go down even further and view the ocean bottom through a glass window near its top. Woe to the man who tried to come up to the surface from such depths too quickly! These poor souls would twist and turn in agony, writhing and screaming in pain, and often perishing in the hot sun on those miserable boats. When this occurred, their bodies were then thrown over the side like some discarded trash. The cruelty of the Spanish never ceased to amaze me, and my resolve grew even stronger to pillage their vessels with the *Pantera* whenever the opportunity presented itself. I swore to myself that I would make them pay dearly. I walked back to camp with dark intentions in my mind.

It was a cool December night. The sight of Dorathea beside me calmed my turbulent thoughts. I kissed her gently as we lay down to sleep. She closed her eyes and snuggled into me, her warm body sending shivers through my skin. I gazed at her, admiring her beauty as she drifted off to sleep and contemplating how wonderful life was with her again. It was as if we had effortlessly resumed the happy life of our childhood after many long years of separation.

Leaning back on my sleeping mat, I stared at the ceiling and thought of my experiences over the last few months. I had spent that time teaching Dorry to appreciate the ways of the *Ais*, whom I believed to have lived here for thousands of years. They had a special use for each and every plant and animal; some practical and some ceremonial. They were not animals who feasted on human flesh, as so many Spaniards had been led to believe, but a culture so adept and finely tuned to their often very hostile environment that they had not only adapted to it, but had flourished.

Dorathea had taken to our hard scrabble life quickly, and had adjusted to the ways of living close to nature. She no longer wore a dress, but had found a pair of breeches and a waistcoat in Caesar's pilfered collection that suited her. She chose not to conform to the submissiveness of the African women, who had done their best to show her everything they knew about domestic life on the wild coast. Dorrie had no desire to cook or mend sails, but wanted only to be with me. It was as if she had put her past life as Allejandro's ornamental prize behind her, and wanted to start again with the same familiar impetuousness and taste for adventure that we had known as we were growing up. I did not allow her to go with us on our "privateering" escapades, even though she protested with tight lipped anger for nearly a week after my return. When we were children she had told me many times that she had secretly wished she had been born a boy. As I felt her warm, curvaceous body next to mine I felt very glad that this had not been the case.

This particular evening, I tried to quiet my mind and sleep, but found it impossible as my thoughts wandered through the many dark corridors of my consciousness. Feeling frustrated, I slipped out of bed, grabbed my shirt from the hook outside the door, and walked out into the cool night air. I made my way to the path that led across the island to the ocean, not even thinking to grab a torch from the red, dying coals of the fire. In a short time, I emerged from the scrub and found myself on our lonely stretch of beach. The moon shone brightly over the silver-tipped waves as the soft breeze blew through my hair. Looking into the southern sky, I saw a small spot of light that did not look like any star; an illumination that was at first nearly undetectable in the distance. Unlike the heavenly bodies around it, it was amber in color and seemed to be pulsating with a sort of energy. I stared for a long time, gradually becoming entranced by it. I then heard something. It was a voice as soft as a whisper, and I felt a spark of fear as I realized that it was calling my name.

"What is this wizardry?" I said aloud to no one.

"*Santos, I am the wind of a thousand years.*"

"What do you want?" I asked.

"*The curse that has been cast upon you is very old.*"

The strange star seemed to be larger and brighter now, growing in intensity as if it were moving closer.
"Why have you chosen me? I asked."

"*You are special, Santos,*" the whisper said, so light and airy that it was barely detectable.
"Why?" I cried, "Why am I special?"
The figure slowly began to take form, and I saw familiarity in its shape. It seemed to stretch out horizontally, and then began to waver and buckle, like some sort of ghostly banner. It glowed brightly, with flashes of green light shooting out from it in all directions. I was now terrified, but transfixed by its beauty. It grew in size in the night sky, and it soon became clear to me what it was.

"*Santos, you are about to endure great change in your life. You need to be strong and overcome it or you will be like your father and his father before him. You must combat this evil with all of your heart.*"

I stood in awe as I took in the enormity of the celestial figure taking form in front of me, and I felt a wave of emotion wash over my body. Tears streamed down my face as I beheld the image of a magnificent panther there in the starry night sky; the totem animal of my beloved Chera.

I awoke with a sudden start, and for a moment did not know where I was. Dorathea was shaking me, her hands clenched around my upper arms.

"Santos! Wake up!"

I looked at her face and saw the fear, and then turned my head toward the doorway of the house, seeing a red glow emanating from somewhere outside. I could hear it now, the tell-tale snapping of flames as they engulfed and consumed branches. The smell of smoke hit me and I scrambled out of bed, slipping on the sandy ground and nearly falling. I stumbled out into the darkness and was stupefied by what I saw. All of the main buildings of the camp were covered with blankets of fire. The flames leapt to the trees above, their glow illuminating the clearing like daylight and emitting a heat so intense that I thought my skin would shrivel and burn. I heard a scream. It was a shriek of pain so intense that my heart leapt in shock. I shouted as loudly as I could in an attempt to warn the others. I saw a small arc of light shooting down from the night sky above the trees, and then another. One of them hit the sand near me with a dull thud. I saw the feathered end of an arrow, and below it a thin wisp of smoke rising where the burning tip lay imbedded in the sand. Anger rose inside me, welling like a tidal surge, as I realized what was happening. Another scream came from the house near me. It was a woman's voice, so I sprinted to it, bursting through the door. The small room was filled with thick, black smoke and I coughed, raising my arm to my face, my eyes stinging and flooding with tears of pain.

"Where are you?" I shouted.

I heard a rasping cough coming from somewhere below me, so I fell to my hands and knees, groping at the ground in front of me. I soon felt one of the posts of the raised bed platform and followed it up. There was a person on the mat; a woman, curled up and coughing uncontrollably. I leapt to my feet and, in one motion, scooped her up and frantically made my way toward where I thought the door was. I could not see anything, so I clumsily smashed into the wall at the door opening, quickly righting myself and stumbling out into the clear night. I ran several yards into a grove of trees and fell to the ground, both of us landing hard. I gasped for breath and rubbed my eyes for several minutes, unable to do anything else. When I was finally able to see, I looked over and recognized the woman I had just rescued. It was Adelena, Abraham's new bride-to-be.

"Are you all right?" I asked, feeling the rising urge to cough again.

She was covered in soot, her body heaving with hysterical sobs.

"Where is Abraham?" I asked her.

She shook her head back and forth. "I don't know," she said, her dirty face tracked with trails from her tears. "He went to hunt pigs this morning. He said he would return tomorrow. What is happening?" she implored, her voice choking.

"We are under attack. I have to go find the others," I said, and started to get up.

"Santos Alvarez!"

The shout was firm and authoritatively calm, ringing out above everything.

"Come into the open now, or we will kill your friends now."

My heart sank as I recognized the voice.

"Adelena," I said in a hoarse whisper, "run into the trees now. Find Abraham and tell him what has happened."

She looked into my eyes for a long moment, fear causing her to not comprehend my words.

"Now!" I said.

She turned her head and scrambled into the trees on her hands and knees I watched as she disappeared into the darkness. When I was sure that she was a safe distance away, I slowly got to my feet and walked around the side of my house into the orange glow of the clearing. There, I found myself looking into the gloating, confident face of Allejandro. He was standing near the fire pit, surrounded by several of his men. In front of him was the kneeling figure of Caesar, his face twisted in pain. I then saw the tight leather garrotte around my friend's neck. Allejandro gripped the small wooden handle, and was now turning it, twisting the thong tighter and tighter.

"You'll kill him, you fool!" I said.

Allejandro threw his head back and laughed out loud, cinching it tighter. Caesar let out a guttural, grunting sound, and slowly began to succumb to the effects of this well applied weapon.

"What is one more–dead slave? The jungle is full of them!" he taunted.

I then felt a crushing blow on the back of my head, and everything went black.

CHAPTER 52
ALLEJANDRO'S REVENGE

I came back to consciousness suddenly, my eyes meeting the grayness of the early morning sky, the air heavy with the briny scent of the sea. I was lying on my back in the in the bottom of the boat with my hands bound behind me, my arms pulled into a very uncomfortable position. Shifting my weight, I attempted to make it bearable. There was much talking and shouting going on, so I tried not to make any sudden moves. I raised my head ever so slowly in an attempt to see behind me. My only view was of the sandaled feet of the rowers. I realized that I was aboard one of the single-masted Spanish salvage boats. The memory of what had taken place came flooding back and my anger began to rise. Throwing all caution to the wind, I shouted out.

"Allejandro! What have you done?"

There was a short pause, and then laughter.

"Aah, the pirate has awakened!" came the high pitched response.

I heard the scuffling of boots on the wooden hull, and soon found myself looking up at the arrogant expression of triumph on Allejandro's face. He was dressed in breeches and a dirty white shirt, and had grown the remnants of a scraggly beard on his freckle-pocked face. He looked exhausted, and appeared to have aged years since I had last seen him. I knew that his haggard appearance was from the duress of life in the wild, but his eyes still gleamed with malevolence. I saw pure hatred in them, and knew that he wanted to see me dead. He suddenly lashed out with his foot and kicked me in the stomach, causing me to double up and groan with waves of nauseous pain.

"I should have killed you when I had the chance," I managed to say between gasps.

"I will finally see you hang, you scum. No longer will you prey on my innocent brothers on the high seas," he snarled.

I struggled for breath for a long time before I managed a reply.

"Where is Dorathea?" I asked.

"You do not need to concern yourself with her, or any other woman for that matter," he snarled. "She has been ill and will be taken back to La Habana for treatment. She is lucky to have survived the forced captivity of you and your depraved pirates," he said.

I began to shake with rage.

"What have you done with her?" I roared, "Where are my people?"

"We have taken care of your pirate lair. I would like to thank you for the many slaves that we took from the place. They will be of great service to King Philip in the future. You have provided well for them, and kept them well fed and healthy. I thank you for that, but it is a shame that you will never reap the rewards of payment, due to your impending appointment with the gallows." It was obvious that he was enjoying the situation very much.

I stared at him, my eyes narrow with fury. "What of Caesar, the man that you held before me?"

"Ah, him," he said, raising his hand to stroke his chin thoughtfully. "Unfortunately, he proved to be unwilling to cooperate with my men, so I felt it necessary to make an example of him to the others. I had him hanged."

I was stunned to silence at these words. I felt a surge of panic rise in my soul and a sense of helplessness that I had never before experienced.

"Hanged? You hung Caesar?" I said in a weak voice.

Sensing my absolute shock, Allejandro smiled.

"Yes, I'm afraid so. He was a pirate, after all," he said in a calm voice.

I cannot describe the emotions that I encountered in those few moments, but I will say that it was indeed the lowest point in my life. I was beyond rage, and experienced a cool clarity of thought that was totally new to me. I looked up at the man, my childhood nemesis, whom had grown into something beastly and seething with hatred.

"Allejandro," I said in a low, even voice, "mark my words."

He simply stared back at me, waiting with a simpering smile on his arrogant face. "Yes?"

"Remember, Allejandro, I will find you and send you to hell," I said.

This was not the response of uncontrolled rage that he had expected, and I saw his face twitch almost imperceptibly.

"That will be difficult to do, since you are going there first," he said, his voice breaking ever so slightly. He paused, and then kicked me viciously in the stomach again.

Many hours later, the skiff slid to a grinding halt on the beach just to the south of the salvage camp. The men jumped out into the shallow water, and pulled the boat further up onto the beach until it slumped at an angle on its hull. I was roughly dragged from it and shoved over the sand toward the crude camp walls. Allejandro walked behind me, repeatedly pushing my back so that I nearly stumbled. As we entered the camp, I could see that conditions had improved only slightly, but there were no longer hordes of destitute survivors scattered about, desperately clinging to life. The smoky camp was now made up of soldiers and a few women, with many *Ais* men performing the most menial work. The soldiers and their slaves had constructed a few more crude buildings for shelter, and were now in the process of organizing and packaging the silver and gold pieces that the salvage crews brought in daily. In the very center of the camp, I noticed two *Ais* men digging a deep hole next to several wooden crates stacked in a pile. Why were they burying the salvaged treasure?

I looked out toward the sea and saw a large galleon anchored about six hundred yards from shore to the north. I scanned the horizon and spotted another to the south about the same distance out. Even though I was miserable, I smiled as I realized that these vessels were the Spaniards plan for protection against men like me.

The soldiers pushed me toward the larger buildings on the far side of the camp just as Admiral Salmon emerged from the doorway. My hands were still tied behind my back, and Allejandro took the opportunity to shove me so hard from behind that I fell forward. I twisted my body so I would not land flat on my face, and slammed onto the hard packed sand on my shoulder.

"*Capitán General*, I have recaptured the prisoner and destroyed the pirates lair," Allejandro proclaimed triumphantly.

The Admiral shook his head approvingly as he looked down at my crumpled form on the sandy ground. I could see that the man had aged considerably in the last few months, his gray hair hanging loose around his unshaven face. His clothes were thin with wear and he had lost considerable weight.

"Ah, you have done well, Allejandro. And the girl, eh, what was her name? Dorathea?" he asked.

"Yes sir, she has been rescued. She was very distraught from being held and ravaged by this scum," he said.

I surprised them by laughing out loud at this.

"What do you say, pirate? You find this amusing?" Salmon asked.

I nearly answered with argument, but a thought suddenly occurred to me. These men had taken Dorathea and were holding her somewhere close by. What would become of her? If I told these men that she had helped me to escape, would she suffer the hand of their cruel retribution? I quickly re-thought my strategy.

"What have you done with my prisoner?" I shouted.

Allejandro looked down at me, his eyes narrowing. "Your prisoner?" he asked.

"The girl was to be used for ransom. I took her by force after I escaped from your miserable jail in the night. I would have returned her, had I been compensated," I said.

Both men laughed out loud at this, as if the mere idea was the most absurd thing ever.

"You are not only a criminal, but a fool as well if you ever thought that you would be paid," Admiral Salmon snuffled. "It was inevitable that my soldiers would rescue the girl from your savage captivity. Allejandro has rid the world of a pestilence," he said, sniffing his nose at me. "We will hang him at dawn tomorrow," he said. He then turned away abruptly and disappeared into the main building. Allejandro remained silent, staring at me with burning hatred.

"Prisoner indeed," he snarled in a low voice. "Nice try, my friend. Do you take Admiral Salmon for a fool?"

I was taken to the very same crude jail that I was imprisoned in many months earlier. The temperature had dropped, and the wind blew in from the sea with a biting coldness. I huddled in the corner and wrapped my arms around my legs in an attempt to stay warm. As the sun went down on the horizon, a great sadness came upon me, for I knew that I was nearing the end of my life. I knew that I had dragged many people with me. My eyes welled up with tears as I thought of my good friend Caesar and his undying loyalty and friendship over the years. I knew that many of the others had no doubt suffered greatly at the cruel hands of Allejandro and his men, and I now blamed myself for this. It occurred to me that the terrible curse on my family was about to come to fruition in my own life, and that the phantom woman from my nightmares would now be gloating with glee. I thought of Abraham and his people, most likely being sent into brutal servitude under these merciless men. What would become of them? I thought of their joyous singing around the fire, and of the absolute devotion they had given me over the years. I thought of Shad and Mike Storm, and their hilarious behavior over the years, and of sad Captain Suarez and his men. I had led them all down this road that had ended in disaster at the hands of the cruel Spanish.

And what of Dorry? What would become of her? I was relieved at the news that she had survived the terrible fire that the soldiers had started. I knew that she would most likely be sent back to La Habana, or perhaps St. Augustine to the north. I could only pray for her good health and happiness. It was for the better, I supposed, because I could never bring her what she deserved out here on the wild coast of La Florida. She would be initially sad at losing me, perhaps for a long while, but she would be in a better place; one that she truly deserved; a place with fine buildings, paved streets and shops. I cursed Allejandro, and the cruelty with which he would undoubtedly unleash on her, but I knew that she was smart enough to eventually gain her freedom from him. The fact that she was alive and safe with the Spanish was the only consolation I felt. Tears streamed down my dirty face as I realized that I would never see the love of my life again. I lay down on my side and closed my eyes, wanting to escape the hellish punishment of my thoughts. Strangely, sleep came to me quickly on that lonely and cold December night.

It was a beautiful summer evening, and we had ventured out to the sea to look at the stars and contemplate our existence, just as we had many nights before. I had spread a blanket out on a low area between two dunes, and we were sitting next to each other, saying nothing, just enjoying one another's company. I looked at her as she gazed up at the stars, her dark hair blowing in the warm breeze and a look of rapture on her beautiful face. It was then that I had realized that she and I were destined by some higher power, perhaps God, or maybe one of the many deities that the Ais prayed to every night, to be together always. I could hear the mournful wails of the holy men as they performed their nightly, sad tribute to the rising moon.

"What a strange, beautiful place this is," Dorathea said softly. "When I first landed on the beach in my soaked dress on that terrible night, I thought that I had arrived in the most remote and savage place on earth."

"Yes," I said, "I will never forget when I first saw you at the camp. I knew then that we were meant to be together."

"I did not reveal my true feelings, Santos," she said. "My heart leapt with joy at the sight of you, even though my actions did not show it. I could not sleep for days as I wondered about you."

"Yes, and you sacrificed it all for me, even though I sometimes wonder why," I said.

"But it is this place, Santos. I look at it differently now. Through you I have grown to see its beauty," she said. Her eyes dropped to the amulet hanging from my neck.

"It is all I have left of my father," I said.

"It is lovely and mysterious. Wouldn't you like to see how it looks around my neck?" she asked.

Her request was out of character for the woman whom I knew rarely put value on such things.

My eyes lifted to hers, and my heart stopped in horror, as if frozen. It was not Dorry sitting next to me at all. My love had suddenly disappeared, and in her place was the witch from my dreams. She looked more frightening than ever with her murky, empty eyes and mottled gray skin. Her wide, evil smile was horrific and showed the black stubs of her broken and decayed teeth. I could even smell the dead stench of her corpse like breath on my cheek. I recoiled in terror, as her unearthly strong grip pulled on the amulet. The chain that held it tightened around my neck, and I felt my head being drawn toward hers.

"OH, KISS ME SANTOS! YOU WILL BE MINE FOREVER!" she said in her dreadful, screeching voice.

"Leave me, witch!" I screamed, trying to pull away from the terrible creature and her cackling laughter.

I woke suddenly to loud screams outside the jail enclosure. It was still dark and cool, and I could see the glow of many torch lights burning throughout the camp. I felt as if I were still dreaming as men ran past me, many of them carrying swords or clumsily trying to load their pistols. I recognized one of them as he rushed by and called out his name.

"Luis! What has happened?" I shouted.

"Hah! As if you don't know," he answered, looking at me with watery eyes, an accusatory expression on his unshaven face.

"What?" I asked again, this time more loudly.

"Your friends are here to kill us and take the King's treasure!"

"My friends?" I asked incredulously.

"A scout has reported that pirates have landed to the south!" he screamed.

CHAPTER 53
A DEAL WITH THE DEVIL

Fear and apprehension spread through the entire camp like wildfire, and the night air was full of shouts as the men frantically tried to prepare for the impending attack. I scrambled to the side of my makeshift jail and gripped two poles, straining my eyes through the darkness to see what was going on. Several men ran as if the hounds of hell were on their tails, and I watched as they disappeared through a break in the palmetto log barrier just to the west of my prison. My heart leapt with excitement, and I shouted at one of them.

"You there!"

He stopped and looked at me, his face twisted in panic. He was a rat-faced man with a long, scraggly beard and eyes that were beady and too close together. His clothes were filthy and torn, and he had a sweat stained bandana tied around his mop of black hair.

"What do you want?" he shouted impatiently.

"Those men coming, they are my brethren. If you free me from this hole I will tell them to grant you mercy, and you won't have to run like those other cowards!" I said.

He looked at me for a moment, hesitating as his mind worked.

"I'll pay you handsomely," I said coaxingly. "Those men will take what you have here. You may as well be on the winning side, my friend."

He looked around quickly, and then ran over to the makeshift door. I met him there and waited for him to cut the leather strap that held it shut. I met his gaze and saw a look of narrow-eyed suspicion.

"How can I trust you, pirate?" he said. "You're scheduled to hang on the morrow."

"Because, friend," I said in a low voice that took him off guard, "I am your worst nightmare!"

As I spoke these words, my hand shot between the poles and gripped his beard tightly. I jerked his head toward me, grinding his face into the grating.

"Aaah!" he screamed, as I reached down and pulled the long knife from the scabbard he wore at his side. I deftly cut the leather thong that held the door fast, then pushed both him and the door backwards, never letting go of his beard. He jeered at me with unintelligible oaths of rage as I squeezed my body through the opening. I let go of him and quickly flew around the open door, my fist raised to strike. I smashed him directly in the face, and he fell backwards onto the sand.

"Your greed has made you a foolish man!" I said to his motionless form before running off into the darkness.

I ran to the trees on the outside border of the camp's west side, doing my best to remain undetected in the mayhem. My only goal was to put as much distance as possible between me and the foul little jail. As the lights of the camp grew small behind me, I began to relax, and my mind started to function again. I remembered the news of the invading pirates, and looked south, searching for signs of their approach. An hour passed without any sight of them, and I began to think that the whole thing had been a false alarm.

A sound came to my ears that didn't fit in. I stopped and listened closely, hearing the sound again over the gentle roar of the sea. I realized that it had the staccato cadence of a drum march. I peered through the darkness south, and my eyes soon detected the glow of torch lights ahead. I moved very slowly around some fallen palmetto trees and bayonet plants until I was parallel to their position. Suddenly, I heard the soft crunch of a footstep behind me. I slowly reached for the knife in my belt. I then heard a sound that was very familiar to me; the strange, halting cry of an owl.

"Dunkirk!" I whispered hoarsely. He was there in an instant, as if he had been standing right next to me. His grinning face in the moonlight was a welcome sight indeed!

"Have you been watching these men?" I asked. He mumbled a few words in his native language and shook his head up and down.

"How is everyone at camp? Are they safe?"

My questions came too fast, and I saw the confusion on his face. I slowed down, trying to enunciate my words.

"Did you follow the men who took me prisoner?" He shook his head "yes."

"Were you watching the *Es-pa-no* who had me?" Again, "yes."

I looked back toward the amber firelight, my mind working furiously. After a few moments, I turned back to him.

"Dunkirk, I need you to do something very important for me. Our lives may depend on it."

I told him of my hastily prepared plan. He shook his head and smiled, showing that he understood and then turned away, disappearing like a ghost into the night.

It was clear, but very dark on that December night, and the cold, unrelenting wind blew in from the sea. There was a large fire burning close to the water's edge, and in its light I could see the outlines of many men unloading small boats that had been pulled up onto the sand. There appeared to be hundreds of them, and even though I was a good distance away I could hear the tell-tale clanking of metal as they walked. They were armed to the teeth with cutlasses, pike poles, and flintlock pistols, ready for battle. They were a swarthy lot, and I knew that the sixty or so Spaniards at the salvage camp would not stand a chance in a fight with them. Most were barefoot and sparsely dressed despite the chill in the air. I heard them speak to one another in low, threatening tones peppered with sporadic bouts of laughter. Most of them spoke in a dialect of English that I could not understand well, but I did recognize a few words due to my association with Shad. I heard phrases like *"Spanish dog bastards"* and *"we'll hang every god-damned one if we have to."* I knew that these were the roughest sort of men; the kind not to be toyed with. There had been many like them on Brattock's ship, and I knew what deviltry they were capable of. I smiled as I thought of Allejandro and the pompous General Salmon, and what they were about to experience. Gathering all of the courage I could, I walked out of my hiding place, approaching them slowly with my hands outstretched to show that I was unarmed. As I entered the amber yellow light of their torches, one of them confronted me.

"Whoa there, mate," said a large man with a completely bald head and heavily tattooed arms as thick as tree trunks. He pointed a flintlock pistol at my face. "Wot's yer business, mate?"

"I am a friend. I was a prisoner of the Spaniards, and have escaped. I beg audience with your Captain. I have information that may help."

The men in front of the rabble were quiet and looked at me suspiciously.

"He's a bloody Spaniard, 'imself," shouted a small man with jet black hair and a short beard. He was carrying a cutlass that was nearly as long as his leg.

"Wait, ye dogs!"

The voice came from somewhere within the crowd. The men in front parted to let someone through. Two dangerous looking fellows, one short and the other tall and rail-thin, stepped out toward me. The shorter man approached me, looking me up and down, as if sizing me up. I guessed that he was of middle age, because his long brown hair was graying at the temples, and the lower half of his face was covered with gray beard stubble. His skin was so sun bronzed that it looked like smooth and worn leather, and he wore his hair long and tied back on his head. His face was plain featured, but his dark eyes flashed with cunning intelligence. He was slender, all but for a slight swelling in his midsection, and wore what was once a fine black waist coat and white breeches complete with large brass buttons that were faded from wear. On his feet were scuffed leather boots that came almost to his knees. In one hand he held a large, gray slouch hat with a wide floppy brim. Around his waist was an impressive brace of pistols and a scabbard for a long, thin dirk that bounced at his side as he walked.

"What is your business here, Spaniard?" he asked in a calm voice. The man displayed the manner more of a refined gentleman than a pirate.

"My name is Santos Alvarez, and I was a prisoner of the Spanish."

His eyes widened at this. "Say that again? Your name, I mean."

"Santos Alvarez."

The man looked me up and down as if appraising me, then smiled widely.

"I have heard of you."

He turned and walked over to the taller man, speaking to him and a few others who had gathered into a small group. I could not hear what was said, but they shook their heads and grunted with low laughter. After a few moments, he turned and strode back to me.

"Are you claiming that you are the great pirate captain that we have heard so much about? The same man that has been the bane of these Spanish bastards for so many years?" he said.

"You know of me?" I asked with surprise.

"Everyone does!" he exclaimed. He turned to his men and raised his hat into the air.

"Gentlemen! We have a distinguished guest with us. I would like you to meet the great Pirate Captain, Santos Alvarez; leader of the cannibals of La Florida!"

There was a short confused silence as the men looked at me, muttering to each other as they beheld my ragged clothes and unkempt hair and beard. I did not know if the man was serious or making fun of me. I wouldn't have blamed them if they didn't believe me. In truth, I expected to be killed at any moment.

"Huzzah!" one of them shouted. The cry was soon joined by another, and the air was filled with a cacophony of voices as the men gathered around, patting me on the back and welcoming me. A wave of relief washed over me, and I did my best to appear brave and strong, even though I felt very weak.

"Captain Santos, it is a pleasure to meet such a man as yourself. I am Henry Jennings of Jamaica, and these are my men. We have come to relieve the Spanish here of the terrible burden of shipping all of that treasure they have reclaimed from the sea," he said with a flourish and a dramatic bow. He swept his hat toward the taller man accompanying him. "This is my first mate, Charles Vane. He is new to my crew, but like you, has no love for the Spanish. Other than their gold, that is!"

Vane was much more imposing in appearance than Jennings. He had long, dark hair and wore a full beard that spread out across his chest. On his head was a black hat with a wide, ornately trimmed brim pinned up on one side. He wore a black jacket with brass buttons over a red blouse, and knee length breeches with black stockings and leather shoes with wide buckles. His face was also dark and tanned from the sun, and his mouth seemed locked in a perpetual sneer. The look he gave me sent a shiver up my spine, and I knew instinctively that he possessed a large capacity for cruelty. Like Jennings, he was heavily armed with at least three pistols, a large scabbard at his side, and a long pike that he used as a walking stick.

"Pleasure to meet your acquaintance, Captain Alvarez," he said in a voice that was low and menacing. "I have heard much about you."

"Men, get the Captain something to eat and a proper coat. This wind is as fierce as a nor'easter," Jennings said in a loud voice.

I realized that I was indeed cold and shivering, so I accepted the military style waist coat that an older man offered me. I was led to the roaring fire, where I took a seat on a palmetto stump next to Captain Jennings. He seemed to be very interested in my story, so I spent the better part of an hour telling him of my life on the beaches of La Florida. He was enraptured by the tale, and never once interrupted me as I spoke. When I finished, he sat back and shook his head as he took it all in.

"An amazing story, Captain. I see that you will want to get your revenge against these bastards. That much I can help you with."

He then told me that news of the wrecked treasure galleons had spread across the Caribbean like a wildfire, and that scores of vessels would soon be descending on the place from each of the islands.

"All of Jamaica flew into a wild uproar at the news of it. Up to five men a day deserted their ships to go "a wrecking" and get their share of the Spanish treasure. I was commissioned by the Governor himself to make haste to this place and dispatch any and all illegal attempts at piracy in the area, and to lay claim to whatever spoil I could obtain. I own property on the island and have many responsibilities to attend to, so I was forced to make hasty preparations for the voyage by hiring men like Vane here, and his crew."

Had he just told me that the Royal Governor of Jamaica had hired pirates?

I looked over at Vane, who was sitting on the other side of the fire, engaged in conversation with several rough looking men. One of them was a huge bear of a man with a beard that was so thick and full that it hung down to his chest in long ropes. He periodically took huge gulps from a large, black onion bottle, and hung on Vane's every word, laughing heartily at everything he said. He was more intimidating than any pirate I had ever seen, except for Abraham.

"Teach, you look as though you just came straight from the gallows," Vane laughingly shouted.

"My lad," roared the bearded man, "that's a brilliant notion! The next time, we shall play a game of gallows and see 'oo can swing the longest on the rope without being throttled!"

The other pirates erupted in laughter. Teach then got to his feet and began to dance around like a clown, spinning in a circle, the bottle still in one hand.

"Aye, you dance just like me own woman back in London!" one man shouted.

Teach froze at this, and silence fell over the group.

"Who sayeth these words?" he said in a low voice.

"T'was me," said one of the pirates standing near him in a quavering voice. "T'was only a joke, me friend."

"You come 'ere, lad. You will dance with me, and we'll both be girls from London."

The man didn't move. Suddenly, with the speed of a wild animal, Teach leapt at him. His huge hands encircled the man's throat, and he shook him like a rag doll. He then dragged the pirate out into the open, and began to dance around with him.

"You like this?" Teach said. He then held the man back and slapped him hard across the face with his open hand. The man fell to the sand in a crumpled heap. Teach stood back and let out a raucous laugh, and all of the others joined in. He reached down and grabbed the man's tunic and jerked him up from the ground. "Now I'm going to 'ave a drink with the lady 'ere."

"Teach is one of the finest men I have. He's rough, but you have to be to lead the Brethren," Jennings said.

I glanced up the beach to the north, in the direction of the salvage camp, my thoughts turning to Dorathea. What if she were to end up in the hands of such cutthroat men as these? The Spanish did not stand a chance against them, so I would have to be ready for anything. Captain Jennings continued to speak.

"I procured the services of several experienced divers. We set sail out of Bluefields nigh upon three and a half weeks ago, with two vessels in our party, my own being the *Barsheba* with eight guns and eighty men, and the sloop *Eagle*, under the command of Captain Wills, with twelve guns and one hundred men. We sailed past the mountains of Cuba with great haste, stopping only briefly at the wild ports of Mariel and Honda for supplies. When we came to an area to the south known as Key Biscayne, we encountered a Spanish mail boat named the *San Nicholas* heading south to La Habana, which we promptly made contact with. The Captain, a man by the name of De la Vega, told us that he had recently moored off the coast very near this place a few days earlier. He also informed us that he had met other vessels in the previous days that had the same questions we were now asking. He did not know the exact location of the camp, but told us that we could not miss it if we simply let the currents in the Bahama Channel carry us north.

I did not have much use for him for he was a typical Spaniard, so I commandeered his ship and had Mr. Vane convince him to see things my way. Sure enough, we discovered that he had been holding out, and we soon uncovered treasure that he had concealed in the ships interior. I have to be honest, son. I've learned to never trust a Spaniard."

"I am a Spaniard, Captain Jennings," I said, smiling resignedly.

"Yes, and I do not trust you. You say you are Captain Santos Alvarez! If you are truly him, those men in the camp yonder would like to see you hang from one of those blasted palm trees."

"With all due respect, sir, I can assure you that this is so."

He looked at me hard for a moment, and then continued his story.

"We were now three ships strong as we made our way along the coast. As we sailed farther north we began to encounter signs of wreckage along the shoreline and the sad remains of the dead. I knew that we were getting closer when I saw wrecks that had been burned to the waterline by the Spanish salvagers. Last night my lookout spotted the light of fires burning, and we located the southern camp."

"There is another camp? I asked. I did not remember this as we walked up the beach.

"Yes, there is one a short distance south of here by a cluster of wrecked galleons. I knew that this was not the main camp because of its small size. We sailed on and sure enough, this camp came into view. We landed here, between the two of them. We will visit both before we are through."

"The Spaniards must have built it very recently," I said.

He paused and gazed at me, a strange expression on his sun burned face.

"I have an idea," he said, stroking his chin and looking at me, then back at the salvage camp.

"We'll make you the negotiator."

His words momentarily stunned me. Was I to face my cruel captors again? I said nothing and looked out toward the sea.

"Come now, Captain Santos, I will not let them harm you, if you are who you say you are," he said with a smile on his face. "If your true identity is confirmed, I will help you escape this place. If you are lying to me, I will leave you to their mercy."

CHAPTER 54
PLUNDER

About an hour before daylight Jennings had his men form a loose military formation, and together they began to plod north through the sand, their torches lighting their progress along the sea. The drummer, a boy of about sixteen years with a sock cap pulled down over his ears, kept time the whole way, the men matching his beating rhythm with their steps. The sun slowly broke the morning gray, rising on the eastern horizon of the ocean in a magnificent flourish of red and yellow. As my senses took in this stunning sight, I thought of how a place so beautiful could be the site of such cruelty and loss.

As the salvage camp came into view in the distance, I took my place next to Captain Jennings at the front of the line. The two galleons were still there, stationed like sentinels on the calm surface of the ocean. We marched to within shouting distance of the sand and palmetto log fortifications of the camp and stopped, some of the men sitting down to rest. I looked around and saw that the majority of them did not seem to be concerned or anxious about the possibility of violence, and were, in fact, laughing and joking with one another.

Captain Jennings conferred with some of his pirates, and a large contingent of them split from the main group, making their way into the trees to the west. I correctly guessed that his intentions were to completely surround the camp, thus sealing off any chance of escape. Jennings and his men then sat back and did nothing, as if waiting patiently for some reaction to our presence from inside the camp. After what seemed like hours, the crude entry gate was pushed open, and three men walked out and slowly made their way toward us across the sand. I recognized Admiral Salmon almost immediately. The other two were soldiers I had seen but could not identify.

Viewing Admiral Salmon from my new perspective, it occurred to me how small and frail the man looked after the months of hardship on the beach. His military breeches were filthy and his stockings were thin and worn, in contrast to the extravagant appearance of his ornately decorated breastplate and morion helmet. Captain Jennings approached him very respectfully, extending his hand in a gesture of greeting. Admiral Salmon refused the pirate captain's courtesy, but removed his helmet in a stiff gesture of military protocol.

"I am Admiral Don Francisco Salmon. What do you want here?"' he demanded.

I was surprised at Salmon's expert grasp of the English language. His accent was thick, but his speech was very clear.

"I am Captain Henry Jennings, official representative of the Governor of Jamaica, and these are my sons. It has been a long journey across the Caribbean Sea to visit this place, and we want only compensation for our efforts," Jennings said coolly. I had to admire the man for the gentlemanly manner in which he was handling the angry Admiral.

"I'm afraid that you will be disappointed," Admiral Salmon said. "There is nothing for you here. The supply ships have already departed for La Habana with His Majesty King Philip's treasure." He gestured out toward the two looming galleons. "The only ships left are *Los buques de la Guardia Real*, which are manned with four hundred of his Majesty's finest battle-tested veteran soldiers."

"Admiral, do you truly believe that a man of my experience would not have been provided with accurate information of your true strength and fighting capabilities here?"

Admiral Salmon's eyes flared defiantly as the pirate captain exposed his lies.

Jennings paused, gazing at the man, and then turned his head to look at the galleons. He then focused his attention on the salvage boats that had been pulled up onto the sand along the shore.

"And you have done nothing since your treasure ships left? Why are you still here? I think that you are not being truthful with me, Admiral. It is my belief that you are hiding more treasure inside those shoddy walls behind you," he said.

The Admiral stared at Jennings intensely as his mind worked. His barely contained rage at being called a liar was obvious by the trembling scowl on his face. Salmon was not a fool. He knew that Jennings and his men would not leave until they were satisfied. The expression on his face softened, and he seemed to shrink a bit.

"I would like to negotiate with you. If you are a gentleman you will realize that I am responsible for the recovery of what is lost. My men and I are prepared to die for it if necessary," he said. "As you can see, my galleons are well disposed for our defense, and I will signal them to fire upon your gang of cutthroats if your actions deem necessary."

Jennings looked at him thoughtfully, and then spoke.

"Let me summon my negotiator. Come here, Captain Santos."

He waved a beckoning hand toward me. The Admiral's head whirled around, his gaze locking on my face. His whole demeanor changed, and he instantly flew into a fit of rage.

"This man is a criminal! He is a traitor to his country! What is he doing here?" he spluttered.

"Do you know who he is, Admiral Salmon?" Jennings asked.

"Of course! He is the bloody pirate Santos Alvarez, and will burn in hell for all of his deeds! I was to hang him just this morning! Oh, what treachery has befallen us?" he cried, throwing his hands into the air and turning away.

The pirates burst into laughter at Admiral Salmon's reaction, and Jennings gave me a nearly imperceptible nod, a knowing smile on his face.

"Unfortunately, Admiral, it is with him you must negotiate. Go ahead, Captain Santos."

Admiral Salmon glared at me, his eyes malevolent. I defiantly returned his stare, looking straight into his gray eyes.

"What have you done with Señora Dorathea?" I shouted, taking both the Admiral and Jennings by surprise. "Speak up, you stupid old fool or I will have you flogged in front of your men!" I said with more anger than I intended. I was trembling with fury at the memory of what they had done to Caesar, and I wanted revenge. The Admiral was momentarily taken aback at my unexpectedly harsh tone, but quickly recovered.

"I will not be spoken to in this fashion by a criminal!" the Admiral spat out indignantly.

Jennings watched his reaction carefully. "Just tell him what he wants to know, Admiral, and we will have an easier time here," he said in a soft voice.

The Admiral paused, a stubborn and almost childish expression on his face.

"I have not seen the girl," he said gruffly. "Allejandro Ruiz is her betrothed and protector. He has rescued her from the likes of you and your rabble and taken her to St. Augustine."

"Allejandro Ruiz! When did he leave?" I demanded sharply.

The Admiral ignored me and looked at Jennings. "I am prepared to make an offer to you and your men."

Jennings laughed gently. "And what would that be, sir? You don't have many bargaining pieces."

"I will gladly hand over twenty-five thousand pieces of eight if you and your "men" turn and go home peaceably and leave us to our business," he said.

Jennings stared at him, an open-mouthed expression of mock awe on his face. "That is a fine sum indeed, Admiral Salmon," he said, "especially since you have already informed me that there is no treasure here."

"We have set aside this amount for protection. It is all we have."

Jennings walked up very close to the proud Spaniard and stared directly into his eyes. He spoke so softly that he could barely be heard, but his words cut to the bone.

"It is obvious that you see me and my sons as a gang of impudent children that you can easily manipulate with your Spanish mendacities. I assure you, Admiral, that many of those I have formerly met in battle would attest that I am no child. What I can tell you is that if you do not reveal to me where you have hidden the treasure you and your men have recently recovered, I will unleash my hungry dogs on this place. If this occurs, I will see that every man, woman, and child here is roasted on a spit for my evening meal. Now, old man, are we ready to talk?"

Admiral Salmon shrunk at these words as the sickening realization came over his face that he truly had no choice. He turned away from the pirates and waved his arm in a signal to the waiting commanders of the galleons, and walked briskly toward the camp. Captain Jennings looked at me and smiled.

"I have grown tired of this game."

At that very moment, there was a thunderous explosion from the sea as the southernmost galleon let loose a broadside. Eight guns simultaneously spewed smoke and a terrific whistling sound filled the air. Back toward the rear of the pirate band the sand seemed to explode, flying high into the air as the ball and chain shot slammed into the beach. Men screamed out in pain when the huge projectiles tore through their bodies as if they were made of paper. I saw one man lose both of his legs and collapse to the beach in a bloody, twisting pile. The pirates seemed to waver, and some of them turned to flee up the beach.

"Those bastards!" I shouted.

Jennings was infuriated. "I will kill every Spaniard here for that!" he seethed.

I looked out toward the warships, and something caught my eye to the south. There was another ship moving quickly shoreward from deep water. I wondered, at first, why the galleons hadn't spotted her. I could then see that the angle of the sun had screened her approach from the galleon's lookouts. Before I could shout out, there was the loud boom of cannon fire from her gun ports. The southern galleon seemed to waver from an unseen impact, and her mainsails fell as if cut by a great blade. I only knew of one weapon capable of such damage.

"Knipple shot! It's my ship, the *Pantera!*" I shouted to Captain Jennings.

"Well I'll be damned!" he exclaimed.

She sailed swiftly passed the disabled galleon, her sails billowing in the breeze; the most beautiful sight I had ever beheld.

"They couldn't see her! She sailed in direct line with rising sun!" I shouted.

Jennings's pirates began to cheer as black smoke started to rise from the damaged ship. The northern galleon frantically tried to turn her bow for a broadside, but the smaller *Pantera* was too quick. She sailed directly between the two Spanish ships and glided to a full stop, unleashing all of her starboard guns at once. Again, the knipple shot proved devastating to the rigging of the larger vessel as the front mast seemed to disintegrate before our eyes; the deck choked with wood splinters, ropes and rigging. The panicked Spaniards had no time to react and ran around the wreckage like ants. Momentum carried the galleon around to face the *Pantera* on her port side.

"No," I screamed. "Don't let her get off a broadside! She'll cut you to splinters!"

"Wait," Jennings said. "I see method in their madness!"

The guns erupted from the ports of the galleon, directly at the *Pantera*.

Then, a miracle happened. It seemed that the northern galleon's barrage of cannon shot had passed through the *Pantera* as if she were a ghost and smashed into the side of the southern galleon, instantly decimating her hull.

"Ha!" Jennings laughed. "The *Pantera's* too low in the water! Their cannons can't aim low enough to hit her!"

Jennings and his mates began to laugh hysterically and danced around like schoolboys.

"Captain Santos," Jennings asked, "who is commanding the *Pantera?*" That was as brilliant a maneuver as I have ever seen!"

"I do not know," I answered. I honestly didn't. What I had just witnessed was amazing. Whoever was commanding her had known that the *Pantera's* deck was below the line of fire, and that the galleon's guns would completely overshoot her.

My thoughts quickly turned toward rescuing Dorathea, and I turned to face Captain Jennings.

"I think that your time has come, señor!" I shouted.

Jennings turned to them, raising his arm high in the air.

"Let us get what we came for!" he screamed.

His men needed no more prodding. A tremendous roar rose from the pirate legion, and they all began to run in a horde toward the salvage camp. As they streamed inside the crude gates, a few hardy Spanish soldiers rose from their hiding places to attack. Their bravery proved to be short-lived, and they were quickly and violently cut down by either sword or staff of the bloodthirsty invaders. I watched as the man called Teach ran directly at one of them, expertly knocking the soldier's musket away. Teach squared off with the terrified Spaniard, and with a single thrust, ran him through with a long pike. The soldier screamed in pain and grabbed the end of the weapon that stuck out before him with both hands as he fell to the ground. Teach, his imposing black beard glistening with perspiration, stood over him and pointed his finger down into the dying man's face, delivering a taunt that I could not hear above the cacophony of sound. The pirate then placed his foot on the soldier's chest and pulled his pike free, already scanning the area for another victim, his eyes gleaming with bloodlust.

The onslaught was complete, and within minutes the camp was swarming with pirates. They proceeded to dismantle, destroy, and pillage every corner of the camp for hidden treasure. Admiral Salmon had no choice but to point out the spot in the center of the camp where the chests were buried, so several men had set about digging up the wooden cases.

The soldiers, divers, and the few women in camp were rounded up and placed inside the same pole jail in which I had been held. Captain Jennings had made it very clear to his men that no innocent people were to be hurt unless they raised a hand in violence, so there were no atrocities committed. The women were left alone.

Snatching up a discarded cutlass I found lying next to a dead soldier, I ran around to all of the buildings, frantically searching for any sign of Dorathea. Near the northwest corner of the camp, I saw a figure run from a small hut fashioned from stout poles with a thatched palmetto roof. I went inside and found a shawl that I knew belonged to Dorry. Grabbing it in one hand, I ran from the house, wildly scanning the trees. I saw movement behind a thick oak, so I quickly ran to it. I leapt around to the other side, my cutlass raised and ready to strike. My heart sank as I found myself standing in front of a very old *Ais* woman. She cowered in terror, her arm raised across her tear-streaked face. She was dirty and dressed in rags, and I knew that she had been taken as a slave. I slowly bent to one knee and put my hand out, showing her that I meant no harm. Doing my best to recall bits of the language, I spoke to her gently.

"Don't be frightened. I am Santos Alvarez, a friend to your people. I mean no harm to you. The beautiful woman with black hair; have you seen her here?" I asked, stumbling on some of the words. She was surprised at this, and her eyes found mine. I saw that she now recognized me.

"Do you remember Chera?" I said and pointed to my chest. Her eyes fluttered and she managed a smile.

I looked skyward. "They all know you, my sweet, sweet Chera," I said aloud. The woman got to her feet and grabbed my hand, pulling me toward a large gap in the fence.

"*Es-pa-no* take her there," she said, pointing north. I gripped the large cutlass tightly, bolted through the breach and into the jungle.

CHAPTER 55
THE CHASE

I darted between the palmetto hammocks and stands of
sea grape and bayonet plants, searching for any signs of
Allejandros' passing. His party proved to be easy to track due
to their inexperience and hasty flight through the dense
foliage. I encountered many broken branches and the faint
outlines of footprints in the low, muddy areas. I knew that
they had a significant head start on me, so I moved as quickly
as I could. One hour became two, and the morning soon
passed into afternoon. I began to fear that I had lost their
trail. My sense of worry increased even more as the shadows
on the forest floor grew longer, and I doggedly searched the
ground for signs.

Just as I was about to give up and start my return trip
back to the salvage camp, I heard a commotion in the trees
above my head. There was a great swooping sound, and
several small oak leaves rained down from the forest canopy
above. To my surprise, I saw a large bird glide into the open
space in front of me and land on the moss-covered branch of a
large oak. It was a magnificent bald eagle, and it focused its
sharp gaze directly on me and let out a cry. I had always been
in awe of these beautiful creatures, so I stood frozen in place.
There was a flash of white at its claw, and then something
delicate fluttered to the ground in gentle spirals. I ran to
where it fell and picked it up, rubbing the fabric between my
thumb and forefinger. It was a piece of white lace that I
immediately recognized. Dorathea had once told me that she
carried with her in the pocket of her breeches for "good luck."
I knew that she had intentionally left it for me to find. I
looked up at the giant eagle and saw that it had taken off

again and was flying to the north between two large stands of live oaks. I ran in the same direction, revitalized by the sign I had been given.

Just as I entered the open area between the trees, I tripped on the protruding root of a huge gumbo limbo and felt my foot sink into a hole. I lurched forward and stumbled to the ground, my foot slipping even deeper into the hidden cavity. I was momentarily stunned and angry, but my blood ran cold as I heard a very familiar sound. The hissing came from below the leaves, and before I could gather my wits to pull my leg free it was too late. The snake struck with blinding speed, sinking its fangs deep. I let out a cry of pain and surprise and scrambled backward, yanking my leg free of the hole. It hung on with the cold tenacity of a killer, its body flailing; its flat, black eyes showing nothing but malevolence. It was almost emerald green in color and had a sharp, red stripe that ran all the way down the length of its body. Time seemed to stop, and there was a terrifying moment when it appeared to be looking directly at me. Then, just as suddenly as it had struck, it pulled loose and slithered away through the underbrush.

I curled up into a ball, instinctively slapping my hand over the wound in a futile attempt to curtail the pain. I could feel its evil venom coursing through my blood as I grimaced in agony. After a few moments my panic subsided, and I tried to quiet my mind and think rationally. I had never been bitten by a venomous snake, but I had seen others who had. I knew what a rattlesnake looked like and the dreaded water moccasin, but this one had been like no other. Its color was unlike any I had ever seen, and its eyes-oh, those horrifying dead, black eyes!

I then heard another sound among the whispering wind in the leaves: a woman's low, mocking laughter. I leaned back up against the tree and massaged the wound on my lower leg, feeling the swelling begin. My head felt woozy with shock, and the stinging soreness in my leg grew steadily. Things in front of me started to appear distorted, as if I were viewing them through some sort of strange tube. The sounds of the forest seemed to echo from a distance as if on the far side of some great chamber. These sensations became more and more intense, and I felt blackness begin to overtake me.

I opened my eyes and saw that late afternoon had come. There was moisture in the air and it was growing cooler. My leg still throbbed with pain and had swollen to nearly twice its normal size, and I was paralyzed with aching nausea. I looked up toward the sky, and saw dark clouds. A storm was moving in. For some reason, I could feel Dorathea's presence near me. I knew that she was not far, but I was helpless to do anything but sit there, clinging to life. Many thoughts clouded my mind; some rational and some not. I imagined that the soldiers travelling with Allejandro were most likely becoming quite desperate in their flight because they were unfamiliar with the ground. The normal route north would have kept them near the shoreline, but the threat of a second encounter with the pirates would have forced them to take their chances inland.

Thunder boomed in the distance, and in a few short minutes I felt raindrops on my forehead. In a very short time the light completely disappeared. Darkness swallowed everything as a deluge of rain began falling. I desperately tried to keep my mind alert, doing my best to stay focused. I soon felt the grip of exhaustion take hold, and I closed my eyes to rest, letting the pain envelope me. I had never felt so alone in my life, and tears sprang from my clouded eyes. Everything I had worked for and loved seemed to be crumbling apart. I would not survive this night and see my love again. The

Spaniards had burnt our homes and killed my people, and I lay dying in this lonely hammock all alone, unable to do anything. Dorathea would never know what became of me.

The rain gradually let up, leaving in its place a damp darkness that made it hard to see anything at all. My head was still spinning, and I noticed a small point of light off in the distant trees that did not seem right. I focused my gaze on it and saw that it seemed to grow larger. I felt a small spark of fear as I realized that it was moving toward me through the forest. The closer it got, the more it began to take shape as its weird, greenish light reflected off the trees and ground below it. A familiar horror rose in me as I saw just what it was, but the effects of the snake's venom had dulled my reactions. I simply curled up against the tree like a child. I helplessly watched as the witch of my nightmares appeared before me with the same black, menacing eyes as the serpent. She floated in front of me, her loose shift and long hair waving about her body slowly as if she were underwater. Her mouth held that hideous grin, displaying those black, decayed teeth. I looked up at her and raised my quivering hands in a useless gesture of defense, my body slowly swaying back and forth with pain and dizziness.

Suddenly, I experienced a detached feeling of surrender that I had never felt during any of my previous encounters with her. My body longed for release from my suffering and wasted condition. I only wanted the agonizing pain and fear to drain away. Just as I was about to give up, thoughts of Dorathea came back to me and reinforced my resolve to survive and find her. I closed my eyes and laid my head back against the tree and tried to dismiss the specter by wishing it away. I reached up and gripped my father's amulet with my shaking hand. It seemed to burn with unnatural heat against my chest.

"*Santos*," the whisper came on the breeze. "*The time has come.*"

"Leave me," I said. "Haven't you tortured me enough?"

"*Did you meet my friend, the snake?*"

"What do you want with me?" I asked in a weak, pleading voice, "Can't you see that I am dying?"

"*You will die when I command it. I am here to collect a debt, Santos.*"

"Just take me now. If I cannot save my love, I am done with this life," I said. I was beyond fear of her.

"*You must know the truth, Santos.*"

She floated very close to me, her horrible breath caressing my face.

"*Come with me to a place very long ago, so that I may show you.*"

I felt myself drifting up into the night, and could see the huge, bright moon very close to me.

TENOCHTITLAN

FIFTEEN-TWENTY

CHAPTER 56
CUALLI'S CURSE

Donato leaned against the wall, a sardonic look on his face as he observed the daily routines of the people in the marketplace by the great "Temple of the Sun." The extreme heat of the day was causing him to sweat, making him very uncomfortable. He was with a group of twelve foot soldiers charged with maintaining a presence in the common areas of the great city square. Unlike most of the other soldiers, Donato was unimpressed by the great city of Tenochtitlan and its native inhabitants. In his opinion, the people were half dressed barbarians who had no regard for civilized behavior. He was twenty-three years old with dark hair and a thick beard, and had a powerful physique under his *camisa* shirt and *Jacqueta De Mala* chain mail and armor. He wore a wide leather belt that supported his scabbard and sword. On his feet were high leather boots, and on his head was the traditional iron *morion* helmet with the flat brim and wide crest that stretched from front to back.

Donato believed that he was, in every aspect, the epitome of what a soldier should be. He had experienced a very troubled childhood in Tarragona, so he had been faced with the choice of either becoming a street urchin or starting his military service for the king at a very early age. He had taken to "soldiering" quickly and, when the opportunity arose, had eagerly volunteered for the sea voyage to Santo Domingo to help protect and expand the new empire. Over the last few years, he had periodically experienced trouble controlling his explosive temper, often ending up being incarcerated. The older he got, the more he realized that it would serve him better if he learned how to contain it. He was fortunate to have been given a reprieve when he had beaten Jose Villa nearly to death just before the ships left La Habana. The small argument at a card game had quickly bloomed into a brawl, and his fiery temper once again proved uncontrollable. He served Spain and God, and he knew that killing many of these beastly natives right here on this sandy ground would be the right thing for both. The priests would try to tame them their own way, by attempting to convince them of the error of their pagan beliefs. As a last resort, they would then torture the stubborn ones to save their sorry souls.

When they had first arrived on the great causeway leading up to the city, that clown fool, "Moctezuma," or whatever he called himself, had personally handed their leader, Don Hernando Cortés, two large discs as a gift: one made of gold, and one of silver. Donato smiled as he remembered the lust on Cortés's face at the sight of those round beauties. The naïve king had then welcomed them in and given them free reign of the city.

"His mistake," Donato thought to himself and smiled.

He admired one thing more than any other about the clown king. Moctezuma's mistress, Cualli, was one of the most beautifully exotic creatures Donato had ever seen. Just looking at her dark, supple form made him breathe hard and break into a sweat. If he ever had the chance to have her, he would do so in a moment. She was always scantily clad, and wore strange, white stripes on her face. He had heard that she was a witch with special powers. He had caught her gaze more than once, and had tried to give her a look of wanton desire. Her eyes were dark and flashing, and had returned his gaze with one of hatred and disgust. Donato would have given five gold pieces to wipe that look from her beautiful face.

Cortés had left a force of one hundred-forty men under the command of Pedro de Alvarado, a man that Donato liked and respected for his no-nonsense leadership and often brutal treatment of the natives. Some of the other soldiers thought that Alvarado's methods were too harsh and cruel, but Donato and his men considered his leadership more effective than Cortés in many respects. Alvarado felt the Aztecs to be akin to animals that needed to be trained.

The soldiers all stood close to each other, leaning on their long matchlock weapons and glaring disdainfully at anyone who passed close by. They formed a semi-circle under the overhang of one of the corners of the temple that offered some shade from the brutal, unrelenting heat.

"These people sicken me," Danato said in a low voice, "they are like dogs."

A few of the others grunted their agreement. In his opinion, the conquest of these animals had been relatively simple. For the most part these *indios*, as Columbus had referred to them, had scattered like birds at their approach, falling to their knees in terror at the intimidating sight of the mighty, armor-clad cavalry soldiers mounted on their great stallions.

"These fools have never seen horses before!" Cortés had proclaimed.

There had been some fighting along the way, but their small force had been both surprised and pleased that there were native people who were willing to join them against the mighty Aztecs.

Donato and his men had been appalled by the way the Aztec people lived, especially their bizarre religious practices. The daily rituals of human sacrifice were the most shocking and brutal things he had ever witnessed. After hours of pomp, prayer and singing, a line of several prisoners taken during battle were led to the top of the highest tower. After much ceremonial chanting and long speeches, one of the men was laid down on his back on a huge stone pedestal, where an ornately dressed priest performed a very bizarre, cruel ritual. While the unfortunate victim was alive and very conscious of what was happening, this priest would use a very sharp and jagged knife made of a white stone to slice through his chest cavity and cut out his still beating heart. The screams were mortifying as the severed organ, still pulsating with involuntary spasms and spurting blood, was then held up as an offering to whatever heathen god they worshipped. The still warm corpse of the sacrifice was then pitched from the top of the temple and sent tumbling to the ground. It was then immediately set upon by many women who cut the body up into small pieces. These pieces were then prepared, cooked and eaten; the fingers and hands said to be the tastiest, most desirable parts.

This was so revolting to the soldiers that they could barely contain themselves. Such acts were an absolute abomination in the eyes of God. Donato complained bitterly to Cortés of this atrocity, but the cagey conqueror insisted on restraint, citing the fact that these savages were only committing these terrible acts on each other, and would face the one, true God in good time. Donato had held his tongue, but still felt indignation at the thought of any sort of acceptance of this abhorrent behavior.

Donato was laughing with the soldiers at some crude joke when he noticed a group of three Aztec men walking up the thoroughfare toward them. They were young, most likely warriors, and were smiling and cajoling each other. Donato focused his attention on the one in the center of the group. He was taller and more muscular than most of his native brethren, with dark brown skin and long, dark black hair tied behind his head. He was not a handsome man. The skin of his face was badly pocked as if ravaged from some childhood disease. His nose was too large, in Donato's opinion, and appeared bent, as if broken in some nameless past clash. He wore a colorful garment tied around his waist and a red cloak over one of his shoulders. As they drew closer, Donato looked directly into his face in an attempt to intimidate, but the man defiantly looked back at him, his gaze hard and his dark eyes shining.

"Ah, what have we here?" Donato said loudly, grinning as he swept his hand through the air in a theatrically exaggerated gesture of introduction. "The city's finest men."

The other soldiers laughed at this.

Donato was bored and more than a little frustrated, so the chance to play with these monkey fools was a welcome diversion. The native men attempted to pass the soldiers' position, but Donato stepped out into the street, directly in their path.

"Hold up. We need to know what you men are doing." he said in a low voice.

The men paused and looked wary, not understanding a word Donato said, but perceiving the threat. The two smaller men raised their hands, palms up in a gesture of passivity, and shook their heads, but the tall man remained silent and stared. Donato, wanting to show off to the other soldiers, pushed the smaller men aside and walked straight up to the tallest one, standing so close that his nose was inches from the man's face. His friend, Luis, caught the subtle hand signal he gave behind his back, and slowly moved behind the three natives.

"You cannot pass this way, my stupid friend," he said loudly, small beads of spittle flying from his lips. "The toll is one gold piece."

Donato reached into his pouch, pulled out a small chunk of gold, and waved it in front the man's face. The Aztec stared back with contempt, slowly shaking his head in a gesture of insolent refusal. Out of the corner of his eye, Donato could see that Luis was ready. With a quick movement, he thrust both hands out at the tall native's chest, giving him a shove that sent him tumbling backward; tripping over Luis's well placed foot. He and Luis then both fell on him, raining vicious blows down on his body without restraint. As the beating progressed, the other soldiers gathered around as if watching some street performance, laughing and taking bets on how long the Aztec could last. A small crowd of people gathered around the scene, but no one dared intervene, even though low grumblings of protest could be heard. After a few minutes, two of the soldiers pulled Donato and Luis away from the bloody, semi-conscious man.

"You should not brawl with men more experienced than you!" Donato jeered at him.

The two smaller Aztecs helped their battered companion to his feet, and started to lead him away as Donato and Luis playfully punched each other's arms, laughing like schoolboys. Donato looked toward the three retreating Aztecs and saw that the beaten man had turned his head back, and was looking straight at him. He felt a slight chill as he noticed that, despite the beating he had just taken, the tall, dark native held that same defiant stare, his eyes focused and his gaze unbroken. A mocking sneer shone through his bloody lips, and he raised his hand and drew it across his neck in a subtle, threatening gesture. He then pointed his finger directly at Donato in a last gesture of defiance.

There was a loud commotion by the temple, so the soldiers gathered their weapons and made their way toward it.

"It's that heathen ceremony," Donato growled angrily, his blood up from the earlier violence. "I can't bear it, I tell you."

The colorfully dressed priests were gathering near the top of the temple's highest tier as the musicians commenced the ceremonial melodies. Huge feathered plumes emerged from the golden headdresses of the holy men as they began their methodical chants. Hundreds of people began gathering to witness the ancient ritual.

The soldiers approached the lower steps of the temple and glared at the natives congregating there. The main part of the great rite had already begun, and the prisoner-sacrifices were being led up the huge staircase to the top. Donato moved closer to the stone step of the temple and was surprised to see two stout native men step in front of him to block his way. They were both strongly muscled and scantily clad in loincloths, with wooden animal masks over their faces. They carried longs spears with wide stone tips tied to the ends. Donato's temper flared out of control, and he reached to pull his sword.

"Get out of my way, you Godless animals," he bellowed as his weapon was freed of its scabbard, "I refuse to watch this vulgar display again. I will stop it!"

The other soldiers, realizing that Donato's temper had once again taken him over, looked warily at the large number of people and reluctantly pulled their sabers. They began moving toward the temple in a tight group, the people moving back and giving them a wide berth. Donato snarled at the two guards and drew his free arm back, swinging at the one on his left. His meaty fist made contact with the side of the guard's head with a loud slap, causing the man's head to jerk back, the long colorful plumes on his head quivering wildly with the force of the blow. The mask came loose and fell askew. The other guard let out a loud cry and lowered his long spear. Before he could use it, Donato brutally thrust his sword into the man's chest. The guard shrieked and grabbed the sword blade with both hands and sunk to his knees, his life quickly ebbing away. Donato placed his foot on the man's chest and pulled his blade loose, and the lifeless body slumped to the ground. He was like an animal now, rage overcoming him and blinding him to any dire consequences of his brash actions.

A great roar erupted among the people, and the soldiers began to realize the gravity of their situation. They responded the only way they knew how: by fighting. They began to slash and thrust indiscriminately at the people around them, pushing their way forward to the great steps. The native guards, though smaller in stature than the Spaniards, threw themselves at the soldiers, thrusting their long spears in front of them wildly. One of the soldiers screamed and spun around violently as his body was penetrated.

Donato let out an angry shout and leapt up the stairs, swinging his blade at anything that moved. The screams of wounded men and women filled the air as he and his men pushed, slashed and shoved their way toward the top tier of the temple. As they reached the pinnacle, the elaborately dressed priests cowered back in fear.

"Kill the heathens in the name of Christ! They must pay for this abomination!" Donato howled; his terrible frenzy of anger at its peak.

The soldiers fell on the priests with a vengeance, releasing all of their zealous frustration. Their weapons rose and fell as they began to slaughter the entire ceremonial group. A few of the native guards tried to put up resistance, but the surprise of the attack and superior steel of the Spaniards was too much. The Aztec holy men tried desperately to escape being cut down; some of them leaping from the height of the great temple itself to their deaths on the hard ground below.

Donato recognized a man wearing a colorful, intricately carved wooden mask cowering on the far side of the temple floor. He was the holy executioner; the same man he had witnessed taking countless lives in the terrible sun ritual several times a day since they had arrived. Donato ran through the horde of people toward him, pushing men who were engaged in battle out of the way. He threw his body at the priest, tackling him to the floor; his sword clattering to the floor's surface and sliding a few feet away. Flipping the man over, he wrapped his strong hands around the masked man's neck. As he did this, the man's right arm thrust upward, and he felt a sharp pain in his side. He felt the warm wetness of blood on his skin and screamed out in rage, tightening his grip on the priest's throat. When the man was dead, he got to his feet and felt the wound. There was a knife protruding from his side, so he grabbed it, yanking it from his body with a quick jerk. He felt his rage boil as he recognized its flamboyantly carved handle. It was the same ceremonial knife that had killed thousands of innocents. He slid it into his belt and leapt to his feet, staggering slightly at the flaring pain in his side.

It seemed as if the whole city were erupting like a great explosion. Donato felt another stabbing pain in his right arm and found that a warrior had thrust his spear and caught him just above the elbow. He managed to hold onto his sword as he looked out over the scene below him. In a few short minutes, the entire area had transformed into violent chaos. His thoughts were suddenly clear, and he instinctively knew that it was time to go. He ran to the edge of the great stairway, and then down them as fast as he could. Hearing a terrible scream, he looked up to see his friend, Luis, being lifted and hurled off the edge of the temple, his body bristling with spears.

"The lord God has to put an end to this!" Donato bellowed with rage as he fled.

When he was back on the ground, he ran from the melee, taking refuge in a very small courtyard at the rear of the temple. It had high walls that bordered the temple, and one small doorway that was easy to guard and blocked him from view. There was another internal doorway that led into a small, empty room underneath the temple that no one had ever used. Wounded in two places, he no longer had the desire to fight. He was bleeding profusely, and felt that he might pass out. There was a great uproar outside, so he carefully peered around the edge of the huge coquina edifice. The sight before him was unbelievable.

The great King, Moctezuma, was being stoned to death by his own people. He had been brave, Donato could give him that. He watched as the King's battered body jerked and convulsed with each blow. Moctezuma staggered over to the edge of the great temple and, with his arms still raised to his Gods above, fell off the side, crashing to the ground below a crunching thud. The King's body had fallen from the rear of the high temple platform, landing right in the same small courtyard where he was hiding. Donato ran to him and kneeled by the crumpled form, noting that the King was still alive. He felt a small streak of pity for him: this pagan clown. He heard screaming outside the doorway, so he got to his feet and moved back into the shadows.

Shrieking like an animal, Cualli ran into the courtyard and fell to her knees next to the twisted remains of Moctezuma. She clutched his face and howled with grief, her tears falling on his face. She placed her trembling hands over the golden amulet that lay on his chest and began to pray. The crowd roared outside the small enclosed area by the temple, but no one could see them.

Donato, smiling at his sudden good fortune, limped out of his hiding place and grabbed the stricken priestess by her arm. She glared at him with wild eyes filled with hatred. She fought like a she-wolf as he dragged her across the ground and through the opening in the empty base of the temple. For the next several minutes, Donato did all of the terrible things to the beautiful priestess that he had always longed to do. As her body was ravaged, she howled with rage, and then began to chant in a low, even voice. Cualli, in the native *Nauhwatl* tongue that she knew the Spaniard could not understand, concocted the most powerful and terrible curse that she had ever produced: one with origins back to her ancient Olmec ancestors. This is a summation of her words.

"I SUMMON ALL OF THE STRENGTH OF THE DARK PLACES! YOUR SOUL WILL BE SLAVE TO MY SPIRIT AND TO THE POWER OF THE OLD ONES FOR ETERNITY! YOU AND YOUR SONS WILL FOREVER SUFFER SWIFT AND TERRIBLE DEATH AT MY HANDS!"

When Donato had finished his ugly business, he strangled her with his bare hands and left her there with the King she would love forever. As if compelled to commit one last act of treachery, he bent and snatched the beautiful amulet from the chest of the dead King, easily snapping the finely crafted chain that held it. He slipped it into the pocket of his breeches and ran from the hidden place, quickly disappearing into the melee.

CHAPTER 57
THE RIGHTEOUS ONE

I felt myself falling through the night sky, my arms and legs suspended in mid-air, the cool wind whistling through my clothes. I looked down into the grayness below me. The images in my mind swirled around as if in a tempest, transforming into nonsensical oblivion. I was falling, but the air felt soothing as it rushed past my body. All around me was dark night sky, and the stars seemed very close. I reached out toward their light; fingers spread wide, the wind's resistance pushing against them. I breathed in slowly, enjoying the sensation of absolute freedom.

An unexpected thought crept in, and a dark realization came to me. If I was falling, then I would soon have to hit the ground! The surface of earth was suddenly there, speedily approaching me, much too fast to allow time for any reaction. My heart leapt with terror. In seconds, I was going to die. I closed my eyes and opened my mouth to scream.

My eyes snapped open again, and the scream came, but it was not mine. I sucked in huge gasps of air and shook my head back and forth to clear it. Was I dead? Was this what happened when life ran from our bodies? Looking around, I found that I was still leaning against the huge gumbo limbo tree in the forest. I looked up and saw that the woman was gone, as if she were made of the mist itself. I looked down at my legs, seeing the same filthy breeches that I had been wearing for weeks. I was not dead at all, but had only experienced one of my terrible visions. This one had been so real that I now questioned my own sanity. It was as if my own reality was slipping away. Had these events actually happened, or was the whole thing a product of the snake venom coursing through my veins?

My confused thoughts were interrupted by another scream from the trees. It was her; it had to be. I leapt to my feet and staggered off toward the source of the sound, still very dizzy and sick. There was a shout of pain, this time from a man. Stumbling through a stand of live oaks, I saw the orange glow of a large fire through the thick undergrowth ahead of me. I nearly lost my balance as I crouched down to peer through some palmetto fronds into a small clearing. Three soldiers were standing in a semi-circle around someone I could not see.

"Let me go, you beasts!" a woman cried. Even in my shattered state, my heart leapt as the recognized the voice. I looked down and cursed softly as I realized that I left my cutlass by the tree where I had been bitten by the snake.

"Be quiet and sit down! You are deluded by infatuation. I know what is best for you!"

"Don't tell me how I feel! I don't want to go with you! You are an evil man!" Dorathea sobbed.

"You must know that this is the right thing for us! A short distance from here, on the river, my boat waits to take us to St. Augustine. I have pilfered enough of the salvaged treasure to give us both a very good life. We can start over again."

This voice was Allejandro's. I slowly made my way around the edge of the clearing, trying to be as quiet as I could. I felt an unexpected wave of dizziness and fell forward, crashing through a stand of cabbage palms and rolling out into the firelight.

"Well, what have we here?" Allejandro said with surprise.

"Santos!" It was the shocked voice of Dorathea. "What are you doing here?"

"Seize him!"

The two burly soldiers ran to me, each one grabbing one of my arms and dragging me out to the open area by the fire. Allejandro sauntered over to me, noticing my swollen leg.

"Ah, a snakebite! This is a fine opportunity indeed to set things right." He drew back his foot and kicked me in the ribs, causing more waves of pain to course through me.

"Don't hurt him! Let him go and I will see that the pirates have mercy on you!" Dorathea cried.

"I don't need their mercy! They will all hang!" he shouted back. He kicked me again, harder than before.

"Allejandro, stop! You'll kill him!" she shouted.

He turned on her, tears of rage on his face. "Why do you defend him?" he shrieked.

Dorathea just looked at him, her own face wet with tears.

"I know why," he shouted. "You love this filthy pirate! You always have! Ever since we were children!"

He looked down at me, his face filled with hatred.

"Tonight it will all end. King Philip will have his revenge. Pedro, I want you to hang this pirate from that oak tree by the fire! I've had enough of his stench," he said bitterly.

"No!" Dorathea cried. "You can't!"

"I will take her away so she doesn't have to see it. You men follow after it is done."

In a haze of pain and delirium, I looked at his booted foot inches from my eyes. He then delivered me a last vicious kick before bending to pick up a torch from the flames. Grabbing Dorathea roughly by the arm, he pulled her away, half dragging her body past the fire pit. They disappeared down the path on the far side of the clearing.

"I hate these pirates," the larger of the two soldiers said. "I'm going to enjoy this."

They dragged my limp body over to the large oak tree and pulled me to my feet. The smaller man, the one called Pedro, produced a roughly hewn rope. He tied my hands behind my back with one end of it, tossing the other end over the lowest branch of the tree. The other soldier, whose name I did not hear, expertly tied a noose and threw it over me, drawing it tight around my neck. My head was spinning with sickness, and I hardly resisted as they pushed me around.

"All right, let's get this done. *Adios pirate!*" Pedro said. They both laughed out loud. The larger man took a few steps back and pulled the slack from the rope, and I felt the roughness of it tighten around my neck.

So this is truly the end of me, I thought. I was going to die here in this lonely place at the hands of these brutal men.

A low, haunting howl rose from the trees, as if from some lost spirit. Both men were startled by the strange cry and looked around warily.

"What was that?" Pedro said.

There was a strange "*thuck*" sound and I turned my head to face the large soldier holding the rope. His bulging eyes stared at me. Something did not seem right. Then I saw it. An arrow, the kind that the native hunters used, protruded from both sides of his neck. The pointed arrowhead was red and shiny with blood. He looked into my eyes, and I saw confusion, as if he were a young child.

What has happened to me?

He made a strange gurgling sound, and then pitched forward to the ground. Pedro, seeing what misfortune had just befallen his partner, spun around and wildly scanned the surrounding trees, a panicked expression on his face. The howl rose again and I saw his body shudder with the impact of a short spear, the kind I had seen the natives use for years. He screamed as he looked down at the spear protruding through his chest, an expression of horror on his face. He then turned around and aimlessly walked a few yards away, as if looking for something, before falling to the ground, his body quivering.

I heard the sounds of someone coming through the trees, and could soon make out the blurry images of several tall, lithe figures hovering on the edge of the amber fire light.

Were these devils from the forest, come to take me to the lower world?

They walked directly to me, crouching in a semi-circle over my crumpled form. Skillful hands quickly pulled the noose from my neck and cut my hands free. I saw that they were not devils, but *Ais* warriors in full body paint, two of which I recognized from the village. One of them was carrying an atlatl, the weapon used to mortally wound the still writhing Pedro. Someone I could not see barked out a command, and they moved stealthily to the two unfortunate Spaniards. The *Ais'* nearly naked bodies glimmered with sweat in the firelight as they worked purposefully, relieving the dead men of the possessions they would no longer need.

I heard the sounds of approaching footsteps, and saw three figures emerge from the forest. As they drew nearer, I felt a familiarity that confused me. I was too weak to acknowledge it, but I heard a deep, reassuring voice.

"Captain Santos; tank God we arrived in time."

It couldn't be.

I found myself looking into the smiling face of Caesar!

"I am dead, I am seeing spirits," was all I could say.

They laughed at this, and I saw that Abraham was there as well, looming behind him.

"Captain, for God's sake, you're a bloomin' mess."

Shad's familiar voice was like a soothing balm to my soul.

"It can't be-you're all here," I said.

"Jes my friend. We not leave ju again!" Caesar said.

"B-b-but Allejandro told me that you had been hung."

Ahh, Captain- what I tell ju before? Ju can never trust the *Es-pa-no!*

His look turned to one of concern as he saw the grave condition I was in. "Ju been snake bit, Captain!" He dropped to his knees next to me, touching my swollen leg gently, causing me to grimace in pain.

"Men," I moaned, "we must go rescue Dorathea. She has been taken by a bad man. Please.."

"Captain, you are in no condition to follow anyone," Abraham said. "I will send the hunters."

"No!" I demanded, pulling myself up to a standing position. "Help me, we must go now. They can't have gone far."

I staggered off toward the trees, my mind swimming sickly. The men stared at me, their faces masks of worry. They knew that I would not be swayed.

"Help him." Abraham said. Caesar ran to me, placing my arm over his shoulder to help me walk. We made our way down the trail with only the bright moon as our guide. The hunters led the way and kept low, stealthily moving along the path. They froze as a voice came from a short distance ahead, near the river. Both of them turned to look at Abraham, their eyes wide with purpose.

"Go ahead," he said in their native tongue, gesturing with his large hand. The warriors disappeared, seeming to melt into the foliage like ghosts. The voices ahead could be heard clearly now.

"Let me go!" Dorathea shouted from somewhere ahead of us. "I hate you!"

There was the sound of a hard slap and a grimace of pain.

"Silence, you stupid woman! You don't know what is best! You will come with me if I have to tie you!" Allejandro's voice was bordering on hysteria. "Go to the boat now!"

My heart sank as I realized that Allejandro's escape vessel was very close, probably tied at the shoreline ahead, ready to whisk them away up the river.

"We need to hurry, men!" I whispered hoarsely.

"Do not worry, Captain," Shad said. "They won't escape. They're just ahead, in that clearing between the mangroves."

I caught the glimpse of torchlight through the trees. There was a shout of anger.

"Get back, you savage! I will kill you right here if you do not stop!"

"The hunters have found them," Abraham whispered to me in a calm voice.

We soon emerged into a clearing between three palmetto stands. Allejandro, looking wild and half mad, stood brandishing a long knife, waving it menacingly at the two hunters who were on each side of him. The warriors stood ready, their lances poised. Seeing that things were hopeless, Allejandro made a very rash decision. He pulled Dorathea to his breast with one strong arm and placed the knife at her throat.

"Santos!" he cried in a voice breaking with panic and desperation. "Call off your animals or I will kill her now. If I can't have her, no man will!"

"Wait!" I cried out in panic. "Allejandro, you don't have to die!"

Dorathea looked paralyzed with fear, her body trembling as the madman tightened his grip around her slender throat.

"The boat is right over there, Santos. If you bar our way or try anything rash, I will kill her," he said, moving them both slowly toward the path.

"Go! Please do not harm her," I pleaded. "Can't you see that this is not the way?"

There was a disturbance in the tall grass directly behind him, and the *Ais* hunters hesitated, shrinking back. Allejandro did not sense it, but continued to glare at me defiantly, dragging Dorry along slowly, the knife still at her throat. Abraham placed his hand on my shoulder.

"Something is there in the grass. Something very big. The warriors sense it," he whispered into my ear.

There was a low rumbling that seemed to originate from the ground itself. The hunters shouted out in fear and immediately bolted, disappearing into the brush like ghosts. Allejandro whirled around, momentarily dropping the hand holding the knife from Dorry's throat. There was movement in the weeds, and something huge swiped out with lightning speed, catching him in the side of the face, instantly knocking him off balance. Allejandro shrieked in pain and surprise, and his grip loosened.

"Dorry, run! Hurry!" I shouted. She broke free and ran toward us. There was a primal cry that filled the air. Allejandro did not have time to think as another blow struck him on the other side, this time hitting him directly on the neck. He silently crumpled to the ground as a huge, golden panther emerged from the grass and descended on his shocked body, its massive head dropping to his exposed neck.

Dorathea ran to me, her face blinded by tears, and fell into my arms, nearly knocking me down.

~ 464 ~

The terrible cries echoed through the still night air as the panther mauled its prey. We all watched reluctantly, transfixed by the brutality of nature in its purest form. For just one moment, the great cat raised its head, directing its gaze at me and baring its bloody fangs in a snarl. In that instant, I knew.

I had seen this creature before.

This was Chera's totem animal, the same that had frightened the Calusa warriors in the forest years before. Chera had saved Dorathea's life. The creature held my gaze for a moment, as if trying to confirm my belief. It then bent its great head and bit in, taking a firm hold on the right leg. The panther slowly dragged the body into the trees. We watched as Allejandro's lifeless hand disappeared into the tall grass.

CHAPTER 58
HOME

Abraham and the *Ais* warriors dragged me back to the salvage camp on a crudely fashioned travois. I was now delirious with infection and close to death. They laid me near a great roaring fire so I could feel its warmth on my fevered skin. Abraham's woman, Adelena, was there; expertly treating my wound by applying a poultice of herbs that she had collected in the forest. She also gave me a dark tea brewed from dried blackberry plants. I faded in and out of consciousness, but Dorathea was always present, gazing down at me, her large eyes full of concern as she clutched my cold, sweaty hand. I could hear the sounds of the pirates all around me as they continued to ransack the camp, but I was past caring about anything.

"Santos, we are going to move you," I heard Dorry say through the haze. "Captain Jennings is giving us a boat. We are taking you home."

These words were welcome to me, but I didn't entirely understand their meaning. Home? We had no home.

The next couple of days were like a painful blur for me. I remember being loaded into a boat amid the clamor of men swearing and chattering to each other, and I recall the swaying feeling of the sea underneath me. The Indian phantom did visit my dreams periodically to show me her hideous grin, but I no longer feared her, and welcomed the possibility of death as an end to my pain and misery.

"A normal bloke'd be dead by now," I heard a man say as the waves hit the side of the small boat.

I remember the feel of the hull sliding onto sand, and the sensation of being picked up and carried a long distance over land. It was sweltering; so much so that the sweat poured from my body in rivulets. After what seemed like forever, I was laid down on some soft ground near another roaring fire. Someone opened my shirt, and I felt skillful hands apply a cool salve to my chest. The same hands then cut my breeches away with a very sharp blade, exposing the area where the snake bite was. I then felt another pasty substance being rubbed onto my wound. This one burned like acid, and I groaned with pain.

"Shhh Santos," Dorry said as she applied a cold cloth to my forehead. "The medicine woman will help you. I don't want you to die and leave me alone," she said in a soothing voice.

"I won't, Dorry, as long as you are here with me," I said in a hoarse whisper.

A long time passed, and I remember the sun rising and falling many times. One morning I opened my eyes, and found that the pain in my leg was still raw and intense, but the dizzy, sick feeling had passed. I felt the warm sunlight on my face as I raised myself up on my elbows. I was on a platform inside a makeshift lean-to covered with a roof made of sailcloth. At first I didn't know where I was, but I soon recognized the place. This was where the *Ais* took their sick; the same hidden clearing in the forest where Chera had worked so diligently to save lives. There were several other people there, all lying in various states of illness near me, but no sign of Dorry or Abraham. A few native women moved about, tending to the sick.

"You there!" I called out to the one nearest me, my voice breaking from being silent for so long. She whirled around and stared at me, not able to comprehend. I felt frustration as I tried to remember the proper phrase in her language.

"Where is Dorathea?"

Her eyes widened in fear, and she ran off up the trail as if she had seen a ghost. I muttered a curse and swung my legs over the side of the platform. As soon as my right foot touched the ground, a stinging pain shot up my leg, and I grimaced and swore aloud.

"Santos! What are you doing?"

It was Dorathea. She ran toward me from the trailhead with the Indian woman close behind, a scowl of anger on her beautiful face.

"You cannot get up!" she protested, pushing my chest with her palm until I lay back down. She placed her hand on my forehead and her expression turned to one of joy.

"The fever has broken!" she said happily, bending to plant a kiss on my bearded face. She then ran to a small area where several glass bottles were lined up next to the creek. She dunked one, filling it with the clean water, and then ran back to me.

"Here, drink this. You need to rebuild your strength."

"Captain!" It was the familiar voice of Abraham, "It is good to see you!"

I hadn't seen him coming, but there he was, standing next to me, a wide grin on his face.

"Yes, my friend." I said, clutching his huge hand.

"I have never been scared of anything, but you put a fright in me like I have never seen!" he said.

Over the next few days I got progressively stronger, and was soon able to walk with the help of a rough crutch. Dorry told me that I had nearly lost my leg to infection, if not for the expertise of the *Ais* medicine women. The pain was still there, but I was soon able to get around pretty well.

The next day, Dorry greeted me with a smile.

"I have a surprise for you," she said. "We are going home."

"Aren't we there already?" I asked. She grinned at me, but did not answer.

We left early the next morning, slowly making our way down the old path. Abraham carried me on his huge back as if I were a child. I had lost so much weight due to my illness that it was not much of a chore for him. Dorathea walked alongside us, carrying a heavy pack strapped to her back. As we walked, I looked at her and felt a pride and gratitude that I had never felt before. Dorry was not the same woman I had seen in the salvage camp with Allejandro. In the short time she had been with us, she had developed a steely toughness that was not visible before. I remembered her as a child, keeping up with my every trip into the wilderness and playing games that young girls would never consider partaking in. I now saw a confidence on her face and in her manner that, I suspected, was lying below the surface, longing to come out. She caught me looking at her and gave me a dirty-faced, wide smile. I actually flushed with embarrassment and felt myself become instantly aroused. It felt like ten years had disappeared and she was here, the love of my life, and we could now be children again. Dorry would have the life that she had always wanted, here with me.

We passed the trail that led to the *Ais* village and continued south. "Abraham, why are we headed back toward Santa Lucia?" I asked. "Wasn't it destroyed in the fire?"

"Yes, it was, Captain. We will soon be there, so be patient."

I grew apprehensive as I recognized the old trail. Just before we emerged into the clearing, we encountered someone walking toward us. It was Samuel and Simeon, the brothers, dragging a long, freshly cut palmetto trunk along the trail. They both broke into wide grins and happily embraced me, each of them talking so fast that I didn't understand a word. After a few moments they broke away, pulling us along, in a hurry to tell the others. Dorry and I followed them up the trail. As we emerged into the clearing, I looked around, lost in stunned fascination. They were in the process of rebuilding Santa Lucia, one pole at a time. Frameworks of houses were already in place, two of them already sporting their palmetto-thatched roofs.

"Aye Captain!"

I heard the booming voice from the trail that led to the dock.

Shad came running up the short rise toward me, followed by the lanky form of Mike Storm.

"Shad! Stormy! It's so good to see you!" I said, barely able to choke back emotion.

They both ran to me with open arms, nearly knocking me to the sand with their welcoming hugs.

"How do you like it, Captain?" Shad bellowed, sweeping his arm in a wide flourish. "After the storm there were plenty of pieces of the King's ships wrecked on the beaches, so we jumped on 'em and split the wood from their hulls," he said, laughing jovially.

I marveled at the amount of work that had already gone into construction of the new shelters. There would soon be four in all, facing each other across the clearing.

"The *Pantera?*" I asked sheepishly, almost not wanting to hear the answer.

Shad's expression turned to one of graveness and he shook his head slowly, at the same time turning toward the waterfront.

"Follow me sir. You 'ave to see this," he said.

I felt dread as I hobbled along after him down the trail to the shoreline. When we got there, I looked out over the surface of the water. My eyes lit up with joy as I gazed at my magnificent ship anchored there in the river, completely intact; her white sails furled, her rigging tight and ready for action.

"Shad, you old sea dog! You fooled me!" I said, laughing and playfully punching the huge pirate on the shoulder.

"Yes, Captain, we patched her up right. The Spanish bastards tried to end 'er, but she's too tough for the likes of them," he said, smiling with pride.

We walked back to Santa Lucia just in time to meet Caesar, who had just returned from a successful fishing trip. He carried a large, golden colored snook that gleamed in the sun. He did not run to greet me, but acted as if I had never left.

"I caught dinner, Captain!" he gloated, holding his prize up high for everyone to see.

I limped toward him and threw my arm around his neck, pulling him close. I was so happy to see him that tears came to my eyes.

"We will have a celebration dis evenin' Captain!" he said.

As we walked toward the fire pit in the center of camp, a thought occurred to me. I pulled Abraham away from the others.

"This is a question that has been nagging me since I started feeling better. Who was commanding the *Pantera* during the fight at the salvage camp?" I asked.

He gave me a wistful look before speaking.

"It was Captain Suarez," he said in a low voice.

"Captain Suarez?" I asked incredulously. This seemed totally out of character for the sad, defeated man I knew.

"Where is he?" I asked.

"After the Spanish took you and burned our homes, Captain Suarez changed. Something seemed to weigh heavily on his mind, and he began to move with more purpose. On the morning we were to set sail for *Palmar De Ays*, he emerged from his shelter dressed in the uniform he had not donned since his liberation from the *Santiago*. He seemed like a different person, and began barking orders for the preparation of the *Pantera*. At first we were resistant to him, but he was so adamant and demanding that we soon realized his intentions. It became clear to us that he was going to lead us into battle against his countrymen. We knew that none of us possessed the knowledge it would take to succeed against so strong an adversary, and began to see in him the fierce, knowledgeable leader that we would need to be successful. We began to follow his orders and instructions to the letter: from the readying of ordinance to the proper set of the rigging."

My eyes began to water again as Abraham spoke. I thought my heart would explode with pride at the news of my friend's transformation.

"Please continue," I said.

Abraham looked at me, a serious expression on his broad face. He began to speak again.

"Captain Suarez looked every bit the conqueror as we sailed that day, and we felt honored to be under the command of such a confident and determined leader. Here was a totally different person than the sad, resigned man you knew, Captain.

From the moment we sighted that first galleon, he became a warrior with purpose. He cheered us on directly into the heat of that battle, fearless of the massively superior firepower of the galleons before us. He led from the bow, fully exposed to the enemy with no regard for his own safety, shouting orders across the wind, which we responded to without question. It was as if he were on a mission to redeem himself to God for the inexcusable behavior of his countrymen. As ball and shot passed over our heads, he shook his fist and screamed in defiance."

"My God what a story!" I said excitedly.

Abraham continued.

"Just after the galleon's broadside missed us and mortally damaged the other, Captain Suarez strode confidently across the deck to me, his eyes wide with excitement and a smile on his face. I thought, at first, that he might have gone mad, but it soon occurred to me that he possessed no fear of death at all. He was actually enjoying the battle. I congratulated him on his brilliant maneuver, and we shook hands. It was a wonderful moment, Captain Santos."

Abraham's eyes began to water as he spoke.

"The wind came up and we drifted dangerously close to the crippled galleon. I noticed that the boy, George, was standing by the rail a few feet from us. He was, like us, caught in the fever of the battle and was raising his fists in the air, shouting oaths at the Spaniards. Captain Suarez stepped toward him; grabbing his arm and pulling him close to chastise him for disrespectful behavior. That was when I looked over at the deck of the galleon and saw one of the Spaniards pointing his musket.

I shouted a warning, and Captain Suarez quickly spun around and saw him as well. He moved in front of George just as the shot was fired. The ball hit the Captain in the chest, and he fell back with its impact, clutching his wound and sinking to the deck. I quickly pulled my small blade and hurled it, finding my mark in the Spaniard's neck. I ran to Captain Suarez and dropped to my knees, pulling his trembling body to mine. There was blood everywhere, and I could see that his wound was indeed very serious. He was bleeding from the mouth, and I could see that he was trying to speak. I bent my head to his and strained to hear his words. He died there, in my arms."

Tears now streamed down my face. "What did he say, Abraham?"

"He said this, Captain. *"Dios salve a la madre España de la tiranía."*

"God save Mother Spain from tyranny," I said.

Captain Suarez had, like me, realized the imperfections and prejudice of his own countrymen. He had made the difficult decision to turn against what he truly believed was wrong. I felt a wave of pride and sadness that I cannot describe. My sad friend had redeemed himself in the eyes of everyone, and it had cost him his life. I was overwhelmed as I realized the true magnitude of his sacrifice.

Shad and Caesar had joined us.

"Did you have a service for our friend?" I asked Shad. He looked at me, thoughtfulness clouding his face.

"Yes, sir. T'was a terrible thing those bastards done to 'im. I'm frightful sorry, sir."

"Where did you put him?" I asked.

"We thought it fitting that we bury 'im at the high place," he said, looking at me with his large, baleful eyes.

"El Lugar?" I asked.

"Yes, sir. That's where 'ee is."

CHAPTER 59
THE VENGEFUL SPIRIT

The African women danced like wild dervishes in the amber firelight. A huge fire crackled and released floating sparks that rose up into the blueness of the night sky, nearly touching the long fronds of the encircling palm trees. Shad and two of Captain Suarez's men grinned, their faces shining with sweat, as they pounded animal skin drums, their hands beating out a syncopated rhythm that was as infectious as it was joyful. The celebration had started early in the afternoon, and had reached a feverish pitch as the wine and rum flowed.

I broke away from the festivities and ambled down to the beach in the moonlight, staggering slightly from the effects of the wine. As I gazed out over the roaring ocean and the brilliant stars in the night sky, my mind retraced everything I had been through. My thoughts inevitably turned to the curse-the scourge that my father had warned me of on his deathbed. I was sure that just before he passed into the abyss, he understood the true nature of it. Like me, he had been shown a glimpse of Cualli's rage. The only difference was that I had survived the vision of our ancestor's terrible deeds, and he had not. I slowly reached behind my head and untied the leather thong that held the amulet. I held it in my right hand, raising it up toward the night sky, its shiny surface dangling in the air.

"Cualli!" I shouted out in a voice that did not quaver in fear. "I do not know why you chose to show me the truth about the terrible scourge that you invoked so many years ago, but I feel for you. What happened to you was terrible, and I know that your anger was justified. I only want to say that my heart feels sad for you every day of my life. I am sorry for what was done to you, and humbly beg for your forgiveness and mercy!"

Nothing happened, and I felt slightly foolish. Two seagulls cried out in the night as they flew over my head. There was no sign that the spirit had heard me. I continued to walk down the beach, the amulet hanging at my side. I decided to try again.

"Cualli, you have every right to want revenge for the wrongs. I am here to make amends for that terrible deed! Please make yourself visible to me!" I said.

Still, there was nothing. I walked a long way, enjoying the cool night air as it blew through my hair. After a while, I paused to rest. I looked out over the sea, transfixed by its forbidding beauty. I sat down on the firm sand and drew my knees up in front of me, clasping my fingers together in front.

"Maybe it is truly over," I said softly, "and you are gone."

I lay back on the firm sand and looked straight up at the stars. I felt more relaxed than I had ever been since that lonely night so many years before when I had found myself stranded on the beach. I began to drift off.

Suddenly, I was startled by a quick movement next to my right arm. At first I thought it was a crab that had gotten too close, but before I could think again, there was an eruption of sand on both sides of me. I saw two long appendages spring free of the sand, and then slam down on my chest so hard that the wind was knocked out of me. I was stricken with horror as I realized what was holding me. They were human arms. The skin was marble white laced with blue veins, and as cold as dead fish. They held me so tightly that I could not move; the pressure on my chest so great that I felt I would be pulled down to Hell itself. Two large figures began to slowly rise from the sand on each side of me as if elevated by some unseen force. I was soon looking wildly back and forth into the faces of two grinning ghouls. The one on my right wore a Spanish *morion* helmet. It had long, black, stringy hair that hung down below its shoulders, and I could see the corroded remnants of chain mail and breastplate that still hung on its withered shoulders and chest. The thing on the right looked to have once been a woman. Her blonde, soaked hair hung down over her decayed face, and what remained of a white, lacy dress covered her exposed upper body, the tattered garment barely covering her gray, cold skin. They stared at me mockingly with stark, flat eyes that were mottled gray in color and had no pupils. As they rose from their graves, their hands pushed my body down, holding me fast in their icy grip.

I then heard the terrible low laugh and the taunting whisper.

"My darling Santos. How do you like my friends? They were once lovers, in another life. Now they reside here, under my care. They unfortunately lost their lives in a terrible disaster that occurred here. Did you hear of it?"

"Cualli," I said, my voice trembling with fear as I stared at the two wretched specters, "please spare my life."

"Why should I listen to you? Do your veins not run with the blood of Donato Alvarez?"

"Yes, yes, this is true! But please, let me speak!"

As the two terrible creatures glared down at me, I could see nothing but a small sliver of night sky between them. Suddenly, the darkness was interrupted with a greenish glow, and the familiar phantom slowly moved into my limited field of vision. Her face held the terrible smile, and her eyes were those same vacant holes. I felt that I would die of fright that very moment. No man, I was sure, had ever seen anything as terrible as these three lonely spirits.

"I know who you are!" I shouted out. "You are a bestowed queen descended of a mighty and ancient people! You were the favorite wife of the great Moctezuma! I saw everything in the vision!"

Her mouth opened so wide that it appeared that her head would split, and she let out a screeching howl of anger.

"*I gave you no such vision, mortal! HOW DARE YOU!*"

Her voice had transformed from a whisper to the tearing rasp of a carpenter's file, her form quivering with pent up rage and centuries of burning contempt.

I continued to shout so that she could hear what I had to say.

"I know what happened that terrible day! I know that you loved the king more than anything on earth! I know what Donato did to you, and I know what he stole from you! It was this!"

I wrenched my arm free of the ghastly soldier's grip and thrust the amulet up, holding it high as I could.

"This is yours!" I screamed. "He took it after he raped and murdered you! He stole it from the king's body!"

The terrible, piercing scream continued, hurting my ears.

"Take it, Cualli! Take it now! I am giving it to you!" I shouted as the grip of the two ghouls tightened even more on my body.

The terrible scream transformed into words that I could understand.

"*YOU DIE NOW, SPANIARD!*"

The wind suddenly picked up dramatically and a torrent of rain began to fall. Lightning flashed, its huge jagged fingers shooting spider-like across the sky, illuminating it completely before disappearing in an instant. The spirit appeared to double in size, its form towering high above me, and its expression of utter malevolence grew more and more terrible. The mouth sneered so widely that it appeared to nearly split the head in two. I felt the rotting hands of the ghouls loosen, and the wind itself began to lift my whole body. I soon felt myself leaving the ground, my body suddenly levitated into the air by an unseen force. I stared upward at the stars, and for a brief moment, wished for time to stop so I could climb up into them and escape. I was then flung violently through the air, my body spinning and turning end over end like a sparrow in a hurricane. My body then hit the hard surface of the sand. I landed with such force that I tumbled across the beach, the wind knocked completely from my lungs. I came to a stop in a jumble, my legs crossed over one another and one of my arms pinned under me in an unnatural position. I felt agonizing pain and thought that it was possibly broken.

"IT IS YOUR TIME TO PAY THE DEBT, SPANIARD!"

The rasping voice came loud and clear, and I could feel the spirit overwhelming me with its hatred. I hid my eyes with my hand and waited for the inevitable final blow that would be the end of my life.

Through the haze of pain came another sound that was different. It was soft and nearly inaudible, but I instantly knew what it was. It was a song. My lips involuntarily moved with the words, even though they were in a language I did not understand. I looked up and saw a distant, celestial light approaching from the sky above the ocean. It glowed brightly, blue and shimmering, and emitted radiance in all directions. The singing grew louder, and I turned to look at the phantom woman. She had stopped, her focus now turned toward the intruding light, which was advancing so quickly that it now illuminated the entire beach. The singing stopped, and a female voice began to speak.

"*Cualli, young one, why are you so vengeful?*" it said.

Cualli said nothing, but hovered there, her ancient, torn shift billowing loosely in the wind. The voice continued to speak.

"*I am of the true ancient people,*" the voice from the blue light said.

Cualli's spirit was obviously affected by these words, and her form began to tremble and vibrate.

"*I was there when you were a small girl, and I saw you emerge from the crevice in the ground. You were special in life, Cualli, and you are now. You must release your hatred of these mortals and become one with me. We are the same.*"

As I watched, the spirit of Cualli began to transform. It seemed to grow smaller, and the loose, flowing garment fell to the sand at its feet. I saw her true form now; the way she had looked in life. She was lovely, and her supple body glowed with the tautness of youth. She looked up, and I saw that the black, vacant holes on her face had been replaced by beautiful brown eyes that were filled with tears. I could now see the beautiful young woman that the great King had chosen for his bride. I gazed at the girl whom I had seen in my dreams ever since childhood.

"*The Tlatoani was my whole being.*"

She said these words in a voice that was human. Gone was the coarse whisper I knew so well. She began to sob, her head bowing down in supplication and surrender.

"*They took him from me.*"

The voice of the new spirit boomed loud, drowning out all other sounds.

"*Cualli, you loved so much in life that it followed you into the night world. You must let your hurt go and move into the great beyond so that you may be at peace. The men from across the big water have left their mark on all of our people, but the fault does not lie on them alone. Men have been compelled to dominate and control others for all time, our own people included. They do not know what they do, and they may not realize the true impact of their actions for many years. What has happened to you is a terrible thing, but we must remember that the Great Spirit has a plan for us, and in time we will all know the meaning of true sacrifice. There are both good and bad forces that we may experience in our time, and we must learn how to tell the difference between the two. This mortal has done nothing to you, and he has no control over the past deeds of his predecessors. In order to find true peace, you must leave him to die on his own when his time comes. It is I who love you Cualli, and I want you to come with me to the home of the Great Spirit.*"

I could tell that Cualli was visibly shaken by these words because her young, lithe body began to waver even more. She hesitated for a moment, and then slowly fell to her knees before the magnificent blue light. I then heard a cry of great sorrow; that of a young woman's spirit in mourning for her lost love; the release of hundreds of years of sadness, mourning, and loss.

The blue illumination slowly began to transform, and I was soon able to see an image. It was a woman; beautiful and naked, hovering in the soft blue light. She slowly turned toward me. I gazed into the face of my beloved Chera. She smiled at me in the same way she always had in life. Slowly, she moved toward Cualli, who had fallen to her knees in the sand, still sobbing into her hands. She reached her hand out to the figure kneeling before her.

"Come, Cualli. We must go."

The two magnificent ghostly figures slowly rose into the air and moved close to each other. Chera's spirit reached out, and Cualli gently took her hand. When they made contact, there was a brilliant flash that brightened everything in sight. Together they floated off into the night sky, their hands joined as they made their way home. Tears streamed down my face as I watched them disappear into the millions of stars.

CHAPTER 60
A NEW BEGINNING

My eyes opened to the warmth of the morning sun on my skin. I rolled onto my side and immediately felt the ache in my head and loss of balance. The screeching of seagulls flying overhead made me wince. The wine had been very strong and I was now paying the debt. A few feet away, sandpipers busily chased the waves as they receded in and out, pecking at the wet sand. The tiny birds reminded me of the day I had washed up on the beach so many years earlier.

"Hello, old friends," I said to them.

I looked up the beach to the north, and saw the calm waves breaking thinly on the sand. The full heat of the day had not yet come, and the morning coolness made me shiver slightly. Gone were the phantoms and spirits, as well as the ghouls from below the sand. There was no sign of any disturbance on the beach around me, and I realized that it had all been a dream. More like a nightmare.

Or had it?

"Never again," I groaned out loud as I rubbed my head.

"Santos?"

The call came from the trailhead at the top of the beach behind me. I turned my head and saw Dorathea walking swiftly toward me, her face etched in an expression of concern. I smiled, waved, and rose to my feet, brushing the sand off my breeches and struggling to keep my balance.

"Hello, my love!" I said as brightly as I could as she walked up and stood in front of me.

"Where have you been? I was worried sick," she said, her voice softening as she looked over my shaking body.

"I must have passed out here." I said. "What was in that wine Caesar brought out?"

"I don't know. Why do you ask?"

"I had the strangest visions. They were terrifying and seemed so real."

"Santos, where is your amulet?"

My hand rose to my chest. As she said, it wasn't there.

"I, I don't know," I stammered. I walked over to the impression in the sand where I had slept. I fell to my knees and ran my fingers through the wet grains. I felt something hard buried just below the surface. Plunging my fingers in, I pulled the amulet up, holding it between my thumb and forefinger.

"Here it is," I said. "I must have dropped it in the night."

I examined its gleaming surface for a long time, turning it over and over in my hand.

"What's wrong Santos? You look as if you've never seen it before."

"Dorathea, I need to tell you a story."

We sat together on the beach, and for the next two hours I told her of the vivid dream I had experienced and the truth behind the curse. When I finished, we both sat there in silence for a very long time. She did not say anything judgmental or tell me that I was insane, which I thought was good.

"There's something I need to do," I said.

I got to my feet and walked down to the water's edge. I held the amulet in my hand, bouncing it up and down as if taking measure of its weight, and then closed my fingers around it. I drew my arm back and hurled it with all of my strength as far as I could out into the waves. I watched it sail out and hit the surface of the water with a tiny splash.

"Santos! What are you doing?" she cried.

"I was wrong. The amulet represents all of the pain and suffering over the long centuries. My father was mistaken about it, as was his father before him. Cualli's love for the King knew no bounds and endured over hundreds of years, long after both of their deaths. I will never think of her the same way I used to."

I placed my arm around Dorathea, and together we walked back toward the camp. As we walked up the trail, I felt a sensation of calm that I had never felt before. Something had changed, and I knew it. We walked into the clearing, and I saw that the men were just rising from wherever they had ended up after the previous night's excesses. Many of them were groaning from the effects of the wine. I laughed out loud as I saw Shad. He was still wearing a ridiculous powdered wig that he had found in one of Caesar's chests. The night before, he had drunkenly danced around the camp in the firelight, causing us to double up in laughter as he proclaimed in a slurred voice that he was now a nobleman and that everyone should address him as "Sir Wallingsworth." As he saw me approaching, he reached up and pulled the ludicrous thing from his head.

"Where the devil 'ave you been, Captain?" he said, gazing at me with bloodshot eyes.

"Everyone gather around, please!" I shouted.

Slowly, the men rose and walked over, forming a circle around me. I scanned their faces, my eyes momentarily stopping on each one.

"I would like to say a few words," I said in an even voice.

"Men, I know that you see me as your leader. For that I am grateful. I often feel that I am not worthy of such a distinction. You have sacrificed a great deal and taken huge risks in being part of this group. We have been through much together over the past few years."

The men looked at one another, grumbling, and I raised my hand to quiet them.

"I would like to say that I have not served with many men, but that you are the best that I could have ever wished for. Our successes have been great, and it is not because of me. The accomplishments we have attained are due to your own efforts. I congratulate you!"

The men all let out a cheer, raising their fists in unison. "*Huzzah! Huzzah!* God save Captain Santos!"

I raised my hands again and continued to speak. My eyes met Caesar's.

"You have been so faithful to me. I was overjoyed when I saw that you were safe. You are one of the finest souls I have ever met, and I will always be grateful to have known you."

He looked at me with his familiar, toothy grin.

Behind him stood the Spaniards; formerly under the command of Captain Suarez. All of them looking worse for wear from the revelry of the night before. The cook, Edmundo, stepped forward.

"Captain Santos," he said, "We will always be in your debt. You have treated us fairly, even after our Captain was killed. For this we will never be able to repay you."

I approached the man, placing my hand on his shoulder.

"Edmundo, your Captain was truly an honorable man. You men have no need to be sad about the loss of your allegiance to kings. You will always be Spaniards in the truest sense. Captain Suarez showed us all that. I hope that you all stay with us and participate in our ventures."

I then looked up at Abraham, who stood off to the side with George, Matthew, Elias, and the others.

"You, Abraham, have proven yourself to be a mighty leader. Your people are fortunate to have you. With you and your men at my side, I can never lose."

He gave me a wide smile, and squeezed the shoulder of Adelena, who stood beside him.

"Captain, I have some good news."

"What is it?" I asked.

He looked at Adelena, and they both burst into laughter.

"What is so funny?" I asked.

"Adelena is with child," he said.

My heart leapt with joy, and I ran to the huge man, grabbing his wrist and shaking it vigorously.

"Oh, God in heaven! That is the best news of the day!"

Later that night, after everyone had found sleep, I ventured out beyond the fire's light, down the path that led to the water. For some reason that I did not understand, I felt compelled to veer down the path to the right, the same one that I knew very well. The mound looked huge in front of me in the near darkness. As I contemplated its looming, blackness, I thought of the many ancient secrets that it must hold. In the time I had been here in the wilderness of La Florida, I had developed a sense of awe and wonder at the people I had encountered. They had made it their home for hundreds, maybe thousands of years before my kind had ever set foot on its shores. Both intelligent and resourceful, they had also proved to be passionate and loving. Knowing them as intimately as I had, I now realized that these doomed people, the *Ais*, had changed my life forever.

I heard a sound from somewhere above me, and looked up into a huge oak tree that stood a short distance away. I found myself staring directly into the lantern green eyes of a great panther. For some strange reason I felt no fear, only a melancholy calmness and understanding, as if this chance meeting were anticipated by both of us. The creature's eyes seemed to glow in the moonlight, and I saw no maliciousness in them, only a look of intelligent knowing. The animal nonchalantly sat in the crook of two large branches, its great paws crossed in front of it. We stared into each other's eyes for a long time, and then the great beast rose to its feet and jumped down from its perch. It slowly loped a short distance down the path away from me, then turned and gave me one last look before disappearing into the forest.

"Goodbye, my darling Chera," I said out loud, tears streaming down my face.

I got up early the next morning with the dawn still gray and made my way toward the river. Caesar's skiff was there, and I was soon rowing across the water. I could see *El Lugar el Alto* looming in the distance and I pointed my bow toward it. It was the beginning of a beautiful day, and the sun reflected silver off the small waves. All around me, mullet periodically leapt out of the water; flying in high, panicked arcs as they tried to escape some predator below before slapping sideways on the surface and back into the depths. A school of huge tarpon rolled past me, their fins appearing, and then disappearing as they traveled lazily toward the inlet. A short distance away, three porpoises played in the morning sunshine, darting back and forth as they fed on small fish. I heard the cry of an osprey overhead, and smiled as I thought of Dunkirk and his perfect talent of mimicry.

I was soon at the opposite shore, and ran the bow of the skiff as high on the sand as I could before jumping out into the shallow water. I pulled it all the way onto the beach and rested the worn paddle inside. There were thick sea grape plants and mangroves on each side of the small beach, and I was surprised at the wide array of birds that had claimed them as their home. There was a large blue heron with the somber expression of a magistrate; his gimlet eyes staring at me suspiciously. I heard the flutter of wings behind me and turned to see three ibis's walking toward me across the beach, steadily picking at the sand with their curved beaks. There were several limpkins around the roots of the mangroves, scouring the water for small shellfish. A cormorant stood guard on a high exposed root, his wings spread out wide and motionless as he dried them in the breeze.

The trail was well marked, so I found it easily and began my ascent through the scrub pine and bayonet plants. As I walked, my mind went back to the first time I came here. I was soon at the summit, and paused to enjoy the magnificent view. I breathed in deep and closed my eyes, trying to connect with the spirits whom I knew resided there. After a while I turned and walked back toward the fire pit. I saw it then; the gravesite that my men had prepared. The earth was not yet overgrown where they had dug, and there was a rough marker that had been driven into the ground at its head. On it was a simple inscription.

HERE LIES CAPITÁN EMILIO SUAREZ
OUR BRAVE FRIEND

1715

It was beautiful in its simplicity. I was so moved that I began to speak out loud.

"Hello, old friend," I said. "I just came to let you know that we all regret your passing. I never got the chance to let you know how I felt about your sacrifice. You not only repaid your debt to me, you have also made all of us better men having known you. Your spirit will live on because we will keep your memory alive. Your name will be our battle cry against the unjust cruelty of those who now control the place of our ancestors. You and I are brothers. Goodbye, my friend."

I stood there for a long time, looking down at his resting place. I then walked over to the edge and once more looked out at the island across the water and the ocean beyond it. I was thinking of returning to camp when something caught my eye to the south. It was very small. . what was it? I strained my eyes. And suddenly felt a charge of excitement. It was a sail!

"Prize ship to the south!" I shouted and ran to the trailhead. I paused and turned back to *El Lugar*.

"This one is for you, *mi amigo!*"

THE END

EPILOGUE

So now you have heard my story. I have not told it all, but the main events that have affected me with the greatest impact have been included in these pages. As I look out through the window onto the bustling street below, I can't help but feel a little forlorn when I recall days gone by. Some of the memories have grown cloudy over the years, but I have resigned myself to the fact that this is one of the symptoms of advanced age.

I do know that the Spanish efforts to retain some of their lost wealth continued relentlessly in the years following the seventeen- fifteen disaster. For five long years they continued with their salvage efforts at *Palmar De Ays* before they declared an end to the effort. One of the largest deterrents to their success was the rampant piracy that was encouraged as more and more of the "Brethren of the Coast" learned of what had happened there. We were far from the only men of our kind to hear of the vast riches strewn across the ocean floor, and often had to compete with others in our efforts to attain it. My crew and I took every opportunity to plunder the wreck sites, often doing so within sight of the Spanish salvage vessels. Their numbers were never great enough to deter us, and our close proximity to the Gulf Stream made hunting very good indeed. I always took great pleasure when the prize was *Es-pa-no*.

Over the years I have made the acquaintance of nearly every pirate of note who ever sailed the Caribbean Sea, from Anne Bonny to Bartholomew Roberts, and had once gotten roaring drunk with Teach himself. I saw him in Jamaica a few years after the disaster and recognized him as one of Jennings's men at *Palmar De Ays*. When I confronted him about it, he

PATRICK S. MESMER

denied ever being there, but I know it was him. I have never met a man more intimidating and full of life than Captain Teach.

The activities of my friends in La Florida continued for many years after I left. I heard stories of a group of fierce pirates who mercilessly preyed on vessels around the reefs of the eastern coast of La Florida. They were said to be cunning and elusive, and were led by two captains of African heritage named Abraham and Caesar. They were feared like no other, and struck terror into the hearts of sailors who traveled in those waters. I could only smile at these tales. They continued to wreak havoc on shipping in the Florida Channel, and were the most sought after men in the Caribbean by pirate hunters like Captain Woodes Rogers of Jamaica. As far as I know they have never been apprehended.

In early seventeen-sixteen, Captain Jennings returned to his home in the English colony of Jamaica. His pirate exploits were well known, but he was left alone by authorities who were sympathetic to his cause and hated the Spanish. Later that year he set out for Cuba with a fellow privateer, the infamous Samuel Bellamy, and illegally took a French vessel as a prize. This attack on a "neutral" ship resulted in Jennings being declared a pirate by his own sovereign, King George. His partner, Bellamy, showed his true character when he betrayed Jennings and pilfered most of the treasure for himself. Captain Jennings was forced to relocate to Nassau, where he lived for the next few years. King George eventually issued a pardon for all pirates who would convert to a legal lifestyle, and Captain Jennings did a complete reversal, becoming a pirate hunter. He was involved in the search for many *boucaniers*, including his one-time understudy, Charles Vane, and countless others who refused to convert. In an incredibly unfavorable twist of fate, Jennings was captured by the Spanish and supposedly perished in one of their terrible prisons. The most admirable thing that I remember about Captain Henry Jennings was that he was a gentleman, and always refused to take English ships as prizes.

As for myself, I stayed in La Florida for a few more years, gradually amassing the fortune on which Dorathea and I lived for many contented years, and on which I survive to this day. Here in Nassau, I am considered a gentleman and an honest citizen. I do not regret a single day of my early life, and wouldn't change any of it. I still hold the government of Spain in high contempt, and sometimes grow bitter if I dwell on their transgressions. Some things never change, I guess.

I grow very melancholy when I think of the *Ais* people of La Florida. Their numbers continued to decline in the years after the shipwreck disaster, and various diseases continued to wreak havoc on them. The advent of slavery depleted them even more. When last I heard, they had ceased to exist as a people. Sometimes in the evenings, as I walk by the shoreline and gaze out at the waning moon over the glimmering water, I can almost hear the sad song of old Canoba on the wind, and I want to sing out myself for the great people who are now lost. The raw beauty and threatening nature of La Florida will survive, but the colorful native people are gone forever. I considered them my family, and I will always mourn their loss. That is why I felt compelled to write this account of my life and my experience with them.

I often walk in the wilderness alone, and find myself growing apprehensive when approaching mysterious burial mounds where the ancient ones are interred. I can still sense Cualli's lonely spirit, and for this reason have never scoffed at any of the beliefs of native people.

For you, patient reader, I thank you for reading this memoir. The events I have shared with you occurred in a land that no longer exists. It is only as it was in my fading memory. The swaying palm trees and colorful sunsets are the canvas on which the happiest adventures of my life are painted. I can only hope that the beautiful and forbidding world of *La Florida* as I knew it will live forever on these pages.

ABOUT THE AUTHOR

Patrick S. Mesmer lives with his wife, Tricia, in the small coastal village of Port Salerno, Florida. He loves history in all forms and spends his weekends exploring ancient sites. He feels that Florida's history must be preserved at all costs, and that education is the answer. It is for this reason that he volunteers at local historical sites as an interpreter and tour guide. He attempts to tell stories that inspire interest in preservation and has a successful lecture series. Patrick and his wife are interested in unexplained phenomena and have a company together called Mesmerized Paranormal Investigations. This is his second book.

OTHER WORKS BY PATRICK S. MESMER

HAUNTED RIVER TALES
FIVE HUNDRED YEARS ON THE LOCHA-HATCHEE
COPYRIGHT 2011

61033310R00275

Made in the USA
Charleston, SC
14 September 2016